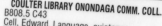

B
808.5   Cell
.C43   Language, existence
           & God

Date Due

DEC 1			
NOV 12 73			

*Language
Existence
& God*

EDWARD CELL *Language*
Existence
& God

Interpretations of
Moore
Russell
Ayer
Wittgenstein
Wisdom
Oxford Philosophy
and Tillich

Abingdon Press—Nashville—New York

ISBN 0-687-21063-1

Library of Congress Catalog Card Number: 71-148079

Quotations from John Hick, Philosophy of Religion,
© 1963, are reprinted by permission of Prentice-Hall,
Inc., Englewood Cliffs, N.J.

SET UP, PRINTED, AND BOUND
BY THE PARTHENON PRESS,
AT NASHVILLE, TENNESSEE,
UNITED STATES OF AMERICA

To Mary

Preface

Some twelve years ago I began reading the analytic philosophers on religious language with the result that my doubts and perplexities concerning religious knowledge were considerably deepened. It seemed to me that their approach was good and would complement what I had learned from the existentialists but that I would lose much of its value unless I started from scratch with a study of their basic position and the process of development that led to it. The result is the studies that comprise this book. They were written in the order in which they appear except that the earlier chapters were partly revised in light of what I learned in the later studies.

My aim has been to understand each philosopher on his own terms and then to ask what application his position has to talk of God. I have not limited attention, then, to those aspects of each position which have immediate application to religious language; the best preparation to consider its application is, I think, simply to study the position as a whole. Nor have I begun with a thesis and used these philosophers to advance an argument for it; even had I had such a thesis this would have forced each position into the mold of the argument and so have limited its full consideration.

These studies, then, are introductory in nature. In places, however, particularly in Chapters VI and VII, important issues about a position have required fairly detailed discussions, and these may be of interest to those who already have a fair knowledge of the matter.

Each chapter is designed so that those with a special interest in that

7

position may turn directly to it. Those relatively unfamiliar with the later work of Wittgenstein, however, may find it advisable to read the expository and critical sections of Chapter VI before reading any of the chapters that follow it. Then, too, although many doubtless will find the earlier analysts of less interest and less direct relevance than their successors to the problem of cognition in talk of God, an understanding of their work is important to an understanding of the later developments. It is against the background of the more negative conclusions of the earlier chapters that the constructive methodological results of the later chapters may best be seen.

Among the many, including several students, who have been so helpful in the course of these studies, I am particularly indebted to Mr. Bruce Keeling, the Rev. John Klindt, and Professors Paul Bosley, William Gillham, Jack Padgett, George Thomas, and John Wisdom. I also wish to thank Miss Mary Melcher and my wife Mary for all their care in typing and proofreading.

Contents

I   Introduction   11

PART ONE: *Analysis Before Wittgenstein's Investigations*

II   G. E. Moore: Analysis and Common Sense   27
III Logical Atomism and Russell: Analysis and
     Language Form   55
IV   Logical Positivism: Analysis and Verification   90

PART TWO: *Wittgenstein*

V   The *Tractatus:* The Limits of Language   117
VI   The *Investigations:* Language-games and Forms of Life 141

PART THREE: *Subsequent Developments*

VII John Wisdom: Paradox, Platitude, and Discovery   215
VIII Oxford Philosophy: Ordinary Language and
      Paradigm-Cases   262

PART FOUR: *Dialogue with Existentialism*

IX Analysis and Existentialism   327
X A Tillichian Analysis of "God Acts in History"   337

Bibliography   383

Index   389

Introduction

Chapter One

Can we human beings say anything meaningful about God? This is the basic question in the tenuous dialogue between linguistic philosophy and philosophical theology. Fundamentally it is a restatement of the traditional question, Can we think about God? That it is now being asked in terms of meaning is indicative of changes that have been taking place in the last half-century in the empirical philosopher's understanding of his task.

"Linguistic philosophy" is commonly understood to designate a conception of philosophy in which the philosopher's task is construed as the clarification of meaning, rather than the construction of a comprehensive world view. The linguistic philosopher, then, does not conceive of himself as belonging to a philosophic "school" in the sense that certain philosophic conclusions are defended as part of an explicitly held world view. He conceives of himself, rather, as participating in a "revolution" in the philosopher's understanding of his subject matter. But if the philosopher is concerned with the clarification of meaning where does he find his access to this datum? According to classical British empiricism, he gains this access simply by looking into his own mind. As one commentator puts it, however, linguistic philosophers "deny such access to an inward oracle. In their view my only access to a man's meaning is through what he *says*, i.e., the datum of analysis is *language*, and this is what philosophy is concerned with." [1]

---

[1] Michael Foster, "Contemporary British Philosophy and Christian Belief," *The Christian Scholar*, Fall, 1960, p. 189.

This change in the conception of philosophy must be understood in terms of the situation that began to force itself upon the empirically minded philosopher after the turn of the century. On the one hand, psychology was rapidly separating itself from philosophy. Yet, on the other hand, under the increasing impact of science and rapid developments in logic, it seemed less and less credible to regard philosophy as dealing with a transcendental world or even as providing any sort of explanation of the universe as a whole. As John Wisdom notes,

as science grew and people saw better how it is based on observation and experiment there grew a suspicion of anyone who professed to have obtained new factual information by anything but empirical methods. There were sneers at the philosophers who were represented as employing arm-chair, *a priori* methods. The deplorable affair of Hegel and the planets was not forgotten. Besides, philosophers could not agree, were in fact in a deadlock—at each other's throats.[2]

But if it is the job of science to produce empirical hypotheses and if philosophy is not a kind of super-science, then is there any point to philosophy at all? It was as an answer to this question that the analytic ideas and practices of G. E. Moore, Bertrand Russell, and Ludwig Wittgenstein were so enthusiastically received. At the same time and under the influence of Wittgenstein, the logical positivists created an alternative view of the nature of philosophical analysis. Increasing dissatisfaction with this general approach, however, led such philosophers as Wittgenstein and John Wisdom at Cambridge, and John Austin and Gilbert Ryle at Oxford to abandon analysis in favor of conceptual elucidation.

It shall be our purpose to examine the significance of these analytic and linguistic positions for the concern of Christian philosophical theology with the question, Can we say anything meaningful about God? We are considering this question in terms of the language of Christianity because Christianity has been the dominant religious force in Western culture, and linguistic philosophy, as a product of Western culture, has been concerned primarily with the meaning of Western language. Indeed, as we shall presently indicate, analytic and linguistic philosophy must be seen in connection with the cultural crisis through which the West is passing.

We shall examine the significance of the philosophic positions we have indicated for the problem of the meaning of statements about God, first of all, in terms of the potential or actual usefulness of their *methodology* for philosophy of religion and, secondly, in terms of the

[2] "Metaphysics and Verification" (1938), reprinted in John Wisdom, *Philosophy and Psycho-Analysis* (Oxford: Basil Blackwell, 1957), pp. 58-59.

results, whether critical or constructive, of those applications which have already been made to the religious use of language. Considering each of these positions in chronological order we shall first present the basic points made by it concerning analysis or conceptual clarification. We shall then examine its significance for a critical understanding of language about God in two ways. First, we shall present a general evaluation of the position, for the strengths and weaknesses of that position with respect to language in general will *ipso facto* be strengths and weaknesses in its application to any part of that language such as the religious.[3] Second, we shall consider the specific application of that position and of our critical evaluation of it to language about God.

We shall conclude our study by applying Paul Tillich's account of the meaning of "God" to affirmations that God is active in human life. I hope to show that Tilllich's interpretation does provide a way of talking meaningfully about God acting, that his view is significantly related to the prophetic dimension of biblical faith, and that his use of the phenomenological method takes him one step beyond the important and related work of John Wisdom in retaining some basic ties with biblical faith. Whether these ties are the essential ones is something concerning which there is no consensus among Christians today and so remains a matter of existential decision. Hopefully our discussion of Tillich will help to clarify the nature of that decision.

We shall focus on assertions about God acting for two reasons. First of all, dialogue between linguistic philosophy and Christian philosophical theology concerning the possibility of meaningful statements about God must inevitably have as its focal point the meaning of the believer's conviction that God acts in history, for it is this belief which is most distinctive of the Christian's way of conceiving things. Second, it is basically in this way that the Christian expresses his beliefs in the reality of God, and it is precisely concerning the reality of God that the existing dialogue becomes most strained. Linguistic philosophers have described religious uses of language as involving various sorts of meaning, as the following typical examples may suggest: "Religious writings . . . are most richly emotionally evocative";[4] "the meaning of a religious assertion is given by its use in expressing the asserter's intention to follow a specified policy of behavior";[5] "the picture of the divine as beyond or behind the world is a model whereby is expressed

[3] Since our concern is whether *any statement whatsoever* about God can be meaningful, we shall use "religious language" to mean both the everyday language of religion and the language of the theologian.

[4] Charles B. Martin, *Religious Belief* (Ithaca: Cornell University Press, 1959), p 164.

[5] R. B. Braithwaite, *An Empiricist's View of the Nature of Religious Belief* (Cambridge: The University Press, 1955), p. 16.

the fullest possible sense of the mystery gleaming in the finite world." [6]
But, as we shall see, when the theologian affirms the reality of God by
saying that "the God whom we find in the Bible is a God who 'does
things,' a prevenient God, who reveals himself, and calls men, and
visits them," [7] linguistic philosophers commonly turn reductionistic.
John Wisdom, for example, asserts that if we ask, "What are our feelings when we believe in God?" [8] we are "reminded of how we felt as
children to our parents." [9] Such beliefs in a God who does things are
largely the "persistent projections of infantile phantasies." [10] One must
agree, then, with Michael Foster's observation concerning contemporary linguistic practices that

the concession of meaningfulness to other uses of language by no means
concedes all that the metaphysician and the theologian require. Is it con-
ceded that metaphysical and theological sentences are able not only to be
meaningful but to be true? *This is surely the crucial issue.*[11]

It is good to underscore the relationship between the question of
the meaningfulness of statements about God and the question of the
meaningfulness of metaphysical statements—statements expressing a
view of reality as a whole—suggested by Foster's statement. Basil
Mitchell, for example, reports that the discussion group called "The
Metaphysicals," which published the "Oxford essays in philosophical
theology" under the title *Faith and Logic,* found that their

unorganized discussions tended, as time went on, to centre upon the nature
and justification of Christian belief. This was natural enough, since for
Christian believers, as we all were, it is at this point that the philosophical
dispute about the possibility of metaphysics assumes decisive importance.
For Christian belief presupposes the existence of God and here, if anywhere,
is a metaphysical problem.[12]

The way in which each of the positions to be considered treats metaphysical language, consequently, will constitute a highly relevant part
of our examination.

Particularly important in the analytic challenge to the meaningful-

---

[6] Ninian Smart, *Reasons and Faiths* (New York: Humanities Press, 1959), p. 43.
[7] Donald Baillie, *God Was in Christ* (New York: Scribner's, 1948), p. 64.
[8] "Gods" (1944), reprinted in John Wisdom, *Philosophy and Psycho-Analysis,*
p. 164. Originally published in *Proceedings of the Aristotelian Society,* 1944. Used
by permission of the editor.
[9] *Ibid.,* p. 165.   [10] *Ibid.,* p. 166.
[11] *Mystery and Philosophy,* in "The Library of Philosophical Theology," ed.
Alasdair MacIntyre and Ronald Gregor Smith (London: SCM Press, 1957), p.
15, n. 4. Italics mine.
[12] "Introduction," *Faith and Logic,* ed. Basil Mitchell (Boston: Beacon Press,
1957; now published by Allen & Unwin, London), p. 1.

ness of religious and metaphysical *assertions* is the contention that the practices of analysis and of conceptual elucidation are metaphysically neutral, and, consequently, that this challenge is not that of a rival metaphysical commitment, but, rather, is simply a report that such statements, upon examination, seem not to possess the purely logical or formal characteristics that assertions must possess. Against this claim that analysis has been a strictly neutral practice is the contention that analysis has involved assumptions that run counter to much religious conviction. According to Michael Foster, "what is to be questioned is 'not the practice of analysis but the belief that nothing is really puzzling and that therefore there cannot be anything unclear that we can legitimatcly want to say.'"[13] It is Foster's own view that "theological thinking, *based on revelation*, may itself be thought of as a kind of analysis, but an analysis proceeding upon different assumptions from those just specified."[14]

It must be emphasized, however, that even if the analysts' challenge concerning the meaningfulness of religious assertions is made by practices in which certain metaphysical judgments are implied, this challenge is not met simply by arguing that the analysts have not shown conclusively that religious assertions are not meaningful. In the words of one Christian apologist, "we often behave as if religious belief (like the Church of England) were firmly established, so that all the believer had to do was to show the attacks of agnostics to be inconclusive; so long as religion could not be pinned down and proved false, the darts of the enemy were vain."[15] But this fails to consider that the challenge is precisely that religious belief does not seem to have any firmly established meaning. Such a challenge can be answered only by showing that religious assertions are meaningful. The question being raised is not whether religious beliefs are true. We are concerned, rather, with the prior question as to whether they are meaningful.

The connection we are suggesting between statements about God and metaphysical statements lies simply in the fact that religion has to do with things as a whole. In my critical evaluation I shall defend as meaningful the type of metaphysics practiced by John Wisdom, and I shall relate this to the philosophical theology of Paul Tillich. However, I shall argue against the meaningfulness of the transcendentalist aspects of metaphysical positions which deal with entities outside of space and time, and I shall similarly argue against the transcendentalist

---

[13] *Mystery and Philosophy*, p. 17. Foster expresses an indebtedness for this point to Ian Crombie.

[14] *Ibid.* Italics mine.

[15] John Wilson, *Philosophy and Religion: The Logic of Religious Belief* (London: Oxford University Press, 1961), p. 74.

or supernaturalist aspects of theologies which speak of a divine being as existing outside of space and time.

My central aim, however, is not to set out a thesis and then to use the analytic philosophers to advance an argument for it, for this would force each position into the mold of the argument and so limit full consideration of that position. Rather I wish to present the basic position of each philosopher on his own terms; consequently, attention is not limited to those aspects of a position which have immediate application to the study of assertions about God but includes whatever seems important to that position as a whole.

We have before us now an outline of our subject. But if we are to understand it properly, we must place it in the context of our cultural situation; for no philosophy can be understood apart from the culture that gave it birth. If by "culture" we mean the way of life of a society—the way in which a people understand and transform reality—then philosophy is an expression of culture, influencing and being influenced by the other forms of cultural expression.

It is a commonplace to remark that our Western culture is in a stage of transition, and it is in this context that we must interpret the contemporary concerns with analysis and with the meaningfulness of statements about God. As Rollo May has expressed it, "We live at one of those points in history when one way of living is in its death throes, and another is being born. That is to say, the values and goals of Western society are in a state of transition." [16]

The Renaissance belief in the sweet reasonableness of the individual, with its emphasis upon the values of individual competition and autonomous reason, seems largely to have lost its hold on modern man as he has lived through barbaric inhumanities and social breakdown, learned to think of reason as deeply influenced by nonrational factors, been confronted with the necessity of working as a member of a large group rather than as a competitive individual, and suffered the anxiety of personal disintegration as he has become increasingly unable to experience a unity of reason and feeling.

But, whatever the correct analysis of the factors involved, what concerns us here is the effect that such a transitional period has on language. We may again take Rollo May as representative of many commentators in his observation that "when a culture is in its historical phase of growing toward unity, its language reflects the unity and power; whereas when a culture is in the process of change, dispersal and disintegration, the language likewise loses its power." [17] The language of

[16] *Man's Search for Himself* (New York: W. W. Norton, 1953), p. 46.
[17] *Ibid.*, p. 65.

our Western culture, then, is marked by confusion and by a loss of effectiveness for personal communication. As T. S. Eliot has put it,

> Our dried voices, when
> We whisper together
> Are quiet and meaningless
> As wind in dry grass
> Or rats' feet over broken glass
> In our dry cellar.[18]

So it is that, in contemporary man's anxiety about the hollowness and disorder of the meanings he communicates, his philosophers are prompted to examine those meanings.

With respect to religious language this situation is given clear expression by Basil Mitchell:

We often hear that the old beliefs have "lost their meaning" and that people to-day no longer find them relevant to the rest of their thought and practice. Christians are accused of a kind of "double-think" by which they contrive to talk two entirely independent languages with no way of relating what is said in one to what is said in the other. The more massive the development of the sciences and their attendant technologies, the more acute the problem of communication seems to become. The philosophical critic with his careful attention to the way in which expressions are used, and his tendency to distrust any but scientific explanations is here representative of a generation which dumbly shares his own perplexities.[19]

What, then, may be said about the relation of analytic philosophy to this situation of cultural transition? Is analysis a creative response to our language confusion, or is it rather a symptom of our inability to achieve new synthesis? Is the emphasis on analysis a constructive road toward renewal of meaning through clarification, or is it a blind alley in which preoccupation with the vestigial meanings of a dying culture diverts energy and talent from the quest for new insight? Doubtless it would be folly to hope for a simple judgment between these alternatives, for this is a complex matter. It may be helpful, then, if we consider briefly some of the facets of this question which most readily present themselves and which the reader may wish to bear in mind as we consider these positions.

On the positive side of the ledger there are three points to be taken into consideration. At one level we have the important task of clarifying the relations between the various sorts of meanings that we are concerned to communicate, such as the religious, ethical, and scientific. As Paul Tillich has suggested, our situation of language confusion

---

[18] "The Hollow Men," *T. S. Eliot: The Complete Poems and Plays, 1909-1950* (New York: Harcourt Brace Jovanovich, 1952), p. 56.
[19] "Introduction," *Faith and Logic*, pp. 7-8.

"has something to do with the fact that our present culture has no clearing house such as medieval scholasticism was, Protestant scholasticism in the 17th century at least tried to be, and philosophers like Kant tried to renew." [20] The concern of contemporary linguistic philosophy to function in this important capacity is indicated by Gilbert Ryle's statement that "the big metaphysicians of the past . . . tried, as we try, to trace and relieve logical stresses between the organizing ideas of everyday and technical thinking; and from their work in these fields we have valuable lessons to learn." [21]

With regard to religious uses of language specifically, these conceptual concerns bring home the lesson that was recognized by classical theology in its doctrine of analogy but which today, according to Michael Foster, is relatively "a new idea, to believers as well as to unbelievers." [22] This is the lesson that theological statements have a *peculiar* character. Foster suggests Archbishop Ussher's conclusion that God created the world in 4004 B.C. as an example of confusing the unique logic of religious language with the logic of another sort of language—in this case, the historical.[23]

Also involved in our situation of language confusion, however, is the presence of a mixture of old beliefs—some of which have lost their meaning—and new beliefs which modern man is coming to affirm. Therefore, as our second point, we may add to the logical task of clarification the existential task of "revealing a man to himself" [24] by helping him to see which of the old beliefs continue to function as the basis of his everyday orientation to life and which do not. By tracing out the implications of a particular belief, analysis may help a man either to see that this is really *not* what he wishes to affirm or to understand more fully this belief that he does wish to affirm. As Michael Foster sees it, for example, analysis "may be part of the task of enabling a man to face and accept what it is that he believes, liberating

---

[20] "The Nature of Religious Language" (1955), reprinted in *Theology of Culture*, ed. Robert C. Kimball (New York: Oxford University Press, 1959), p. 53.

[21] "Final Discussion," *The Nature of Metaphysics*, ed. D. F. Pears (New York: St. Martin's Press, Inc.; Macmillan & Co., Ltd., 1957), p. 164. By "we" Ryle refers to his fellow Oxford philosophers.

[22] "Contemporary British Philosophy and Christian Belief," p. 191.

[23] *Ibid.* Whether this rediscovery that there are important differences in the sorts of language we use is, at the same time, the rediscovery "that there are levels of reality of great difference"—a rediscovery which Tillich sees as coming from some of the present studies of meaning—is the issue we have already alluded to as decisive for our study: namely, does contemporary analysis find that some utterances about God are not only meaningful but also capable of being true. ("The Nature of Religious Language," *Theology of Culture*, p. 54.)

[24] Foster, "Contemporary British Philosophy and Christian Belief," p. 190.

him from dogmas which he could no longer wholly accept, but which haunted him because he had not faced them." [25]

The third contribution concerns yet another sense in which linguistic philosophers have not uncommonly seen their task to be that of revealing a man to himself, namely, by helping a man to see that certain aspects of his ways of thinking and speaking represent distorted perceptions of reality explainable as due to certain anxieties that he has refused to face. This is most clearly seen in the analysts' antipathy toward metaphysics. Just as, according to Erich Fromm, Marx and Freud "believed that most of what men consciously think is 'false' consciousness, is ideology and rationalization," [26] so at least some of the analysts believe that "metaphysical speaking is rooted in anxiety." [27] In one of the strongest expressions of this belief we read that

metaphysics only *seems* to disclose the "real" structure of the universe, and actually exposes deeply hidden strivings which lead men to speak metaphysically. For instance, the craving for a closed system unveils the remarkable compulsion to claim that there *must* be a well-ordered, recognizable pattern behind the distressing manifoldness of things. A metaphysician just cannot stand the idea of a universe which cannot be grasped, either by reason, by meditation, or by intuition, for it would fill him with horror.[28]

Although one, perhaps, should be cautious about making such judgments for any but one's own thinking, the many who subscribe to the concept of "false consciousness" in one form or another will welcome the possibility of the use of analysis or conceptual elucidation at least to raise this question at those points where it seems most warranted.

But, there are also certain possible negative evaluations of analytic and linguistic philosophy as a response to our cultural situation to be borne in mind as we examine these positions. Perhaps the most common charge is that linguistic philosophy tends toward an irrelevance to life. As Gilbert Ryle admits, a "unanimous grumble is that, even inside our constricted horizon, we are diligent about trivialities and neglectful of things that matter." [29] But, it is not simply that the concerns of many analysts often seem to be very remote from the concerns that we have when we are not doing philosophy. The danger is also seen to be that excessive emphasis on analysis will stifle the quest for new vision. The virtue of precision may become a substitute for the value of un-

[25] *Ibid.*

[26] *Marx's Concept of Man* (New York: Frederick Ungar, 1961), pp. 20-21.

[27] Willem Zuurdeeg, *An Analytical Philosophy of Religion* (Nashville: Abingdon Press, 1958), p. 137.

[28] *Ibid.* For an interesting comparison of certain metaphysical doubts with neurotic doubts see John Wisdom, "Philosophy, Metaphysics and Psycho-Analysis, *Philosophy and Psycho-Analysis*, pp. 281-82.

[29] "Final Discussion," *The Nature of Metaphysics*, p. 156.

derstanding, and the scrutiny of present outlooks may become the excuse for failure to search for new insight. In the words of one critic, "Instead of employing [critical acumen and scrupulous precision] to sift one's own wheat from one's chaff, one has abandoned any effort to grow wheat." [30]

Secondly, the skeptical attack on constructive metaphysics may be a double-edged sword. If, as a number of analysts allege, metaphysics carries the danger of becoming a pretentious mask by which a man avoids facing himself, then there is a genuine need for a philosophy which, "like psycho-analysis, punctures self-conceit" [31] in that it "destroys the pretensions of the speculative reason, and emphasizes the human, all-too-human character of our deepest convictions." [32] However, this sort of pretension-destroying philosophy may, in turn, pose a psychological temptation of its own which, in our age, is of even greater danger than the temptation that it is attacking. Rollo May reports that the fundamental psychological condition of our day is one of a deep feeling of emptiness and lack of personal worth. This has the consequence that many people turn to self-condemnation as the "quickest way to get a substitute sense of worth," [33] for this is, in effect, a way of saying to oneself, "I must be important that I am so worth condemning." [34] In May's judgment,

many of the arguments in our day against pride in one's self, and many of the homilies on alleged self-abnegation, have a motive quite other than humility or a courageous facing of one's human situation. A great number of these arguments, for example, reveal a considerable contempt for the self.[35]

Is there a point, then, at which analytic philosophy slips from a healthy concern for humility into an attack on the value of the human being? [36] J. V. L. Casserley believes that such a point is reached in the attack on metaphysics as beyond the scope of human reason:

Our ideas about the dignity of man, his role in life, the purpose of his existence, his relation with ultimate reality, cannot but be vitally affected by

---

[30] Walter Kaufmann, *Critique of Religion and Philosophy* (New York: Harper, 1958), p. 25.

[31] H. A. Hodges, *Wilhelm Dilthey: An Introduction* (London: Routledge and Kegan Paul, 1952), p. 106.

[32] *Ibid.*, p. 107.   [33] *Man's Search for Himself*, p. 98.

[34] *Ibid.*, p. 99.   [35] *Ibid.*, p. 98.

[36] This danger may also be seen in the attacks on human pretension by certain neo-orthodox theologians. This becomes particularly relevant to our study at the point where some theologians dismiss the challenges of analytic philosophers concerning the meaningfulness of religious language as merely the expressions of sinful pride. Cf. Thomas F. Torrance, "Faith and Philosophy," *The Hibbert Journal*, April, 1949.

our speculative estimate of his intellectual capacities. In fact we observe that scepticism and agnosticism, positivism and relativism, have produced an anti-humane tendency in Western thought, a progressive "debunking" of that traditional stress on the dignity of the human spirit which went hand in hand with metaphysical and religious assumptions and preoccupations in philosophy, a tendency which in our brutal twentieth century has begun to produce tragic practical results.[37]

It becomes clear that psychological judgments work both ways. If the "speculative" metaphysician is in danger of becoming "pompous" in his affirmations,[38] the skeptic may become equally pompous in his denunciations. Or, if the metaphysician is charged with an inability to face himself, he may, in turn, charge the skeptic with an inability to commit himself.

The third, and perhaps most serious, question that may be posed concerning the adequacy of analysis as a philosophical response to our cultural situation is whether, as it is practiced, analysis does not presuppose precisely that depersonalized attitude which many believe to be the heart of our contemporary spiritual crisis. According to this belief, our concern with science and technology has had, as a by-product, the result of reducing the consciousness of Western man to a largely objective mode, so that our response to the world is largely a response to a world of things rather than to a world of persons. This is closely related to the judgment that the road of Western consciousness has been "a road toward ever-increasing *loss* of religious consciousness." [39] Is it not symptomatic of this waning of personal and religious consciousness that "almost every man can name the parts of an automobile engine clearly and definitely; but when it comes to meaningful interpersonal relations, our language is lost: we stumble, and are practically isolated as deaf and dumb people who can only communicate in sign language"? [40] Insofar, then, as analytic philosophy tends to be preoccupied with, and even to raise to a normative position for language generally, the language of objective matter of fact, must not this philosophy be judged as itself a symptom of our illness rather than a creative response to it? Is it not further symptomatic of this same depersonalized consciousness that, for many, analysis is itself something that can be carried on anonymously; that the philosopher's convictions, his point of view, are to be kept in a compartment separate from his philosophical activity?

One of the marks of this depersonalized consciousness, it is common-

[37] *The Christian in Philosophy* (New York: Scribner's, 1951), p. 176.
[38] Willem Zuurdeeg, *An Analytical Philosophy of Religion*, p. 142.
[39] Paul Tillich, "The Two Types of Philosophy of Religion" (1949), reprinted in *Theology of Culture*, ed. Robert C. Kimball, p. 12.
[40] May, *Man's Search for Himself*, p. 64.

ly held, is the fragmentation of the personality in which the reasoning, feeling, and willing functions of the personality have been separated, so that the person no longer functions as a total personality. This is in marked contrast to the cultural situation of the seventeenth century, for example, when "reason" in the work of Spinoza meant "an attitude toward life in which the mind united the emotions with the ethical goals and other aspects of the 'whole man.'"[41] Perhaps, then, the claim of contemporary analysis to distinguish between cognitive, emotive, and conative aspects of meaning more carefully than often was true of earlier philosophy must be viewed not only as a clarification of meaning but also as a symptom of a consciousness which, because it has torn these things asunder, is able to achieve little clarity about the sort of meaning which is experienced when the person is responding as a whole person.

We shall follow this question of the relation of analysis to the allegedly depersonalized consciousness of Western man particularly in the form that it takes concerning the nature of cognitive meaning: Has preoccupation with impersonal, technical meanings resulted in too narrow a conception of cognition? In addition to the objective meaning of those statements whose truth is determined by certain observations, there is the existential meaning of the picture of reality as a whole by which we organize the totality of our experience and commit ourselves to a way of life defined in terms of that way of ordering experience. Is such existential meaning also to be regarded as cognitive? Do our metaphysical pictures of reality as a whole give us knowledge of a pattern in things-as-a-whole as it is apprehended from a given finite perspective? Or is such a picture an arbitrary, purely conventional, conceptual scheme for which it is theoretically possible to substitute many others which would do equally as well. If a metaphysical picture is not arbitrary but is, rather, one whose adequacy must be tested by the process of living by it to see how far the expectations it embodies are reliable and fulfilling, then the very fact of such a test seems to necessitate the classification of this sort of metaphysical picture as cognitive. Belief is genuinely cognitive if it is verifiable, and verifiable means testable. But such a test of a metaphysical picture would be a very different sort of verification than is the verification of statements of objective matter of fact, and the sort of knowledge to be claimed depends on the sort of test possible. We may consider Paul Tillich as a leading exponent of this wider sense of cognition:

Every cognitive assumption (hypothesis) must be tested. The safest test is a repeatable experiment. . . . [But] verification can occur within the life-

41 *Ibid.*, p. 50.

process itself. Verification of this type (experiential in contradistinction to experimental) has the advantage that it need not halt and disrupt the totality of a life-process in order to distil calculable elements out of it (which experimental verification must do). The verifying experiences of a nonexperimental character are truer to life, though less exact and definite.[42]

It is easy to see that experiential tests are not only "less definite," but very indefinite—a fact that, to many, seems to make the cognitive value of statements so tested very doubtful. We might put this another way by saying that the cognitive value of the religious or ultimate concern expressed in a metaphysical picture will depend upon the extent to which this religious *concern* involves religious *expectations* that may be either frustrated or realized by actual experience. Because of the far-reaching significance of this cognitive issue, it will be of considerable importance to see whether and how each of the positions to be considered treats existential meaning.

We have been saying, then, that, in an age marked by confusion concerning meaning and value—especially concerning ultimate or religious meaning and value—it is understandable that philosophy should turn its attention to the task of the clarification of meaning. But, if what is required in an age of cultural transition is that we work to "lay the groundwork for the new constructive society which will eventually come out of this disturbed time, as the Renaissance came out of the disintegration of the Middle Ages," [43] are the analytic and linguistic conceptions of philosophy ones that allow for the fullest possible use of the talents of philosophers to meet this need? Concerning the analytic philosophies of logical atomism and logical positivism and the views of some linguistic philosophers, our study will indicate a negative answer to this question. With little qualification we may say of analytic philosophy particularly that it neglected problems of meaning that are most important to everyday life and was itself a symptom of the depersonalization of our time in that it assumed an impersonal standpoint from which to make its analyses and so dealt only with what can be objectified. There are many, however, who hold similar opinions about the later work of Wittgenstein and Wisdom. Our study shall be especially concerned to show that this is mistaken and that these men have made important contributions toward the renewal of meaning in our time.

---

[42] *Systematic Theology,* 1 (Chicago: The University of Chicago Press, 1951), 102. Volume I © 1951 by The University of Chicago.
[43] May, *Man's Search for Himself,* p. 79.

PART ONE: *Analysis Before Wittgenstein's Investigations*

G. E. MOORE: *Analysis & Common Sense*

Chapter Two

The work of G. E. Moore has been one of the main sources of linguistic philosophy, not because of any results he achieved, but because of the methods he used. His practices were influential because philosophers were ready to welcome a method that would be unique to philosophy and that could achieve results on which philosophers could agree. Moore occupied himself with "the work of analysis and distinction" because he believed that, in philosophy, "the difficulties and disagreements, of which its history is full, are mainly due to a very simple cause —namely, to the attempt to answer questions without first discovering precisely what question it is to which you desire an answer" and also "what kinds of reason are relevant as arguments for or against any particular answer." [1] In approaching philosophic statements, then, Moore attempted to clarify issues and expose confusions in several ways. First, he simply raised all the questions he could think of about their precise meaning and about reasons for believing them. Second, he often examined them in terms of a sharp distinction between analytic and synthetic statements. Third, he argued that certain statements must be confused because they contradict commonsense beliefs which, he insisted, we know with certainty. Above all, however, Moore attempted to solve certain philosophic problems by his technique of analysis or definition.

The influence of Moore's analytic approach to philosophy began with the appearance in 1903 of "The Refutation of Idealism" in which

[1] George E. Moore, *Principia Ethica* (Cambridge: The University Press, 1959), pp. vii, viii.

he broke with the movement of Bosanquet, Bradley, and McTaggart which had dominated English philosophy since 1870.[2] In attempting to establish their central and important conclusion that the universe is spiritual, Moore said, the modern idealists had failed to give separate consideration to each of the large number of properties that define "spiritual" and so had left much unexamined. But even more important, the basic proposition on which idealism finally rests—to be is to be perceived—involves a type of confusion of which "all philosophers and psychologists" have been guilty when producing "their most striking and interesting conclusions." [3] This conclusion, which occurs in what have been called necessary synthetic propositions, is one in which a distinction between subject and predicate is both affirmed and, "in a slightly more obscure form of words," denied.[4] The idealist asserts that being and being perceived are the same. Yet he also believes that this assertion is interesting, that it gives us information about the nature of reality, and this is the case only if being and being perceived are not the same. In other words, at some point the idealist identifies the perceived object and the perceiving subject:

When he thinks of "yellow" and when he thinks of the "sensation of yellow," he fails to see that there is anything whatever in the latter which is not in the former. This being so, to deny that yellow can ever *be* apart from the sensation of yellow is merely to deny that yellow can ever be other than it is; since yellow and the sensation of yellow are absolutely identical. To assert that yellow is necessarily an object of experience is to assert that yellow is necessarily yellow—a purely identical proposition and therefore proved by the law of contradiction alone. Of course, the proposition also implies that experience is, after all, something distinct from yellow—else there would be no reason for asserting that yellow is a sensation: and that the argument thus both affirms and denies that yellow and the sensation of yellow are distinct, is what sufficiently refutes it.[5]

Careful analysis of perception, Moore believed, would remove this error of identifying the experience and the object perceived. The idealist, he said, analyzes perception as the occurrence of a sensation with some sort of content. The correct analysis of perception, however, will follow commonsense realism in distinguishing between consciousness and an objective reality of which one is conscious. To perceive yellow is not to have a sensation with a yellow content; rather, it is to be conscious of an objectively real yellow color.[6] The correctness of this analysis cannot be proved, but it was Moore's hope that it would enable

---

[2] Reprinted in Moore, *Philosophical Studies* (London: Routledge and Kegan Paul, 1922).

[3] *Ibid.*, p. 5.   [4] *Ibid.*, p. 16.   [5] *Ibid.*, pp. 13-14.   [6] *Ibid.*, pp. 21, 27.

the reader to "see" that this is what perception really is. The idealists lost sight of this whenever they consciously reflected on the nature of perception, because they unconsciously brought to that reflection a preconceived notion of the sort of thing consciousness must be if it is to be judged as distinct from its object. It must be the sort of thing that they could compare with its object in the same way in which they could compare two different colors. But, when we try in this way "to fix our attention upon consciousness and to see *what*, distinctly, it is, it seems to vanish." [7] Moore wished to expose this faulty model by reminding the reader of the truth of Bishop Butler's principle, "everything is what it is and not another thing." [8] At a later time Moore might have described this confusion by saying that the idealist, without realizing it, sometimes follows his commonsense knowledge that consciousness is distinct from its object but at other times, when he is arguing his most important conclusions, he denies this commonsense distinction. Although Moore later rejected this analysis as "full of confusions" [9] it was important as an example of an analytic approach to philosophy.

Moore's attack on necessary synthetic propositions was based on his acceptance of a rigid distinction between analytic and synthetic propositions. An analytic proposition, as he saw it, is one in which subject and predicate are identical and so to deny it would be contradictory: "X is not X." But, if this is true, then these propositions cannot convey information about reality. Such information can only be given where subject and predicate are distinct, that is, by synthetic propositions. One cannot have it both ways. A proposition cannot be at once necessary (analytic) and synthetic. Therefore, "all the most striking results of philosophy" are seen to have "no more foundation than the supposition that a chimera lives in the moon" [10] for they have been based on the ambiguity of certain key propositions whereby the proposition is sometimes used in its analytic sense and sometimes in its synthetic sense according to the need of the moment. Taken in its analytic sense, it could be used to advance conclusions; to assert, for example, "that yellow is necessarily an object of experience is to assert that yellow is necessarily yellow—a purely identical proposition and therefore proved by the law of contradiction alone." [11] Once analytically established it is taken in its synthetic sense that yellow does not really exist independently of my experience. It is when taken in this sense that the proposition becomes interesting because it allegedly gives us new knowledge.

[7] *Ibid.*, p. 25.
[8] From the title page of Moore, *Principia Ethica*.
[9] *Philosophical Studies*, p. viii.
[10] *Ibid.*, p. 5.
[11] *Ibid.*, p. 14.

This claim to new knowledge by an *a priori* method is, from Moore's point of view, exposed as nothing more than a confused and contradictory use of a proposition.

A highly influential side of Moore's approach to many philosophic statements is his way of opposing them by a defense of common sense. When Moore was a student at Cambridge in the 1890s, ordinary, everyday beliefs were typically dismissed—in the fashion of Zeno—as confused and even self-contradictory; it was held that such beliefs regarded as real what is mere "appearance." At that time, Moore related,

Russell had invited me to tea in his room to meet McTaggart; and McTaggart, in the course of conversation had been led to express his well-known view that Time is unreal. This must have seemed to me then (as it still does) a perfectly monstrous proposition, and I did my best to argue against it.[12]

Moore's way of arguing against this proposition is well illustrated in his article "The Conception of Reality":

What would most people mean by this proposition? . . . To define *exactly* what can be meant by saying of an entity of that sort it is unreal does seem to offer difficulties. But if you try to translate the proposition into the concrete . . . there is, I think, very little doubt. . . . If time is unreal, then plainly nothing ever happens before or after anything else.[13]

Having given this interpretation Moore simply exclaimed that surely we cannot sensibly deny that we have breakfast before we have lunch. How, then, can we deny that time is real?

Similarly, if anyone questioned the existence of material objects and, consequently, the existence of external things—things which, unlike toothaches, exist independently of our experience of them—Moore was ready to reply:

I can prove now, for instance, that two human hands exist. How? By holding up my two hands and saying, as I make a certain gesture with the right hand, "Here is one hand," and adding, . . . "And here is another." And by doing this I have proved *ipso facto* the existence of external things.[14]

---

[12] "An Autobiography," *The Philosophy of G. E. Moore*, 3rd ed.; ed. Paul A. Schilpp (New York: Tudor Publishing Co., 1952; now published by The Open Court Publishing Co., LaSalle, Illinois, 1968), pp. 13-14.

[13] *Philosophical Studies*, pp. 209-10.

[14] "Proof of an External World," *Proceedings of the British Academy*, 1939, p. 295. Concerning Moore's argument in its complete form, Douglas Lewis argues: "Since the commonsensical difference between hands and after-images is that while the former are continuants, the latter momentary entities, rather than that the former are public and the latter private, Moore's proof falls to the ground. . . . The 'proof' of an external world is, in other words, coherence. It does not follow, however, that one is not certain in such situations as that described . . . that there is an external thing." Laird Addis and Douglas Lewis, *Moore and Ryle: Two Ontologists* (Iowa City: University of Iowa Press, 1965), p. 183.

How like Dr. Johnson's disproof of Berkeley by kicking a stone! At first reading, these arguments seem to have missed the point. When Bradley or McTaggart maintained that time is unreal they realized that they had breakfast before they had lunch; when Kant concluded that we must take the existence of an external world on faith until we know his philosophical proof of its existence he knew that we can easily show that our hands exist. And yet in explaining the pointlessness of Moore's reply we are pointing out how little, if any, the philosopher's contentions affect these facts of our everyday lives. Moore's use of concrete cases suddenly makes these philosophic statements seem very peculiar. Consequently, we now ask just what point *they* have if they make no difference to my knowledge that I have a hand with which I can pick up a pen and write, as I am now doing, and that later today I have a meeting to attend. At the very least this forces the philosopher to get clear about what he is saying;[15] perhaps he will find that what he is saying is of less consequence than he supposed. In this way, for example, Russell was led to give up idealism. "The emperor was seen to have, if not quite no clothes, at least not very many. . . . Why should one try to believe that Time is not real? There was quite suddenly seen to be no reason at all." [16]

By his arguments, then, Moore called into question the very nature of philosophical assertions and explanations. But he did this by insisting that we do know the everyday facts that we think we know. This he discussed at length in his "Defence of Common Sense," which he began with a long list of "truisms" that he claimed to know with certainty: "There exists at present a living human body, which is *my* body. This body was born at a certain time in the past. . . . I am a human being . . . . I have had dreams." [17] According to Moore, those philosophers who have maintained that some of these commonsense beliefs are false or that we do not know them with certainty have not succeeded in arguing their view consistently; their arguments imply that they too accept these beliefs as certainly true, much as I imply that there is someone home if I argue with someone knocking at my door that there is no one home.[18] Furthermore, against the contention

---

[15] Cf. John Wisdom, "Moore's Technique," *The Philosophy of G. E. Moore.* "When he [the philosopher] does this," says Wisdom, "the queerness of his negative hypothesis and its likeness to an analytic statement comes out." (P. 442)

[16] G. J. Warnock, *English Philosophy Since 1900* (London: Oxford University Press, 1958), p. 17.

[17] *Contemporary British Philosophy*, ed. J. H. Muirhead, II (London: Allen and Unwin, 1925), pp. 194-95.

[18] Such a philosopher, for example, "asserts with confidence that these beliefs *are* beliefs of Common Sense, and seems often to fail to notice that, *if* they are, they must be true; since the proposition that they are beliefs of Common Sense is

of some philosophers that commonsense propositions have contradictory implications Moore argued that "all the propositions in [my list] are true; no true proposition entails both of two incompatible propositions; therefore, none of the propositions in [my list] entails both of two incompatible propositions." [19] Moore admitted that there is no logical contradiction in holding the first premise of this argument to be false, and this led him to ask, "Do I really *know* all the propositions in [my list] to be true? . . . In answer to this question, I think I have nothing better to say than that it seems to me that I *do* know them, with certainty." [20]

But even though we do know many things with certainty, nonetheless we are "in this strange position," Moore confessed, that "we do not know *how* we know them, i.e. we do not know what the evidence was." [21] We do not, that is, know "the correct *analysis* of such propositions." [22] More than to any other problem, Moore devoted his attention to that of providing correct analyses.

A large number of Moore's commonsense propositions have to do with material objects, and it was particularly with their analysis that he was concerned.

Two things only seem to me to be quite certain about the analysis of such propositions . . . namely that whenever I know or judge such a proposition to be true, (1) there is always some *sense-datum* about which the proposition in question is a proposition . . . and (2) that, nevertheless *what* I am knowing or judging to be true about this sense-datum is not (in general) that it is *itself* a hand, or a dog, or the sun, etc., etc., as the case may be.[23]

In other words, we know with certainty the existence of many material objects, and we see or touch or taste or smell sense-data. But we do not know how these two things are related. Despite persistent attempts Moore was never able to solve this problem. Yet his way of proceeding, his concern to be precise and clear, has been an example of considerable influence.

In addition to this sort of epistemological analysis Moore also concerned himself with another sort, which we may illustrate by his favorite example, "The concept 'being a brother' is identical with the concept 'being a male sibling.'" [24] The distinction between this analysis and epistemological analysis corresponds to that which we shall find Moore's disciple John Wisdom making in his atomistic days between

---

one which . . . logically entails the proposition that many human beings . . . have had bodies, which" . . . and so on. (*Ibid.*, p. 205.)
[19] "Defence of Common Sense," *Contemporary British Philosophy*, p. 204.
[20] *Ibid.*, p. 206.   [21] *Ibid.*
[22] *Ibid.*, p. 216.   [23] *Ibid.*, p. 217.
[24] "A Reply to My Critics," *The Philosophy of G. E. Moore*, p. 664.

same level and new level analyses. Brothers (or male siblings) and hands are objects of quite a different sort from sense-data.

Despite this difference Moore thought that all correct analyses would share the same pattern. "To define a concept," he believed, "is the same thing as to give an analysis of it"; [25] and the definition of something is the enumeration of its "different properties and qualities" and "their definite relations to one another." [26] This means that a definition can be given only of complex things, and is possible logically only if there are non-complex elements—the "parts" to be enumerated:

You can give a definition of a horse, because a horse has many different properties and qualities, all of which you can enumerate. But when you have enumerated them all, when you have reduced a horse to his simplest terms, then you can no longer define those terms. They are simply something which you think of or perceive, and to any one who cannot think of or perceive them you can never, by any definition, make their nature known.[27]

Such indefinables include "good," "yellow," and presumably, "consciousness" and "being." Each of these concepts can be used in giving an analysis of a complex concept but are themselves not analyzable.

Since analysis is definition, an analysis will be expressed by an analytic proposition. Moore's theory of analysis, then, is closely related to his distinction between analytic and synthetic propositions. In his *Principia Ethica*, for example, Moore used his theory of definition and his analytic-synthetic distinction to argue that most ethical theories have been guilty of a serious error. This error is typified by the hedonist proposition that "good is pleasure." As a necessary synthetic proposition this involves the confusion of both affirming and denying a distinction. It is also an attempt to define what is indefinable, or, in other words, to analyze what is unanalyzable. Good simply is what it is and not another thing. To equate good with something non-moral or naturalistic is to commit the "naturalistic fallacy" of attempting to define an undefinable moral concept.[28]

We have focused on Moore's defense of common sense and his analytic practices because they are important sources of linguistic philosophy. But in his *Principia Ethica*, along with his analyses he enquired about those things which are worthy of human aspiration and ought to exist. He also maintained that "the most important and interesting thing which philosophers have tried to do" is to provide "a general description of the *whole* of the Universe" [29] and, in breaking

[25] *Ibid.*, p. 665.
[26] *Principia Ethica*, pp. 7-8.
[27] *Ibid.*
[28] *Ibid.*, p. 59.
[29] *Some Main Problems of Philosophy* (New York: Macmillan, 1953), p. 1.

with idealism, both he and Russell defended a realist metaphysics. Moore held that neither mind nor matter could be reduced to anything else, that talk about a universal such as "tree," for example, is not just a shorthand way of referring to all the particular trees there are, that the goodness of things is a characteristic they possess much as they possess a certain color or shape, and that the nature of a thing may be logically independent of at least some of its relations to other things— that the yellow I experience, for example, is what it is quite independently of my experience of it. Even in defending commonsense beliefs, then, Moore was involved in metaphysics, for he was defending such things as the reality of time and space. Unlike some of the analysts, neither Moore nor Russell ever rejected metaphysics.

Critical Evaluation

Both Moore's analytic practices and his defense of common sense raise a number of problems. First of all, Moore was able neither to state clearly the nature of an analysis—just how understanding a proposition differs from knowing the correct analysis of its meaning—nor to provide adequate criteria for judging the correctness of an analysis. Moore says that analysis is definition, but just what philosophical purpose does such definition serve? In the case of his epistemological analyses, to analyze the meaning of a proposition seems to be the same thing as to show how we know its truth. In these cases he seems to hold the view expressed by John Wisdom that "epistemology—puzzles of the form . . . 'How do we really know?'—and ontology—puzzles of the form 'What is it that we claim to know'—are one." [30] Moore contended, for example, that "if the propositions you choose to analyse . . . tell you something about reality, . . . then I think the analysis of them will tell you something about reality too." [31] Yet Moore, to my knowledge, neither explicitly identifies epistemology and ontology[32] nor discusses the relation between epistemological and other analyses. For an analysis to be correct, according to Moore, there must be a necessary relation between the concept being analyzed and the concepts in terms of which it is analyzed. But, since necessary relations, for Moore, are relations of identity it is difficult to see how a correct analysis can be informative. An analysis, that is, must be expressed by

[30] "Note on the New Edition of Professor Ayer's *Language, Truth and Logic*," *Mind*, 1948, reprinted in *Philosophy and Psycho-Analysis*, p. 229.
[31] "A Reply to My Critics," p. 676.
[32] Moore's lack of clarity about this is reflected, for example, in the fact that one of his commentators first identifies correct analysis with knowing how we know but then, later, distinguishes them. (See Maxwell John Charlesworth, *Philosophy and Linguistic Analysis* [Pittsburgh: Duquesne University Press, 1959], pp. 22, 40.)

an analytic statement in which the subject (the concept being analyzed) has the same meaning as the predicate (the concepts in terms of which it is analyzed). To be informative the predicate must add something, in which case the analysis would be incorrect. Of this "paradox of analysis" [33] Moore confessed that "I am not at all clear as to what the solution of the puzzle is," but he suggested that

for a full discussion of the subject it would be necessary to raise the question how an "analytic" necessary connection is to be distinguished from a "synthetic" one—a subject upon which I am far from clear. It seems to me that there are ever so many different cases of necessary connection, and that the line between "analytic" and "synthetic" might be drawn in many different ways. As it is, I do not think the terms have any clear meaning. [34]

In asserting that the only necessary relation that may exist between subject and predicate is one of identity, Moore undermined not only the "necessary synthetic" propositions of traditional philosophy but also his own analyses.

One way out of this dilemma would be to interpret the predicate as expressing one dimension of the complex, multidimensional meaning of the subject. This relation would be necessary without being one of identity. "To be is to be perceived" could be interpreted in this way to assert that the possibility of being perceived is an inseparable part of what we mean by "being." Aquinas, one could then say, pointed to another dimension of meaning by stressing that being is act. [35] Berkeley himself asserted, "I know or am conscious of my own being and that *I myself am* . . . a thinking, active principle." [36] Yet another dimension would be that expressed by the ontologist, such as Paul Tillich, in asserting that being is the negation of nonbeing; our sense of being is seen to be inseparably tied up with our experience of threat to that being, whether in the form of death, dissolution of personality, or the guilt of failing *to be* all that we are capable of being—such as being fully a person to other persons. [37] Whether even this view of analysis makes sense in light of Wittgenstein's work on meaning will be discussed in Chapter IX.

Moore's model of philosophical analysis as definition, then, suffers

[33] Cf. C. H. Langford, "The Notion of Analysis in Moore's Philosophy," *The Philosophy of G. E. Moore*, p. 323.

[34] "A Reply to My Critics," p. 667. On the preceding page Moore stipulates that in a correct analysis subject and predicate must express "in some sense" the same concept but that the predicate must "explicitly mention" concepts not explicitly mentioned by the subject—as in the case of "brother" and "male sibling."

[35] Cf. *Summa Theologica*, Vol. I, Q. 3, a. 1.

[36] *Three Dialogues Between Hylas and Philonous*, ed. Colin M. Turbayne (The Library of Liberal Arts; New York: Liberal Arts Press, 1954), p. 80.

[37] *Systematic Theology*, I, 163-64.

from his failure to show clearly how such definition can be informative. But his theory of definition as the *enumeration* of the *simple* properties (and their relations) of whatever is being analyzed is also open to criticism. First of all, since the properties and their arrangement of, say, any two horses are not the same, a separate definition would be required for each horse, and so the word "horse" could only be applied to one particular horse.[38] Second, the concepts simple and composite do not have the absolute standing that this theory suggests. Wittgenstein was later to make the point in this way:

What are the simple constituent parts of a chair?—The bits of wood of which it is made? Or the molecules, or the atoms?—"Simple" means: not composite. And here the point is: in what sense "composite"? It makes no sense at all to speak absolutely of the "simple parts of a chair." [39]

What may be taken as a simple in one universe of discourse may lose this standing in another. And Moore himself admitted to being very unclear about just what qualified as a simple.[40]

Third, the theory that analysis is the enumeration or naming of simple parts and relations presupposes that meaning is the same thing as naming. Words, that is, simply name various things, and if those things are complex their analyses may be carried out by naming their simple parts. As we shall see, the difficulties that Moore and, later, the atomists encountered in attempting analyses on the basis of this theory of meaning have led the language analysts to interpret meaning in terms of use. It will suffice for now to point out that if words are names then we must understand language in terms of nameable things. But this view that language is concerned only with things and their relations—at the most basic level, with qualities and their relations—fits language about material objects far better than it fits other sorts of language. To say that good is a quality in the sense that red is a quality and consequently that ethical statements are factual in the sense that statements about red books are factual is surely to make a very strained comparison between "good" and "red"—an attempt to see all language as following the pattern of language about material objects. More precisely, it is an attempt to understand the ethical use of language as some sort of descriptive use.

From the point of view of contemporary analytic practice Moore's problems find their solution in the achievements of Wittgenstein.

[38] Cf. Charlesworth, *Philosophy and Linguistic Analysis*, p. 24.
[39] *Philosophical Investigations*, 2nd ed. (Oxford: Basil Blackwell, 1953), par. 47. See also L. Susan Stebbing, "Moore's Influence," *The Philosophy of G. E. Moore*, pp. 527-28.
[40] "Hume's Philosophy" (1909), reprinted in *Philosophical Studies*, p. 165.

Moore has himself said of Wittgenstein that "he has made me think that what is required for the solution of philosophical problems which baffle me, is a method . . . which he himself uses successfully, but which I have never been able to understand clearly enough to use it myself." [41] For Wittgenstein, the difference between understanding a meaning and knowing the correct analysis of it becomes that between knowing how to use a word and being able to describe that use by displaying the rules that govern it. Here meaning is no longer a non-linguistic entity (i.e., a concept or idea),[42] philosophical analysis is no longer the statement of an equivalence, and language is no longer something that follows a basic pattern. The model "a brother is a male sibling" seems, then, not to have the extensive application that it might were our language more uniform and that Moore believed it to have.[43] Nor are "good" and "red" as similar in meaning as Moore was encouraged to think when he classified them together as indefinables. When one asks instead about their use one begins to see the philosophically important differences between them.

That Wittgenstein made it possible in this way to say something about the meaning of good and of other "indefinables" is also important in connection with another of Moore's problems, namely, that his principles of analysis made it impossible to say anything about the meaning of an indefinable—except to contend that it is in fact indefinable. This problem is apparent in the *Principia Ethica*, for example, when Moore speaks of good as that which "ought to exist." [44] This, as H. J. Paton remarks, "indicates some sort of necessary connection between goodness and existence," [45] and so it contradicts both Moore's sharp distinction between analytic and synthetic propositions and his view that the concept good is absolutely simple and unanalyzable.

From this point of view, then, Moore's confessed inability to adopt the Wittgensteinian solution to his difficulties is perhaps traceable to the persistence of old habits of thought. And yet it seems prudent to wonder whether Moore was not concerned, among other things, with

[41] "An Autobiography," p. 33.

[42] For example, in Wittgenstein's *Philosophical Investigations* we read: "You say: the point isn't the word, but its meaning, and you think of the meaning as a thing of the same kind as the word, though also different from the word. Here the word, there the meaning. The money, and the cow you can buy with it. (But contrast: money, and its use.)" Par. 120.

[43] The analysis of "brother" into "male sibling" is what we have termed same level, and it is instructive that whatever successes Moore had in constructing analyses—and he himself thought them meager—seem also to have been same level. Cf. Stebbing, "Moore's Influence," pp. 528-29, and Moore, "A Reply to My Critics," p. 677.

[44] P. 17.

[45] "The Alleged Independence of Goodness," *The Philosophy of G. E. Moore*, pp. 116-17.

something involved in our use of words to which Wittgenstein's method is also inadequate. We shall explore this briefly in Chapter IX.

Much controversy surrounds the interpretation of Moore's defense of what he called "certain fundamental features of the Common Sense view of the world." Moore himself seems very unclear about what he was doing, which is what one would expect when new trails are being blazed. It is difficult to determine precisely what Moore was defending or just how his defense works.

Moore's use of the expression "common sense" is rather different than our ordinary uses of it—such as to indicate good judgment.[46] In his "Defence" he said that the beliefs of common sense are beliefs "very commonly entertained by mankind";[47] and in an earlier work he spoke of beliefs that "are so universally held that they may, I think, fairly be called the view of Common Sense." [48] In Moore's use, then, "common sense" refers to beliefs that are universally held, and he defended certain of these which he contended we know with certainty. Moore did not say, however, that it is their universality that makes these beliefs certain, but only that the certainty with which they are believed is universal. In fact there are "some things about which the views of common sense have changed," [49] such as the former belief of savages that "sometimes when a man was dreaming, his mind or soul used to leave his body." [50] And in his "Defence" Moore admitted that "the phrases 'Common Sense view of the world' or 'Common Sense beliefs' (as used by philosophers) are, of course, extraordinarily vague; and, for all I know, there may be many propositions which may be properly called features in the 'Common Sense view of the world' or 'Common Sense beliefs' which are not true." [51] Moore defended the common sense view, then, only in certain of its "fundamental features," yet he did not make explicit any further criteria for determining just which features qualify. Whatever it is that Moore defended, he defended it quite conclusively, he believed, simply by pointing out that we do know it with certainty. Analysis is needed if we are to see how we know it, but neither this nor any other justification is necessary for the claim that we do in fact know it.

Moore's interpreters, for the most part, do not find his views on "common sense" defensible unless he may be taken to have done in an unclear way what later philosophers, such as Wittgenstein, have learned

---

[46] See Norman Malcolm, "George Edward Moore" in Malcolm, *Knowledge and Certainty* (Englewood Cliffs, N.J.: Prentice-Hall, 1963), pp. 168-70.

[47] P. 204.

[48] *Some Main Problems of Philosophy*, p. 2.

[49] *Ibid.*, p. 3.

[50] *Ibid.*, p. 7.

[51] "Defence of Common Sense," p. 207.

from him to do, namely, to defend the correctness of ordinary language against critics.[52] According to Wittgenstein, "philosophy may in no way interfere with the actual use of language . . . [and] it cannot give it any foundation either" [53] for "every sentence in our language 'is in order as it is.' " [54] And in his "Defence" Moore explains that he is defending the statements in his list of commonsense beliefs as they are understood in ordinary usage. Furthermore, in claiming to know their truth with certainty he is apparently also using "know," "truth," and "certainty" as we use them in ordinary language. This use of ordinary language, these interpreters maintain, has the result of showing the senselessness of attacking the ordinary ways in which we use language. What is to determine the correctness of these uses if not the fact of their everyday usefulness? Understood in this way, Moore's appeal to ordinary language is held to be what is really important about what he was doing.

To be fair, however, we must carefully distinguish what has been learned from Moore and what is to be attributed to him. Moore always took great pains to explain what he meant, and he has never said either that he was defending the correctness of ordinary language against those who wanted to change it or that ordinary use is necessarily correct use or that ordinary use may serve as a formal criterion for meaning.[55] Concerning the analysis of meaning, Moore said, "What I have talked of analysing has always been a concept or proposition, and *not* a verbal expression." [56] Then, too, when Malcolm presents examples of Moore's method of proving the falsity of philosophical statements, Moore accepts his examples with the qualification that "in the case of the proposition 'Nobody knows [*for certain*] that there are any material things' [57] it does seem to me more obvious that some further argument is called for, if one is to talk of having proved it to be false, than in the case of 'There *are* no material things.' " [58] But Moore's qualification is incompatible with Malcolm's claim that "the actual efficacy of Moore's reply,

[52] See Norman Malcolm, *Knowledge and Certainty*, pp. 180-83, or Malcolm, "Moore and Ordinary Language," pp. 343-68, and L. Susan Stebbing, "Moore's Influence," p. 529 (both in *The Philosophy of G. E. Moore*); George Nakhnikian, *Readings in Twentieth-Century Philosophy*, eds., W. P. Alston and G. Nakhnikian (New York: Free Press of Glencoe, 1963), pp. 218-20.

[53] *Philosophical Investigations*, par. 124.

[54] *Ibid.*, par. 98.

[55] Cf. G. J. Warnock, *English Philosophy Since 1900*, pp. 21-24; G. A. Paul, "G. E. Moore: Analysis, Common Usage, and Common Sense," *The Revolution in Philosophy*, A. J. Ayer, *et al.* (London: Macmillan, 1957; New York: St. Martin's Press), pp. 67-68; Charlesworth, *Philosophy and Linguistic Analysis*, pp. 42-44.

[56] "A Reply to My Critics," p. 661. Cf. *Philosophical Studies*, p. 217.

[57] Malcolm's statement is actually, "We do not know for *certain* that there are other minds," but Moore regards it as similar to the one he quotes here.

[58] "A Reply to My Critics," p. 669.

his misnamed 'defence of common sense,' consists in reminding us that there is a proper use for sentences like . . . 'It is known for certain that he drowned in the lake' ";[59] for Malcolm presents just such reminders, and Moore asks for further argument. Moore understands himself to be defending the *truth* of certain propositions that are expressed in ordinary language rather than the correctness of that way of speaking.

Similarly, in considering John Wisdom's interpretation of Moore we must again distinguish the way Moore has influenced philosophers from his true position. Wisdom concludes an astute analysis of Moore's confusion concerning analysis by emphasizing that "for the metaphysical and Copernican discovery of how nearly philosophy *is* really logic Moore did as much as, and perhaps more than, any other man." [60] But when Wisdom asserts that philosophers "escape the power of Moore's proof only by making 'Does Matter exist?' an analytic issue and thus claiming that what they have been doing is what Moore says they should have been doing, namely analysis, . . ." [61] and when he also speaks of "Moore's account of philosophy as analysis," [62] Moore replies that "analysis is by no means the only thing I have tried to do." [63]

Maxwell Charlesworth says of Moore's "appeal" to ordinary language simply that "for him, the fact that a philosophical position is expressed in a grammatical form which we would not employ in ordinary everyday language, is a rough and ready sign that 'common sense' is being violated." [64] Yet even this limited interpretation is open to question because of the vagueness of "would not employ." In the articles most frequently cited concerning his appeal to ordinary language, for example, Moore followed special philosophic usage in speaking of "common sense," "sense datum," "mental fact," "having an experience" and "mind." [65]

We perhaps do least violence to Moore's position if we interpret his appeal to ordinary language not in terms of Wittgenstein's belief that ordinary use is necessarily correct use but in terms of an insight underlying this belief. According to Wittgenstein,

when I talk about language (words, sentences, etc.) I must speak the language of every day. Is this language somehow too coarse and material for what we want to say? Then how is another one to be constructed? . . .

---

[59] *Knowledge and Certainty*, p. 181.   [60] "Moore's Technique," p. 450.
[61] *Ibid.*, p. 439.   [62] *Ibid.*, p. 425.   [63] "Reply to My Critics," p. 676.
[64] *Philosophy and Linguistic Analysis*, p. 15. Charlesworth then maintains, incorrectly I think, that Moore's views on common sense are important *only* because they call "into question the whole traditional conception of the nature of philosophical explanation and justification." (P. 19)
[65] Cf. "A Defence of Common Sense," pp. 207-10, 217-18; "Proof of an External World," pp. 289-91.

In giving explanations I already have to use language full-blown. . . . Yes, but then how can these explanations satisfy us?—Well, your very questions were framed in this language.[66]

Now Moore neither concerned himself with words and sentences nor limited himself to the language of everyday. Nonetheless, this passage illuminates Moore's position because here Wittgenstein draws our attention to the fundamental place that certain *meanings*[67] expressed in our ordinary discourse occupy in our language as a whole. They are presupposed by our more technical ways of speaking, for at some point in defining our technical meanings we must make use of these ordinary meanings. It is senseless, then, to use technical meanings to attack the ordinary meanings that they must presuppose; it is senseless, to borrow a metaphor from Wittgenstein, to believe that we can use ordinary language to climb up to technical language and then throw away the ladder. This throws light on Moore's defense of common sense against attempts to deny the reality of material things, of space, of time, and of the self.[68] The philosopher is able to ask whether material objects exist, for example, only because the distinction between material and nonmaterial is meaningful. Similarly he can examine the nature of time only because it is meaningful to say that we had carrots *before* we had cake. Moore did not say that we could never find reason to alter any of the meanings expressed in ordinary language.[69] But these meanings in some form are basic to the human enterprise as we know it.[70] Consequently any attempt to do away with the ordinary ways in which we use these meanings would simply result in their reappearance in a new form. Were we to decide, for instance, not to use the terms "earlier" and "later" or "above" and "below" we should have to express their meanings in some other way.

Similarly, when Moore claims to know for certain the truth of his commonsense propositions, he is using "know" and "certain" to express meanings so basic to our language that the philosopher must presuppose them in order to call them into question. Were we to decide never to say, "I am *sure* there is cheese on the table," we should have to find some other way of saying that we are sure. Certainty, in other

---

[66] *Philosophical Investigations*, par. 120.
[67] Wittgenstein, as we shall see, preferred to speak of uses rather than meanings.
[68] "A Defence of Common Sense," pp. 200-201.
[69] For example, we might wish to change some of the inferences concerning the relation of mind and body which are based on the ordinary meaning of "mind" and "body."
[70] It is fundamental to our way of responding to experience, for example, to group hands, chairs, and walls as physical objects that we can shake, sit on, lean against, but not walk through, and to distinguish between these merely physical objects and a person as something else besides.

words, is relative to the language we are using, and it would not serve the purposes that our ordinary language is used to serve if, for example, we were to express uncertainty about the existence of Moore's hand when, under ordinary circumstances, we see him gesturing with it. If there are special philosophical purposes in terms of which uncertainty is warranted—uncertainty, say, about *how* we know something—then we should be careful not to confuse the ordinary and special senses of "certainty." The commonsense meanings that Moore defends, then, are those for which it will be universally true that, having become clear about what they are, we will not attempt to alter them.[71]

There is, however, another side to Moore's use of "common sense," for the propositions defended as "features in the 'Common Sense view of the world'" are quite varied. As Michael Foster has shown, Moore's belief that "the 'Common Sense view of the world' is, in certain fundamental features, *wholly* true" [72] seems in places to be an "affirmation of faith." [73] Moore's frequent use of such phrases as "we now believe," "we all commonly believe," "we all cannot help believing," [74] seems to constitute an existential affirmation of "certain views about the nature of the Universe," [75] particularly about man and his place in that universe—and it is from this affirmation, argues Foster, that Moore's philosophy flows:

"We," then, in the mouth of a modern philosopher, seems to mean "we men." The kind of philosopher he is will depend upon what he believes a man to be. Thus "we" for Kant meant "we rational beings, who are bound by our human condition to a physical nature." To say "we" in Kant's sense is to affirm ourselves to be members of the intelligible world. But when Moore speaks of "human beings with human bodies" who have lived upon the earth, this expresses a different conception of what man is. "We" now commits me to membership of a differently conceived society, and involves me in a different affirmation of my own being. Is not this new anthropological affirmation really what is basic to Moore's philosophy? Other philosophers had gone on talking the language of a spiritual anthropology which no longer resonated with what they or their hearers were prepared to affirm existentially. Moore refused to say what he could not authentically affirm.[76]

---

[71] Earlier we cited Moore's reply to Malcolm that "in the case of the proposition 'Nobody knows that there are any material things' . . . some further argument is called for . . . than in the case of 'There are no material things.'" If Moore's proofs finally depend on showing the fundamental standing of the meanings involved, then he must here be interpreted as believing that the basic status of "know" in this case cannot be established as quickly as can that of "material."

[72] "A Defence of Common Sense," p. 207.

[73] "'We' in Modern Philosophy," *Faith and Logic*, ed. Basil Mitchell, p. 205.

[74] *Some Main Problems of Philosophy*, pp. 3, 115.

[75] *Ibid.*, p. 2.

[76] "'We' in Modern Philosophy," p. 210.

It seems, then, that the commonsense meanings or language uses which analysis is to clarify are those which express the philosophical point of view that really holds conviction for those modern men ("we") among whom Moore places himself in this respect. Analysis presupposes an "initial act of affirmation" on the part of the analyst, and it results in making "clearer what the initial affirmation involved; indeed it will be only after the analysis that the speaker fully realizes what it was that he was affirming." [77] If Moore's analyses are common sense seeking understanding, some of them may also be seen as faith seeking understanding.

Moore's emphasis on common sense as a starting point for analysis serves the valuable function of insisting that philosophy should not lose touch with life as we actually live it. The meanings philosophy analyzes should be meanings that men actually use, and the beliefs that philosophy tries to clarify should be beliefs that men are actually living by, even if the questions that philosophy asks about these meanings and beliefs are not always those which men might ordinarily ask.

Yet Moore's focus on areas that afford certainty and universal agreement also carries with it the danger of leading to a neglect of meanings about which we are confused and of beliefs concerning which there is widespread disagreement. Furthermore, there is the danger that an emphasis on commonsense beliefs will result in a failure to be sufficiently critical of these beliefs, leaving confusions, half-truths, and prejudices unexamined. Moore's refusal to champion ordinary language *per se*, however, made him less susceptible to this latter mistake than has been true of some ordinary language philosophers.

Closely related to these difficulties in Moore's views on analysis and common sense is his frequent failure to do justice to the views of his philosophical opponents. So careful a historian of philosophy as Richard McKeon has charged that Moore has never used the "simple device of asking a philosopher what he meant before saddling him with self-contradictions and absurdities." [78] And another critic has asserted that Moore "forgets that what in the world a philosopher *means* cannot be decided unless one pays careful attention to the argument behind what he says." [79] These charges are striking in light of Moore's revelations that "what has suggested philosophical problems to me is what other philosophers have said" [80] and that consequently he has always been "very keenly interested . . . [in] trying to get really clear as to what on earth a given philosopher *meant* . . . [and in] discovering what real-

[77] *Ibid.,* p. 201
[78] "Propositions and Perceptions," *The Philosophy of G. E. Moore*, p. 475.
[79] Nakhnikian, *Readings in Twentieth-Century Philosophy*, p. 222.
[80] "An Autobiography," *The Philosophy of G. E. Moore*, p. 14.

ly satisfactory reasons there are for supposing that what he meant was true, or alternatively, was false." [81] How are we to understand the fact that Moore contends he has been asking all his life what philosophers meant, yet critics can charge that he has never used this "simple device"?

To begin with, we may see here one of the dangers of piecemeal analysis. In paying attention to a single sentence, the analyst may misunderstand it because he has failed to give sufficient attention to the whole philosophy of which it is a part. Before searching for "really satisfactory reasons" for a philosopher's statement, one must consider fully that the reasons given by the philosopher himself go a long way toward determining what he means.[82]

More important, however, is the question whether philosophers have been as clear about what they meant as McKeon's criticism implies they have. Moore admitted to being unclear about what other philosophers have meant, but he believed that they were themselves confused. He admitted, for example, that perhaps most philosophers who have said "there are no material things" have not meant anything contrary to what he proved in drawing attention to his hand. As Wittgenstein reportedly said of Moore's proof, "Those philosophers who have denied the existence of matter have not wished to deny that under my trousers I wear pants." But Moore also insisted that some philosophers have meant to deny this and quoted, as an example, McTaggert's assertion that "matter is in the same position as the gorgons and the harpies." [83] And, while conceding that some who have denied the existence of matter have really been asserting the truth of a certain kind of analysis, Moore suggested that "perhaps the truth is that most have confused several different meanings with one another." [84] Philosophers have been particularly prone, he believed, to confuse the question of the truth of a proposition with that of its correct analysis.[85] Perhaps the best case in support of Moore's contention is made in the work of John Wisdom, who maintains that both Moore and his opponents were confused about the nature of metaphysical sentences, for, we shall find Wisdom contending, they are neither definitions nor empirical assertions.[86]

One side of Moore's failure to do justice to the views of his opponents is his inability to show why they were confused. The meta-

---

[81] *Ibid.*

[82] One must also consider the ways in which he uses his statement and, particularly, the inferences he draws from it.

[83] John Wisdom reports this in "Moore's Technique," p. 439.

[84] "A Reply to My Critics," p. 670.

[85] Cf. "A Defence of Common Sense," p. 216.

[86] Cf. *Philosophy and Psycho-Analysis.*

physician will remain unconvinced by criticism that leave out of account the point he is trying to make. Here again we shall find the work of John Wisdom illuminating.

At bottom, Moore's difficulties are those of a transitional figure. In theory he seemed to think of philosophy in traditional terms as concerned finally with general truths about the universe. But, in practice, Moore implied an analytic view of philosophy, for he emphasized the confusions of traditional philosophy and occupied himself particularly with the goal of clarification.

Some Applications to Talk of God

We may turn now to consider some applications of Moore's position and of our criticisms of it for religious language. At an early age Moore himself became "a complete Agnostic," [87] but this apparently was not one of the doubts that he found philosophically interesting, for we find little attention given to religious questions. As we have seen, however, the major importance of Moore's work is to be found not in any results he may have achieved but, rather, in the method that he practiced, and so it is to this methodology that we have given our attention. Consequently, the significance of our discussion for philosophy of religion must be sought in the conclusions that we have drawn concerning analysis as a method.

On the positive side, we have considered: (1) Moore's painstaking inspection of particular statements to guard against any equivocation on their meaning, (2) the analysis of the precise meaning of the question we wish to answer, (3) the way in which Moore's appeal to common sense often points up the dependence of our language on certain fundamental meanings, and (4) another meaning that "common sense" seems to have for him whereby analysis becomes a clarification of the beliefs that modern man is prepared to affirm in his actual living. From our criticism of Moore we have concluded that: (1) Moore's conception of analysis was inadequate, and that the analytic statements of philosophy are significantly different from statements in which the predicate term is equivalent in meaning to the subject term; and (2) that the value of analyzing a single statement carries with it the danger of forgetting that an adequate understanding of a single statement requires an understanding of the entire point of view from which it is made.

The importance, first of all, of painstaking examination of particular statements or questions can scarcely be overemphasized. As we shall find John Wisdom arguing, in our thinking our final appeal must al-

[87] "An Autobiography," *The Philosophy of G. E. Moore*, p. 11.

ways be to particular cases, and much important discovery and clarification has come only by careful attention to the particular. This is true not only of our conceptual understanding but also of our self-understanding. Self-deception thrives on generalization. The application to religion is evident, and we shall consider it only briefly.

As we have seen, Moore tried to show that many of the most important conclusions reached by past philosophers were achieved only by using words at times in a highly technical sense and then returning at other times to their ordinary meaning. He was convinced, for example, that "even if Mr. Bradley is using the words 'Time is unreal' in a *highly unusual and special* sense, he does mean *as well* what ordinary people would mean." [88] But if vacillation between ordinary and special senses of a word is a danger in philosophy it can scarcely be less a danger in religion, for when the words we ordinarily use of human beings are used with reference to God they too have an "unusual and special sense."

For example, when the believer says that God acts in history he takes the word "acts" in a special sense. Perhaps he follows here some of the thinking of Thomas Aquinas. Aquinas asserts that "as long as a thing has being, so long must God be present to it, according to its mode of being," [89] which means that "God works in things in such a manner that things have also their proper operation." [90] God acts in things, according to Aquinas, in that he is the cause of their actions in each of the following special senses: first, as the source of the good that motivates the action; second, "by giving the form which is the principle of action"; and, third, "as conserving the forms and powers of things." [91] Here, then, is an attempt, by means of Aristotelian categories, to say that God acts in the special sense of being the ultimate source or basis of all particular actions. Somewhat similar are Paul Tillich's statements that "the divine life participates in every life as its ground and aim," [92] and that God is "the power of being in everything"—not one power but the source of every power.[93]

But now, having adopted a technical definition of this sort in the course of his critical reflection, perhaps in another context the believer vacillates to the ordinary meaning of "act" and draws the implication from this ordinary meaning that he may properly hope and pray for an act of divine intervention such as preventing a child from dying of his serious illness, or, at some future time after his death, bringing the believer back into being again. Rationally the believer may be unable to accept the idea of divine interventions in which God is con-

---

[88] *Philosophical Studies*, p. 208.
[90] *Ibid.*, Q. 105, a. 5.
[92] *Systematic Theology*, I, 245.
[89] *Summa Theologica*, Vol. I, Q. 8, a. 2.
[91] *Ibid.*
[93] *Ibid.*, p. 236.

ceived of as one of the many causal agencies at work in certain situations, but stories of divine intervention learned in childhood may continue to be the basis of some of his religious practices because he has not carefully examined them.

Another feature of Moore's analytic practices which is methodologically significant for philosophy of religion is the way in which his appeal to common sense often had the effect of drawing attention to the dependence of our language on certain fundamental meanings. The point is that to question these meanings is to question the way of life to which they are fundamental, so that it does not make sense to challenge them unless one really wishes to envision a radical upheaval of that way of life. Furthermore, since the more specialized or technical aspects of our language are dependent on these basic meanings, to challenge the latter on the basis of a technical or specialized usage is to put the cart before the horse. From this relation of dependence it would also seem that special uses of these basic concepts cannot make a complete break with the meaning they ordinarily have, since they are dependent upon this ordinary meaning. In "To be is to be perceived," for example, "to be" cannot be given a radically new meaning, because its power to communicate depends upon the place that it has in our ordinary speech community. To attempt to break completely with the original meaning, Moore argued, is to end up with the tautology, "To be perceived is to be perceived."

With respect to religious language, it is commonly agreed that when we say that God acts, that he loves, delivers, calls, judges, and the like, we are using terms that we have first learned to use concerning finite persons and that we have subsequently extended to these religious uses. If this is true then our discussion of Moore indicates that religious uses of these concepts must keep significant contact with their ordinary meanings. If we are meaningfully to say, "God exists," for example, "exists" must retain some connection with the meaning that it has when we speak of hands and chairs. Ian Ramsey makes this point in saying of religious assertions that, although "we cannot expect, even in the simplest case, that an adequate logical setting will be given by reference to assertions which relate *only* to public behavior," it is none the less true that

theological assertions must have a logical context which extends to, and is continuous with, those assertions of ordinary language for which sense experience is directly relevant. From such straightforward assertions theological assertions must not be logically segregated: for that would mean that they were pointless and, in contrast to the only language which has an agreed meaning, meaningless.[94]

[94] "Contemporary Empiricism," *The Christian Scholar*, Fall, 1960, p. 181.

In the chapter on the later Wittgenstein we shall use some of his procedures to examine more fully the relation of religious and ordinary nonreligious meaning.

Moore's point that to question the fundamental meanings on which our language depends is to question our entire way of life is of significance, however, not only concerning meanings basic to the speech community of an entire culture, but also for meanings basic to that portion of language used only by a smaller speech community within that culture. To question certain meanings fundamental to the language of a religious community, then, is to question the way of life of which that language is an expression.

John Hick, for example, argues that

the biblical writers were (sometimes, though doubtless not at all times) as vividly conscious of being in God's presence as they were of living in a material environment. . . . It would be as sensible for a husband to desire a philosophical proof of the existence of the wife and family who contribute so much to the meaning in his life as for the man of faith to seek a proof of the God within whose purpose he is conscious that he lives and moves and has his being.[95]

Yet another example is the contention of J. J. C. Smart that

the question "Does God exist?" has no clear meaning for the unconverted. But for the converted the question no longer arises. The word "God" gets its meaning from the part it plays in religious speech and literature, and in religious speech and literature the question of existence does not arise.[96]

For the believer, according to Smart, God must necessarily be thought to exist not because of any imagined logical necessity—which would be a contradiction in terms—but because "it would clearly upset the structure of our religious attitudes in the most violent way if we denied [God's existence] or even entertained the possibility of its falsehood." [97] Smart concludes that "the question 'Does God exist?' is not a proper question." [98]

Just as questions about time or material objects presuppose a meaningful use of these concepts in our ordinary language, so questions about God, if they are meaningful, must have their place in the language of a community in which the word "God" has a meaningful use.

[95] *Philosophy of Religion* (Foundations of Philosophy Series; Englewood Cliffs, N.J.: Prentice-Hall, 1963), p. 61.
[96] "The Existence of God," *New Essays in Philosophical Theology,* ed. Antony Flew and Alasdair MacIntyre (New York: Macmillan, 1955), p. 41. Originally in the *Church Quarterly Review,* Vol. CLVI, No. 319 (April-June, 1955).
[97] *Ibid.,* p. 40.   [98] *Ibid.,* p. 41.

Tillich has put it, "God is the presupposition of the question of God." [99]

Against the rationalist tradition in philosophy, empiricists and existentialists alike maintain that the basic meanings by which we live neither need nor have some sort of philosophical justification. In everyday life "know" has a meaning or meanings which take us to a more fundamental level than what can be proved. Just as some things are presupposed when we raise questions, so some things are presupposed when we construct arguments and proofs—"the chain of reasons has an end." [100] Some meanings we discover, upon reflection, to be basic to our form of life—to the human enterprise as we know it—and this is necessarily our final court of appeal. Moore drew attention to the basic standing of such concepts as time and matter. The reality of time and of the external world are known quite apart from philosophical proof, he argued. Similarly some philosophers of religion draw attention to the basic place of the term "God" in the life of the community of believers. God is known, they contend, quite apart from philosophical proof. Existentialist philosophers of religion, for example, frequently quote Pascal in indicating that their concern is with the "God of Abraham, God of Isaac, God of Jacob, not of the philosophers and scholars."

The parallel, however, between the common sense views defended by Moore and belief in God has the important limitation that belief in God lacks the universality that is characteristic of the views he defended. In other words, belief in God is not basic to the human enterprise in the way that Moore's common sense views are. This difference throws light on the fact that a religious community must struggle with doubt, a struggle which has both existential and logical dimensions. Existentially it is significant that the believer also belongs to a wider cultural community. Insofar as the experience of this wider community has called into question the meanings basic to his religious community, the believer will also feel this question in himself. Indeed, where the culture manifests a widespread defection from the meaningfulness of belief in God in favor of a competing system of belief such as naturalism, the nonbeliever may well wonder whether the believer is not attempting to live by two pictures of reality which are mutually incompatible. The believer, in turn, may judge that his religious meaning is more adequate than its competitors and yet that it has not, in his own life, won a decisive victory.

The believer's doubt may also concern the logical adequacy of his religious language, for, as is widely held, in speaking of God he must

[99] "The Two Types of Philosophy of Religion," *Theology of Culture,* p. 13.
[100] Wittgenstein, *Philosophical Investigations,* par. 326.

borrow terms from the langauge of his wider speech community, and the relation of their religious use to their nonreligious use is likely to be very complex and open to much confusion. If, for example, the believer conceives of God as existing, the question of the relation of this to the ordinary uses of "exist" will be most difficult.

Smart's contention, then, that "in religious speech and literature the question of existence does not arise" fails to consider both the place given to theological reflection in the religious community and the many expressions in religious literature of the dark night of the soul. The fact that "the word 'God' gets its meaning from the part it plays in religious speech and literature" will lead to mistaken inferences if one assumes an existential and logical segregation of the life of the religious community. Moreover, if religious faith includes cognitive elements, these elements exercise a cognitive function only in being subject to some sort of test of their adequacy to reality. The fact of this test represents the threat that they will be found meaningless.

On the other hand, Moore's defense of common sense has shown the importance of recognizing the basic standing in our language of certain meanings, and the meaning of "God," in the judgment of the believer at least, is not derived from any other meanings. It may simply be that the procedures of the linguistic philosopher are not by themselves adequate to clarify some of the meanings—or, as we shall come to say in later chapters, to explicate the rules governing some of the language uses—which are most important to us. Specifically, we may require as well the work of the phenomenologist to help us recover awareness of certain meanings that are quite basic to our forms of life but that we have lost sight of and so have failed to capture some of the vitality that our form of life might afford. In the cases defended by Moore, we can easily see that if we were to do away with one form of expression it is inconceivable that another would not take its place to express the same meaning. Our way of life is such that we need to be able to distinguish between being sure there is cheese on the table and being unsure whether there is. But it is not readily clear whether the meaning of "God" is indispensable in the same way. In contrast to Smart, for example, Tillich presents analyses to show that the form of life not only of the believer but also of the nonbeliever at least implicitly involves an immediate awareness of God; indeed he argues that this awareness affords a meaning that prevails even when the word "God" loses its meaning for the believer—even when factors combine to "upset the structure of our religious attitudes in the most violent way."

Another point that we have made concerning Moore's method was that he seemed to regard analysis as common sense seeking under-

standing, where "common sense" means those beliefs concerning the
nature of the universe which really hold conviction for those modern
men ("we") among whom Moore places himself in this respect.
Analysis presupposes an "initial act of affirmation" on the part of the
analyst and results in making "clearer what the initial affirmation involved; indeed it will be only after the analysis that the speaker fully
realizes what it was that he was affirming." [101] By helping us in this
way to get clear about what it is we wish to affirm, analysis can reveal
whether we "repeat forms of words without meaning them, or only
half meaning them," [102] verbally clinging to vestiges of beliefs that, for
us, have died with the passing of a previous cultural period. With respect to the Christian tradition specifically, analysis can help us to
determine whether and in what way it is true that, for us, "God is
dead," where "God" is understood as indicative of certain beliefs
affirmed in earlier periods. This is the significance of Moore's agnostic
attitude toward traditional Christian beliefs as an example of his refusal "to say what he could not authentically affirm." [103] We find
him declaring, for example, that "common sense has *no* view on the
question whether we do know that there is a God or not." [104]

From this point of view, for example, Rudolf Bultmann's controversial program of demythologizing the Bible can be regarded as an
analysis of biblical language. This analysis, on one hand, is based on an
affirmation of the belief that "the world and human life have their
ground and limits in a power which is beyond all that we can calculate
or control," and, on the other hand, it is based on a rejection of the
"mythological" belief in "the intervention of supernatural powers in
the course of events." [105] We can regard Bultmann, then, as attempting, like Moore, to clarify what it is that "we believe." This is expressed
in the following statement by Bultmann: "*Modern men* take it for
granted that the course of nature and of history, like their own inner
life and their practical life, is nowhere interrupted by the intervention
of supernatural powers." [106] "Modern man is in danger of forgetting
two things: first, that his plans and undertakings should be guided not
by his own desires for happiness and security, usefulness and profit,

[101] Foster, " 'We' in Modern Philosophy," p. 201.
[102] *Ibid.*
[103] *Ibid.*, p. 210.
[104] *Some Main Problems of Philosophy*, p. 17. See also his repudiation of belief
in immortality and in the divine creation of the world in "A Defence of Common
Sense," *Contemporary British Philosophy*, II, 216. It is interesting to note that
Moore regarded the meaning of "God" as one more entity that some allege must be
mentioned "if you are to give any complete description of the sum of things."
(*Some Main Problems of Philosophy*, p. 17.)
[105] *Jesus Christ and Mythology* (New York: Scribner's, 1958), pp. 19, 15.
[106] *Ibid.*, p. 16. Italics mine.

but rather by obedient response to the challenge of goodness, truth and love, by obedience to the commandment of God which man forgets in his selfishness and presumption; and secondly, that it is an illusion to suppose that real security can be gained by men organizing their own personal and community life." [107]

We may take as another example of this role of analysis in religious belief the not uncommon reinterpretation of the traditional arguments for the existence of God as "analyses or clarifications of propositions which religious persons antecedently believe." [108] Austin Farrer, for example, believes that "the grateful re-appropriation by religion of the philosophical arguments . . . is the best evidence we can have that those arguments in their essentials were a true clarification of the relation with God which religion had always confusedly known." [109] As Farrer sees it, "the theist's first argument is a statement; he exhibits his account of God active in the world and the world existing in God, that others may recognize it to be the account of what they themselves apprehend—or, if you like, that others may find it to be an instrument through which they apprehend for perhaps apprehension here is not separable from interpretation." [110] To this we may add, as another example, the claim of Paul Tillich that "the real and extremely productive meaning of the cosmological way in the philosophy of religion" is based in part on "the first step of the old cosmological argument, namely the analysis of the finitude of the finite in light of the awareness of the Unconditioned." [111] As Tillich sees it, "medical psychology, the doctrine of man and the Existential philosophy have contributed to this negative way of recognizing the unconditional element in man and his world." [112]

This view of analysis also carries important implications for our treatment of both philosophies of religion of the past and those of the present from which we differ. As Michael Foster argues,

even if we regard [philosophers of the past] as having been themselves engaged unconsciously in analysis of linguistic use (I think it legitimate up to a certain point to think of them like this), we shall not be able to attribute all the divergences of their results to faults of analysis unless we assume that we have independent knowledge of their analysandum. But, this, it seems clear, we have not got. On the contrary, the result of their analysis is part of the evidence which reveals to us what their analysandum was. [113]

[107] *Ibid.*, p. 39.
[108] H. H. Price, *Some Aspects of the Conflict between Science and Religion* (Eddington Memorial Lecture), (Cambridge: Cambridge University Press, 1953), p. 18.
[109] *Finite and Infinite* (London: A. & C. Black, 1959), p. 4.
[110] *Ibid.*, pp. 9-10.
[111] "Two Types of Philosophy of Religion," *Theology of Culture*, p. 26.
[112] *Ibid.*, pp. 26-27.
[113] " 'We' in Modern Philosophy," p. 202.

If analysis is a clarification of initial commitments, then many of the divergent results of analysis must be understood as evidence of different commitments. Criticism of differing analyses from the standpoint of our own perspective will not be less significant as a clarification of the issues, but this view of analysis "will require us to reveal our own presuppositions and to confront the others with them, committing ourselves in witness. We shall not be able to confine ourselves to refutation from the vantage-point of a technical superiority." [114]

A further implication for the analysis of religious language to be drawn from our discussion of Moore's method is to be found in our criticism of Moore's conception of analysis as inadequate because of his failure to see that the analytic statements of philosophy are significantly different from those in which the predicate term is equivalent in meaning to the subject term. Statements that are philosophically analytic function to show how the basic meanings of our language are related, and, so, each deals with just one dimension of the meaning of its subject term. Taken as analytic in this sense, "God is love," for example, asserts that our experience of agape love is a significant dimension of the complex meaning of the term "God." It need not mean that this experience is all that we mean by "God," any more than "To be is to be perceived" need mean that being perceived is all that we mean by "being"—as though "God" and "exists" could be dropped out of our language. Similarly, "God is Being-Itself" may be taken to assert that statements about God may be analyzed significantly in terms of the language of ontology. Rather than asserting that "God" can be reduced to this one dimension, this analytic statement functions to lay the foundation for relating the religious and ontological points of view—a philosophic task for which Moore's doctrine does not provide.

Our analyses of terms like "God," in other words, must recognize that the meanings they are used to express are not confined to one special area of language but are found to permeate many or even all portions of language. As John Wild charges against Moore's approach to value "as a very peculiar, simple, and unanalyzable property, . . . what we refer to by the term 'value' refuses to let itself be confined within any special compartment or region but seems rather to run through various regions, even getting itself involved in whatever it is that enables us

[114] *Ibid.*, p. 203. For further discussion of the role in analysis played by the standpoint or perspective of the analyst, see H. A. Hodges, *Languages, Standpoints and Attitudes* (London: Oxford University Press, 1953); and Willem Zuurdeeg, *An Analytical Philosophy of Religion.*

to distinguish between different regions, each of which is for some end." [115]

The final point of significance for method in philosophy of religion is contained in our criticism that the value of analyzing a single statement carries with it the danger of forgetting that an adequate understanding of a single statement requires an understanding of the entire point of view from which it is made. As we have seen, it is frequently charged that Moore consistently misunderstood what philosophers had meant by the statements he examined. Is this not the inevitable danger inherent in failing to place the statement to be examined both in the context of the philosopher's position as a whole and, finally, in the context of the entire cultural situation in which it was made?

[115] *Existence and the World of Freedom* (Englewood Cliffs, N.J.: Prentice-Hall, 1963), p. 55.

LOGICAL ATOMISM
AND RUSSELL: *Analysis & Language Form*

Chapter Three

Moore led the revolt against idealism and pointed to the need for an analytic approach in philosophy. But his own analyses were on an *ad hoc* basis. It remained for others to construct a systematic program of analysis and to justify this in terms of a developed philosophical point of view. To accomplish this, the analysts drew from two sources: classical British empiricism and the mathematical achievements of Russell and Whitehead in the *Principia Mathematica*. The result was that the practice of analysis was successively justified from two different metaphysical viewpoints, logical atomism and logical positivism, which we shall consider in turn. The metaphysics of logical atomism was, in effect, an attempt to use the new tools of logic to rethink the empiricist viewpoint.

We shall first examine the general characteristics of this position and then turn to the particular contributions of Bertrand Russell, who originated its leading ideas in his work before 1920. The work of another major figure in this movement, Ludwig Wittgenstein, will be considered in a separate chapter because of its importance to his later developments in which the present linguistic approach to philosophy had its birth. In considering the general position of logical atomism we shall examine, in order, its empirical aspects, its logical aspects, and the sort of justification of analysis that these were used to provide.

The General Nature of Atomism

Because it is fundamentally a program of analysis, empiricism was a natural candidate for the job of providing analytic practice with a rationale. Hume had been concerned to analyze our thinking into those simple elements—the sensations, emotions, and operations of the mind and the ideas that are copies of them—which he interpreted as the ultimate "contents" of our minds. By this analysis he sought to show that our ideas of the world do not reach any farther than our senses and that complex ideas are simply the way in which the mind is naturally disposed to associate the simple elements.

Since the work of Hume and his follower, John Stuart Mill, however, philosophy and psychology had been busy disengaging themselves from each other. The atomists were particularly influenced in this matter by the work of the logician Frege and the idealist Bradley.[1] It was their position that philosophy was not properly concerned with the psychological operations of our minds but rather should restrict itself to the study of the meanings with which these operations are concerned; the subject matter of philosophy is not the mental vehicle but the meanings it conveys. As the idealists had long been insisting, the classical empiricists misunderstood the nature of thinking when they analyzed it as the successive occurrence of ideas and, so, failed to see that thinking is always a judgment about objective reality. To *mean* something is to *refer to* something. Bradley and Frege further argued that thought, therefore, is "a functioning unity, possessing, of course, distinguishable features but not composed out of detachable pieces." [2] The subject matter of philosophy is not ideas but the meanings expressed by propositions or judgments.

The atomists, consequently, saw their task not as the psychological analysis of ideas but as the logical analysis of the meanings of propositions. Complex propositions were to be analyzed into those absolutely simple or atomic propositions which are their constituents. These atomic propositions expressed facts about the atomic or indivisible particles or substances of which the world is composed—namely, sense-data. Such a proposition would have as its subject the name of a sense-datum, and its function would be to predicate of that substance a simple quality or relation which it would name. "This is red," asserted of a patch of color, and "This is right of that," asserted of two patches of color are examples of atomic propositions. And so we see that the analytic movement became what it has continued to be, an empiricism founded not on ideas but on judgments or propositions.

This program of analysis, however, was developed not only by draw-

---

[1] See F. H. Bradley, *The Principles of Logic*, 2nd ed. (London: Oxford University Press, 1922), I, x; and *Translations from the Philosophical Writings of Gottlob Frege*, ed. Peter Geach and Max Black (Oxford: Basil Blackwell, 1952).

[2] Gilbert Ryle, "Introduction," in A. J. Ayer, *et al.*, *The Revolution in Philosophy* (New York: St. Martin's Press, Inc.; Macmillan & Co., Ltd.), p. 7.

ing from traditional empiricism but also by borrowing from the extraordinary logical advances of the *Principia Mathematica*. Russell and Whitehead showed that the whole of mathematics was reducible to a set of simple statements, statements which until 1931 were classified as a part of logic.[3] Complex mathematical statements were now seen as shorthand forms of combinations of these basic statements. It was further held that this logic could express all forms of argument and that its statements "are the skeletal forms of ordinary statements taken in abstraction from their content." [4] From this the atomists reasoned that since all these forms are reducible to a few basic forms then all statements of our language—or at least all significant rational statements—must be reducible to statements having these basic forms.

Just as Russell and Whitehead, then, had shown that irrational numbers $(\sqrt{-1})$ were derived from rational numbers (-1), which in turn were similarly built out of real numbers (1), and these were still further constructions out of simple "logical" statements, so the atomist would show, for example, that a statement having "state" as its subject was reducible to a series of simpler statements about men, which in turn were constructions out of simple statements referring to sense-data. Terms such as "state," "man," and "chair" do not denote entities other than the corresponding sense-data, but are indirect or shorthand or "elliptical" ways of referring to such data.

The justification offered for this sort of analysis was openly metaphysical. Under the leadership of Wittgenstein, the atomists formulated a theory that the simple sense-data propositions "pictured" the facts they expressed—a kind of one-to-one correspondence in which the subject of the proposition simply named or pointed to a simple substance, and the predicate named a simple quality or relation. This simple form of proposition was preferred metaphysically, because it alone showed the form that the world really had. If language is conceived by the analogy of a map, then here is, allegedly, a kind of photographic map, a map that is somehow drawn without using any particular method of projection. In this way philosophy serves the purpose of enabling us to see more clearly the nature of our knowledge about the world. As John Wisdom expressed it, the nature of philosophy "does not consist in acquiring knowledge of new facts but in acquiring new knowledge of facts." [5] So, although verbal in method, philosophy remained metaphysical in its aim of giving new insight into facts.

[3] Cf. W. C. Kneale, "Gottlob Frege and Mathematical Logic," *The Revolution in Philosophy*, p. 36.
[4] J. O. Urmson, *Philosophical Analysis* (Oxford: The Clarendon Press, 1958), pp. 96-97.
[5] "Logical Constructions," *Mind*, 1933, p. 195.

The world, then, was pictured as having a form corresponding to the "truth functional" or "extensional" form of mathematical logic, since this logic provided the model in terms of which the atomists conceived the nature of our everyday and scientific propositions. To refer to mathematical logic as "extensional" means that the truth or falsity of any one simple proposition bears *no necessary relation* to the truth or falsity of any other. The kind of world pictured is, consequently, one in which no simple entity stands in any necessary relation to any other.[6] The world is comprised, in this view, of self-contained, unique, irreducible elements—a conglomeration of monads, as they might well have been called.

It may be noted that this vision of the world is directly antithetical to that of idealism, in which the world is interpreted as a system of necessary relations. To the idealist the relations of any one thing to the rest of the world are an intrinsic part of the very nature of that thing. To consider anything apart from its relations is to falsify its true nature. Consequently any attempt, such as that of the atomists, to analyze what is really an organic whole into separate parts results in distortion. Indeed, the very term "atomism" implies a rejection of idealism.

Against idealism, the atomist believed that his picture of the world as "an aggregate of separable things, qualities and relations, which are, as it were, particles" was justified epistemologically in that

if you did not know what these particles were like, you would never be able to understand statements in which their names occurred. And the particles must be separable from one another; for, if you could not get to know some of them separately, you could never get to know any of them.[7]

With this sketch of the general nature of atomism, let us turn to consider the particular contributions of Bertrand Russell to philosophizing about language.

Bertrand Russell and Language Form

Russell acknowledged a great indebtedness to Moore, especially to the lead that Moore took in bolting idealism in favor of a conception of philosophy in which its main business was seen as a piecemeal or small-scale analysis. He was greatly encouraged in this view of philosophy by the fact that the spectacular progress in mathematics

---

[6] Cf. Wittgenstein, *Tractatus Logico-Philosophicus* (London: Routledge and Kegan Paul, 1922; New York: Humanities Press, Inc.), 2.061, 4.211, 5.134.
[7] D. F. Pears, "Logical Atomism," *The Revolution in Philosophy*, p. 50.

to which he had greatly contributed had been achieved through "patient detailed reasoning." Yet, like Moore, he did not claim that analysis is the sole method of philosophizing. It is with analysis that philosophy begins, but a subsidiary role is to be given to "comprehensive construction." [8]

Russell also joined Moore in his respect for common sense: "Bradley argues that everything that common sense believes in is mere appearance; we reverted to the opposite extreme." [9] But, unlike Moore, he regarded common sense as a rough, pre-critical version of scientific knowledge, so that analysis is required if we are to have an adequate understanding of common sense beliefs.

Russell's principal contribution to linguistic philosophy, however, was made through his severe criticism of the ordinary language in which common sense is enshrined. It has been one of his lasting convictions that

we ought not in our attempts at serious thinking, to be content with ordinary language, with its ambiguities and its abominable syntax. I remain convinced that obstinate addiction to ordinary language in our own private thoughts is one of the main obstacles to progress in philosophy.[10]

This is because "language misleads us both by its vocabulary and by its syntax." [11] Although he dealt with the way in which both vocabulary and syntax influence our thinking, it is his work concerning the latter which has been of prime importance. It is only with great mental vigilance, Russell believed, that we can prevent the syntactical form or grammatical construction of a statement from becoming a mental straitjacket for our thinking processes. From the fact that "any proposition can be put into a form in which it has a subject and a predicate united by a copula," for example, "it is natural to infer that every fact has a corresponding form, and consists in the possession of a quality by a substance." [12] From this it may be reasoned that since any relation between two things is an attribute of each of them, those things are not really distinct. The logical outcome of this is monism, since to view the entire world as a *fact* is to see it as a subject (the Absolute) with attributes (everything finite). Russell said of Spinoza, Hegel, and Bradley that if their "purely logical doctrine that every proposition has a subject and a predicate . . . is rejected,

---

[8] Bertrand Russell, "Logical Atomism," *Contemporary British Philosophy*, I, 360.

[9] "My Mental Development," *The Philosophy of Bertrand Russell*, ed. Paul A. Schilpp ("The Library of Living Philosophers"; New York: Tudor, 1951; now published by The Open Court Publishing Co., LaSalle, Ill.), p. 12.

[10] "Reply to Criticisms," *The Philosophy of Bertrand Russell*, p. 694.

[11] Russell, "Logical Atomism," *Contemporary British Philosophy*, I, 368.

[12] *Ibid.*

the whole foundation for the metaphysics of these philosophers is shattered." [13]

We can see, then, how we can be misled by the syntactical form of a statement. Let us say that some statements having the form of a subject and predicate united by a copula do refer to the possession of a quality by a substance. Other statements that do not have this sort of reference nonetheless seem to have it, because they too have the subject-copula-predicate form. These latter statements, Russell reasoned, should have a form that shows the different nature of their reference. The form that meets this requirement he called their logical form. In this way Russell distinguished between the form in which a proposition might appear in ordinary language—syntactical form—and the form that would show what sort of proposition it really is, the sort of thing it really refers to—logical form. The syntactical requirements of ordinary language are so loose that the syntactical form of a statement may be only its *apparent* logical form and not its *real* logical form—a distinction first appearing in Gottlob Frege's *Foundations of Arithmetic*.[14] The form of a statement becomes a mental straitjacket when we allow its ordinary grammatical construction to deceive us about its logical form.

To avoid this tyranny of form in matters of important thinking, it is necessary, Russell believed, to reformulate ordinary language in terms of an "ideal" or "philosophical" language in which the syntactic requirements are so strict that the syntactic form of a statement would always coincide with its logical form. This ideal language would serve a twofold metaphysical purpose: "first, to prevent inferences from the nature of language to the nature of the world, which are fallacious because they depend upon the logical defects of language; secondly, to suggest, by inquiring what logic requires of a language which is to avoid contradiction, what sort of structure we may reasonably suppose the world to have." [15] Ordinary language, in short, was to be translated into the metaphysical language of the atomist in which language form corresponds to or "pictures" the form of the reality referred to.

The problem was to develop systematic means of applying the distinction between apparent and real logical form to concrete instances. Russell's approach was to see whether an expression that functioned meaningfully in one statement could function meaningfully in another statement of an apparently similar form. If not, the two statements were not of the same logical form. Russell then referred to the ex-

[13] *Ibid.*, p. 360.
[14] (Oxford: Basil Blackwell, 1950), pp. 39-40.
[15] "Logical Atomism," *Contemporary British Philosophy*, I, 377.

pression in question as of a different "logical type" than the expression
for which it was substituted in the other sentence:

A and B are of the same logical type if, and only if, given any fact of which
A is a constituent, there is a corresponding fact which has B as a constituent,
which either results by substituting B for A, or is the negation of what so
results. To take an illustration, Socrates and Aristotle are of the same
type, because "Socrates was a philosopher" and "Aristotle was a philosopher"
are both facts. . . . To love and to kill are of the same type, because "Plato
loved Socrates" and "Plato did not kill Socrates" are both facts.[16]

It follows from this that there are a very large number of different
logical types. There is not, Russell maintained, "one relation of meaning
between words and what they stand for, but as many relations of
meaning, each of a different logical type, as there are logical types
among the objects for which there are words." [17]

Russell gave special attention to two important cases of confusion
due to discrepancy between the real and apparent logical forms of
a statement. To remove these confusions he developed his theory
of types and his theory of definite descriptions.

The theory of types was first developed to deal with certain logical
paradoxes. These paradoxes were generated due to the way in which
certain sorts of statement seem to refer to themselves. Russell's theory
is really an attempt to provide grounds for denying that these statements are self-referring. We may take as one example the rule that
there is an exception to *every* rule. Paradoxically, if there is an exception
to this rule itself, then the exception will be a rule that has no exception.
According to the theory of types, the confusion here is that rules are
of two logical types: (1) rules about rules are one logical type; (2)
rules about things other than rules are another logical type. The rule
that there is an exception to every rule refers only to rules of type 2,
that is, to rules that are not about rules. This rule, then, does not
refer to itself. To see it as applying to itself is to make the mistake
of placing it logically among rules that are not of its logical type.
This mistake is similar to that of thinking that verbs and nouns are
of the same logical type and so allowing them to occupy the same
place in a sentence.[18] In this way, paradoxes of this sort were shown

---

[16] *Ibid.*, pp. 369-70.
[17] *Ibid.*, p. 370.
[18] Bertrand Russell and Alfred North Whitehead, *Principia Mathematica*, I
(Cambridge: The University Press, 1910), 60, 77. As another example, we may
consider the paradoxes generated by Plato in the *Parmenides* by predicating one of
the Ideas or Universals of itself (see section 132, for example). The confusion here
is that a Universal does not itself belong to the class of particulars of which it is
predicated and, so, is not to be predicated of itself. It is of a different logical type.
To take yet another example, when the Cretan Epimenides asserted that *all* Cretans

to be resolvable by clearing up the confusion of logical types on which they were based. This confusion was often due to the failure to distinguish the difference in logical type between words and the objects they referred to.

In his article "Logical Atomism," Russell extended this logical tool to cover similar confusions outside the field of logic. Statements are sometimes made which are actually meaningless because they contain an expression of a logical type that is logically out of place in a statement of that form. Since a verb cannot function as a noun, for example, "Hit hit a home run" is nonsense. Also meaningless are the statements "Attributes are not relations" and "Facts cannot be named," because in each case a confusion of logical types may be detected. The function of attribution is logically different from the function of relating, yet the first sentence places them together. Similarly, since a fact is that which a proposition refers to, it is of a different logical type than are the subjects of propositions, yet the second sentence uses "fact" as a subject. But, *since* words are of the same logical type, these confusions can be removed by translating these sentences to read "Attribute words and relation words have different uses" and "The symbol for a fact is not a name." [19] In these translations the apparent and true logical form coincide.

In Russell's ideal language, these confusions would be avoided because the form of a symbol would correspond to the form of the thing symbolized. Concerning the logical status of a fact, for example, he explained that

if we are to have a language which is to safeguard us from errors as to types, the symbol for a fact must be a proposition, not a single word or letter. Facts can be asserted or denied, but cannot be named. . . . This illustrates how meaning is a different relation for different types. . . . The way to mean a simple is to name it. Obviously naming is different from asserting.[20]

Since a simple fact is comprised of a sense-datum and one of its qualities or of two sense-data [21] and one of the relationships between

---

are liars his statement did not belong to the class of *all* statements by Cretans being referred to, because it was a statement about this class and, so, functioned at a different logical level.

[19] Russell, "Logical Atomism," *Contemporary British Philosophy*, I, 372-73.

[20] *Ibid.*, p. 373.

[21] Russell referred to these as "particulars"—"such things as little patches of colour or sounds." (*The Philosophy of Logical Atomism*, A Reprint of a Series of Articles Published in the 1918 and 1919 Volumes of the *Monist* [Minneapolis: University of Minnesota Press, n.d.]; also reprinted in Alston and Nakhnikian, *Readings in Twentieth-Century Philosophy*, p. 299). It was Wittgenstein who pushed the consideration as to the metaphysical status of these "patches" to the

them, a proposition will show or "picture" this, since it will contain the name for that substance and the name for its quality or the name for each of the two substances and the name for their relationship. However, if the word "fact" were used as a symbol for a fact, it would not show this form.

The theory of definite descriptions was developed to deal with a very commonly used grammatical form that is misleading because it appears to name something and, so, to imply its existence. This is any phrase of the form "*the* so and so," referred to by Russell as a "definite description" because it can describe only one thing, as contrasted with an indefinite description of the form "*a* so and so." For example, "*the* present King of France" can be used to describe only one thing, while "*a* king" lacks any such definite reference. It is easy to see the sort of difficulty to which this grammatical form can give rise when one considers such definite descriptions as "the round square" and "the present King of France." What does "round square" name? Would it be meaningful to deny the objective reality of the round square named, since this would raise the question as to what it was whose reality was being denied? This sort of difficulty had led men like Mill, Meinong, and the early Russell to affirm the objective reality or subsistence of an object corresponding to every possible definite description.

Russell's move to resolve this metaphysical problem was to translate any sentence containing a definite description as its grammatical subject into an equivalent sentence that does not have this grammatical subject. "The round square does not exist" becomes "It is false that there is an object X which is both round and square." [22] While the original proposition appeared to be about an object having certain properties, the proposition into which it was translated is seen to be about those properties themselves, and the bogus object has disappeared. Technically, the object is now seen to be a logical construction out of those properties.

A very interesting feature of this translation is that the word "exists" apparently disappears as a predicate. This suggested to Russell the truth of Kant's position that "exists" is not really a predicate at all and that the failure to realize this was the source of the metaphysical

---

conclusion that they were themselves facts, consisting of a simple substance and the quality red or blue or the like which it possessed. (*Tractatus Logico-Philosophicus,* pars. 2.01, 2.032). John Wisdom put forward an intermediate position: "An account of the world in terms of things, . . . in terms of facts, and . . . in terms of events is just an account of the world in three languages." Cf. Urmson, *Philosophical Analysis,* pp. 55 ff.

[22] Russell and Whitehead, *Principia Mathematica,* I, 66.

problems thought to arise in connection with this word.[23] It was thought that perhaps the most important consequence of the theory of descriptions is that the metaphysical problem of existence apparently evaporated in this way when exposed to logical analysis. In the case of names, the fact of existence is expressed by the very act of naming, and, so, the addition of "exists" is redundant and without significance —in a word, meaningless. It follows from this, for example, that "the fact that you can discuss the proposition 'God exists' is a proof that 'God,' as used in that proposition, is a description and not a name." [24] In cases other than names, such as a definite description, "exists" could be translated into non-existential terms. For example, "The author of Waverley exists" becomes "One (and only one) value of the propositional function 'X is the author of Waverley' is true." In both of these cases it turns out that "existence is essentially a property of a propositional function," [25] and, so, it would be a confusion of logical types to apply "to the individual that satisfies a propositional function a predicate which applies only to a propositional function." [26] From this Russell concluded that "the ontological argument and most of its refutations are found to depend upon bad grammar." [27] He was later to remark that "this clears up two millennia of muddle-headedness about 'existence' beginning with Plato's 'Theaetetus.' " [28]

The theory of types and the theory of definite descriptions provide techniques for the translation of certain statements from our ordinary language into an ideal language so that the ordinary language form of these statements will not mislead us. We remember, however, that it is not only the syntax of ordinary language but also its vocabulary that may be misleading. To use an example supplied by Urmson, Russell's theory of definite descriptions reformulates a statement such as "The modern age is materialistic" into "There is one and only one thing which is a modern age and it is materialistic." But this translation leaves us with the entities "modern age" and "materialistic beliefs." The empiricist metaphysics requires that these be reduced. It was the theory of definite descriptions which suggested to Russell the means of accomplishing such a reduction. Concerning the theory of definite descriptions, John Wisdom notes that "once it had been seen how the inmates of the universe of legend and of dream, imagination, and thought were *logical constructions* out of ordinary things so that statements about them could be checked with our eyes and ears as

[23] "Logical Atomism," *Contemporary British Philosophy,* I, 365.
[24] Russell, *The Philosophy of Logical Atomism,* p. 45.
[25] *Ibid.,* p. 34.   [26] *Ibid.,* p. 35.
[27] "Logical Atomism," *Contemporary British Philosophy,* I, 365.
[28] *A History of Western Philosophy* (London: Allen and Unwin, 1945), p. 860.

well as any statements about spades and lions it quickly occurred to Russell and Whitehead that the same might be true of other things including spades and lions." [29] "Modern age," then, must be reduced to something like "most people living now," and this, in turn, is to be translated into statements about that very large number of sense-data to which we are really, if indirectly, referring when we refer to people. "Materialistic beliefs" must be similarly reduced.[30] This reductionistic procedure, which Russell called the "method of logical constructions," may be thought of as comprised of three principles: (1) "wherever possible, substitute constructions out of known entities for inferences to unknown entities"; [31] (2) take all known entities to be sense-data and universals; [32] and (3) use the model of the philosophy of mathematics, in which rational and irrational numbers are reduced to natural numbers, as a guide.[33]

The reductive analyses of the method of logical constructions were clearly metaphysical, since they involved a judgment as to what sorts of entity really exist. The analyses that concerned only the grammatical construction of statements, however, were regarded as metaphysically neutral. Since they did not involve a change in the semantic level of the statements, a change, that is, in the sort of entity referred to, but were rather a technique to prevent the looseness of ordinary grammatical construction from misleading us, these analyses did not seem to be based upon any sort of metaphysical judgment. To emphasize this metaphysical neutrality these analyses were often referred to as "same-level" or "logical," while the translations that dealt with vocabulary were variously referred to as "new-level," "philosophical," "directional," or "reductive."

Critical Evaluation

Our critical examination of Russell's philosophy of language and of atomism in general must naturally take as its central focus the notion of logical form, for it was in connection with this concept that Russell and his followers made their most important contribution

---

[29] "Bertrand Russell and Modern Philosophy" (1947), reprinted in Wisdom, *Philosophy and Psycho-Analysis*, p. 204. Wisdom adds in a footnote that "Jeremy Bentham first introduced logical constructions."

[30] Urmson, *Philosophical Analysis*, pp. 39-40.

[31] "Logical Atomism," Contemporary British Philosophy, I, 363.

[32] Russell, "Knowledge by Acquaintance and Knowledge by Description" (1910-11), reprinted in *Mysticism and Logic* (London: Allen and Unwin, 1917), p. 223. Russell adds that we may, perhaps, also include ourselves among the entities we know. (*Ibid.*)

[33] Russell, "Logical Atomism," pp. 363-65.

to contemporary analytic philosophy. This contribution was the persuasiveness of their argument that, as Russell put it,

the influence of language in philosophy has, I believe, been profound and almost unrecognized. If we are not to be misled by this influence, it is necessary to become conscious of it, and to ask ourselves deliberately how far it is legitimate.[34]

It was to become conscious of this influence that Russell developed the distinction between grammatical and logical form.

To determine the value, then, of Russell's philosophy of language for the philosophic study both of meaning in general and of particular sorts of meaning other than those explicitly dealt with by Russell, we are not interested, primarily, in the particular applications of his theory of logical form that he was concerned to make—the theories of logical types and of definite descriptions—but, rather, in the theory of logical form *per se*. According to this theory, as we have seen, the danger of being misled by the grammatical form of certain statements is to be accounted for by postulating for each of these statements the existence of another form that has for it a kind of absolute propriety—a form that is the only correct or true form by which to express that meaning. Furthermore, this correct or real form is to be determined by purely logical considerations, considerations that are not founded upon any particular metaphysical view. If this position is true, then the requirements of the atomists' extensional logic or of Russell's modified version[35] of it become the procrustean bed that every sort of language—including the ethical, the metaphysical, and the religious—must either be shown to fit or be discarded as meaningless. The fundamental question, then, concerning the wider philosophic signif-

---

[34] *Ibid.*, p. 367.

[35] Russell did not share the view of the majority of the atomists that logical syntax could be completely extensional, thereby dispensing with quantifiers such as "some" and "all." Wittgenstein and others tried to interpret a general proposition like "all swans are white" as equivalent to an extensional series of particular propositions each asserting the whiteness of one particular swan. In addition to the fact that the series could not be completed, Russell objected that the general proposition means more than what is given by this series, namely, that these are all the swans. Reluctantly, Russell also came to hold the view that certain particular statements could not be made to fit the requirements of the extensional view that the truth of any statement involving more than one fact depends on the truth of each of the facts expressed. For example, the truth of "I hope he is home" does not depend on the truth of "He is home." In general the truth of statements about wishing, believing, hoping, thinking, and the like does not seem to depend in any way on the truth of what it is that is wished, believed, etc. The same may be said of statements of implication in which one fact is put forward as the ground for another. The truth that one implies the other does not depend on the truth of that other. (See Umson, *Philosophical Analysis*, pp. 62 ff., and Russell, "My Mental Development," *The Philosophy of Bertrand Russell*, p. 15).

icance of Russell's theory of logical form is whether the formal requirements that any particular sort of language, such as the religious, must meet in order to be meaningful may be determined without an examination of the meanings of that language itself, or whether translations into another form are simply *ad hoc* devices to avoid confusion between two different sorts of meaning, because they are expressed in similar grammatical forms.

I shall contend that the belief that these translations are not simply useful devices but actually restore sentences to their true logical form is based upon several errors. The most fundamental error is the failure to see that the form of a sentence cannot be separated from the meaning of that sentence because one must understand the meaning before one can understand the form. It follows from this that to make the form of one sort of language normative for all language is to make the meaning of that language normative for all meaning. This selection of the formal characteristics of one sort of meaning as normative for language as a whole is not, then, metaphysically neutral but finds its justification in the metaphysical picture of the world derived from or underlying that particular use of language—the picture of the world as a conglomeration of monad-like entities. Moreover, in making one such picture absolute in this way, the atomists failed to recognize that any such picture is relative to one of the limited perspectives from which men experience their world. My contention, then, will be that the formal characteristics of any sort of language must be determined by examining the meaning of that language, and that, because Russell's translations are expressions of his atomistic metaphysics, the applicability of these translations to any sort of meaning, such as that of religious language, is a metaphysical issue.

After criticizing the metaphysical nature of Russell's methods of "same-level" translation, this criticism of his metaphysics will be extended to his method of logical construction. Finally, consideration will be given to the possible usefulness of language translation once it is reinterpreted apart from the absolutist metaphysics of logical atomism.

Russell's use of the concept of logical form, then, is problematic in several respects. First of all, the claim that syntactical translations from ordinary grammatical form into ideal logical form are metaphysically neutral seems to be false. The reason for preferring Russell's ideal syntax is the metaphysical judgment that this form corresponds to or pictures the form of the real world. If one does not accept this metaphysical judgment, he will not concur in this translation, unless, of course, other reasons for it can be given. The other reason that Russell gives for this translation is a corollary of the first, namely, it will prevent us from being misled by the syntax of ordinary language into making false metaphysical judgments. But, one will accept this reason only if he accepts the metaphysical judgment that the metaphysical judgments in question are false. And, even if one believes that these are false, he will accept Russell's translations only if he believes that they will not themselves lead to false metaphysical inferences. These same-level translations would truly avoid metaphysical judgments only if they were used merely as devices to raise the question of whether one has been misled by a particular statement by showing a possible alternative formulation.

To be specific, the syntax of the atomists' ideal language of purely logical forms was derived from extensional logic in which the truth of any simple statement has no necessary relation to the truth of any other. The sort of world which this syntax "pictures," then, is one consisting of "an aggregate of separable things, qualities and relations." [36] But many, including the linguistic analysts of today, would reject the adequacy of such a view. As one analyst has recently said of the atomists' view, "the reaction against the idealists has gone too far. Certainly we should reject their notion that everything is logically connected with everything: but it does not follow that some things are not logically connected with anything." [37]

The metaphysical nature of the atomists' "logical" translations is illustrated by those syntactical translations which get rid of the word "exists" and allow Russell to define existence as a property of a propositional function. Although his use of "existence" as the subject of a statement violates his theory of types, his meaning is clearly that the word "exists" merely has the force either of asserting that one or more values of a propositional function are true or of asserting that a name may be applied. To show that this is the function of "exists," statements such as "The author of Waverley exists" and "Lions do not exist" are to be translated into "There is at least one person and at most one person who wrote Waverley" and "The term 'lions' does not apply to anything." These translations evoke the sort of objection raised by Charlesworth, however, that "existential sentences can never be wholly translated, without remainder, into non-existential sentences and, in one form or another, they are bound to recur sooner or later in spite of all the circumlocutions used to get rid of them." [38] Of the translation concerning the author of Waverley, Charlesworth asks,

What is the force of "there is" in the translation, for it is certainly not the "is" of the logical copula. And if the translation is significant, is it not

---

[36] Pears, "Logical Atomism," *The Revolution in Philosophy*, p. 50.
[37] *Ibid.*, p. 52.
[38] *Philosophy and Linguistic Analysis*, p. 67.

because in the last resort we can say something like "The author of Waverley exists"? [39]

Similarly, of the second translation he asks, "And why does not the term 'lions' apply to anything?" [40] Must we not here agree with Charlesworth that "the only answer is, 'Because lions do not exist' "? [41] So viewed, existence is not a property of propositions but is something that may be expressed by them. And, our need for the word becomes, at the very least, a serious question when we add to Charlesworth's observations not only the existentialists' discussion of the personal meaning of one's existence and of threats to that existence such as death, but also the significant use of "exist" in ordinary language, such as its use to ask "Does John exist?" where the alleged existence of a rich uncle John is in question. Russell's translations would be neutral if they merely served as a device to remind us of the now commonly recognized fact that "exists" is very different from other predicates, for this would leave it open to accept a judgment such as Wisdom's that, now that "the relevant oddities of this predicate have been set out," we may "go back to saying that existence is a predicate provided we don't forget its peculiarities." [42] In any event, Russell's treatment of "exists" is but another instance of the perennial metaphysical attempt to define concepts such as existence, truth, value, and the like. As P. F. Strawson remarks, the atomist's "search for definitions of problematic ideas was almost as old as philosophy itself." [43]

Russell's use of the concept of "logical form" is defective, however, not only with respect to the claim of metaphysical *neutrality* but also with respect to the status of this concept as a norm for the *meaningfulness* of statements. To be meaningful, statements must be constructed in accordance with the syntactic rules of whatever language is being spoken. "Into hit a home run" is meaningless because it violates the syntactic requirements of ordinary language by making a preposition function as a noun. In order to avoid the ambiguities of ordinary grammar, Russell makes the syntactic requirements governing logical form far more strict than those governing ordinary grammatical form, with the result that many statements, such as "A fact cannot be named," which do not violate ordinary syntax do violate Russell's logical syntax and, so, are meaningless judged by these new requirements.

[39] *Ibid.*
[40] *Ibid.*, p. 68.
[41] *Ibid.*
[42] "Bertrand Russell and Modern Philosophy," p. 200.
[43] "Construction and Analysis," *The Revolution in Philosophy*, p. 100.

The major difficulty is that the strictness of this syntax has the effect of stultifying communication. As Max Black has put it:

Any interpretation that will be faithful to [Russell's] intentions requires the impossibility of substituting two words for one another in even a single context to be regarded as sufficient cause for their segregation into mutually exclusive types. The consistent elaboration of this leading idea involves the making of ever finer distinctions of "meaning" between words not customarily regarded as ambiguous. So stringent does the requirement prove that it becomes difficult, if not impossible, to state the theory itself without contradiction, such a difficulty being only a single instance, though a striking one, of a general tendency to produce a paralysis of the general statements of which philosophical discussion so largely consists.[44]

The problem, for example, in stating the theory may be seen if we consider the statement "Expressions are of different types." Expressions and types of expressions are of different logical types and, so, cannot be used together as they are in this statement. More generally, we may take as an example of the extensive restrictions that are placed on language the syntactic requirement that a statement have as its subject the name of a simple substance. As a consequence, Russell could not allow philosophical statements of the sort "A fact cannot be named." To meet this difficulty, a distinction was made between first and second order propositions, those about non-linguistic facts and those about linguistic facts, and by translation we get second order propositions of the sort "The symbol for a fact is not a name." Carnap was to conclude from this that all philosophical statements are second order or "formal mode" propositions.[45] But there are difficulties with this way out. Pushed to its logical conclusion, Russell's position results in an unbridgeable gap between first and second order propositions. If the symbol for a fact must be a proposition and not the word "fact," then we cannot speak meaningfully of "the symbol for a fact," for to do so is to use "a fact" to symbolize or refer to a fact. If only a proposition can symbolize a fact, then it becomes strictly impossible to use the word "fact" and, so, to say anything at all about a fact including the sort of symbol it has. Difficulties of this sort have led Carnap to abandon the position that philosophy can restrict itself to formal mode statements. And Wittgenstein concluded his own philosophical discussions in the *Tractatus* by insisting that "he who understands me finally recognizes them [my propositions] as senseless." [46]

[44] "Russell's Philosophy of Language," *The Philosophy of Bertrand Russell*, p. 239.
[45] See Rudolph Carnap, *Philosophy and Logical Syntax* (London: K. Paul, Trench, Trubner, 1935).
[46] *Tractatus Logico-Philosophicus*, par. 6.54.

These difficulties stem from Russell's insistence that words be *syntactically identical,* capable of the same syntactical function in all possible uses, before they can be allowed the same function in any statement. If communication is not to be seriously impaired, syntax must have something of the *flexibility* that we find it to have in ordinary discourse. Max Black refers to "certain polygamous contexts able to receive words of the most diverse syntactical types without degenerating into nonsense. It is proper to say both 'I am thinking about Russell' and 'I am thinking about continuity.'" [47] Russell's position, in effect, categorizes as meaningless a large number of statements merely because their syntax displays that flexibility which is necessary if we are to avoid paralysis in our discourse.

The theory of types involves the further difficulty that it prevents statements from referring to themselves. A rule about rules, for example, is held to be of a different logical type than the rules to which it refers. However, as Frederic Fitch and others have argued, many important propositions are self-referential in nature.[48] Consider a theory about the nature of theories or a proposition about the nature of propositions or a statement about the possibility of knowing the truth of any statement. In these cases self-referential inconsistency seems very damaging indeed. W. V. O. Quine presents an attractive solution the general nature of which we may at least suggest: since "the idiom 'the class of all entities x such that . . .'" leads to the sort of paradox with which Russell was concerned, this idiom is revised to read "the class of all *membership-eligible* entities x such that . . ." [49]

However, Russell did not apply the theory of types as rigorously as Wittgenstein or Carnap but sought to avoid the difficulties concerning philosophical statements that resulted from this theory by limiting its status to that of a methodological device by which to prevent false inferences. Russell also seems willing to regard the theory of descriptions and the notion of an ideal language in much the same way. But this has the consequence of undercutting much of the force of Russell's theories. If, for example, any philosophical statements are to be allowed which do not conform to the requirements of the theory of types, it becomes inconsistent to use this theory to judge other philosophical statements as meaningless. More generally, the translations provided by these theories had been offered as means not simply to prevent false inferences but to show that all significant language really had the sort of structure the atomists envisioned. The

[47] "Russell's Philosophy of Language," pp. 237-38.
[48] Cf. Fitch, *Symbolic Logic* (New York: The Ronald Press, 1952), pp. 217-25.
[49] *Mathematical Logic,* rev. ed. (Cambridge: Harvard University Press, 1958), pp. 130-31.

claim could then be made that this form pictured the structure of reality, and it was this claim that provided the metaphysical justification of analysis. As Urmson says of atomism generally,

language had been conceived as a clear-cut truth-functional structure, securely based on atomic propositions; given this view of language indefinite statements, though their occurrence could not be ignored completely, had seemed to be aberrations presenting a very special problem. Such a view of language had seemed essential to empiricism, since it showed how the edifice of our knowledge was securely based on experience.[50]

A third deficiency in Russell's concept of logical form is his tendency to hypostatize it as separable from the meaning of the statements in which it is embodied. As the linguistic analyst P. F. Strawson has put it: "We are inclined to think of the logical form of a statement as a sort of verbal skeleton which is left when all expressions, except those selected as logical constants, are eliminated from a sentence which might be used to make that statement, and replaced by appropriate variables." [51] But, he objects, "logical form is not a property which statements have *on account of which* (or in virtue of which) they have certain formal powers. Their possession of a certain form *is* their possession of those powers." [52] We do not know, that is, the logical form of a sentence unless we first know its meaning. We may take, as an example, Moore's objection to the theory of descriptions that it cannot be applied to all statements of the grammatical form "the so-and-so." To quote Russell:

Mr. Moore points out quite correctly, that the theory of descriptions does not apply to such sentences as "The whale is a mammal." For this the blame lies on the English language, in which the word "the" is capable of various different meanings.[53]

Now the point of the translations provided for by this theory was to show that the subject of the sentence being analyzed does not have the same sort of meaning, the same logical function, as a name. Once translated into its logical form, it "shows, pictures, reveals the form of the fact which the other formulation obscures." [54] We see, however, that we must already know the sort of meaning that this subject has before we know that the theory is applicable.

That meaning and form cannot be separated may be seen also if we consider that "logical form" really refers to a system of classification in which statements are grouped according to certain similarities of

[50] *Philosophical Analysis*, p. 159.
[51] *Introduction to Logical Theory* (London: Methuen, 1952), p. 49.
[52] *Ibid.*, p. 56.
[53] "Reply to Criticisms," p. 690.
[54] Urmson, *Philosophical Analysis*, p. 24.

meaning. We can classify a statement, in other words, only by comparing its meaning to that of other statements. We determine, for example, that the statement "The whale is a mammal" cannot be translated according to the theory of descriptions only by comparing its meaning with the meaning of statements of the sort that have been translated in this way. To utilize a system of classification is to have in mind for each category one or more specific instances which are held as normative for that category. We then classify anything by determining to which of these norms it is most similar. It is necessary to say "similar" here since the meanings of natural language are so extremely varied. One may find a continuum of meanings which begins with one category and shades off gradually into another. At a certain point in the continuum, instances may be regarded as borderline cases, and a decision to include them under a given category has the effect of broadening that category.

To illustrate, we may take the categories "semantic" and "syntactic" as applied to the meaning of words. To distinguish the sort of meaning a word like "chair" has, which refers to something beyond the statement in which it is used, and the sort of meaning a word like "but" has, which merely performs a function within a statement, we may take "chair" and "but" as normative instances of the categories semantic and syntactic. Between words having these two sorts of meaning there exists a continuum such that we have, for example, borderline cases like the auxiliary "must" and the relative pronoun "that." "Must" is conventionally categorized as syntactic although it has reference, beyond the statement in which it occurs, to necessity as characterizing the case referred to, whether in a moral or some other sense. "That" is conventionally categorized as semantic, although, as a *relative* pronoun, its meaning might seem to be largely that of a function within the sentence. In both cases there are similarities and differences when compared with "chair" and "but." [55]

[55] To illustrate further, we may consider the category analytic. This category may be drawn narrowly or more broadly depending, for example, upon which of the following statements are included as normative: "A triangle is not not a triangle"; "A triangle is a three sided plane closed figure"; "Man is a rational animal." The first two are nearly alike in the relationship of identity between subject and predicate except that in the second the subject does not make the explicit reference to three sides that the predicate does. In the third, the relationship between subject and predicate is somewhat less clearly that of identity. If, for example, one also means by "man" psychologically repressed animal, this characteristic is not implicit in "rational animal" in the way that, say, "three interior angles" is implicit in "three sided closed figure." As G. E. Moore has concluded, "The line between 'analytic' and 'synthetic' might be drawn in many different ways." ("A Reply to My Critics," *The Philosophy of G. E. Moore*, p. 667). This question of the nature of categories of classification will be pursued at greater length in our study of John Wisdom.

A fourth defect in the conception of logical form is the belief that this form pictures the form of reality. This belief fails to take into account an element of truth in the idealists' position that the knower affects the known, namely, that any one language does not deal with reality as such but with certain *aspects* of reality taken in abstraction from all other aspects. As Urmson points out, the atomists' position involves a belief in "clear-cut ready made facts." That "A resembles B more than C" is simply a fact "out there in the world." [56] But this is true only of a certain aspect of A, B, and C. It may be true of their color but not of their size, true of their function but not of their durability. The metaphor of *picturing*, then, is misleading. Language is more like a map than like a picture, for a map represents only certain aspects of the area with which it is dealing. To this objection we must add that the atomists admittedly were unable to give an adequate account of just what was meant by "picturing" and that the work of the logicians in creating many different logical systems greatly undermined the conviction that the form of any one of them shows just what reality is really like.

The atomists, then, were metaphysicians in the broad sense in which a picture of reality as a whole is treated as having cognitive status. But they were also metaphysicians in that sense against which contemporary analytic philosophers are arrayed, namely, the sense in which metaphysicians "ontologized; that is, they essayed to prove assertions of existence from conceptual considerations"; [57] they attempted, that is, "to get beyond the limits of ordinary, hypothetical and incomplete human knowledge to something absolutely satisfactory and complete." [58] According to Russell, for example, one of the purposes of the construction of an ideal language was that "by inquiring what logic requires of a language which is to avoid contradiction," one would be determining "what sort of structure we may reasonably suppose the world to have." [59] However, once this belief that we can deduce an "absolutely satisfactory and complete" picture of reality from conceptual considerations is rejected, the question remains whether pictures of reality which are ordinary, hypothetical and incomplete may not be regarded as cognitive insofar as they are subjected to a *test* of their efficacy in the attempt to live by them.[60]

[56] *Philosophical Analysis*, p. 105.
[57] Ryle, "Final Discussion," *The Nature of Metaphysics*, p. 164.
[58] Mary Warnock, *ibid.*, p. 143.
[59] "Logical Atomism," *Contemporary British Philosophy*, I, 377.
[60] Tests of coherence and of adequacy to the facts are, in one sense, a part of the test of the efficacy of such pictures to the life-process, for, insofar as a metaphysical picture carries contradictory implications, or fails to show the relation between facts, or leads us to expect what is not the case, to this extent it will be inadequate to live by.

The fifth criticism to be made of the atomists' use of the concept of logical form is really of one piece with the basic criticism of their position as a whole. The basic defect of atomism is that one use of language, the language with which we deal with physical objects, is made the norm for all other uses of language—or, at least, for all uses of language which are of interest to the philosopher. In connection with logical form, this means that the syntactic requirements established by a study of one use of language are simply imposed on all other uses, a practice obviously connected with the belief that form is separable from meaning. In the words of one of the later analysts, "what Russell and Wittgenstein did in this period was to glimpse traces of a pattern in our experience, and then, taking their eyes off the facts, to develop this pattern far beyond what is warranted by the facts." [61]

The effect of making one use of language—the description of fact—the norm for all language was varied. The host of ordinary statements such as exclamations, promises, personal greetings, etc., which are not descriptive remained largely veiled from notice by the preconception that all genuine language must be descriptive. Other sorts of language—such as the religious, metaphysical, ethical, and psychological—which could not but be noticed, either had to be discarded or else made to conform. Concerning psychological language, for example, Urmson notes that "statements about knowledge, belief, wishes, intentions, and hopes could only be kept going by the construction of a psychic machinery, facts about which such statements described, or else by a blatant philosophical behaviourism; that they were descriptions of something could not be doubted." [62]

With regard to ethical language, if the only legitimate use of language is to report facts, then it becomes hard to avoid the conclusion drawn by Wittgenstein that "there can be no ethical propositions." [63] "It is clear," he said, "that ethics cannot be expressed. Ethics are transcendental." [64] The alternatives to this rejection, for the atomists, were either to reduce ethical to empirical statements, a move that Moore had criticized as the "naturalistic fallacy," or to follow Moore in holding that there also were irreducible ethical facts. Dissatisfaction with these alternatives played a significant part in the downfall of logical atomism.

[61] Pears, "Logical Atomism," *The Revolution in Philosophy*, p. 46.
[62] *Philosophical Analysis*, p. 199. We may recall here the problem of translating intensional statements such as "John believes that . . ." or "John thinks that . . ." into extensional form. The truth of such statements does not seem to depend in any way on the truth of what it is that is believed, thought, etc., while, according to the extensional view, the truth of any statement involving more than one fact depends on the truth of each of the facts expressed.
[63] *Tractatus Logico-Philosophicus*, par. 6.42.
[64] *Ibid.*, par. 6.421.

The assumption that language can only be used to report facts had similar consequences for metaphysical language. Since metaphysics does not report empirical fact, if it is to have any significance it would have to be conceived of as reporting another sort of fact, a sort lying beyond this cave of appearances to which the ordinary, non-metaphysical man is confined. If one did not wish to give up the empiricist's position that all facts are either logical or empirical, then, to be consistent, he had to reject metaphysical language. It mattered little whether the metaphysical reference was to Plato's ideas, Kant's things-in-themselves, or the atomist's objects of sense experience. It was Wittgenstein who first saw this and said of his own metaphysical propositions in the *Tractatus* that "he who understands me finally recognizes them as senseless," [65] a conclusion which others did not quickly accept.

The atomists did violence to the nature of our language not only by attempting to make all uses conform to what was merely one of its uses but also by assuming that the only way in which words can refer is that in which names such as "Mary" and "Fido" do. Russell, particularly, maintained that all intelligible propositions consist of names of things with which we are immediately "acquainted," the subject, for example, naming a sense-datum of the speaker's private experience.[66] Moreover, this particular version of the naming function of language has the additional difficulty that such propositions could not be understood by anyone else, since private experience cannot be shared by another.[67] Wittgenstein was quick to see an implication

---

[65] *Ibid.*, par. 6.54.

[66] "Knowledge by Acquaintance and Knowledge by Description," p. 223. Russell came to this view because if a name applies to more than one experience of a thing we must have in mind certain characteristics of that thing which enable us to identify it and so apply the same name to it at different times. He concluded that these identifying characteristics become part of the meaning of the name and so the name becomes a disguised description. For example, the ordinary proper name "Socrates," he held, really stood for the description "the master of Plato" or "the philosopher who drank the hemlock." But only logically proper names—not descriptions—may be the subjects of atomic propositions. Russell's conclusion about ordinary proper names, however, seems unwarranted. The fact that we need descriptions to be able to apply names does not mean that descriptions and names are used in the same way (i.e., have the same sort of meaning). Cf. P. F. Strawson, *Introduction to Logical Theory*, Part III, chap. 6, section 10.

[67] In *The Philosophy of Logical Atomism* Russell argues that "it would be absolutely fatal if people meant the same things by their words. It would make all intercourse impossible . . . [because] since different people are acquainted with different objects, they would not be able to talk to each other." (P. 312) And elsewhere he explains that although no two people in a room "have exactly the same sense-data, yet there is sufficient similarity among their data to enable them to group together certain of these data as appearances of one 'thing.' " The things seen by two different people are often closely similar, so similar that the same

of this which gained general recognition somewhat later: "In fact what *solipsism* means is quite correct, . . . that the world is *my* world . . . [and] the limits of the language (*the* language, which I alone understand) mean the limits of my world." [68] In any event, we shall find the later Wittgenstein extensively criticizing both the naming view of language and the idea that language can be private.

We may turn now from our focus on the central concept of logical form to consider the theory of logical constructions. As some of the analysts have recently noted, "we constantly find the entities favored in any particular metaphysical system being accorded the rank of substances, while everything else is given some inferior, dependent status, or is even declared to be mere appearance." [69] Favoring the sense-datum, the atomists sought to show that statements about all other objects could be reduced to statements about sense-data. The trouble was that no one succeeded in doing this. While it was true that "Wisdom had indeed analyzed the llama in terms of (ordinary) llamas, and, for good measure, the average plumber in terms of (ordinary) plumbers," nonetheless, the metaphysically important analyses of things and people into sense-data were not forthcoming.[70] It was this failure which, more than any other single factor, led to the abandonment of reductive analysis.

This failure to produce satisfactory analyses stemmed from the demand that all analyses provide translations that are exactly equivalent in meaning to the statement being analyzed. The statement "The average plumber has 3.4 children" is equivalent to (i.e. a logical construction out of) "Plumber one has two children," and "Plumber two has five children," and so on for all the plumbers. This sort of analysis became the norm for analyzing statements about things and persons into statements about sense-data. If the relation between a chair and the corresponding sense-data could be shown to be exactly the same as that between the average plumber and all the plumbers, then, just as we can infer, subsequently, that the average plumber does not exist, we could infer, similarly, that the chair does not exist. The trouble is that the relation between sense-data and chairs is not just the same as that between all the plumbers and the average plumber, and, so, the metaphysical program of getting rid of all entities other than sense-data failed.

The "fruitful idea" behind the theory of logical constructions could

---

words can be used to denote them." ("The Relation of Sense-data to Physics," reprinted in *Mysticism and Logic* [New York: Doubleday, n.d.], pp. 149, 153.)

[68] *Tractatus*, 5.62. First italics are mine.

[69] H. P. Grice, D. F. Pears, and P. F. Strawson, "Metaphysics," *The Nature of Metaphysics*, ed. D. F. Pears, p. 10.

[70] Urmson, *Philosophical Analysis*, p. 150.

be put to good use, it was found, once the atomists' metaphysics
was abandoned. The principles of analysis which the atomists developed
were based on the vision of a very *uniform* language that underlies,
or is the real form of, our ordinary language. The problems connected
with these principles showed that our language, really, is multiform.
As Wisdom concludes after examining the difficulties surrounding the
doctrine of logical construction and other difficulties of a similar nature,
"the trouble arose from deducing how a sentence *must* work from a
rule which fitted like cases to date, while the trouble was removed
by reminding ourselves of how the sentence does work." [71] The difficulty, he explains, is

not that rules are wrong, but that they easily grow too powerful. Without
them there is no order, no connecting one thing with another. But it is
only too easy to substitute the manipulation of rules for looking carefully
at the individuals they cover.[72]

Classifications, therefore, must be drawn more broadly. It may be useful
to include things such as the relation between statements about sense-
data under the classification logical construction "provided we keep
on remembering that not all inferences legitimate in the older, narrower
application of the words in question will still be legitimate." [73] It is
useful in that it gives us a new way of looking at these statements.
Philosophers, according to Wisdom, "had often represented us seated
sadly guessing from the images in the mirrors of our minds at what
was happening in reality." [74] Following Berkeley's lead, Russell gave
us a different representation of our noetic situation:

He substituted for an old and muddling model of the connection between
realities and appearances a new model. For to say that a chair is a logical
construction out of appearances of a chair is to say that a chair is related to
its appearances *not* as a thing is related to the images of it in a mirror, . . .
but as the average plumber to plumbers, as a family to its members, as
energy to its manifestations, as electrons to the evidence for electrons.[75]

This use of the classification logical construction, then, helps us to
see that just as it is "silly to say 'Confined as we are to individual
plumbers how can we claim knowledge of the average plumber?'" so
it is also silly to lament "Confined as we are to our own sensations
how can we claim knowledge of spades?" [76]

The final evaluation to be made of the atomists' general position
concerns their method of translations into statements of equivalent

---

[71] "Bertrand Russell and Modern Philosophy," p. 207.   [72] *Ibid.*, p. 208.
[73] *Ibid.*, p. 206.   [74] *Ibid.*, p. 204.
[75] *Ibid.*, p. 205.   [76] *Ibid.*, p. 207.

meaning. In his assessment of this method, Urmson comments that "one way of finding out what job a sentence does is to find another sentence equivalent to it about whose job we are not perplexed." [77] Over against this, however, Urmson notes two mistakes, one of which "was to think that this method was the only proper method; another was to think that there was some absolute propriety about the one formulation and some impropriety in the other, and to invent a metaphysical explanation of this absolute propriety and impropriety; but the method itself is not faulty." [78] We may, for example, be helped in this way to see that a definite description, such as "The present king of France," may have connotation without having denotation. But, to make a judgment about the equivalence of any two statements we must determine the meaning of each of them, and, if we are able to do this for the original statement to begin with, why should we regard its formulation as improper? The value of this method does not lie in a mechanical translation into a proper form. Rather, the very process of making this comparison is itself a process of getting clear about the meaning of the original statement. Moreover, when we look at the method in this way it is not hard to see that any instance of its use that is philosophically significant will involve the philosophic position of the one making the comparison, for his judgment about the meaning of the two statements involved is what will have philosophic significance.

The method of providing a translation of exactly equivalent meaning has other limitations. Not only are the number of cases for which such equivalences can be provided rather restricted in number, but this device would not prove helpful where the philosophic problem involves very complex meanings. To judge the equivalence of meaning would be possible only after one had gotten clear about this complexity in both of the formulations involved, but the difficulty in doing this is part of the problem to begin with. What is required is a method by which to unravel the complexity a little at a time. One such method would be that of translations each of which deals with only one of these strands of meaning. This method was touched on in our comments on Moore, and we shall consider it further in Chapter IX. The concept man, for example, may be analyzed from many different perspectives— the psychological, sociological, religious, ontological, etc.

To summarize, I have argued, first of all, that the syntactical translations of Russell and the atomists from ordinary grammatical form into ideal logical form are not metaphysically neutral, because the justification of these translations was the metaphysical judgment that the "logical form" pictured the form of the real world. Second, Russell's

[77] *Philosophical Analysis*, p. 180.   [78] *Ibid.*, pp. 180-81.

interpretation of logical form makes the syntactic requirements for meaningfulness far less flexible than they must be if communication is not to be impaired seriously. Third, the atomists' belief that the logical form of language pictures *the* form of reality overlooks the fact that any metaphysical picture is relative to the limited perspective of the persons using that picture and, so, represents certain aspects of reality at the expense of others. Fourth, the atomists' use of the logical form of one sort of language as a norm for all language, in effect, makes the meaning of that language normative for all meaning, and tends to conceal the existence of other sorts of meaning important to our ordinary living. Fifth, the atomists' understanding of logical form was based on the false assumption that the function of nouns is that of naming, an assumption which, as we shall see, was to be criticized thoroughly by Wittgenstein in his later work, the *Philosophical Investigations*. Sixth, the atomists' attempt to show that statements about all other objects could be replaced by statements about sense-data simply failed. Seventh, translations such as those aimed at by the theory of logical constructions or the theory of logical types, once they were shorn of the atomists' metaphysics with its requirement that the translation provide an exact equivalence of meaning, could be useful devices for the clarification of meaning. Finally, and most fundamentally, the atomists' conception of logical form fails to recognize that the formal characteristics of a statement cannot be understood apart from the meaning of that statement and, so, are a distinguishable but not a separable aspect of that meaning.

Some Applications to Talk of God

We may turn, finally, to consider some implications of this position, and our discussion of it, for religious language. Russell himself, in the words of Edgar Brightman, "abandoned religion at an early age for slender reasons—evidence of an initially loose grip on religious thought and experience," and his "critical philosophy of religion consists largely of considerations leveled against historical Christianity" such as the charge that "the Christian religion, as organized in its churches, has been and still is the principal enemy of moral progress in the world." [79] It was true of Russell and of the other atomists that the subject of religious language was simply ignored.

Religious language, of course, would have fared no better on the procrustean bed of the atomist's language requirements than ethical or metaphysical language. The extensional logic of the atomists rep-

---

[79] "Russell's Philosophy of Religion," *The Philosophy of Bertrand Russell*, pp. 540, 542, 543.

resented the formal requirements of a language whose purpose was to report facts about the separable, self-contained entities that constituted the world as pictured by their metaphysics. If the meaning of language is, in this way, the qualities of and relations between finite entities which it reports, then religious language must either be discarded or be shown to report facts about a finite entity or entities. Statements about God, then, to be meaningful, must either report facts about a finite entity to which the word "God" refers or else, if "God" does not have this sort of reference, statements with "God" for a subject must be reduced to statements that do report facts about finite entities. Any claim that there are special religious facts would have been no better received than was Moore's claim that there were ethical facts, because it was the metaphysical judgment of the atomists that sense-data are the only real entities. Furthermore, the religious man would insist that the reality to which "God" refers is not a finite entity but, rather, a reality that transcends all finite entities. Then, too, even if God were conceived of as one monad among others, so that language about God would possess the required formal characteristics, religious language would, in this way, become nothing more than a set of propositions, whether arrived at by metaphysical reasoning or divine revelation, to which one might or might not give intellectual assent. But what of other sorts of meaning which the religious man alleges his language to have, such as the expression of existential commitment, worship, and the like? These possibilities are entirely neglected by the atomists' treatment of language.

The issues with which we have been concerned in our critical evaluation, therefore, are important for the question of the meaningfulness of religious language. As we have noted, the significance of Russell's thought for the philosophic study of meaning in general and of particular sorts of meaning, such as the religious, with which Russell does not explicitly deal is to be found primarily not in his special theories of logical types and of definite descriptions but in his theory of logical form of which these special theories are applications. Since religious language is apparently unable to meet the requirements for meaningfulness that constitute his use of this theory of logical form, it is, indeed, a crucial issue for religious language as to whether the formal requirements that any particular sort of language, such as the religious, must meet if it is to be meaningful may be determined without an examination of that language itself.

If, as I have argued, the formal characteristics of a statement may be distinguished but not separated from its meaning, then the formal requirements for religious language must be determined by a study of the meaning of that language. The failure of the atomists to recognize this had the result of a tyranny, in their thought, of one use of language over all uses, because the formal characteristics of that use became normative for all language—they were held to constitute *the* logical form of any meaningful language. A study of the formal characteristics of one sort of language—such as the scientific—whose meaning is judged to be cognitive does not show the form that any statement *must* have if it is to be cognitive. Rather it shows only the form that the statements of that particular language *do* in fact have. To examine the claim that statements with "God" as their subject are cognitive, one must first determine the formal characteristics of these statements. The issue is then whether these characteristics are to be regarded as cognitive. This cannot be settled simply by showing that this form is not the same as that of some other language regarded as cognitive. This would merely be to point out that the meaning of religious statements is, of course, religious rather than something else and, so, if religious language is cognitive, it is cognitive of a religious reality and not of a reality of some other sort. We can certainly agree that languages that are regarded as cognitive must have something in common that justifies placing them all in this classification, but the issue may well turn on deciding what feature or features are essential to cognitive status. It may be decided that cognition requires the sort of tests that are applicable to assertions about isolatable segments of reality, that the *expectations* concerning possibilities of future experience are such as may be (or at least theoretically could be) frustrated or realized by a definite and repeatable procedure. The claim that the cat is on the mat by the doorstep may be tested simply by going to the doorstep and looking at the mat to see if there is a cat on it, perhaps also touching the cat, and so forth. If I wish to, I may go back to the doorstep and look again, or someone else may repeat this procedure. Such a decision that cognition is limited to isolatable segments of reality obviously eliminates statements about God where God is not conceived to be merely another segment of reality. However, it may be decided that to be cognitive a statement need only express *some* sort of expectations concerning future experience of the life-process either in one of its aspects or as a whole. If "God" has to do not with a part of reality but with reality as a whole, then statements about the nature of God will have their test, in some sense, in the whole of experience rather than in one area of it.[80] Consequently, such statements will be judged cognitive if it can be shown that the life-process as a whole can actually serve as some sort of test of them. We shall

---

[80] However, statements about particular actions or other manifestations of God will directly concern only particular segments of experience, although they will imply the truth of general statements about the nature of God.

provide an example in the final chapter. But just how valuable these statements are cognitively—the extent to which they are cognitive—will depend upon how definite the expectations are which they involve. How valuable statements are existentially will depend not only on their *cognitive* value but also on how much or in what way we are *concerned* about what these statements express. Our religious or ultimate concern, then, will be cognitive to the extent that it involves religious or ultimate expectations that our experience will either frustrate or realize.

Whether a religious or any other statement has cognitive meaning, then, cannot be determined in a metaphysically neutral way by simply appealing to formal requirements. The judgment that certain formal characteristics are cognitive is finally a metaphysical judgment.[81]

On the positive side, however, there is one very important lesson to be learned from Russell and his followers of this period, namely, that our response to statement forms becomes habitual, and this habit may result in the error of treating two statements as more alike than they are. If, for example, we allow our habitual way of treating statements like "John is forgiving" to carry over uncritically into our understanding of "God is forgiving," we make the error of treating them as far more similar in meaning than critical examination shows them to be. Indeed, not a few contemporary analysts believe that statements about God are typically spoken or written in a cognitively meaningless way and that those who believe them to be meaningful are being misled by a certain feel of meaningfulness which religious assertions derive from sharing the form of words of our statements about human beings.

It is in connection with this danger that Russell's distinction between grammatical and logical form is of value once it is separated from the metaphysical interpretation that "logical form" refers to a sentence form that has some absolute propriety for the meaning being expressed.[82] The usefulness of this distinction, we have argued, is as an *ad hoc* device either to raise the question whether two grammatically similar statements possess the same formal characteristics or to raise the somewhat similar question whether a statement that has a meaningful grammatical form nonetheless harbors certain formal confusions.

The dangers of being misled by the form of language—failing to

---

[81] Epistemology, in other words, concerns the relation of knower to known, and this, in turn, involves judgments about the nature of the knower and the nature of the known.

[82] Many statements having "God" as their subject term would violate Russell's insistence that words be capable of the same syntactical functions in all statements in which either can be used, before they can be allowed the same function in any statement. Consider, for example, the statements: "God delivered the Israelites," "Moses delivered the Israelites," "God was in Christ," "Moses was in Christ."

recognize logical differences—and the usefulness of developing techniques, such as that of translation, to guard against these dangers, have received particularly strong attention in Ian Ramsey's work on religious language. The Christian is in constant danger of falling into logical confusion because he uses two different sorts of language about certain persons or events. His language practices with respect to Jesus, for example, imply "the logical claim that two languages of different logical status can nevertheless be used of the one object." [83] For example, he uses our ordinary language about human beings in saying that Jesus wept, prayed, was crucified, and the like. But the Christian also uses theological language in saying of Jesus that "God was in Christ reconciling the world unto himself"; Jesus' actions, in effect, are regarded as also the actions of God. From this practice, there easily arises the sort of logical confusion which resulted in Patripassianism, for example. As Ramsey analyzes it,

patripassianism becomes not an error but an absurdity, a confounding of logical areas, a violation of syntax. For it uses "crucify," a word significant only at the Jesus of Nazareth level, of the Father. The truth . . . is that we cannot say significantly that God suffers. But neither can we significantly say that he does not. Each claim is a misuse of language.[84]

Similarly, talk about a man's relation with God does not have just the same sort of logic as talk about his finite relations, but the two are sometimes confused. When the Christian, for example, claims that God justifies the sinful, "some have been tempted to read words such as 'justification' as though they belonged to the language of morality," and so have supposed "that 'being justified' is a logical synonym for 'being good,'" and have tried to link them together in posing questions of the sort "Can we do wrong after justification?" [85] One may be misled here by the fact that such questions look like the question "Can we contract diphtheria after inoculation?" Ramsey analyzes the confusion in this way:

That some sort of connection can be discovered on the theistic map between "justification" and moral behaviour is undeniable. But it is of a most complex kind, which makes the question: 'Can we do wrong after justification?" just as improper and misleading as the question: "Can we contract diphtheria after baptism?" We need not deny that what "justification" talks about will have some sort of connection with moral behaviour; we need not deny that since "baptism" concerns the "whole man," it will have some sort of connection with health; but what is characteristic and distinctive about "justification" and "baptism" belongs to different logical areas altogether.[86]

---

[83] *Religious Language*, "The Library of Philosophy and Theology," ed. Alasdair MacIntyre and Ronald Gregor Smith (London: SCM Press, 1957), p. 168.
[84] *Ibid.*, pp. 169-70.   [85] *Ibid.*, pp. 180, 181.   [86] *Ibid.*, p. 181.

It would be a similar confusion to ask "Does light ever travel by train?" for this would be to confuse the logical function that "travel" has in ordinary language and the function it has in the language of physics when it appears in the sentence "Light travels in a straight line."

The Christian, then, requires from theology logical guides by which to keep clear about how the logically different languages he is using in connection with his faith are related to one another and, so, avoid being misled by logical confusion. This requirement is, in fact, one that was felt very early in the history of the church. In proclaiming that God had acted decisively in Jesus, the Kerygma employed "a riotous mixture of phrases . . . belonging intrinsically to so many different logical areas." [87] Jesus was spoken of as "God's servant, child, Christ, Lord; as the Holy and Righteous One; as Saviour, Prince, and Author of Life; as raised from the dead." [88] But the language of those to whom this preaching was directed contained no adequate guides for understanding these phrases, no adequate "framework of ideas against which their logical edges could be aligned, and their appropriate claims made evident." [89] First, the Jews could not relate the crucifixion to their convictions about the Messiah, and then the Greeks could not conceive of how the term "God" could be given a logic whereby it could be used with reference to a man. It was to meet this need—in effect, a need for "analysis and teaching"—that Christian doctrine came into being. It "began by bringing alongside these various phrases some *interpretative rule* which might be as abstract and general as some dominant metaphysical idea, or as concrete as some particular relationship." [90] Such ideas as sonship or *Logos* were made to function as "models," or "illuminating pictures" whereby one was guided in the logical complexities involved.

The analogy of father and son, to take the first example, suggests both a distinction and a logical connection. Father and son are not identical, but to speak of a son *implies* a father as well. This picture, then, warns us that language about Jesus—eating, praying, being crucified—and language about God are logically different. We may say that Jesus prayed but not that God prayed. Yet this picture also points to a connection of logical necessity between the words "Son" and "Father." In talking about God, in other words, we are not to proceed as though "God is to be altogether distinguished from, and be apart from, his Son." [91] This subordinationism would not "do justice to what is 'disclosed' in worship." [92] Just as many who knew the historical Jesus of Nazareth felt in his presence the presence of God at the same time, so the worshiper fastens his attention on Jesus in

[87] *Ibid.*, p. 154.   [88] *Ibid.*   [89] *Ibid.*, p. 156.
[90] *Ibid.* Italics mine. [91] *Ibid.*, p. 157. [92] *Ibid.*, p. 164.

such a way that in this life and person he also encounters God. This concept of a "disclosure" will be examined more fully in our consideration of Oxford philosophy. In connection with Russell, we are merely concerned to indicate the way in which his ideas about the danger of being misled at the logical or formal level of language have been developed fruitfully in connection with theological language.

The danger of being misled in connection with theological models such as sonship lies in the fact that they express "important logical point[s] *misleadingly in the material mode.*" [93] "God sent his Son," for example, appears to report an actual occurrence in the way that "The King sent his representative" does, while it is actually a second order statement referring to religious *language.* This was the sort of confusion, for example, that resulted in the Arian heresy: "Arius did not realize that words like 'son' and 'father' only provided models." [94] Failing to understand the logical status of these terms, Arius reasoned, in effect, that "'sons come after fathers,' so that if we are to talk about Jesus in terms of sonship, we cannot escape some degree of subordination if we are to use words meaningfully." [95]

To guard against subordinationist interpretations, "qualifiers" were added to the model in order to stress the logically necessary connection between "Father" and "Son" which constituted one of the rules of the orthodox use of this religious language. Thus, the Son was said to be "eternally generated" by the Father. But here, too, the logical point was put "misleadingly in the material mode" as though what were being talked about was something that "goes on at all times in some sort of heavenly laboratory, or labour-ward." [96] It must be recognized that, if Arius was logically confused, "the orthodox, from their side, were far from being clear about what they were doing." [97]

It becomes obvious that one way to avoid such confusion is to use Russell's technique of a translation from the material mode into the formal mode. We may take, as an example, Ramsey's recommendation that theological "talk of the Fall as 'pre-mundane' is best understood by changing in the first place to the formal mode" in which it "can be taken as saying that 'The Fall' does not belong to 'mundane language.'" [98] In this way we avoid any suggestion that the Fall is an event. The logic of this story is not that of observational language but rather that of providing linguistic guides by which to relate, consistently, talk about evil and talk about God as the source of all that is. By speaking in the formal mode, we show clearly that this story has to do with problems of language consistency rather than with a historical event.

[93] *Ibid.*, p. 158.   [94] *Ibid.*, p. 159.   [95] *Ibid.*
[96] *Ibid.*, p. 158.   [97] *Ibid.*, p. 159.   [98] *Ibid.*, p. 82.

To this account we may add that this story has also an existential function of illuminating the believer's personal struggle with the problem of his own egocentricity, his unwillingness to accept the limitations of his finitude—"you will be like God" (Gen. 3:5). A translation into an existential mode, such as that found in the writing of Martin Heidegger, would show more clearly this function of speaking about every man rather than a man named Adam. We see, then, that such translations need not imply that there is some absolute logical propriety about the form into which the translation is being made. Language about the Fall performs more than one function—expresses more than one meaning—and we know what sort of translation will draw attention to one of these functions only because we have already grasped that meaning through the original form of expression. Indeed, the existential function is no doubt best performed by the rich imagery of the story form, so that it is to this form that the believer will return after the translation has done its reminding and clarifying work. As John Hutchison points out, "The mode of religious or mythical thinking consists in the occurrence in the mind of the religious person of compelling or authoritative images," [99] images by which "men get their orientation or take their bearings in existence." [100]

Ian Ramsey's work, then, is illustrative of the usefulness for the philosophic study of the meaning of religious language of Russell's distinction between what *prima facie* often seems to be the function of a statement and the function which that statement really performs. When the theological models or illuminating pictures designed to guide the believer through the logical complexities of his language are expressed in the material mode they may seem, at first glance, to be referring to actual persons and events, for this is most often the function of statements of that mode. Or the statement "Can we do wrong after justification?" seems to be in order logically, but actually fails to make sense because it mixes terms that get their meaning from languages of very different formal characteristics.

It must be emphasized once again, however, that these translations are not metaphysically neutral. The meaning that they seek to safeguard from confusion due to grammatical form is the meaning that they are interpreted as having from the translator's point of view. Thus, Ramsey says of God's creation of the world, "Whereas creation *ex nihilo* seems on the face of it, and from its grammar, to be talking of a great occasion in the past, it is rather making a present claim about

[99] *Faith, Reason, and Existence* (New York: Oxford University Press, 1956), p. 56.
[100] *Ibid.*, p. 57.

God, and its logical grammar must be understood appropriately." [101]
Alasdair MacIntyre, however, sees the matter very differently:

Schleiermacher, for example, suggests that when we say that God created
the world we are really saying something about our inner experience of
absolute dependence. But if we use the words "God created the world"
in their ordinary sense then the rules of meaning and syntax in English
preclude us from referring them to inner experience.[102]

MacIntyre adds that "if one wishes to mean something other than
what they would mean, *taken as they stand*, it would seem *misleading*
to use this form of words." [103]

We may consider, also, the suggestive value for conceiving the
nature of our knowledge about God of what Wisdom and others have
shown to be the "fruitful idea" behind the atomists' doctrine of
logical constructions. If it is "silly" to lament "Confined as we are to
the evidence for electrons how can we claim knowledge of electrons?"
to what extent do we have similar reasons for doubting the appropriateness of the question "Confined as we are to the manifestations of God
in our experience of the finite world how can we claim knowledge of
God?" How far can it helpfully be argued that the relation of God to
finite events is more like the relation of electrons to the evidence for
electrons than it is like the relation of things-in-themselves to their
images on the mirrors of our minds or the relation of objects to their
shadows on the wall of a cave? We shall see some initial explorations
of this question when we consider the philosophy of John Wisdom.

But there is another implication of the doctrine of logical constructions for the student of religious language. Russell's principle: "Wherever possible, substitute constructions out of known entities for inferences to unknown entities" [104] displays one of the basic thrusts of
the empiricism of the analytic movement. As Ian Ramsey puts it
with respect to religious language, if anyone "thinks that logical
empiricism will have a tendency to make theology 'verbal,' he is right
if he means by this that it would invent no 'entities' beyond necessity." [105] And elsewhere we are warned,

[101] *Religious Language*, p. 75. According to Ramsey, creation *ex nihilo* evokes
"a sense of creaturely dependence." (*Ibid.*)

[102] "The Logical Status of Religious Belief," *Metaphysical Beliefs*, Stephen
Toulmin, Ronald W. Hepburn, and Alasdair MacIntyre (London: SCM Press,
1957), p. 176. Italics mine.

[103] *Ibid.*, pp. 176-77. Italics mine. The question might well be raised whether
"created" *can* be taken in any ordinary sense in "created the world."

[104] "Logical Atomism," *Contemporary British Philosophy*, I, 363.

[105] *Religious Language*, p. 185.

Let us not suppose that any and every theological word describes a separate feature of the supernatural scene. Theological language can be made significant and empirically grounded without its nouns having to talk of particular landmarks in the way they would do if it was ordinary matter-of-fact language. Indeed, the curse of much theological apologetic is that it talks as if theological language worked like ordinary matter-of-fact language.[106]

Insofar, then, as theology is influenced by contemporary analysis, it will seek to interpret "the creation," "the fall," "the eschaton," "heaven," "hell," "satan," and the like in such a way that these terms are not taken as referring to particular events, places, or persons. At this point, then, analytic philosophy is at one with the concern to demythologize the Bible.

[106] *Ibid.*, p. 82.

LOGICAL POSITIVISM: *Analysis*
&
Verification

Chapter Four

As we have seen, the metaphysics of logical atomism functioned as a justification of its program of analysis. That is, it explained why one form of words is to be preferred over another. But this metaphysics proved to be inherently unstable. The metaphysical view that the sole function of language is to picture facts and that there are no metaphysical facts eliminates itself from what is statable. This was first made explicit by Wittgenstein when he stated that his own statements were not statable—that is, did not deal with anything statable. As this anti-metaphysical strain gained ascendency the reaction was, in the words of Frank P. Ramsey, that "we must then take seriously that it is nonsense, and not pretend, as Wittgenstein does, that it is important nonsense." [1]

Now if the metaphysics of logical atomism was to be rejected, an alternative justification was needed for the work of analysis. Such an alternative was developed by the logical positivists, whose analysis was otherwise like that of the atomists.

Rather than giving insight into the structure of *facts*, analysis was construed, by the positivists, as clarifying the structure of the *languages* of science and common sense. This clarification amounted to showing that the propositions of these languages are reducible to more basic propositions which are roughly equivalent to the atomic propositions of the atomists. Whenever the prevalent language left unclear, or even

[1] *Foundations of Mathematics and Other Logical Essays*, ed. R. B. Braithwaite (London: K. Paul, Trench, Trubner, 1931), p. 263.

90

misled one about, its relation to these basic propositions, it was the philosopher's job to reform that language.

The important feature of these preferred propositions is that they can be verified directly. "This is red" is verified simply by looking and seeing if the referent is in fact red. The program of analysis, then, was the same as that of the atomists, except that it had to be explicated by a consideration of language which somehow did not raise the question of the relation of language to the reality experienced. If their statements were to avoid being metaphysical, the positivists had to avoid talking about the relation of language to fact.

One way of getting into the positivists' point of view, and indeed into the empiricist point of view in general, is to consider how a child learns a language or how an adult might, without benefit of explanation, determine what others mean by terms that he has never heard before. Attending a basketball game for the first time, one would not at first find intelligible the remarks of others about goals, fouls, palming the ball, and the like. But by noticing what conditions obtain when the various remarks are made, one could gradually learn the meaning of the terms. He could gradually come to see that the meaning of an assertion that player x is palming the ball is that a circumstance of one special sort is observed. Moreover, it is just this observation that verifies the statement about palming the ball, i.e., that provides an answer to the question "Is it true that x is palming the ball?" If one were sitting behind two metaphysicians, however, and overheard a discussion as to whether basketballs were substances, it seems that one could not similarly learn the new meaning. No special type of circumstance could be detected as that which was meant. One could not detect anything empirical that would count in favor of an answer to the question. To be sure, it is true that often meanings are explained to us by someone else, but these explanations must make use of meanings that we have already grasped, constructing the new meaning from them. It seems, then, that any system of meaning depends ultimately upon those meanings which we can grasp without requiring an explanation but simply in some such way as suggested above, a way that is applicable to empirical things but not, apparently, to things that allegedly transcend experience.

Consequently, the meaning of an empirical statement seems to be one or more observations concerning an empirical state of affairs. If I say, "The cat is on the mat in the next room," do I not mean that under certain conditions—i.e., entering the next room, looking toward the mat, etc.—one will have certain experiences such as seeing the cat and hearing the cat purr? Since these observations are also this statement's verification, the logical positivists contended that the meaning of an empirical statement *is* its method of verification, the method by which its truth is established. This, in incipient form, is the famous "verification principle," which constituted the heart of the positivists' position.

There proved to be many difficulties, though, in formulating this principle so that it would be adequate to its task of clarifying the language of common sense and, especially, the language of science, while yet eliminating as meaningless metaphysical talk of realities that transcend experience. For example, the positivists found that by identifying meaning and verification they had reduced the meaning of a statement about an event in past history to the method by which the historian verifies it, that is, rummaging through historical documents and the like. If verification meant nothing more than direct empirical observation, then statements about past and future were eliminated. They found also that if conclusive or complete verification were required, then general propositions, such as those of natural science, would be eliminated. In fact, the only empirical propositions that can be verified in this strong, conclusive sense are those basic propositions which simply report a single experience; all others, such as "This book is red," are "hypotheses which are continually subject to the test of further experience." [2] Yet if they adopted the weaker requirement that some observations merely must be *relevant* to the statement's truth or falsity, they might open the gate to metaphysics.

A. J. Ayer's formulation in the second edition of *Language, Truth and Logic* is representative of the later revisions: "A sentence [has] literal meaning if and only if the proposition it expresses is either analytic or empirically verifiable." [3] "Empirically verifiable" meant that an empirical observation or sense experience should be conceivable that would be *relevant* to establishing truth or falsity. [4] Unless further qualified, though, this formulation allows meaning to every conceivable statement. Ayer points out that "the statements 'the Absolute is lazy' and 'if the Absolute is lazy, this is white' jointly entail the observation-statement [i.e., basic proposition] 'this is white.'" [5] Observations about the whiteness of the object referred to by "this" are relevant to the truth both of "The Absolute is lazy" and of "If the Absolute is lazy, this is white." To avoid this consequence, Ayer tightens the requirements:

A statement is directly verifiable if it is either itself an observation-statement, or is such that in conjunction with one or more observation-statements it entails at least one observation-statement which is not deducible from these

---

[2] A. J. Ayer, *Language, Truth and Logic*, 2nd ed. (London: Victor Gollancz, 1946), p. 9.

[3] *Ibid.*, p. 5.   [4] *Ibid.*, pp. 35-38, 11.   [5] *Ibid.*, p. 11.

other premises alone; and . . . a statement is indirectly verifiable if it satisfies the following conditions: first, that in conjunction with certain other premises it entails one or more directly verifiable statements which are not deducible from these other premises alone; and secondly, that these other premises do not include any statement that is not either analytic, or directly verifiable, or capable of being independently established as indirectly verifiable.[6]

All significant propositions, then, "are to be incorporated in the system of empirical propositions which constitutes science."[7] Given these requirements, we cannot use "If the Absolute is lazy, this is white" to show the meaningfulness of "The Absolute is lazy" nor can we use the latter to show the meaningfulness of the former. Similarly, we cannot use "If God exists, then repentence leads to new life" to establish the meaningfulness of "God exists."

Statements that are not empirically verifiable, then, do not qualify as meaningful unless they are analytic. The category "analytic" covers the laws of logic and mathematics and the positivists' own philosophical statements, including the verification principle itself, none of which are empirically verifiable. According to Ayer, an analytic proposition is one that is true by definition. It has meaning only in the sense that it "illustrates" the way we use our language; it "calls attention to linguistic usages of which we might not otherwise be conscious."[8] From this point of view, logic and mathematics have

the important function of making it clear to what our use of symbols commits us. That we use them as we do is a matter of convention; but once these conventions are established, we are bound by them, not morally but in the sense that the infraction of them is self-stultifying.[9]

The concept of analyticity, then, has meaning only if it is used in reference to a given language. The verification principle, for example, is analytic with respect to the languages of science and common sense because its function is to elucidate the structure of these languages. "It purports to lay down the conditions which actually govern our acceptance, or indeed our understanding, of common sense and scientific statements."[10] The positivists, in short, saw philosophy as "nothing more and nothing less than the analysis of language; and since analysis is done in sets of equivalences, which are tautologies, philosophy is even to be equated with logic."[11]

The language of common sense, however, includes moral and other value statements, which seem to be neither analytic nor empirically

[6] *Ibid.*, p. 13.   [7] *Ibid.*, p. 120.   [8] *Ibid.*, p. 79.
[9] "The Vienna Circle," *The Revolution in Philosophy*, pp. 76-77.
[10] *Ibid.*, p. 75.   [11] Urmson, *Philosophical Analysis*, p. 118.

verifiable. Statements of this sort were understood, generally,[12] to be simply emotive; they express and evoke feelings.

Concerning ethical language, Ayer maintained, for example, that

if I say to someone, "You acted wrongly in stealing that money," I am not stating anything more than if I had simply said, "You stole that money." In adding that this action is wrong I am not making any further statement about it. . . . It merely serves to show that the expression of it is attended by certain feelings in the speaker.[13]

This is the emotive theory of ethics, according to which an ethical dispute is cognitively significant only if it is a dispute as to the true nature of the facts toward which a moral attitude is taken. Clarification of fact may lead to a change of attitude, but it is pointless to dispute the attitude as such. According to Ayer, "if our opponent happens to have undergone a different process of moral 'conditioning' from ourselves . . . then we abandon the attempt to convince him by argument." [14]

Positivistic analysis, then, maintains that there are just three kinds of sentence: the empirically verifiable, the analytic, and the emotive. Failing to qualify as empirical or analytic, metaphysical sentences are consigned to the purely emotive category. As Rudolf Carnap expressed it, metaphysical propositions "are, like laughing, lyrics and music, expressive." [15] They are extremely deceptive, however, because they have the appearance of being empirical.

This was the positivism that offered those who were practicing analysis an allegedly nonmetaphysical justification of their methods.

Critical Evaluation

An evaluation of the adequacy for the entire range of language of this approach to analysis must deal with two closely related questions: (1) Have the positivists succeeded in eliminating metaphysics as meaningless on purely logical grounds? (2) How adequate for the whole of language is the threefold classification empirically verifiable-analytic-emotive?

First, were the positivists successful in their attempt to discuss language in complete *separation* from the question of how language is related to fact or reality? Were they consistent in their claim to have substituted logic for metaphysics by simply limiting their consideration

---

[12] Schlick, for example, interpreted ethical statements in terms of facts about the achievement of human happiness. Carnap interpreted them as commands.

[13] *Language, Truth and Logic*, p. 107.   [14] *Ibid.*, p. 111.

[15] *Philosophy and Logical Syntax*, p. 12.

to the languages of common sense and of science and, then, by limiting their own philosophical statements to those which were analytic with respect to these languages? Let us consider two main difficulties that lead to a conclusion that they were not.

In the first place, if philosophical statements are to be restricted to the purely analytic, the positivistic philosopher cannot accomplish his purpose, which is the clarification of language. This clarification, allegedly, is a matter of showing that all meaningful indicative language can be reduced to—is constructed out of—certain basic or protocol sentences. But the difficulty is that an analytic statement cannot do the job of indicating what sentences these are. As Urmson puts it,

> If one means by a protocol sentence a sentence from which other scientific sentences are logically derived but which is not itself derived from any other sentences, which is roughly the explanation usually given, and then, when asked how science gains its protocol sentences, answers that science accepts as protocols those sentences which are records of direct experience, this cannot be a tautology if it is to count as an answer at all. . . . It seems, then, that taken at face value it is metaphysics—nonsense. . . . It is the attempt to talk about the relation of language to fact.[16]

In a position he later felt forced to abandon, Carnap, for example, tried to stay within the limits of logical syntax by saying that protocol statements are those having the same type of syntax as statements like "joy, now" and "there, red." But since he could not further define these sentences as those which directly report reality—for this would be to go beyond syntax—questions were raised as to why sentences of this syntactic form should be selected and how one then is to decide which sentences of this form to accept. Carnap held that it is simply a matter of convention that this form is selected, the protocols accepted being those accepted by accredited scientists. However, as Urmson points out, "we could now go on to ask why we accept the protocols of accredited scientists, why they are accredited, and how we know within syntax that these or those are accepted by accredited scientists." [17]

Protocol statements, in fact, seem not to be statements at all. As Ayer admits, "the mere recording of one's present experience does not serve to convey any information either to any other person or indeed to oneself; for in knowing a basic proposition to be true one obtains no further knowledge than what is already afforded by the occurrence of the relevant experience." [18] But this sentence is contradictory. If

---

[16] *Philosophical Analysis*, p. 122. The attempt to legislate certain reforms of scientific and commonsense language also seems to require a judgment as to the relation of language and reality.

[17] *Ibid.*, p. 126.   [18] *Language, Truth and Logic*, p. 10.

no information is conveyed, then one does not know the proposition to be true. It cannot be true because it cannot be false. No experience could count against it. And if it cannot be true or false it is not a proposition.

The other main difficulty is this: If all philosophical statements are analytic and an analytic statement simply illustrates part of the logic of one sort of language, then a philosophic statement cannot eliminate any sort of language as meaningless. To draw attention to characteristics of one sort of meaning does not tell us anything about another sort of meaning except that it is another sort.

The verification principle was put forward in the form of just such an analytic statement; it was intended as an elucidation of the logic of the language of science and of certain usages referred to as common sense. To say that it defines literal meaning or indicative meaning is simply to decide to use these terms to refer to the logic of these languages alone.[19] For example, when Ayer says that a nonanalytic statement is literally meaningful "if and only if it is . . . empirically verifiable," [20] he means by this that unless a nonanalytic statement "satisfied the principle of verification it would not be capable of being understood in the sense in which either scientific hypotheses or common-sense statements are habitually understood." [21] Or, as Wisdom translates this statement, "Unless a statement has the sort of verification a scientific or common-sense statement has it won't be a common-sense or scientific statement." [22] This opens the door to Wisdom's contention that "after study of [the verification principle] we come to its complementary platitude 'Every sort of statement has its own sort of meaning.' " [23] Clearly, on a strictly analytic interpretation, the verification principle eliminates neither metaphysics nor any other sort of language but only shows that metaphysical statements are not verified in the same way that scientific statements are verified.

Why, then, did the positivists think they had eliminated metaphysics? Urmson suggests that they "had been led by superficial grammatical resemblance into thinking that any expression having the same grammar as the empirical statements with regard to which the verification principle seemed most plausible must either have the same logical character as they had or else be faulty, nonsensical." [24] The positivists, in other words, saw language as something uniform. In the earlier identification of meaning and verification, especially, empirical state-

[19] This is a departure from ordinary, commonsense usage, for we do not, in our ordinary language, refer to value statements as nonsense or meaningless.

[20] *Language, Truth and Logic*, p. 9.   [21] *Ibid.*, p. 16.

[22] "Note on the New Edition of Professor Ayer's *Language, Truth and Logic*" (1948), reprinted in Wisdom, *Philosophy and Psycho-Analysis*, p. 245.

[23] *Ibid.*, p. 246.   [24] *Philosophical Analysis*, p. 168.

ments are represented as basically just alike; empirical statements ultimately[25] must all be verifiable in essentially the same way. Metaphysical statements are not verifiable in the way that scientific statements are, and so they are not verifiable. As had been true of the atomists, the positivists assumed that language was fundamentally a rather tidy logical system. Whether or not similarities in grammatical form were the causes of this view they would certainly reinforce it.

The positivists' belief that they had eliminated metaphysics seems also to have been strongly encouraged by the emotive form in which they cast their definitions. C. L. Stevenson drew attention to this in his article "Persuasive Definitions":

But do their distinctions take us more than *half way* to a full rejection of metaphysics? Are we led to go the other half by the word "nonsense," defined so that it may cast its objectionable emotive meaning upon metaphysics, without being predicated of it untruthfully? [26]

In such a "persuasive definition," Stevenson contended, we find an "interplay between emotive and descriptive meaning" which "is used, consciously or unconsciously, in an effort to secure . . . a redirection of people's attitudes." [27]

Not only did the positivists fail to eliminate metaphysics, but little clarification of the nature of metaphysics can be gained by using Ayer's empirical-analytic-emotive scheme of classification. And this is true of many other sorts of language use as well. Since, as the analysts have come to see, language is richly complex and varied, the positivists' attempts to treat language as neatly divisible into three uniform groupings necessarily did violence to many sorts of meaning.

We may helpfully begin by considering how such a classification system actually functions. A formal language category is formulated by the selection, as paradigmatic or normative, of a sentence or set of sentences about whose formal characteristics those who will use the category are relatively clear. For the positivistic categories one might select "The cat is on the mat" (empirical), "A triangle is a plane figure bounded by three sides" (analytic), and "Phooey on metaphysics" (emotive). To classify a sentence under one of these categories is to make the judgment that its formal characteristics are more like the formal characteristics of the paradigm sentence of that category than they are like those of the paradigms of the other categories.

The adequacy of a positivistic analysis, then, depends upon how

[25] Indirect verification is simply an extension of the pattern of direct verification.
[26] *Mind* (1938), p. 340.
[27] Charles L. Stevenson, *Ethics and Language* (New Haven: Yale University Press, 1944), p. 210.

much clarification of the formal characteristics of our various sorts of sentence is achieved by the comparisons it utilizes. How much are we helped to understand the logic of sentences that are neither analytic nor strictly subject to empirical verification by the positivists' practice of comparing them to "laughing, lyrics and music"? Negatively, the reminder of what the sentence is not may be helpful at times, but the positive comparison of the sentence with the purely expressive may be of very limited value or even misleading. The category became so broadly inclusive that, as Ayer notes, the positivists came to "mean by emotive simply not cognitive." [28] They included in this category the language usage of metaphysics, religion, ethics, and aesthetics. In analyzing these uses as emotive they did not give us any clarification as to how each differs from the others. By what criterion are we to distinguish an ethical from, say, an aesthetic attitude? May not such a criterion (or criteria) elucidate a function of that language that is of more central importance to it than its function of expressing or evoking attitude or emotion, however inseparable these functions may be?

Some question must also be raised concerning the adequacy of the positivistic conception of the emotive function itself. Does its subjectivistic-relativistic value theory give an adequate account of the relation between emotion and understanding—between the attitude and the reality toward which that attitude is directed? Can our attitudes be judged appropriate or inappropriate without reference to the nature of the reality toward which they are directed? If not, does not the positivistic claim that our attitudes are purely a matter of taste obscure this point? John Wisdom says of Ayer's analysis of ethical statements that

though light is thrown on their peculiar logic or verification by representing them as a mixture of empirical statement, exclamation and exhortation, this account of them still misleads. For it suggests that such statements . . . could be proved by establishing the relevant points of fact and then giving our opponent a "shot" of some drug which would make him feel like us about what we are talking of. Yet this, it is certain, would not be altering his attitude in the way we also call "showing him . . . the wrongness of the act." For to do this his attitude must be altered by *rational* persuasion. And this is done by drawing attention rhetorically to the features of what we are talking about, insisting upon how different it is from this, how like to that, passing insensibly from the purely factual through the semi-factual, semi-critical, to the critical predicate at issue.[29]

---

[28] *Language, Truth and Logic*, p. 346.
[29] "Note on the New Edition of Professor Ayer's *Language, Truth and Logic*," p. 246.

This is not to say that the appropriateness of attitudes can be deduced from judgments concerning matters-of-fact. It is to say, rather, that there are other sorts of rational relation than those of deduction and induction. By deduction, Wisdom explains,

we may pass from statements of one type to statements of the same type, but not from statements of one type to statements of another type. . . . We cannot pass, neither by deduction nor by induction, from statements of fact, whether about things or about words, to logical statements. Nevertheless the basis of logical statements is experience. . . . It is the same with ethical statements.[30]

An attitude or emotion, then, is directed to some aspect of reality or to reality as a whole, so that to distinguish different sorts of attitude is, by implication, to distinguish different aspects of reality, and to speak of an attitude as appropriate is, by implication, to speak of reality in one of its aspects as being of such a nature as to make that attitude appropriate. Similarly, that we have an attitude toward things as a whole presupposes that we have some understanding of the whole, and to judge such an attitude appropriate is to say something about the nature of that whole. As Ferré has put it, "Why adopt the attitude of unlimited adoration unless it is believed to be *in some sense* appropriate to reality?" [31] Failing to clarify the nature of this objective reference of our attitudes, the positivists' fail to provide the criteria needed to distinguish religious, moral, aesthetic, or other sorts of attitudes from one another.

Our question concerning the adequacy of the positivists' understanding of the emotive functions has as its focal point their relativistic view of human values. Our ethical attitudes, we are told, are simply what we have been conditioned to hold. But this surely is a metaphysical interpretation of the empirical data of moral experience. We must, then, reject Ayer's claim concerning the emotive theory of ethics that "the theory is entirely on the level of analysis," [32] unless all that he meant was that this theory concerns itself with the formal characteristics of the ethical language practices of *only* those persons who hold a deterministic view of the nature of man and who regard ethical attitudes merely as a matter of taste. When this theory is applied to all ethical language it becomes legislative; it assumes the truth of the deterministic view of man and the appropriateness of the moral attitudes that this view implies.

[30] *Ibid.*

[31] Frederick Ferré and Kent Bendall, *Exploring the Logic of Faith* (New York: Association Press, 1962), p. 69.

[32] "On the Analysis of Moral Judgments" (1949), reprinted in Ayer, *Philosophical Essays* (New York: St. Martin's Press, 1954), pp. 245-46.

The positivists' analytic-empirical division is also inadequate insofar as meaning and verification are identified because it is based upon a narrow preconception of the sort of thing a nonanalytic statement must be—the sort of relation it must have to the evidence for it. When I speak of another's behavior my evidence is basically observation of that behavior. But when I speak of another's state of mind my evidence is not observation of his state of mind; my evidence is rather his behavior. But this does not fit the required pattern; the evidence is of a different logical type than that for which it is evidence. How can observations of behavior serve as evidence for statements about anything other than that of which they are observations? Talk of another's state of mind, then, must really be talk of his behavior—a rather uncommonsense description of commonsense statements but one that shows that they do fit the acceptable pattern of verification. Statements, such as those of ethics or religion or metaphysics, which cannot be made to fit this pattern—at least not very plausibly—were dismissed as not really statements at all. They are not similar enough to the type of statement by which the statement category was defined to qualify for inclusion in that category.

When we consider the work of John Wisdom we shall find extensive criticism of this "idea that the justification of a statement must be either of the *inductive* sort we have when we notice familiar symptoms and reckon, for example, that a patient is suffering from a certain disorder, or of the *deductive* sort we have when we have carried investigation so far that it would be senseless to deny that he is suffering from that disorder." [33] For now, however, we shall simply note that the positivists' failure to see any but these sorts of relation between a statement and its evidence prevented them from giving an adequate account of even their own analytic statements. To say that an analytic statement, such as the statement of the verification principle, is true by definition does not make clear how we know whether such a statement is true. The early version of the verification principle, for example, was thought to be true by definition but was subsequently revised in light of certain facts of language use. What is needed is an account of how these facts support the revised version and count against the original, and if such an account is fully given it can then be argued that metaphysical statements follow the same pattern of justification so that the verification principle turns out to be metaphysical. Our discussion of Wisdom will enable us to explore this more fully.

Whatever the inadequacies of the positivists' treatment of analytic

[33] "Philosophy, Metaphysics and Psycho-Analysis," in *Philosophy and Psycho-Analysis*, p. 268.

and metaphysical statements, however, it was the violence they did to many characteristics of ordinary language use which revealed most strikingly the narrowness of their preconceptions about language. We do in fact talk about another's feelings as well as about his behavior. We also talk about ethical statements as making sense; we do not say they are nonsense as the positivists did. Then, too, we frequently say we are absolutely certain about the truth of an empirical statement, whereas the positivists contended that we can only know empirical statements as highly probable because we can never obtain the unlimited evidence for an empirical statement which is theoretically possible. By our everyday standards I may be able properly to say, for example, "I am certain that John is taking logic this semester" even though I have not checked the registrar's records, asked John and the other members of the class, checked with his parents and friends, made an exhaustive search for a withdrawal slip, etc. Since it is logically possible that any or all of these further tests would tell against this belief, the positivists concluded that it is contradictory ever to claim certainty in such cases. As we shall see, the typical reaction of ordinary language philosophers to this is that "a philosophical theory that has such a consequence is plainly false." [34]

In addition to distorting these and other sorts of ordinary use, the positivists largely overlooked sentences that are neither cognitive nor emotive. "I vote yes" and "I promise to come" are examples that fit neither of these categories; and when we consider these further sorts of ordinary use we find once again that there are cognitive issues involved in language-uses that do not fall under the positivist's category of the cognitive. Compare, for example, the petitions "Deliver us Oh Absolute" and "Deliver us Oh King." Such petitions are meaningful only if one knows what it is that is being requested or, in other words, what sorts of experience would count for and what against belief that the petition has been fulfilled. The positivists were not entirely unaware of this, but their formulation of their theory of meaning was inadequate to such cases.

Some Applications to Talk of God

We may turn now to consider implications of this position and of our criticisms of it for the analysis of religious language. In his brief treatment of religion in *Language, Truth and Logic*, Ayer claims that the possibility of religious knowledge "has already been ruled out

[34] Norman Malcolm, "The Verification Argument," in *Knowledge and Certainty*, p. 56.

by our treatment of metaphysics." [35] The existence of God, he points out, cannot be deduced from *a priori* propositions, for these are tautologies, and from tautologies we may deduce only further tautologies.[36] Neither can the existence of God be proven probable or improbable, for, Ayer argues, if this were possible "the proposition that he existed would be an empirical hypothesis," [37] and this is not the case, for the religious man

would say that in talking about God, he was talking about a transcendent being who might be known through certain empirical manifestations, but certainly could not be defined in terms of those manifestations. But in that case the term "god" is a metaphysical term. And if "god" is a metaphysical term, then it cannot be even probable that a god exists. For to say that "God exists" is to make a metaphysical utterance which cannot be either true or false.[38]

Whether the religious man appeals to "a certain sort of regularity in nature" [39] or to a mystical intuition of God, he does not succeed in saying anything intelligible about a transcendent God, for he fails to provide tests in actual experience that would verify or falsify—and hence give meaning to—this transcendent reference. He succeeds only in talking about the alleged regularity in nature or his experience of a religious emotion. In the latter case, the religious man "does not give us any information about the external world; he merely gives us indirect information about the condition of his own mind." [40]

Why the religious man should want to make such references to a transcendent God is not discussed by Ayer, but we find the following intimations of what his answer to this question would be:

The mere existence of the noun ["God"] is enough to foster the illusion that there is a real, or at any rate a possible entity corresponding to it.[41]

One of the ultimate sources of religious feeling lies in the inability of men to determine their own destiny; and science tends to destroy the feeling of awe with which men regard an alien world, by making them believe that they can understand and anticipate the course of natural phenomena, and even to some extent control it.[42]

Those philosophers who fill their books with assertions that they intuitively "know" this or that moral or religious "truth" are merely providing material for the psycho-analyst.[43]

[35] *Language, Truth and Logic*, p. 114.
[36] *Ibid.*, pp. 114-15.   [37] *Ibid.*, p. 115.
[38] *Ibid.*   [39] *Ibid.*
[40] *Ibid.*, p. 119.   [41] *Ibid.*, p. 116.
[42] *Ibid.*, p. 117.   [43] *Ibid.*, p. 120.

These passing observations suggest a psychological reductionism in which God is viewed as a psychological projection that is motivated by feelings of insecurity and that is aided and abetted by the popular belief that for every noun there exists a corresponding entity.

There is, however, the possibility of constructing a purely humanistic version of Christianity within this philosophic context. This is seized upon, for example, by Paul Holmer. Belief in a transcendent God, according to Holmer, must be dismissed because "metaphysics reflects not 'Being' and its attributes but the will of the philosopher and his non-cognitive insecurities," [44] and because the belief that certain qualities "are *known* to be of a divine being" is a confusion that "the structure of language seems to have invited . . . and many other features of reflective and linguistic usage have sustained." [45] Holmer proposes a way of translating statements about God in which they cease to be metaphysical and become instead truly cognitive. A sentence, for example, that says that there was a man who is God should be understood to mean that there was "a man who is (or announces) a new possibility, a new way of life." [46] So interpreted, "religious sentences are cognitive . . . of a possible way of constituting one's life and daily existence" [47] and of the historical figure who has embodied this possibility. The word "God," then, is reduced to meaning a possible way of life or "passion," as it is elsewhere called. But Holmer makes a sharp distinction between this merely cognitive meaning of the term and its religious use: "The difference between cognitive assent to the truth of the possibility and being a Christian is the distance between conceiving a passion and being passionate." [48] "To put the sentence to a truly religious use," in other words, is to use it to express an "enthusiasm and interest in becoming the possibility" which it describes.[49] Under this proposal, then, if one uses language as a Christian, "the meaning of saying that Jesus is God is that in that historical person . . . I find the possibility which I am willing to actualize." [50]

Now the application of our previous criticisms to Ayer's positivistic account of language about God is fairly evident. If the verification

---

[44] "Philosophical Criticism and Christology," *Journal of Religion*, 1954, p. 94.

[45] "The Nature of Religious Propositions," *Review of Religion*, 1955, p. 146.

[46] *Ibid.* Holmer cites Kierkegaard as having demonstrated that a way of life or existential "passion" can be cognized: "Kierkegaard's own literature is the evidence that the passions of man do, in fact, have form and order. . . . One can have universals about the particulars which passions they are." ("Kierkegaard and Religious Propositions," *Journal of Religion*, 1955, p. 142.) Although enlisting Kierkegaard in support of his program, Holmer does not, in the four articles I have seen, make the claim that Kierkegaard himself did not believe in a transcendent God.

[47] *Review of Religion*, p. 140.   [48] *Journal of Religion* (1955), p. 143.

[49] *Review of Religion*, p. 145.   [50] *Journal of Religion* (1954), p. 99.

principle is strictly analytic, an account of the formal characteristics of language about empirical matters-of-fact, then in showing that language about God does not meet the requirements of this principle Ayer is entitled to conclude only that language about God is not language about empirical matters-of-fact. No warrant is provided, then, for his claim that the religious man's talk about his experience of God "merely gives us indirect information about the condition of his own mind." [51] Ayer's contention that statements about God are not informative—cannot be either true or false—can consistently be interpreted to mean no more than that religious statements are not informative in just the same way that statements conforming to the verification principle are. Ayer's insistence that an utterance is informative only if it expresses some sort of expectation about what under certain conditions future experience will be like is, I think, important and correct. These expectations, however, are far more varied than he and the positivists recognized. There are many different ways in which statements are supported by experience.

Furthermore, experiences other than sense experience may well enter into our expectations concerning future experience in such a way that they play an important role in verifying certain types of assertions. If the value relativism of the positivists is false and values are not simply a matter of how we have been conditioned to feel, then the value dimensions of experience—including the religious—may constitute an important part of our knowledge of ourselves and our world. In other words, the facts basic to my day-to-day existence—such as the fact that this is my wife, that these are my children, that this is my study, that it is 8:45 Tuesday morning—may not be reducible to facts of the scientific sort, and yet the latter are the only sort recognized by the positivists. Many, for example, would at the very least argue that in reducing reality to that which can be apprehended through the objective, detached stance of the scientific observer, the positivist fails to consider that dimension of reality which can be apprehended only through a personal, involved mode of responding. Martin Buber distinguishes between the dimensions or "worlds" of "It" and "Thou." [52] God, he maintains, is known only in terms of the world of Thou.

The positivistic formulation of the verification principle not only fails to consider the personal dimensions of knowledge but also is inapplicable to the Christian's conception of God as mysterious. Michael Foster points out two assumptions underlying positivistic

---

[51] *Language, Truth and Logic*, p. 119.

[52] *I and Thou*, trans. Ronald Gregor Smith (New York: Scribner's, 1937), p. 37. See also Karl Heim, *Christian Faith and Natural Science* (New York: Harper, 1953).

analysis[53] which eliminate the possibility of saying anything intelligible about what is inherently mysterious. First, there is the assumption that significant belief requires clarity "in the Cartesian sense of 'clear and distinct perception.' " [54] This assumption rests on "the belief that nothing is really puzzling and that therefore there cannot be anything unclear that we can legitimately want to say." [55] Moritz Schlick, for example, has claimed that "there is no unfathomable mystery in the world." [56] Second, it is assumed "that all thinking, and therefore all philosophical thinking, consists in solving problems" [57] in the sense of providing verifiable answers to clearly formulated questions.[58] These assumptions, however, are rejected by a great many of those who use some form of the Christian language. Gabriel Marcel contends that "a genuine problem is subject to an appropriate technique by the exercise of which it is defined: whereas a mystery by definition, transcends every conceivable technique." [59] Consequently, the charge that statements "about" God are characterized by "a sort of inherent and necessary incomprehensibility" [60] will be admitted, provided that by "comprehensibility" is meant the sort of clarity demanded by the verification principle. As Frederick Ferré notes,

a proposition which is not fully comprehensible need not be entirely without significance. The degree of theoretical comprehensibility required for a proposition depends on the function intended for it. . . . If there are more uses for theological assertions than theoretical belief alone, perhaps even a high degree of theoretical incomprehensibility is compatible with the meaningful employment of such language.[61]

Ayer's requirement, then, that a significant statement must either be or, in conjunction with one or more observation statements, entail a report of a sense experience is too narrow.

What is needed, consequently, is an analysis that will make clear the extent to which and ways in which statements about God are subject

[53] Foster maintains that these assumptions have been retained throughout subsequent developments in linguistic philosophy.
[54] *Mystery and Philosophy*, pp. 16-17.   [55] *Ibid.*, p. 17.
[56] "Meaning and Verification," *Readings in Philosophical Analysis*, ed. Herbert Feigle and Wilfred Sellars (New York: Appleton-Century-Crofts, 1949), p. 156.
[57] *Mystery and Philosophy*, p. 18.   [58] *Ibid.*, pp. 22, 24.
[59] *Being and Having*, trans. Katherine Farrer (Westminster: Dacre Press, 1949), p. 117.
[60] Bernard Williams, "Tertullian's Paradox," *New Essays in Philosophical Theology*, p. 187. Statements about God have this character, it is explained, "because the concepts required—of fatherhood, for instance, and of love, and of power— are acquired in a human context." (P. 204.) When applied to God the meaning must be extrapolated from this context, but this "is an extrapolation to infinity, and in even trying to give sense to this we encounter the incomprehensibility."
[61] *Language, Logic and God* (New York: Harper, 1961), p. 57.

to verificational criteria. It will then be an existential decision for each person to make whether this degree of comprehensibility is sufficient warrant for regarding these statements as an adequate basis, intellectually, for belief. As Austin Farrer has put the matter,

the analytical part of philosophy ought to be a matter of agreement. If we refrain from judging systems of thought on preconceived grounds, and examine them from within, we ought to be able to agree where the system works and where it breaks down, as we may, for example, in the case of Spinozism, since this is a matter of logic. It is at the next stage where agreement ceases; when, assuming that all systems have flaws, we ask which, taken as a whole, is least unsatisfactory as an account of what is, or when one of us refuses to philosophise at all outside the area where he thinks exact demonstration to be possible, whereas another is prepared to extend a crepuscular and imperfect reasoning into a crepuscular fringe of our experience and belief.[62]

Purely humanistic analyses of the sort offered by Holmer may be welcomed, then, by the theologian as helpful clarifications of one dimension of language about God without any necessary acceptance of their reductionistic use. But Holmer's rejection of talk of a transcendent God as non-cognitive seems to me correct insofar as "transcendent" means outside of human experience. Only insofar as God is conceived as truly immanent in human experience will talk of God express expectations concerning future experience and so be subject to verificational criteria. In our discussions of Wisdom and Tillich we shall explore conceptions of God's transcendence which do not place God outside of experience.

Not only does positivistic analysis fail to show that statements about God are not cognitive in some wider sense of that term and fail to provide the means for investigating this possibility, but, further, the psychological reductionism that we have seen in Ayer, for example, is open to additional question. What is the warrant for Ayer's claim that those who make religious assertions "are merely providing material for the psycho-analyst"? Does a fruitful application of the tools of psychological analysis to religious language show that other sorts of analysis are not also needed? In what way does the presence of a psychological dimension of meaning imply that there are not other dimensions of meaning, including, possibly, even some sort of cognitive meaning? If, as psychoanalysis maintains, all our statements are psychologically conditioned, then this must include the statements both of the psychoanalysts and of the positivists as well as those of the theologians. Consequently, the cognitive status of a statement must

[62] *Finite and Infinite*, p. 5.

be determined on grounds other than the fact of its psychological conditioning.

Furthermore, in his reductionistic account of religious experience, Ayer seems implicitly to be making a judgment that religious awe is inappropriate to the sort of world in which we now know ourselves to be. But a judgment as to the nature of the world as a whole—which in turn makes possible a judgment as to the appropriateness of an attitude toward things as a whole—is surely a metaphysical judgment and, so, one that the positivist cannot consistently permit himself. According to Ayer,

science tends to destroy the feeling of awe with which men regard an alien world, by making them believe that they can understand and anticipate the course of natural phenomena, and even to some extent control it. The fact that it has recently become fashionable for physicists themselves to be sympathetic towards religion is a point in favour of this hypothesis. For this sympathy towards religion marks the physicists' own lack of confidence in the validity of their hypotheses.[63]

These statements imply the judgment that there is nothing about the world which would appropriately inspire religious awe once men have learned that at least large ranges of phenomena can be subjected to predictive hypotheses. But such a judgment is naturalistic, and if it is meaningful, then so may alternative metaphysical judgments be meaningful. Moreover, the fact that scientific pursuits not infrequently become the occasion for religious awe is not self-evidently to be explained as a failure of nerve—a lack of confidence that man can understand and "to some extent even control" natural phenomena. Was it such "lack of confidence" that led Einstein, for example, to say that the true scientist "attains that humble attitude of mind towards the grandeur of reason incarnate in existence, which, in its profoundest depths, is inaccessible to man"? [64]

A reductionistic account of religious language, however, is not the only possibility inherent in the positivistic position. Positivism may be used to drive a wedge between the concerns of faith and the concerns of philosophy, so that both theologian and philosopher can get on with their work without bothering with each other. If "cognitive" is defined to mean either analytic or descriptive of empirical matter-of-fact, and if the domain of philosophic concern is limited to the cognitive in this narrow sense, then the positivist will not be concerned with religious language once he has shown that it is non-cognitive. But if the positivist, then, simply excludes religious language from his concern because it is

---

[63] *Language, Truth and Logic*, p. 117.
[64] Albert Einstein, quoted by Paul Tillich, "Science and Theology: A Discussion with Einstein" (1940), reprinted in *Theology of Culture*, p. 130.

neither analytic nor descriptive of empirical matters-of-fact, may not the theologian conclude that his work is in no way interfered with? If theological concerns are excluded from philosophy, then it follows that philosophic concerns are excluded from theology. That these concerns are not merely different but divorced becomes plausible provided that the "emotive" category is left very vague so that it comes to mean merely non-cognitive in the positivistic sense of cognitive and does not come to mean that the possibility of a wider cognitive function is being excluded.

However, some who take this path of immunizing religious language from philosophic criticism are understandably unhappy about the ambiguous and problematic nature of the "emotive" as a wastebasket category. It is open to a reductionistic interpretation, and it fails to offer means for the clarification of the differences between religious, ethical, metaphysical, poetic, and any other languages thrown together under the "emotive" label. Why may not other categories be introduced to provide this additional clarification and to guard against the danger of slipping from descriptive analysis into metaphysical reduction? Why may not the analytic philosopher describe the way in which religious language is actually being used without appropriating to philosophy any right to criticize that use?

The possibility, within positivism, of this line of development has been explored at some length by Willem F. Zuurdeeg in his *Analytical Philosophy of Religion*. Zuurdeeg is at one with traditional positivism in its "understanding that analytical philosophy means an approach which can analyze and *only* analyze" and in its "disqualification of metaphysics and ontology," [65] but argues that its "emotive" category is not adequate for the analysis of religious and similar languages.[66] To label a man's religious utterances as emotive obscures the fact that typically not only do his

emotions, will, and persuasive intentions come into play, but so also does his intellect, and other aspects of his personality as well. That is to say: his whole person is involved, and it is not easy to say where the boundaries of "a whole person" are to be found. One cannot think of him apart from his wife, his children, his work, or his home.[67]

Positivistic analyses have assumed in all cases that it is necessary only to analyze the language itself, but to give an adequate account of religious language one must replace this sort of "logical analysis" by a "situational analysis" in which one gives an "account of the language situation, to which belong: (a) the person who communicates, (b) the

[65] *An Analytical Philosophy of Religion*, pp. 16, 17.
[66] *Ibid.*, p. 24.   [67] *Ibid.*

community within which the language functions, (c) the (subjectively) objective references of the languages, (d) the 'worlds' within which these elements are related, (e) the historical background of these elements." [68]

The category that Zuurdeeg develops for this purpose is termed "convictional" where "conviction" is taken to mean "all persuasions concerning the meaning of life." [69] A central part of having convictions is the experience of being convicted or "overcome" by "somebody or something"—a "convictor." Concerning this convictor, however, analytic philosophy can only show that our convictions are alleged to have some such objective reference. Philosophy cannot evaluate or discuss the reality of these convictors. For the task of analysis, "the only thing which counts is whether the objective reference is a reality *for the believer.*" [70]

The theoretical justification for this restriction apparently rests on the principle that faith is a matter of commitment rather than of objective understanding. As Zuurdeeg expresses it, religious language is not something that the believer *uses* but is rather something that he *is*. To be a person is to establish a certain relationship with the world—with "all that is"—a relationship that embodies what one judges to be the meaning of life. The self establishes that relationship—and, so, establishes its existence as a self—by speaking religious or convictional language. Convictional language does not merely express that relationship. It *is* itself a central part of that relationship. Therefore, since the self cannot be separated from its relationships with the world, it cannot be separated from the convictional language that it speaks. The languages that the positivist classifies as cognitive may be regarded as tools that the self uses. Their meaning is their use. But convictional language is not a tool that one uses. It is part of the relationship with reality that one establishes in becoming a self. Therefore, to analyze the meaning of convictional language is not to analyze a use but rather to analyze what it means to be a self. This is not to deny that people often do "merely use" convictional language, but in such cases, Zuurdeeg points out, the speaker is not "a real, authentic self" but a "masked person." This observable distinction between authenticity and mask is an important tool for the analyst. [71]

What it means to establish one's existence by speaking a convictional language can be analyzed only insofar as it is something "we can observe about people." [72] The facts that we can observe are what comprise the convictional language situation: "Since people *are* their convictions, the analysis of convictional language immediately leads to a consideration of the person who speaks the language and of all the other elements

⁶⁸ *Ibid.*, p. 17.   ⁶⁹ *Ibid.*, p. 26.   ⁷⁰ *Ibid.*   ⁷¹ *Ibid.*, pp. 56-57.   ⁷² *Ibid.*, p. 13.

of the convictional situation," [73] especially the convictor or hierarchy
of convictors, the relationship to which comprises the basic meaning
of life. A convictor, however, cannot itself be dealt with because it
cannot be observed: "The origin of the convictions is acknowledged as
lying in a domain which is inaccessible to rational understanding." [74]
In thus bracketing the question of the objective reference of the convictional experience, Zuurdeeg's approach leads to a sort of phenomenological account of the convictional experience, except that his analysis
seeks to include the unconscious as well as the conscious factors of that
experience. Convictional language, then, involves the intellect, since
it involves a belief about something, but the questions as to what sort
of reference this is and what counts for or against such a belief are
removed from analytic consideration, because such questions are open
to objective examination only in the case of use language in which
observations concerning this reference are possible. In convictional
language the speaker is his language, and there are observations available
concerning the speaker but not concerning the object of his belief.

But we must ask whether there is not a confusion involved in
attempting, in this way, to isolate rational belief from questions concerning the rational criteria governing this belief. Does not rational
belief by its very nature involve rational criteria, and do not such
criteria, in turn, expose such belief to objective examination and
challenge?

It must be questioned whether Zuurdeeg has not drawn too sharp
a distinction between "is" language and "use" language, between being
a language and using that language. To refer to a person as being
his language does have the merit of drawing attention to one of the
important functions of that language, namely its function in enabling
a person to define himself in terms of his ultimate convictions. But
this function should not be confused with the cognitive function of
that language in expressing belief about something. In this latter
function the language is used, and, consequently, one may ask about
the criteria that govern this referential use. Zuurdeeg, for example,
claims that "the evidence in the meaning of empirical, factual evidence
is not decisive for one's convictions." [75] The Christian conviction, he
maintains, "is independent of 'evidence.' " [76] But, insofar as conviction includes rational understanding, it becomes an open question
how far the demands of the intellect can be satisfied if one suspends
the criterion of adequacy to the facts. Innumerable systems having
little or no bearing upon reality could satisfy the demand for internal
coherence, and a broadly pragmatic criterion cannot by itself distinguish

---

[73] *Ibid.*, p. 64.
[75] *Ibid.*, p. 29.
[74] *Ibid.*, p. 135. Cf. pp. 291, 292, 295.
[76] *Ibid.*, p. 30.

between acting as if something were true and believing that it is true. Zuurdeeg admits that his point "is not to say that evidence does not play any role at all," [77] but in this case one will wish to know just what role it does play. He points out that "many times people are convinced in spite of the so-called facts," [78] but the question will then be in what sense such a conviction continues to involve rational understanding as one of its dimensions. Rational assent doubtless is not the same thing as shaping one's very being as a self in terms of that assent, but, if rational assent is to be part of what is meant by "conviction," then an analysis of conviction will include an examination of its rational criteria.

It must further be questioned whether Zuurdeeg's treatment of metaphysical language is consistent either with his claim that analysis can have no bearing upon the question of the reality of the convictor or with the closely related claim that it is improper for philosophy in any way to evaluate religious or any other language. He devotes much space to a strongly negative evaluation of metaphysics as an "objectionable way in which man can speak" convictionally.[79] This denunciation is based on Hume's insight into "the phenomenon of 'overreaching' the range and possibilities of certain types of thinking." [80] Metaphysics, in other words, is "a matter of the misuse of language and of confusion of its functions" [81] in which the use of reason and certain of its concepts appropriate to one sort of language, typically the scientific or logical, is erroneously transferred to language of quite a different sort—the convictional.[82] Comparison with those linguistic errors analyzed by Freud "strongly suggests" that these metaphysical errors are to be accounted for as the result of a wrong attitude, a wrong way of relating to the world, on the part of the metaphysician.[83] "Metaphysical speaking is rooted in anxiety," is the inference that is drawn, and so such speaking

only *seems* to disclose the "real" structure of the universe, and actually exposes deeply hidden strivings which lead men to speak metaphysically. For instance, the craving for a closed system unveils the remarkable compulsion to claim that there *must* be a well-ordered, recognizable pattern behind the distressing manifoldness of things. A metaphysician just cannot stand the idea of a universe which cannot be grasped, either by reason, by meditation, or by intuition, for it would fill him with horror.[84]

Such is the way of speaking of the metaphysician, "homo pomposus." [85]

---

[77] *Ibid.*, p. 29.   [78] *Ibid.*, pp. 29-30.   [79] *Ibid.*, p. 130.
[80] *Ibid.*, p. 129.   [81] *Ibid.*, p. 19.   [82] *Ibid.*, p. 130.
[83] *Ibid.*, p. 129.   [84] *Ibid.*, p. 137.   [85] *Ibid.*, p. 142.

What must be noted about this highly emotive "analysis" is that the alleged confusion is not something that can simply be observed. It is a judgment that rests squarely on the convictions of the analyst, "the 'analytical' understanding of man," [86] in which positivistic views on the limitations of reason occupy a central place, as do existential views on the relation between anxiety and self-awareness. Metaphysical language must rest on (cowardly) confusion *because* reason simply cannot do what the metaphysicians try to make it do.[87] This judgment about the limitations of reason is, moreover, at the same time a judgment about the reality of those "structures of the universe" to which the metaphysician is referring. For example, the account of the development of Zuurdeeg's analytic position which is given on the jacket of his book states that he moved toward analysis because he "became suspicious of the existence of such eternal laws." His analysis, we see, includes a judgment concerning the objective reference of the metaphysician's convictor—the basic structure of things. If our judgment be right, then, this analysis of metaphysics contradicts Zuurdeeg's principle that analysis must not evaluate.

Nor must the analyst persuade. Yet consider, for example, the operation of Zuurdeeg's convictions in the "description" of metaphysics in which, in the space of less than one page, one finds the following "descriptive" language: "unmask these confusions," "guilty of," "indulges," "vague," "barren," "rationalistic," "sweepingly," "completely vague," "habitually insensitive," "privileged," "most charitably interpreted," "an unclear combination . . . which is then dignified with," "meaningless verbalisms," and "arrogantly." [88] The emotive quality of these terms suggests not description[89] but persuasive definition.

The analogies of metaphysical language are thus, upon "philosophical analysis," condemned as language confusions, while the analogies employed by convictional language of the revelational sort personally spoken by Zuurdeeg [90] are placed beyond such analysis. Revelation, for example, is claimed to be a kind of "language-like unobservable" but this analogy is not to be examined. The analyst must be satisfied with the fact "that this 'language' means something to the believer." [91] Again, it is claimed, we remember, that faith includes reason, but how and whether this is so is left unexplained and unexamined, although the similar claims of the metaphysician are attacked. How is it that the often far less emotive efforts of some of the analysts to show that the Christian's language appears to be based on language confusions can be rejected as nonanalytic, while Zuurdeeg employs similar attacks on metaphysics? And if the metaphysician's language confusion is to

[86] *Ibid.*
[89] *Ibid.*, p. 129.
[87] *Ibid.*, pp. 121, 129, 132.
[90] *Ibid.*, p. 283.
[88] *Ibid.*, pp. 127-28.
[91] *Ibid.*, p. 295.

be compared with Freud's analysis of language slips, why is not Freud's analysis of the Christian convictor as illusory also to be used? The latter affords a much more plausible comparison—one used in fact by Wisdom and others in analyzing Zuurdeeg's sort of revelational language—because the similarity between slips of the tongue within a language and the "mistake" of using an entire language seems, at best, rather distant. This unequal treatment of revelational and metaphysical sorts of convictional language seems accountable only as an expression of Zuurdeeg's own convictions, in which case his analysis of metaphysics becomes, to a considerable extent, an *argumentum ad hominem*.

Broadening the conclusions drawn from our examination of Zuurdeeg's position, we may say that the attempt to exempt the cognitive claims of religious language from philosophic criticism and analysis on the basis of the positivist's limitation of philosophic concern with cognition to language reporting empirical matters-of-fact does not succeed. Even on this interpretation of positivism one must still ask whether this limitation of concern is simply arbitrary or whether it is based on an implicit belief concerning the nature and limits of reason. If the limitation is arbitrary, then those interested in the analysis of religious language may ignore it and proceed to examine the cognitive nature of that language. If the limitation involves a view of the limits of reason, then it must be shown that the cognitive claims made for religious language are consistent with this view. To put the point in its most general terms, if a cognitive function is claimed for religious language, it becomes necessary to supply the cognitive criteria that give meaning to this claim. To believe that the existential functions of a language—the functions of defining and affirming one's being as a self—exempt the rational functions of that language from philosophic examination is simply to confuse these two sorts of function.

Perhaps the root of this confusion of existential and cognitive functions is the tendency of analysis to separate rather than to relate, to show the differences between languages rather than the similarities. The "open convictional views" that are championed by Zuurdeeg, for example, are defined as "those wherein the author admits both to his reader and himself that his convictions possess a unique character, are *sui generis*." [92] But to show that the cognitive function of religious language, whatever it is, is not the same as the cognitive function of the language of empirical matter-of-fact, is not to show that religious language does in fact have a cognitive function, nor to show in what sense the two functions both deserve to be called "cognitive."

[92] *Ibid.*, p. 135.

In summary, we have argued that, if the verification principle is interpreted as strictly analytic, then it can show us that religious language is not the empirical matter-of-fact language of science, but cannot show us that religious language is not cognitive in some other sense. The "emotive" classification seems to be simply a wastebasket category for whatever does not meet the verification criterion. In the analysis of religious language, it seems questionable to assume either "clear and distinct perception" as a criterion for significant belief or detached observation as the only approach to testing such belief. Once the verification criteria actually operative in theological language have been set forth, it is a matter of existential decision whether such criteria provide an intellectually adequate basis for belief. Ayer's psychological reduction of religious meaning, therefore, was seen as going beyond his explicit principles and as resting on the naturalistic and relativistic metaphysical views implicit in his position. An alternative interpretation of positivism as limiting the domain of philosophic concern in such a way as to immunize the cognitive claims of religious language from philosophic criticism was rejected on the ground that significant belief, by its very nature, involves verificational criteria and that such criteria expose belief to rational examination and challenge. To fail to see this is to confuse the existential and cognitive functions of religious language.

PART TWO: *Wittgenstein*

THE TRACTATUS: *The Limits of Language*

Chapter Five

It was in the early work of Ludwig Wittgenstein, his *Tractatus Logico-Philosophicus*,[1] that logical atomism reached its fullest and most rigorous expression. In this work what the atomists viewed as the limits of language was most sharply drawn. Consideration of the distinctive ideas that Wittgenstein contributed to atomism has been reserved for separate treatment in this chapter not only because his relation to the metaphysics of atomism is somewhat problematic but, even more, because it is as an outgrowth of these ideas that his later work in the *Philosophical Investigations* must be understood.

We remember that, according to the atomists, a proposition *expresses* or pictures a fact, and what is *expressed by* a proposition cannot be the *subject of* a proposition. Fact, therefore, cannot be talked about, cannot be made the subject of a proposition, since it is expressed by a proposition. For example, "This is red" expresses a fact. The subject of this proposition is the object named by "this." But the fact expressed by "This is red" cannot itself be the subject of a proposition. There are no facts about facts for a proposition to picture. In Wittgenstein's terminology, a proposition cannot *say* anything about a fact but rather *shows* a fact. Language is limited to subjects about which something can be *said*.

What can be said, what can be talked about, is a *particular* state of affairs, such as the cat being on the mat, the table being green, etc. Now in asserting something to be the case we are excluding the pos-

[1] Paragraph numbers will be used in all references to this book.

117

sibility that it is not the case. To assert that "The table is green" is also to deny the denial of "The table is green." In other words, we can meaningfully affirm a proposition only if we might also meaningfully deny it: "the possibility of denial is already prejudged in affirmation." (5.44) A sentence that is compatible with every possible state of affairs does not say anything about the world: "I know nothing about the weather when I know that it is either raining or not raining." (4.461)[2] I know something about the world when I know that the fact pictured by "This is red" actually exists or when I know that this fact does not exist. "The sense of a proposition is its agreement and disagreement with the possibilities of the existence and non-existence of the atomic facts." (4.2)

This principle of exclusion—which becomes, in Wittgenstein's later work, the principle of contrast—is fundamental to Wittgenstein's position. The idea is really quite simple, but it is of great consequence. It is informative to say "It is raining," because it might not be raining. It is informative to say "The dagger you see is an illusion," because not all daggers we see are illusions. But it is not informative to say "All is illusion" or "Everything is in flux," because there is then no possibility of pointing to something real or something not in flux. This dagger is an illusion compared to what? Well, to that dagger. All is illusion compared to what? A statement is uninformative if we cannot conceive of the conditions under which we would say it is false. As we shall see, not only does Wittgenstein hold that metaphysical statements are uninformative for this reason, but many hold that statements about God are uninformative for the same reason. This becomes the criterion of meaning: that we know what it would be like for the proposition to be true and for it not to be true.[3]

---

[2] Wittgenstein continues, "Tautology [e.g., either P or not-P] and contradiction [e.g., both P and not-P] are not pictures of the reality. They present no possible state of affairs. For the one allows *every* possible state of affairs, the other *none*." (4.462) And in 5.61 we find: "We cannot therefore say in logic: This and this there is in the world, that there is not. For that would apparently presuppose that we exclude certain possibilities."

[3] Against Russell, Wittgenstein argued that what objects there are determines what can be the case, but not what actually is the case. If a red patch were an object, then its existence would determine that something is the case—that something is red. (2.0231) For Wittgenstein, then, the subject of "This is red" is a metaphysical substance whose very nature or essence it is to have some sort of color but not necessarily the color red. "This is red" says something about the world because it excludes the possibility that it is not the case that this is red. But for Russell "This is red" is necessarily true because the subject "this" refers to a red patch. Russell's atomic propositions, then, were metaphysical *in the sense* of being both factual and necessarily true, and for this reason Wittgenstein rejected them. See Urmson, *Philosophical Analysis*, pp. 57-59 and Dennis O'Brien, "The Unity of Wittgenstein's Thought" (1966), reprinted in K. T. Fann, ed., *Ludwig Wittgenstein* (New York: Dell, 1967), pp. 396-97.

As the early Wittgenstein saw it, only statements about particular states of affairs in the physical world can meet this criterion of meaningfulness. "The right method of philosophy would be this. To say nothing except *what can be said, i.e., the propositions of natural science,* i.e., something that has nothing to do with philosophy." (6.53, italics mine). Philosophical statements are not meaningful, because they do not *exclude* their denial; their denial is inconceivable—we could not know what we meant by it, anymore than we could know what we meant if we denied that "either it is raining or it is not raining." Philosophical statements are not concerned with particular states of affairs but, rather, with the structure of the world which determines that there are these possibilities rather than some others. But we cannot conceive what *might have been* possible. We cannot talk about what *might have been* the structure of reality. For this would be to conceive the impossible as possible; or, since what is possible is what is logical, it would be to conceive the unlogical (*Unlogische*) as logical. Since we think in terms of logic, in terms of the possible, we cannot think what is unlogical or impossible. We cannot step outside of the structure of our thinking, the structure of our world, and, so, we cannot talk about that structure. "*The limits of my language* mean the limits of my world." (5.6)

One can talk, then, about particular states of affairs *in* the world but not about the world, because to talk about the world would be to conceive it as a limited whole—that is, as a totality that is limited by something and consequently is not a totality. Thought cannot transcend its own limits. (5.61)

We can think only what we can conceive to have been other than it is, namely, whatever is in the world—particular states of affairs. It follows that tautologies do not say anything about what is thinkable. They do not say anything about what is in the world. They exclude no possibilities. Tautology and contradiction "present no possible state of affairs. For the one allows *every* possible state of affairs, the other *none.*" (4.462) In other words, only the contingent can be talked about. What is *necessarily* so, what we cannot conceive to be otherwise, does not refer to something *in* the world.

In Wittgenstein's conception, then, the human mind, and so the language it uses, is capable of dealing *only* with particular states of affairs in the physical world. But if so, why do we attempt to use language to deal with other things? According to Wittgenstein, there are two reasons for this. The first of these places us on familiar ground. The meaningless statements look like those which are meaningful, and so we treat them as meaningful. That is, the meaningless statements *appear* to have the logic of those that are meaningful. It is only when we look more closely, with the aid of Wittgenstein's criterion of meaning, that we see that this is not the case. Only then do we see that the meaningless statements do not embody the *real logic* of our language. In short, the meaningless statements do not *exclude* any possibilities and so say nothing about what is the case in the world. For example, philosophers ask meaningless questions about things like existence and objects because "exists" and "object" look similar to terms like "runs" and "table" which we use in talking about particular states of affairs. "What is an object?" looks like the same sort of question as "What is a book?" but really is not because it does not have its locus in the language we use to assert particular states of affairs.[4] We see here the dependence on Russell. "Russell's merit," Wittgenstein acknowledges, "is to have shown that the apparent logical form of the proposition need not be its real form." (4.0031)

But this alleged confusion of form does not account for the way these meaningless sentences could come into being in the first place. Why are we tempted to speak in a meaningless way? Where do we get the mistaken idea that there is any subject matter other than particular states of affairs in the physical world? It is just here that we come to what is perhaps the most interesting[5] and certainly the most baffling side of Wittgenstein's thought. "There is indeed," he maintained, "the inexpressible. This *shows* itself; it is the mystical." (6.522) We have a mystical or intuitive grasp of what lies beyond those particular states of affairs with which alone language is capable of dealing, and it is a subject matter that we are tempted to try to talk about. Here, then, is the second source of meaningless language.

What "shows itself" is exemplified by such matters as logic, beauty, morality, religion, and the relation of language to reality. One can point to a picture, but one cannot point to its beauty. The beauty simply shows itself in the picture. Sentences can be written which exemplify a logical structure. But, after the relevant features of these sentences have been indicated, one cannot go further and point to the logic of these features. Attention may be called to aspects of certain actions which we feel exemplify a moral principle, but no reply is possible to one who then asks why we refer to these aspects in moral

---

[4] Wittgenstein distinguishes between formal concepts, such as "object," and proper concepts, such as "book." Formal concepts are a part of the structure of our language while proper concepts are expressed by our language. We cannot use language to talk about the structure which that use presupposes and, so, formal concepts can only be shown in the use of proper concepts. When we talk about a book we think of it as an object. See *Tractatus*, 4.126-4.12721.

[5] Most interesting, one might even say most important, because it attempts to deal with the most illusive element of language, the intuitive awareness that underlies our ability to make distinctions.

terms. Again, notice can be taken of certain elements in behavior which are designated as religious, but one cannot, in addition, point to the religiousness of these elements. And, by way of final illustration, in considering the relation of language to reality, one can write or speak a word and then point to some of the objects to which that word is related as a sign, but one cannot, in addition, point to this *relationship* of signification.

What language can be used to say, then, is only what can be pointed to. What can be pointed to may show something else, but, since this cannot be directly pointed to, language cannot say anything about it. (Here we see again the atomists' error of believing that the naming-describing function of language is its only function.)

Now since, according to Wittgenstein, nothing can be said about the relation of language to reality, the atomists' position that "picturing" is the metaphor most appropriate to the language-reality relationship cannot itself be stated. What the atomists meant could only show itself.

What the picture must have in common with reality in order to be able to represent it after its manner—rightly or falsely—is its form of representation. . . . The picture, however, cannot represent its form of representation; it shows it forth. (2.17, 2.172)

Urmson uses the example of a portrait:

Imagine someone who looks at it and complains that he cannot see the likeness. It would be ridiculous if the complaint was that the likeness was not drawn in with the eyes and nose, if he demanded that it should be added to the picture, or that a supplementary picture of the likeness of the picture to the original be drawn. Clearly the likeness cannot be represented, at least *in pari materia*. We can but draw pictures of things and the likeness must show itself. I can draw things having a certain structure, but I cannot draw the structure on its own.[6]

The further implication is that sentences

cannot represent what they must have in common with reality in order to represent it—the logical form. To be able to represent the logical form, we should have to be able to put ourselves with the proposition outside logic, that is outside the world. (4.12)

We cannot think unlogically, i.e., by some principle other than what is logical, and, therefore, we cannot get outside the logical structure of what we say to say something about this structure. If everything

[6] *Philosophical Analysis*, p. 91.

were green we could not point to the color green. Wittgenstein concludes that "all propositions of logic say the same thing. That is, nothing." (5.43) In short, logical propositions are senseless.[7]

This distinction between what can be said and what shows itself casts further light on the question of the relation of language to the world as a whole as distinguished from a part of the world. According to Wittgenstein, nothing can be said about the world as a whole, since to think about the totality would be to think of it as limited by something that is excluded from it. But "propositions can represent the whole of reality" because "the propositions show the logical form of reality." (4.12, 4.121) In other words, the logical structure of a sentence *shows* itself, and this, in turn, *shows* us something *about the world*. Of course, *what* it *shows* we cannot say. That the logic of our language makes it possible for us to describe states of affairs in our world indicates that the world is of such a nature that the logic of language makes this possible. "It is clear that it must show something about the world that certain combinations of symbols . . . are tautologies." (6.124) Wittgenstein also says of the world that

the fact that it can be described by Newtonian mechanics asserts nothing about the world; but *this* asserts something, namely that it can be described in that particular way in which as a matter of fact it is described. The fact, too, that it can be described more simply by one system of mechanics than by another says something about the world. (6.342)

Critical Evaluation

Critical comment must be made both on the way in which Wittgenstein establishes the limits of language and on the adequacy of the view of language which results. Wittgenstein sometimes refers to what can be said in terms of the language of natural science to which it is limited and sometimes in terms of the logical requirement that if anything (P) is really being said to be the case another possibility is thereby being denied as untrue—namely, the denial of P. If I assert it is raining I am also excluding the state of affairs in which "it is not raining" would be true. This has resulted in two different interpretations of Wittgenstein's position, metaphysical and logical. Until recently the metaphysical interpretation, which is shared by Russell, was little challenged. This view regards Wittgenstein as establishing the limits of language on the basis of an empiricist metaphysics. According to D. F. Pears, for example, "Wittgenstein, in the *Tractatus*,

---

[7] One is reminded a little of Greek realism in which it was held, for example, that an "idea" of beauty is present to the mind, functioning as the norm whereby the relative beauty of various objects is judged, yet not itself susceptible to judgment.

makes it clear that this doctrine [that there must be absolutely simple particulars] is a new version of the old theory of individual substances." [8] It is this side of the *Tractatus* that leads Max Black to the interpretation that "to say that p 'says' something is to say that p is empirical; to say that p 'shows' but does not 'say' anything is to say that p is not empirical." [9]

On the other hand, much recent interpretation has held that Wittgenstein's *Sachverhalten* or "facts" are logical possibilities rather than atomic facts in the metaphysical sense. Charlesworth, for example, says that "while the positivist 'elimination of metaphysics' is based upon an *a priori* assumption, namely, that we only know sense-data, Wittgenstein claims that his criterion of meaningfulness is based upon a purely formal *logical* examination of language." [10] On this interpretation, "fact" means "that which is logically required in order that the proposition should 'propose'"; and "'objects' are simply logical postulates; they are logically required for the name to name or refer." [11] The idea is that Wittgenstein establishes the limits of language by purely logical considerations. The language of natural science just happens to be the only language meeting these requirements, but this is incidental to Wittgenstein's position.

The merit of this logical interpretation is that Wittgenstein, in fact, does define what can be said in terms of the logic of our language concerning particular states of affairs. But this is precisely the basic error in Wittgenstein's position, for, as we have argued in connection with Russell, the logical or formal characteristics of language cannot be separated from the *meaning* of the particular language in which they are embodied. Logic is a *distinguishable*, rather than a *separable*, aspect of the meaning of a language. That the language of natural science just happens to be the only language meeting the requirements of Wittgenstein's logic is due to the fact that this logic is nothing more than an aspect of this meaning to begin with.

Separated from the meaning of some part of our language, logic becomes a meaningless manipulation of a given set of figures or marks. What does Wittgenstein *mean* when he says that "the sense of a proposition is its agreement or disagreement with the possibilities of the existence and non-existence of the atomic facts"? Must he not admit the extra-logical meaning implicit in "agreement with" "possible existence" etc.? How else could it be determined whether an alleged assertion met this requirement? If this determination could not be made, Wittgenstein would not be saying anything at all about prop-

[8] "Logical Atomism," *The Revolution in Philosophy*, p. 53.
[9] *Language and Philosophy* (Ithaca: Cornell University Press, 1950), p. 150.
[10] *Philosophy and Linguistic Analysis*, p. 90.
[11] *Ibid.*, p. 84.

ositions. Wittgenstein's statements in this respect are meaningful because these terms are derived from a study of the language of natural science and, consequently, are understood with reference to that language. The same can be argued for all the *fundamental* terms of the *Tractatus*, such as "world" and "fact." As Charlesworth notes, Wittgenstein "at times . . . goes beyond a purely logical definition of 'facts' and identifies 'facts' with *empirical* facts, the facts of the natural sciences." [12]

We see, then, that in making the *logic* of the language of natural science normative for all language, Wittgenstein is, in effect, making the *language* of natural science normative. The "logic of language" is equated with the logic of the language of natural science. This is the large element of truth in the metaphysical interpretation of his position. Wittgenstein's metaphysics, then, is not established by purely logical considerations, because the formal characteristics of the language of natural science do not become normative merely by being described or "shown." His use of this logic is based, rather, on the prior metaphysical judgment that it is to be given a normative status for all language. This question of the role played by Wittgenstein's metaphysics is so crucial that it merits further examination, for, as Charlesworth points out, Wittgenstein's attempt to base his criterion of meaningfulness on considerations devoid of extra-logical assumptions is due to his desire "to escape the paradoxes of the positivist anti-metaphysics (he who denies metaphysics must nevertheless use metaphysics to deny it) and, in general, from the impasses of traditional philosophical argument." [13]

The extra-logical assumptions implicit in the *Tractatus* are evident not only in the normative position that is given indirectly to the language of natural science but, also, in the justification that Wittgenstein offers for his own philosophical statements. Although his statements do not say anything and, so, are nonsense, they are not entirely meaningless, i.e., mere "jabberwocky," because they do show something: "My propositions are elucidatory in this way: he who understands me finally recognizes them as nonsensical, when he has climbed out through them. . . . He must surmount these propositions; then he sees the world rightly." (6.54)

Wittgenstein's philosophizing, then, is to culminate in a right view of the world, i.e., Wittgenstein's view. But this view of the world furnishes the final criterion for distinguishing those nonsense statements which show something from those which do not and, so, are completely without meaning. Wittgenstein's statements are meaningful because they show the world as it really is, i.e., as Wittgenstein

---

[12] *Ibid.*, p. 99.   [13] *Ibid.*, p. 90.

believes it to be.[14] Statements of opposing metaphysicians, of course, by this criterion, would "show" nothing. But, if the judgment that other metaphysical statements are strictly meaningless depends in this way on the acceptance of Wittgenstein's metaphysics, then the "impasse" between opposing metaphysical views has not been avoided after all. Wittgenstein's philosophy is put forward as a process of elucidation which is self-authenticating. If one sees, for example, that a particular system of logic displays or pictures the real structure of our world, then one sees it. But, if other philosophers, after reading Wittgenstein, still see the world differently than he does, the "impasse" scarcely seems to have been avoided as Wittgenstein had hoped. To put the matter another way, Wittgenstein's judgment that other philosophical statements are merely language confusions, whereas his statements, though nonsense, are elucidatory, has his view of the world as its basic criterion. A nonsense statement is elucidatory only if it shows the world as Wittgenstein sees it. One such confusion, for example, is the attempt to talk about the world as a whole by means of our language, which is able only to treat objects *in* the world. Yet Wittgenstein sets aside his own references to "the world" as elucidatory. They are meaningful because, by means of them, "one sees the world rightly." [15]

Not only is Wittgenstein involved in the very metaphysical "impasse" he sought to avoid, but his position widens the impasse by removing itself and opposing positions in principle from rational criticism. One cannot think, we are told, about anything but particular states of affairs. Wittgenstein himself, however, does much reasoning about past metaphysics as involving confusion, especially in its attempts to think about the limits of an unlimited totality. Moreover, his own position has, in fact, been subjected to highly rational criticism. One may point to the criticisms offered by Wittgenstein himself in the *Philosophical Investigations*. Or one may consider the criticisms that Urmson makes of the following passage:

The gramophone record, the musical thought, the score, the waves of sound, all stand to one another in that pictorial internal relation, which

[14] As Wittgenstein sees the world, for example, "what solipsism *means* is quite correct" (5.62), and propositions picture facts.

[15] In connection with Wittgenstein's treatment of language confusion, Charlesworth asks, "What is the difference between holding (according to the traditional view of philosophy) that we cannot know the 'facts' as they really are save by means of philosophical explanation and saying (with Wittgenstein) that we cannot know the 'facts' as they really are without first removing, by means of philosophical analysis, the confusions which make our thoughts 'opaque and blurred'?" Explanation and analysis seem to differ only in that Wittgenstein believes that philosophy would not be necessary if there were not confusions. (*Philosophy and Linguistic Analysis*, p. 90, n.)

holds between language and the world. . . . There is a general rule by which the musician is able to read the symphony out of the score. . . . The rule is the law of projection which projects the symphony into the language of the musical score. (4.014, 4.0141)

Among Urmson's criticisms is the following:

If a law of projection is all that we require for similarity of structure, then the fact that we can find a law of projection connecting any drawing with any object reduces the significance of the demand for identity of structure almost to the vanishing-point.[16]

In addition, Wittgenstein's position removes from rational treatment all concerns outside the sphere of the natural sciences—concerns, that is, about what shows itself. "We feel," he tells us, "that if *all possible* scientific questions can be answered, the problems of life have still not been touched at all. Of course there is then no question left and just this is the answer." (6.52) "Problems" here apparently means questions or doubts about what shows itself. But there can be no problems, in this sense, about what shows itself, "for doubt *can* only exist where there is a question; a question only where there is an answer, and this only where something can be *said*." (6.51) Clearly one cannot doubt what shows itself in the immediacy of mystical experience. The supposition that there are problems or concerns of an extra-scientific nature is alleged to be the product of mere language confusion—the attempt to talk about what can only show itself.

But Wittgenstein's attempts to limit language in this way involve him in an ambiguity concerning what shows itself, which is, at the same time, an ambiguity in his use of the term "world." We have already noted the ambiguity between the logical and extra-logical meanings of this term. But Wittgenstein also vacillates between using "world" in such a way that its reference is limited implicitly to the physical world, *Weltbild*, and extending its meaning to the wider sense of world view, *Weltanschauung*, in which one is concerned also with judgments of purpose and value. "*The limits of my language,*" he says, "mean the limits of my world." (5.6) Now since "the world is the totality of facts" (2.04) and therefore what can be said is limited to "the propositions of natural science" (6.53), what shows itself as my world is what shows itself through the language of natural science. Philosophy "will mean the unsayable by clearly displaying the sayable." (4.115) What is shown is *Weltbild*. That we might employ statements that are "profound nonsense" for the purpose of drawing attention to the logical aspects of these natural science statements is

---

[16] *Philosophical Analysis,* p. 90.

not entirely unintelligible. But Wittgenstein also deals with value questions, as in the following:

The sense of the world must lie outside the world. In the world everything is as it is and happens as it does happen. *In* it there is no value—and if there were, it would be of no value. If there is value which is of value, it must lie outside all happening and being-so. . . . It is clear that ethics cannot be expressed. Ethics is transcendental. (Ethics and aesthetics are one.)[17] . . . There must be some sort of ethical reward and ethical punishment, but this must lie in the action itself. (6.41-6.422)

He attempted to justify these statements on the same basis as he did those which draw attention to characteristics of the *Weltbild*, namely, that they show something. This must mean that there is something to be shown beyond what is shown by the propositions of natural science, that is, beyond what is meant by the world as *Weltbild*. But what function of language is such that "the ethical" is shown through what is said? This aspect of Wittgenstein's thought becomes intelligible only in terms of an implicit recognition of functions of language other than that of reporting particular facts. If, for example, one can distinguish between actions that in themselves contain "ethical reward" and those which contain "ethical punishment," then one, surely, can use words to indicate this difference; and even from Wittgenstein's point of view about ethics it would seem important to be able to use words in this way at least in the task of the moral nurture of the young. Ethics is also immanental.

When Wittgenstein said, "My propositions are elucidatory in this way: he who understands me finally recognizes them as nonsensical [*unsinnig*]" (6.54) Max Black interprets him to have meant that "their absurdity is irredeemable, and their ultimate fate must be rejection."[18] Black concurs in this judgment in the cases of many—but not all[19]— of Wittgenstein's propositions. But these absurdities, according to Black, served the important function of allowing Wittgenstein to determine that they were absurdities:

Wittgenstein is trying out a new way of looking at the world, which forces him to twist and bend language to the expression of his new thoughts. His own conclusion that the new vision is incoherent was a result that had to

[17] When I see the world as a whole in terms of my life (5.621), my happiness, I see it in terms of ethics; when I see the world as a whole as an object of contemplation, I see it in terms of aesthetics.
[18] *A Companion to Wittgenstein's "Tractatus"* (Ithaca: Cornell University Press, 1950), p. 382.
[19] See *ibid.*, p. 381: "For example, when Wittgenstein says that a proposition is not a complex name, he draws attention to an important feature of the grammar (or the 'logic') of the word 'proposition.' "

be won by severe mental labour, and could not have been achieved by any short-cut—such as the automatic application of some principle of verifiability.[20]

When Wittgenstein says, then, that value "must lie outside the world" Black comments that "this is irredeemable nonsense, not the nonsense that arises through the attempt to say what can only be shown. For how could it be shown that there is 'value' outside the world?" [21] This leads Black to interpret Wittgenstein as concluding from the failure of his attempt to revise our language that "the problem of life," or of life's meaning, "can be solved only by causing it to vanish (6.521)—by extirpating the metaphysical craving for a 'higher' answer." [22]

This interpretation seems to me mistaken. Wittgenstein *follows* his statement about "the vanishing of this problem" (6.521) by a reference to "men to whom after long doubting the sense of life became clear" (6.521) (e.g. Tolstoy) and by the contention that "there is indeed the inexpressible. This *shows* itself; it is the mystical." (6.522) Even his concluding comment, "Whereof one cannot speak, thereof one must be silent" (7), seems to indicate that there is something about which one cannot speak.

Rather than uprooting any felt need for the mystical, Wittgenstein seems rather to have been providing the way to satisfy this need. By attempting to demonstrate that in our use of ethical, aesthetic, and religious terms we do not succeed in saying anything, Wittgenstein was seeking to turn our attention to the root of our attempt to use these terms. "Man has the urge to thrust against the limits of language," he once said to Moritz Schlick, and "I regard it as very important to put an end to all [this] chatter. . . . But the tendency, the thrust, *points to something*." [23] Once we stop reducing our quest for meaning to the level of a problem we have cleared the way to seek meaning at its proper level—we have cleared the way for wonder. Later, in his 1929 "Lecture on Ethics," Wittgenstein said

If I want to fix my mind on what I mean by absolute or ethical value . . . it always happens that the idea of one particular experience presents itself to me which is therefore, in a sense, my experience for excellence. . . . The best way of describing it is to say that when I have it *I wonder at the existence of the world.*[24]

[20] *Ibid.*, p. 386.   [21] *Ibid.*, p. 370.   [22] *Ibid.*, p. 373.
[23] "Notes on Talks with Wittgenstein (1929)," *Philosophical Review*, trans. Max Black, Jan., 1965, pp. 12-13.
[24] "Wittgenstein's Lecture on Ethics," *Philosophical Review*, 1965, p. 8.

As Black recognizes, " 'the urge toward the mystical' . . . is one of the chief motive powers of the book." [25] In the *Notebooks*, part of Wittgenstein's preparations for writing the *Tractatus*, he remarks, "The urge towards the mystical comes of the non-satisfaction of our wishes by science." [26] These are wishes for something absolute, something permanent: "If there is a value which is of value, it must lie outside all happening and being-so. For all happening and being-so is accidental." (6.41)

One's life or world takes on meaning and value not by an active involvement in a transformation of the world but by a transformation of oneself in which one sees the world "*sub specie aeternitatis* from outside." [27] To do this is to "make myself independent of the world—and so in a certain sense master it—by renouncing any influence on happenings." [28] To do this is to become the happy man. "In this sense Dostoevsky is right when he says that the man who is happy is fulfilling the purpose of existence." [29] Such a man "no longer needs to have any purpose except to live" and so no longer fears death.[30] He lives in the eternity of the present, not in time, renounces the amenities of the world, lives the life of knowledge and of the contemplation of the beautiful.[31]

All this and more Wittgenstein says about value, yet concludes that the saying of it is nonsense (*unsinnig*). One must agree with George Pitcher that "this evaluation cannot be accepted; Wittgenstein has said these things and therefore they can be said." [32] But in claiming that Wittgenstein "has said these things" we must mean that he has at the same time excluded other things that might be said; and many uses of mutually excluding terms are found explicitly in his discussions of value. For example, Wittgenstein speaks of ethical reward and punishment, something acceptable and something unacceptable, good

[25] A *Companion to Wittgenstein's "Tractatus,"* p. 374. In response to a letter from Russell concerning the *Tractatus* Wittgenstein wrote, "Now I'm afraid you haven't really got hold of my main contention, to which the whole business of logical propositions is only corollary. The main point is the theory of what can be expressed . . . and what . . . only shown." Quoted by G. E. M. Anscombe, *An Introduction to Wittgenstein's Tractatus* (London: Hutchinson, 1959), p. 161.

[26] *Wittgenstein Notebooks 1914-1916*, ed. G. H. von Wright and G. E. M. Anscombe, trans. G. E. M. Anscombe (New York: Harper, 1961), p. 51.

[27] *Notebooks*, p. 83. According to Wittgenstein, "The work of art is the object seen *sub specie aeternitatis*; and the good life is the world seen *sub specie aeternitatis*." (*Ibid.*) See also p. 73 and, in the *Tractatus*, 6.421-6.43, 5.632.

[28] *Notebooks*, p. 73.   [29] *Ibid.*   [30] *Ibid.*, pp. 73-74.

[31] *Ibid.*, pp. 74, 81, 86. See also, in the *Tractatus*, 6.4311, 6.4312. A somewhat comparable neo-stoicism is found in Bertrand Russell's "A Free Man's Worship" (1903), reprinted in *Mysticism and Logic*.

[32] *The Philosophy of Wittgenstein* (Englewood Cliffs, N.J.: Prentice-Hall, 1964), p. 155.

and bad willing, the world of the happy and the world of the unhappy, eternity and temporal duration, facing death with fear and without fear, will in the ethical sense and in the sense of "that which sets the body in motion." [33] And in his "Lecture on Ethics" Wittgenstein distinguishes ethical from other experience and says, "I will describe this experience in order, if possible, to make you recall the same or similar experiences, so that we may have a common ground for our investigation." [34] That even after giving these descriptions he says "the verbal expression which we give to these experiences is nonsense" [35] strongly points to a deep-seated unwillingness to give up his metaphysical system. For the distinction between what can and what cannot be said is basic to that system and the system serves Wittgenstein's purpose of disengaging himself from the world of time and change and suffering and death: "Suppose that man could not exercise his [ethical] will, but had to suffer all the misery of this world, then what could make him happy?" [36]

Finally, Wittgenstein was himself driven to revise his position in the *Tractatus* because of its inherent instability. As we have seen in the previous chapter, the atomists were unable to state their views without using language in a way that their views did not allow. We remember, for example, that if a fact can be symbolized only by a proposition and not by a word, then it becomes strictly impossible to use the word "fact" and, so, to say anything at all about a fact, including the sort of symbol it has. Wittgenstein was the first of the atomists to see this when he concluded that "he who understands me finally recognizes [my propositions] as nonsensical." (6.54)

But Wittgenstein's view of the nature of the world also contained a fatal inconsistency. He shared the atomists' view of the world as having a form corresponding to the form of "truth functional" or "extensional" logic. That "atomic facts are independent of one another" (2.061) corresponds to the logical tenet that elementary propositions are independent of one another: "it is a sign of an elementary proposition, that no elementary proposition can contradict it." (4.211) Yet Wittgenstein later notes that "the assertion that a point in the visual field has two different colours at the same time, is a contradiction." (6.3751) In other words, "This is red and this is blue" is a contradiction where "this" refers in both cases to the same point in a visual field. Wittgenstein is driven in this passage to the conclusion that propositions of the sort "this is red" are not elementary propositions; elementary propositions cannot contradict each other. No wonder, then, that Wittgenstein failed to give even a single example

---

[33] *Tractatus*, 6.422, 6.43, 6.4311, 6.423; *Notebooks*, pp. 75, 76, 77.
[34] "Lecture on Ethics," p. 8.   [35] *Ibid*.   [36] *Notebooks*, p. 81.

of an elementary proposition, for similar difficulties seem to arise for any quality that one might attribute to an object.

As early as 1929 Wittgenstein was lead by this problem to say "atomic propositions, although they cannot contradict, may exclude one another";[37] and those who know truth functional logic will see that, as Wittgenstein pointed out, in cases of mutually excluding propositions one line will be missing from the truth table.[38] With this revision he had begun the surrender of the "truth functional" conception of the independence of elementary propositions; and in 1930 he had begun the related transition to his later emphasis on seeing any given proposition as belonging to a "system" of language or language-game: "I do not apply the *proposition* as a measuring-rod to reality, but the *system* of propositions." [39] As we shall see, the place of a proposition in the language "system" is marked by the range of propositions which it excludes and which therefore provides it with contrast.

To summarize, first of all, I have criticized Wittgenstein's claims to have established the limits of language on purely logical grounds. He has, in effect, made the extra-logical, metaphysical judgment that the logical characteristics of the language of natural science are normative for all language. Then, too, the justification of his own philosophical statements, together with the concomitant judgment that the statements of other philosophers are meaningless, rests on the extra-logical criterion that a statement may be said to "show" something only if it enables us to "see the world rightly."

Second, I have criticized the view of language which results because it removes from rational discussion all concerns outside the area of natural science, including the concerns both of philosophy and of ethics. Moreover, if we are to "mean the unsayable by clearly displaying the sayable" (4.115), and if the sayable is limited to the

[37] "Some Remarks on Logical Form," *Aristotelian Society Supplementary Volume* (1929), p. 168.

[38] If P and Q are two propositions that exclude each other, the truth table for their conjunction becomes

$$P \cdot Q$$
$$T \quad F \quad F$$
$$F \quad F \quad T$$
$$F \quad F \quad F$$

Max Black comments that "here we have to envisage some 'rule of syntax' that makes the missing line (TFT) 'nonsense'" and that Wittgenstein therefore says in his *Philosophische Bemerkungen* (34, 5), "The grammatical rules for 'and,' 'not,' 'or,' etc., are indeed not exhausted by what I said in the *Tractatus*, but there are rules for truth-functions that also concern the elementary parts of the proposition." (*A Companion to Wittgenstein's "Tractatus,"* p. 369).

[39] *Philosophische Bemerkungen*, ed. Rush Rhees (Oxford: Basil Blackwell, 1965), (34,6).

propositions of natural science, then the only thing unsayable that we can mean is the limits of the world described by natural science. There is nothing that can be said which would mean such unsayable matters as ethics or the relation of logic to the world. This view of language implies a view of man as not having any problems other than those relating to scientific fact. Beyond these there are only pseudo-concerns generated by language confusion, which dissolve upon a return to mystical experience. But those who remain convinced that there are significant problems of life will find it surprising if man has not developed other sorts of language to deal with them.

Third, I have pointed to an inconsistency in the *Tractatus* which proved fatal to its system, namely, the apparent impossibility of complete independence between all elementary propositions.

Some Applications to Talk of God

We may now turn to ask about the implications of Wittgenstein's early position and of our criticism of it for religious language. Bertrand Russell gives us the following information about Wittgenstein's personal attitude toward religion:

He was, in the days before 1914, concerned almost completely with logic. During or perhaps just before the first war, he changed his outlook and became more or less of a mystic, as may be seen here and there in the "Tractatus." He had been dogmatically anti-Christian, but in this respect he changed completely. The only thing he ever told me about this was that once in a village in Gallicia during the war he found a bookshop containing only one book, which was Tolstoy on the Gospels. He bought the book, and, according to him, it influenced him profoundly.[40]

In the *Notebooks* of the 1914-16 period Wittgenstein said that "the meaning of life, i.e. the meaning of the world, we can call God" and that "to pray is to think about the meaning of life." [41] And in his "Lecture on Ethics" Wittgenstein related the meaning of "God" to the experiences of wondering at the existence of the world and "of feeling absolutely safe" so that "nothing can injure me whatever happens":[42]

For the first of [these experiences] is, I believe, exactly what people were referring to when they said that God had created the world; and the experience of absolute safety has been described by saying that we feel

---

[40] "Ludwig Wittgenstein," *Mind*, 1951, p. 298. See also Paul Englemann, *Letters from Ludwig Wittgenstein* (Oxford: Basil Blackwell, 1967), pp. 75-80.
[41] *Notebooks*, p. 73. See also pp. 74, 75, 79.
[42] "Lecture on Ethics," p. 8.

safe in the hands of God. A third experience of the same kind is that of feeling guilty and again this was described by the phrase that God disapproves of our conduct.[43] Thus in ethical and religious language we seem constantly to be using similes. But a simile must be the simile for *something*.[44]

Although he believed that these remarks are nonsensical, Wittgenstein commented to Schlick that "nevertheless we thrust against the limits of language. Kierkegaard, too, recognized this thrust and even described it in much the same way (as a thrust against paradox)." [45]

In light of these comments we may consider the basic religious content of the *Tractatus* which Wittgenstein gave in the following statements:

If by eternity is understood not endless temporal duration but timelessness, then he lives eternally who lives in the present. . . . (6.4311)

The solution of the riddle of life in space and time lies *outside* space and time. . . . (6.4312)

How the world is, is completely indifferent for what is higher. God does not reveal himself *in* the world. . . . (6.432)

Not *how* the world is, is the mystical, but *that* it is. (6.44)

The contemplation of the world sub specie aeterni is its contemplation as a limited whole. The feeling of the world as a limited whole is the mystical feeling. (6.45)

For an answer which cannot be expressed the question too cannot be expressed. *The riddle* does not exist. . . . (6.5)

Scepticism is *not* irrefutable, but palpably nonsensical, if it would doubt where a question cannot be asked. . . . (6.51)

There is indeed the inexpressible. This *shows* itself; it is the mystical. (6.522)

By "God," then, Wittgenstein meant the mystical or the sense of life's meaning, that which cannot be expressed but which shows itself when we contemplate the fact that the world exists. There are no religious questions or problems but only the fact of mystical experience about which one must remain silent. The belief that there are religious questions or problems to be struggled with is simply the product of a language confusion, the attempt to say something about what can only show itself. Michael Foster comments that "this is to deny not God, but Revelation; or more accurately, it is to deny that language can be

---

[43] Compare "Conscience is the voice of God." (*Notebooks*, p. 75.)
[44] "Lecture on Ethics," p. 10.
[45] Moritz Schlick, "Notes on Talks with Wittgenstein," p. 13.

the vehicle of revealed truth." [46] As he says elsewhere, "What Wittgenstein seems not to believe is that God has spoken." [47]

Wittgenstein's rather cryptically expressed views on "the mystical" are developed by Thomas McPherson in his article "Religion as the Inexpressible." [48] McPherson finds support for the religious portions of the *Tractatus* in Rudolf Otto's *The Idea of the Holy*.[49] He suggests that Wittgenstein's "feeling of the world as a limited whole" has "clear affinities with Otto's 'creature-feeling' " [50] and that for both it is the inexpressible, feeling side of religion that is important and essential:

Otto conceived himself in *The Idea of the Holy* to be recovering the essential element in religion—which had been in danger of being lost under a cloud of rationalizing. What is essential about religion is its non-rational side, the part that cannot be "conceptualized"—that is, the part that cannot be put into words. Otto travels the same road as Wittgenstein. Are we to call Otto an enemy of religion? Why not call Wittgenstein its friend?[51]

Although granting that Otto does not depreciate the conceptual side of what is rightly meant by "the holy," McPherson argues not only that Otto believes that all that is "essential" in religion is the non-rational, numinous element but also that, by implication, he would seem to agree with those who question the possibility of a meaningful religious language. He sees Otto to be saying, in effect, that "there is much nonsense in Christian doctrine" and that "there are some things that cannot be said; so let us not try to say them." [52] This is offered as "not an unreasonable interpretation" [53] in view of what Otto says about "concept," namely, that "all language in so far as it consists of words, purports to convey ideas or concepts;—that is what language *means*; . . . and hence expositions of religious truth in language *inevitably* tend to stress the 'rational' attributes of God." [54]

It is these judgments about the essential and the nonsensical in religion that are marshalled in support of Wittgenstein's position. We should realize, according to McPherson, that Wittgenstein offers a "way out" for those who are worried about the meaningfulness of religious "beliefs," yet feel that these beliefs have to do with some-

---

[46] "Contemporary British Philosophy and Christian Belief," p. 196.
[47] *Mystery and Philosophy*, p. 28.
[48] (1954), revised and reprinted in *New Essays in Philosophical Theology,* pp. 131-43.
[49] Trans. John W. Harvey, 2nd ed. (London: Oxford University Press, 1950).
[50] "Religion as the Inexpressible," p. 137.   [51] *Ibid.*, p. 139.
[52] *Ibid.*, 136-37.   [53] *Ibid.*, p. 137.
[54] *The Idea of the Holy*, p. 2. The italics are those added by McPherson.

thing "very important" which should not be lost. This way out, as we have seen, is a "retreat into silence." Now, even though Otto does not hold that silence is necessary, his primary concerns are seen to coalesce with Wittgenstein's way out in two crucial respects. In maintaining that "there is indeed the mystical," Wittgenstein, it is alleged, is preserving all that Otto regards as essential to religion. Then, too, in maintaining that the mystical cannot be talked about, Wittgenstein removes both the danger that our sense of the mystical will be lost behind a screen of nonsense, and the constant danger, stressed by Otto, of an overemphasis upon the conceptual, which language introduces by its very nature.

Such an account, however, distorts Otto's position and obscures the crucial point at issue that separates his position from that of Wittgenstein. McPherson has seriously understated the place of the conceptual in Otto's thought. In his foreword, Otto warns against those who are "too ready to evade the arduous duty of clarifying their ideas and grounding their convictions on a basis of coherent thought. . . . I feel," he stresses, "that no one ought to concern himself with the 'Numen ineffable' who has not already devoted assiduous and serious study to the 'Ratio aeterna.' "[55] He then opens his discussion with the same emphasis:

It is essential to every theistic conception of God, and most of all to the Christian, that it designates and precisely characterizes deity by the attributes spirit, reason, purpose, good will, supreme power, unity, selfhood. . . . The nature of deity described in the attributes above mentioned is . . . a rational nature; and a religion which recognizes and maintains such a view of God is in so far a "rational" religion. Only on such terms is *belief* possible in contrast to mere *feeling*. . . . We count this the very mark and criterion of a religion's high rank and superior value—that it should have no lack of *conceptions* about God; that it should admit knowledge—the knowledge that comes by faith—of the transcendent in terms of conceptual thought, whether those already mentioned or others which continue and develop them.[56]

Only after defending, "with the most positive emphasis," the conceptual as essential to religion at its highest, does Otto go on to warn against "the view that the *essence* of deity can be given *completely* and exhaustively in such 'rational' attributions."[57] Otto says here not that the conceptual gives nothing of the essence of God but that it does not give everything.

Otto maintains not only that language can be used meaningfully with reference to the rational dimensions of the holy but also that

---

[55] *The Idea of the Holy*, Foreword by the author.
[56] *Ibid.*, p. 1. The first use of italics is mine.   [57] *Ibid.*, pp. 1-2. Italics mine.

language can be used symbolically in analyzing "the *feeling* which remains where the *concept* fails." [58] Of this nonrational element, he argues that

> though it eludes the conceptual way of understanding, it must be in some way within our grasp, else absolutely nothing could be asserted of it. And even mysticism . . . does not really mean to imply that absolutely nothing can be asserted of the object of religious consciousness; otherwise, mysticism could exist only in unbroken silence, whereas what has generally been a characteristic of the mystics is their copious eloquence. [59]

Wittgenstein's belief, then, that language has no place in mystical matters is shared neither by Otto nor, if Otto is right, by the mystics in general.

The issue here as to whether language is essential to religion—whether something essential would be lost by a "retreat into silence"—is really an issue as to whether there are religious problems and concerns interwoven in the fabric of everyday life. If there are such problems, then it is essential that we have a language by which to deal with them. To retreat into silence would be to remove religion from everyday concerns, making "the mystical" irrelevant to other dimensions of experience. Wittgenstein's retreat into silence is of one piece with his conviction that there is no "problem of life." [60] But, contrary to this, as McPherson admits, in following Otto "we do not lose the sense that there is a problem of life." [61] And the difference is not only that Otto regards religious questions as real, but also that he sees them somewhat differently than McPherson does when the latter remarks that "the sort of questions that religious people ask are questions about the fact that there is a world at all. ('Why is there a world anyway?')" [62] This understanding of religion neglects to consider the existential nature of the questions commonly asked by religious people. The sense of religious wonder that finds expression in the question "Why does the world exist?" passes over into existential concern when the question becomes "Why do I exist?" And the closely related question, "What must I do to be saved?" is one that grows out of Otto's "creature-feeling" rather than out of wonder at the existence of the world.

Hutchison puts the matter in its broadest terms:

[58] *Ibid.*, Foreword.   [59] *Ibid.*

[60] Although at one point McPherson does say that, for Wittgenstein, there are no religious questions, at many other points in his discussion he softens this and merely says that the religious questions cannot be asked or answered "in words."

[61] "Religion as the Inexpressible," p. 139.

[62] *Ibid.*, pp. 137-38.

Will religion be significantly related to the various concerns of the common life, or will it shut itself off in a corner apart from the other concerns of a culture? If it takes the latter course, it condemns itself to triviality and irrelevance. Taking the former course, it will need a language in which it may relate itself intelligibly and pertinently to the different areas and interests of culture.[63]

Similarly, in expressing the relevance of religion to the ethical concerns of culture, Otto maintained that when "the notion has ripened and *reached the highest stage* in its development . . . this 'holy' then represents the gradual shaping and filling in with ethical meaning, or what we shall call the 'schematization,' of what was a unique original feeling-response.[64]

Now Wittgenstein, we remember, placed the ethical and the aesthetic, as well as the religious, in the category of that about which nothing can be said. Yet he also said that "there must be some sort of ethical reward and ethical punishment, but this must lie in the action itself." (6.422) Earlier we remarked that, if there is in this way a difference between actions which are ethical and those which are unethical, then, surely, we can use language to indicate it. Similarly, we may now ask whether there is not also a distinction to be made between responses which are religious and those which are irreligious. If there is not this distinction, then the religious or the mystical is irrelevant to everyday life. If there is this distinction, then surely we can use language to indicate it also, and we can go on to ask philosophically about the logic of this aspect of language.

Wittgenstein ruled out the possibility that a religious way of speaking can be meaningful by his assumption that all meaningful language must share the same formal or logical characteristics. But this assumption cannot be maintained if, as we have urged, the formal characteristics of a statement are a distinguishable but *not a separable* aspect of the meaning of that statement. The formal characteristics of religious language cannot, therefore, be determined except by attention to the *meaning* of religious language. If there are religious questions, then their logic will differ from that of scientific questions—otherwise they would *be* scientific questions; consequently, whether there is such a logic cannot be determined by examining the language of science.

The formal characteristics of religious language which make it possible to say something—and so to ask something—about religious matters must be such that in saying something we thereby rule out some other things that might have been said. We must know, that is, what is involved in accepting one statement rather than another.

---

[63] *Faith, Reason, and Existence*, p. 131.
[64] *The Idea of the Holy*, p. 6. Italics mine.

According to the *Tractatus*, a statement such as "This book is red" says something because it excludes finding the book not to be red. Since Wittgenstein, and the atomists generally, had assumed that naming was the only function of language, so that we refer to a fact by putting together names of its constituent elements, the only sort of exclusion by which sense can be given to a statement seemed to be limited to that of naming one constituent element and thereby ruling out the absence of that element. But if the function of language is not restricted in this way, we must be open to other sorts of difference which make statements mutually exclusive. The statement, for example, that one is justified by faith is understood by those who use Pauline language to exclude the claim that one is justified by works and not by faith. Each of these statements says something provided that one knows what is involved in accepting it rather than its denial.

Religious questions are meaningful, then, insofar as one comes to see what is at issue between accepting one possible answer as opposed to another. But this means, of course, that one must have come to some awareness of the numinous so that one will know what religious questions are questions about. As Otto said concerning the question of salvation, "Everywhere salvation is something whose meaning is often very little apparent, is even wholly obscure, to the 'natural' man," i.e., to the man in whom the numinous feeling has not yet been awakened.[65] It is only the religiously alive mind that knows it "for what it is behind the obscure and inadequate symbols which are its only expression." [66] Those who use religious language, then, commonly analyze it as exercising a symbolic function in which the religious shows itself. "Everything religion says about God . . . has a symbolic character." [67] One attempts, that is, to talk about the finite world in such a way that the numinous shows itself. And, just as Wittgenstein said that the fact "that it can be described more simply by one system of mechanics than by another says something about the world," [68] so we can add that the fact that some religious symbolism is more adequate than other religious symbolism shows something about God.

Such religious symbolic statements may refer to particular states of affairs, or they may refer to the world as a whole. And in statements of this latter type we have striking examples of the importance of judging religious language in terms of its own logic. Analyzed from the

----

[65] *Ibid.*, p. 35.   [66] *Ibid.*, p. 36.
[67] Paul Tillich, *Systematic Theology*, II (Chicago: The University of Chicago Press, 1957), 9. This statement itself is exempted as nonsymbolic, although there are problems with this in that it appears to be a second order statement, i.e., a statement about *statements* about God rather than a statement about God.
[68] *Tractatus* . . . , 6.342.

standpoint of language whose point it is to give information about particular states of affairs, statements such as "The world is separated from God" are judged to be empty, for they exclude no particular fact and, so, do not give us information in the ordinary sense of asserting that this rather than that is the case. But this is to misunderstand their logic. The task of seeking to understand religious language on its own terms is well illustrated by Ninian Smart's discussion of the words of the *Isa Upanisad*, "Brahman is outside all this":

We might for instance suppose that all this is everything that there is. But this is hardly helpful, since (i) Brahman is said to exist and is outside all this: so there will be something that exists apart from everything that there is; and (ii) "everything that there is" seems a logically malformed phrase, for "exists" is not a (logical) predicate and hence the expression "that there is" does not define a class in the way "blue" does. "Everything blue" is intelligible, "everything existent" is not (at least immediately).[69]

To understand these words from the *Upanisad*, we must see them as having quite a different point from words defining a class of particular states of affairs. Their point is to present a picture that is of great significance for worship: "The picture of the divine as beyond or behind the world is a model whereby is expressed the fullest possible sense of the mystery gleaming in the finite world." [70]

Wittgenstein was himself soon to recognize that language did have, as an important function, the task of showing the ethical, aesthetic, and philosophical dimensions of things. G. E. Moore reports that, in his lectures between 1930-1933, Wittgenstein put the matter this way:

Reasons, he said, in Aesthetics, are "of the nature of further descriptions": e.g. you can make a person see what Brahms was driving at by showing him lots of different pieces by Brahms, or by comparing him with a contemporary author; and all that Aesthetics does is *"to draw your attention to a thing,"* to "place things side by side." He said that if, by giving "reasons" of this sort, you make another person *"see what you see"* but it still "doesn't appeal to him," that is "an end" of the discussion. . . . And he said that the same sort of "reasons were given, not only in Ethics, but also in Philosophy." [71]

Perhaps the reason that Wittgenstein had not recognized this function in the *Tractatus* was that he had not yet seen the full complexity of the patterns that show themselves. As D. F. Pears notes,

what Russell and Wittgenstein did in this period was to glimpse traces of a pattern in our experience, and then, taking their eyes off the facts, to

---

[69] *Reasons and Faiths*, pp. 35-36.   [70] *Ibid.*, p. 43.
[71] *Mind*, Jan., 1955, p. 19. Italics mine, except the first.

develop this pattern far beyond what is warranted by the facts. They had fixed their eyes on logic . . . and where they failed to discover clarity and order, they invented them.[72]

Given a relatively monolithic pattern—"*the* logic of our language"—which shows itself in everything that can be said, the development of a special language whose function would be to show this pattern would not be anticipated. But given many different sorts of patterns and concerns—ethical, aesthetic, epistemological, religious, etc.—and given the complexity of each of these patterns, so that after some features of, say, the religious terrain have been noted, there are yet many other features to map, the development of special ethical, religious, and other languages is inevitable. We may at least note here that if analysis points out certain features of a subject which may have been overlooked, if it "gives reasons" in this sense, it may result in a change of our language habits—a change in our understanding of a subject matter. One may, in other words, agree with Wittgenstein that "my world" is relative to my language, but see language as a growing, changing instrument, an instrument whose growth and change are governed by man's interaction with his environment in conjunction with analytic reflection on that instrument itself.

To summarize, the position of the early Wittgenstein, in effect, rules out the possibility of religious language by making the logic of natural science normative for all language. We have argued, however, that the formal characteristics of a language are an inseparable part of the meaning of that language, so that the logic of religious language must be ascertained by a study of its meaning rather than the meaning of natural science. McPherson's contention that a "retreat into silence" might not be damaging to what is essential in religion has been challenged as implying that there are no religious problems and concerns interwoven in the fabric of everyday life, for if there were we would need a religious language to deal with them. Wittgenstein's position that there are no religious problems is not shared by a majority of those who actually use religious language. To deal with such problems, religious language must meet at least two requirements. First of all, what is involved in accepting one statement must be incompatible with what is involved in accepting certain other possible statements, for if a statement is incompatible with nothing, it would lose its point as an answer. Secondly, religious statements must perform the symbolic function of showing the religious dimension that gives rise to them.

[72] "Logical Atomism," *The Revolution in Philosophy,* p. 46.

THE <u>INVESTIGATIONS</u>: *Language-games & Forms of Life*

Chapter Six

> The sickness of a time is cured by an alteration in the mode of life (*Lebensweise*) of human beings, and it was possible for the sickness of philosophical problems to get cured only through a changed mode of thought and of life.[1]

Running throughout the positions considered so far is the belief that the task, or at least a main task, of philosophy is the reduction of language to a set of basic propositions. Their differences were with respect to the philosophical justification of the reductive analysis, the atomists seeing the goal as insight into the structure of facts, the positivists interpreting their work as clarifying the structure of the language of common sense and science. Whatever the difficulties connected with such justification it was the failures of reductive analysis itself, the lack of fruitfulness of the method, which led to the present positions in analytic philosophy. We have already noted certain forms of sentences which cannot be given a truth-functional interpretation. In addition we have seen the lack of any satisfactory treatment of statements concerning value. Most damaging, however, was the inability of the analysts to provide so much as a single satisfactory reductive analysis of the sorts of statement that were of fundamental importance to their program. No one succeeded in the reduction of statements about nations into statements about people or

---

[1] Wittgenstein, *Remarks on the Foundations of Mathematics*, ed. G. H. von Wright, R. Rhees, and G. Anscombe, trans. G. Anscombe (Oxford: Basil Blackwell, 1956), Part I, App. II, No. 4.

the reduction of statements about people or things into statements about sense-data. In such a reduction, the meaning of the first sentence was to be exactly equivalent to the meaning of the sentence or sentences to which it is reduced. But, in Urmson's example, the statement "England declared war in 1939" is "clearly not equivalent to 'All Englishmen declared war in 1939'" and is understandable without knowing the actions of any one person, such as the Foreign Secretary, or of any group of people.[2]

Forced to conclude that natural language is not open to reductive analysis, there were two alternatives open to the analytically minded empiricist. First, the method of reductive analysis could be retained by rejecting natural language as a proper concern for the philosopher and concentrating instead on the construction of languages that meet the structural requirements of this analysis. This was the alternative chosen by many outside England, such as Carnap. Second, one could look for non-reductive approaches to the clarification of natural language. This was the path followed by the English analysts, and it is with this alternative that we shall now be concerned.

The leading exponent of this new development in English philosophy was, once again, Ludwig Wittgenstein. Wittgenstein's work in this direction was getting underway in 1929 but has gradually been published only since his death in 1951. In order of chronological development we now have available: "Some Remarks on Logical Form" (1929);[3] "Wittgenstein's Lectures in 1930-33";[4] *Philosophishe Bemerkungen* (1930);[5] *The Blue and Brown Books* (1933-35);[6] *Wittgenstein: Lectures and Conversations on Aesthetics, Psychology and Religious Belief* (1938);[7] *Remarks on the Foundations of Mathematics* (1937-44); *Zettel* (1929-1948, but principally 1945-1948);[8] *Philosophical Investigations* (Part I finished in 1945; Part II: 1947-1949).

This new position is really a profound revision of that of the *Tractatus*. Wittgenstein now sees language to have many different uses or purposes that are *not reducible* to any other. We are not, as in the *Tractatus*, limited to the one particular use exemplified by science.

[2] *Philosophical Analysis*, p. 151.

[3] *Aristotelian Society Supplementary Volume* (1929).

[4] G. E. Moore, *Mind*, Jan., 1954; July, 1954; Jan., 1955; reprinted in Moore, *Philosophical Papers* (New York: Macmillan, 1959).

[5] Ed. R. Rhees (Oxford: Basil Blackwell, 1965); English translation by Anscombe forthcoming.

[6] 2nd ed., ed. R. Rhees (Oxford: Basil Blackwell, 1960).

[7] Ed. Cyril Barrett (compiled from notes taken by R. Rhees, Y. Smythies, and J. Taylor); (London: Basil Blackwell, 1966).

[8] Ed G. Anscombe and G. H. von Wright; trans. G. Anscombe, 1967. Originally published by the University of California Press. Quotations reprinted by permission of The Regents of the University of California, and Basil Blackwell, Ltd.

But, the all-important concept of the limits of language is preserved by speaking in terms of various "language-games," each with its own limits; and with this concept is preserved the attack on metaphysics as meaningless. The concept of use and the analogy of a game are the focal points around which Wittgenstein's position must be considered, together with their use to dispose of metaphysics and the techniques developed for this purpose.

Wittgenstein takes us to the heart of his position when he says: "For a *large* class of cases—though not all—in which we employ the word 'meaning' it can be defined thus: *the meaning of a word is its use* in the language." (43)[9] By thinking in this way of meaning as use, he introduces a Copernican revolution into analytic philosophy, a fundamental change of perspective on the philosophical question as to the meaning of meaning. Up to this point the analysts, and most other philosophers as well, had regarded meaning as the relation of standing for or naming. The meaning of a proposition is its referent. For the positivists it is the sensory experience referred to. But, if we ask ourselves why we human beings speak, would it make sense to say that we do so simply to refer to something? What good would this do us? If we wish to refer to something, it must be that we have a purpose that is served in this way. In the course of an operation, a surgeon utters the word "scalpel." What does he mean? Well, his purpose is that his assistant hand him that instrument. Is this not what we understand if we understand his meaning? What the surgeon means by "scalpel" here is not a static standing for a certain sort of object. The word has a job to do. The utterance is not simply a reference but a reference-for-a-purpose. It commands, and that command, that function in the course of the operation, is its meaning. In short, words and sentences do not have any meaning unless people use them to mean something, and, consequently meaning cannot be understood apart from the human purposes for which language has been created. "The essence of language," argues Wittgenstein, is "its function." (92)

The reductive analysis, then, of logical atomism (including the *Tractatus*) had been fundamentally mistaken in believing that meaning is the thing named. Wittgenstein insisted that "the word 'meaning' is being used illicitly if it is used to signify the thing that 'corresponds' to the word. That is to confound the meaning of a name with the *bearer* of the name." (40) It is true that we do sometimes ask what

[9] References to the *Philosophical Investigations* will be placed in the text, giving section numbers for Part I and page numbers for Part II. Italics mine, except for the first. An important example of the type of statement not included in this class is that having to do with intention, e.g. "I meant to do that."

something is called. But the answer gives us only the name and not the meaning of the name. "Nothing has so far been done, when a thing has been named." (49) Learning a name is significant only as a preparation for using it. Names would not exist were it not for the purposes they serve, and we would not ask about them or teach them were it not for their potential application to these purposes. "Only someone who already knows how to do something with it can significantly ask a name." (31) There would be no point in learning the name of a tool if we were not able to use that tool, or in hanging a label on things if we had no purpose that would be served by labels. Words do not just refer. They have various "kinds" of reference, and to know what sort of reference a word has is to know its use. (10)

Descriptions, for example, are among the uses to which our language tools are put. We should be careful to distinguish describing from naming, "for naming and describing do not stand on the same level: naming is a preparation for description." (49) There are, moreover, "many different kinds of things called 'description': description of a body's position by means of its co-ordinates; description of a facial expression; description of a sensation of touch; of a mood." (24)

In addition to describing, Wittgenstein suggests such language uses as giving orders, reporting an event, testing a hypothesis, telling a joke, asking a question, offering a prayer, cursing (23), and telling a lie. (249) There are, indeed, "countless kinds" of uses. (23) Plainly, it is folly to attempt to specify *a priori* what sort of use or uses language must have to be meaningful. In any given case, rather, we must attempt to see what sort of use those words are put to. The kind of reference, for example, that a moral statement makes to the situation with which it is concerned need not be that of a description of a special sort of moral fact. Perhaps its use is to express or evoke an emotion toward that situation. Perhaps it offers, in that situation, a rule to guide choice and draws attention to the aspects of that situation which allegedly make that rule applicable.[10]

The meaning of a word, then, is its use, and this use has three aspects: syntactic, semantic, and pragmatic. In one passage Wittgenstein referred to the syntactic aspect as "surface grammar": "In the use of words one might distinguish 'surface grammar' from 'depth grammar.' What immediately impresses itself upon us about the use of a word is the way it is used in the construction of the sentence." (664) As we shall see, Wittgenstein's interest in surface grammar is limited to the

---

[10] See, for example, Iris Murdoch, "Metaphysics and Ethics," *The Nature of Metaphysics*, ed. D. F. Pears, p. 103. On the preceding page we read that "the notion that the meaning of a word is its use—a notion which in other fields we may associate with the name Wittgenstein—did, I think arise independently in the field of ethics, as a development and refinement of the emotive theory."

way the philosopher is so easily deceived by it. Depth grammar includes both semantic and pragmatic aspects of use. The semantic aspect concerns the conditions that must hold if a word is used to refer to something: "Let us see . . . what the situations are in which we use this expression, what sentences would precede or follow it (what kind of conversation it is a part of)." [11] The pragmatic aspect concerns the jobs that words can do, the purposes they are made to serve. Wittgenstein's concern is with the semantic and pragmatic aspects of use and especially the latter.

The fundamental mistake of the reductionistic philosopher is to assume that words function in only one way. Although many of the terms that are of special philosophic interest have various uses, the reductionist simply asks about *the* meaning of the term. One may ask, for example, about *the* nature of truth or about *the* meaning of meaning or about *the* definitions of time, space and simultaneity. Wittgenstein refers, in this respect, to the treatment in the *Theaetetus* of the term "primary" (i.e., noncomposite):

Socrates says in the *Theaetetus:* ". . . In consequence it is impossible to give an account of any primary element; for it, nothing is possible but the bare name; its name is all it has. But just as what consists of these primary elements is itself complex, so the names of the elements become descriptive language by being compounded together. For the essence of speech is the composition of names." Both Russell's "individuals" and my "objects" (*Tractatus Logico-Philosophicus*) were such primary elements. But what are the simple constituent parts of which reality is composed?—What are the simple constituent parts of a chair?—The bits of wood of which it is made? Or the molecules, or the atoms?—"Simple" means: not composite. And here the point is: in what sense "composite"? It makes no sense at all to speak absolutely of the "simple parts of a chair." (46-47)

Language-Games and Language Confusion

As a corollary to the principle that the meaning of a word is its use, we are asked to think of language by means of the dramatic analogy of a game. We are to consider different uses of language as different sorts of games, as different *"language-games."* (7) We may compare words to the pieces in a chess game and sentences to the moves that are made with those pieces: "the question 'What is a word really?' is analogous to 'What is a piece in chess?'" (108) Just as an object of wood or ivory does not have the status of being a piece except in the context of the chess game, so a sound is not a name except as it is a part of a language-game. (49)

There are three main purposes served by this analogy between lan-

[11] *The Brown Book,* p. 179.

guage and games. First, it expresses the pluralistic nature of
Wittgenstein's view of language. To the charge that "You talk about
all sorts of language-games, but have nowhere said what the essence
of a language-game, and hence of language, is," Wittgenstein replies:
"This is true.—Instead of producing something common to all that
we call language, I am saying that these phenomena have no one
thing in common which makes us use the same word for all,—but
that they are *related* to one another in many different ways." (65)
Wittgenstein illustrates this by examining our uses of the word "game."
There does not seem to be any one feature common to football,
solitaire, throwing a ball against a wall to catch it, and ring-around-the-
rosy, for example. The same is true of "language," "understanding,"
and other words put to varied use.

We see a complicated network of similarities overlapping and crisscrossing:
sometimes overall similarities, sometimes similarities of detail. I can think
of no better expression to characterize these similarities than "*family
resemblances*"; for the various resemblances between members of a family:
build, features, colour of eyes, gait, temperament, etc. etc. overlap and
criss-cross in the same way.—And I shall say: "games" form a family.
(66-67)

Wittgenstein has, in effect, added the various sorts of language uses
to the family of activities called games. "One might say that the
concept 'game' is a concept with blurred edges" (71); it is a concept
whose use lacks definite boundaries. (68) To say that language uses
are games is simply to blur the edges of the concept "game" a bit more.

In addition to expressing the pluralistic nature of language, the
concept of the language-game also serves to point up that just as in
playing golf or chess so in using language we are doing something
in accordance with rules.[12] According to Wittgenstein "the person
of whom we say 'he has pain' is, *by the rules of the game*, a person
who cries, contorts his face, etc." [13] These rules provide possible uses
or moves. This is illustrated by a discussion of "My arm is broken"
and "I have grown six inches":

There is in these cases the possibility of an error, or as I should rather put
it: The possibility of an error has been provided for. The possibility of
failing to score has been provided for in a pin game. On the other hand, it
is not one of the hazards of the game that the balls should fail to come up
if I have put a penny in the slot. . . . To ask "are you sure that it's *you*

[12] This claim seems to conflict with Wittgenstein's belief that language phenomena have no one thing in common. Whether Wittgenstein maintains the latter
with consistency is much debated; however, at this point the conflict is removed
if the phenomena of acting in accordance with rules also have no one thing in
common.
[13] *The Blue Book*, p. 68. Italics mine.

who have pains?" would be nonsensical. Now, when in this case no error is possible, it is because the move which we might be inclined to think of as an error, a "bad move," is no move of the game at all. (We distinguish in chess between good and bad moves, and we call it a mistake if we expose the queen to the bishop. But it is no mistake to promote a pawn to a king.) [14]

When philosophers talk about language in the way proper to philosophy, "we talk about it as we do about the pieces in chess when we are stating the rules of the game." (108) Just as one cannot play chess or most other games without rules, so one cannot use language without some criteria that determine sense, some agreement in how we use words which enables the hearer to grasp the speaker's intent and, so, to make an appropriate response. The necessity of rules in language is humorously illustrated in Alice's conversation with Humpty Dumpty:

"I don't know what you mean by 'glory,'" Alice said. Humpty Dumpty smiled contemptuously. "Of course you don't—till I tell you. I meant 'there's a nice knock-down argument for you!'"
"But 'glory' doesn't mean 'a nice knock-down argument,'" Alice objected.
"When I *use* a word," Humpty Dumpty said, in rather a scornful tone, "it means just what I choose it to mean—neither more nor less."
"The question is," said Alice, "whether you can make words mean so many different things." [15]

Alice's confusion is further compounded when, a few puzzling moments later, Humpty Dumpty exclaims "Impenetrability!"

"Would you tell me please," said Alice, "what that means?" "Now you talk like a reasonable child," said Humpty Dumpty, looking very much pleased. "I meant by 'impenetrability' that we've had enough of that subject, and it would be just as well if you'd mention what you mean to do next, as I suppose you don't mean to stop here all the rest of your life." "That's a great deal to make one word mean," Alice said in a thoughtful tone. "When I make a word do work like that," said Humpty Dumpty, "I always pay it extra."
"Oh!" said Alice. [16]

Humpty only makes sense when he follows the rules for making sense that have been learned by Alice and the rest of us. Otherwise his language-moves are like moves made in a chess game which are not in accord with the rules of chess. Such moves are senseless, and the opponent cannot make meaningful responses. Consider, then, that

[14] *Ibid.*, p. 67.
[15] Charles Dodgson [Lewis Carroll], *Through the Looking Glass*, in *The Complete Works of Lewis Carroll* (The Modern Library; New York: Random House, n.d.), p. 214.
[16] *Ibid.*

to know the rules for the use of the king in bridge is not necessarily to know the rules for its use in pinochle; similarly, to know the rules for the use of the word "love" in language about persons is not necessarily to know the rules for its use in language about God. Different rules must be learned for the two games, although they may have a close family relationship to each other.

Suppose, for example, I say "I'll give Smith an analysis of the problem tomorrow." The thing that makes this a promise,[17] that gives it that sort of meaning, is that I am acting in accordance with a number of rules or agreements that I share with my hearers. (Compare what makes the movement of a piece of wood a chess move.) These rules require that certain conditions are fulfilled: (1) Something in the situation singles out the problem, e.g., we have just been talking about it; (2) Something in the situation singles out a certain person named Smith; (3) Something in the situation shows that there is some point in my doing this; (4) I am able to make such an analysis and to give it to Smith tomorrow; (5) I intend to do these things; (6) Such and such is the sort of thing we are now calling an analysis; (7) Such and such is what we now mean by "tomorrow," e.g., during working hours; (8) Such and such is what we now mean by giving it to Smith, e.g., it is to be written rather than verbal but Smith will need only a brief outline rather than a detailed presentation in order to understand the analysis.

Rules 6, 7, and 8 are what Wittgenstein calls criteria, and it is with rules of this sort that he is particularly concerned. A criterion is a linguistic convention or rule governing the correct application of a word; it is our agreement about the use of a word to refer to something. "It is part of the grammar of the word 'chair' that *this* is what we call 'to sit on a chair'; . . . in the same way to explain my criterion for another person's having toothache is to give a grammatical explanation . . . concerning the meaning of the word 'toothache.' "[18]

Sometimes, however, we apply a word on the basis of a symptom rather than a criterion: "I call 'symptom' a phenomenon of which experience has taught us that it coincided, in some way or other, with the phenomenon which is our defining criterion."[19] We may say "The home team has won" simply by seeing people leave the ball park in an exuberant way, although this is not what we mean by "The home team has won." It is criteria and not symptoms which "give our words their common meanings."[20] We learn criteria when

---

[17] "Promise" may be too strong here. Perhaps I should say simply "an agreement to do something."

[18] *The Blue Book*, p. 24.   [19] *Ibid.*, p. 25.   [20] *Ibid.*, p. 57.

we learn to use language; we learn symptoms from our experience of the thing to which our language refers.

Often there is not a single criterion for the application of a term but many criteria. If, for example, between 4:00 and 4:30 I expect B to come to tea, my expectation "does not refer to one process or state of mind going on throughout the interval, but to a great many activities and states of mind." [21] What actually takes place may be this:

At four o'clock I look at my diary and see the name of "B" against today's date; I prepare tea for two; I think for a moment "does B smoke?" and put out cigarettes; towards 4:30 I begin to feel impatient; I imagine B as he will look when he comes into my room. All this is called "expecting B from 4 to 4:30." And there are endless variations to this process which we all describe by the same expression.[22]

These criteria, we see, do not have any single feature in common. "They have family likenesses which are not clearly defined." [23] And whether any one of these is a criterion will depend upon the circumstances. For example, if I exclaim "I'm longing to see him" this may be a criterion of expecting B. On the other hand, if this explanation followed some self-observation, Wittgenstein suggests, it might mean "So, after all that has happened, I am still longing to see him." (586) The meaning of the exclamation will vary according to the context.[24]

Learning these rules is a matter of training, of acquiring a skill. "To understand a language means to be master of a technique." (199) Consequently, we cannot clarify the meaning of a word by introspection without regard to the rules governing its use. "It would be as if without knowing how to play chess, I were to try and make out what the word 'mate' meant by close observation of the last move of some game of chess." (316)

Wittgenstein warns us, however, against possible misunderstandings of the sense in which language-games are played according to rules. First of all, he does not mean that rules are directly *involved* in playing the game in the sense that we consciously refer to them—as we might, for example, refer to some sort of table of values in the course of a parlor game. We may play *"in accordance with"* rules without being consciously aware of them or even being able to state them if asked to do so.[25] As G. E. Moore pointed out, to understand the meaning of a sentence is not at all to be able to give an account of that meaning.

[21] *Ibid.*, p. 20.   [22] *Ibid.*   [23] *Ibid.*
[24] For another example see *The Brown Book*, p. 115: "We may say 'Under certain circumstances "He can continue . . ." means he knows the formula.'"
[25] Cf. *The Blue Book*, pp. 13-14, 25; also the *Investigations*, 240.

Wittgenstein gives a second warning of great importance when he contends that "the application of a word is not everywhere bounded by rules." (84) A concept, we remember, may well have blurred edges, its extension "*not* closed by a frontier." (68) Wittgenstein asks, for example, "What still counts as a game and what no longer does? Can you give the boundary? No." (68) For most of the cases in which we use the word "game" the application we are making of it has been established by long practice; everyone customarily or habitually just does call the thing in question a game. But sometimes one person may go beyond established practice in calling something a game, and his listener may simply catch on to this new use because he senses a significant similarity with the established use. In reading poetry, for example, the reader must frequently catch on to new uses in this way. One must also do this in playing dolls with a child or in the case of a fairy tale in which "the pot too can see and hear." (282) At other times the new use may have to be explained, its connection with established use pointed out.[26]

But it is not only new uses that take us beyond the routine and well established. Think, for example, of the variety of cases we might call "irresponsible behavior." Some will be unusual, and we may in some cases be hesitant about whether to call an act "irresponsible." Life is such that our language must be flexible and partially open. "I say 'I am afraid'; someone else asks me: 'What was that? A cry of fear; or do you want to tell me how you feel; or is it a reflection on your present state?'—Could I always give him a clear answer? Could I never give him one?" (P. 187) Some of the things we say, then, may not be placed neatly in one language game or another; I may use an expression "as it were between the games." (P. 188) In his lectures on religious belief, for example, Wittgenstein contends that "there can easily be imagined transitions where we wouldn't know for our life whether to call them religious beliefs or scientific beliefs." [27] Indeed some words "are used in a thousand different ways which gradually merge into one another." [28] To underline this point Wittgenstein asks "and do I always talk with very definite purpose?—And is what I say meaningless because I don't? (P. 188) [29]

We must, then, hold onto two sides of Wittgenstein's position here: (1) we may use language quite flexibly and creatively but (2) this

---

[26] Cf. *The Blue Book*, pp. 9-10.

[27] Barrett, *Wittgenstein: Lectures and Conversations* . . . , p. 58.

[28] *The Blue Book*, p. 28.

[29] Contrast the *Tractatus* (4.112): "Without philosophy thoughts are, as it were, cloudy and indistinct: its task is to make them clear and to give sharp boundaries." (George Pitcher's translation.)

flexibility depends on use that is routine and well established.[30] In his book, *Wittgenstein's Definition of Meaning as Use*,[31] Garth Hallett distinguishes between "occasional use"—individual speech acts—and "institutional use." When Wittgenstein talks of the meaning of a word in our language, Hallett points out, he means the institution of language—our conventional, well established use—rather than individual speech acts.[32] It is this, the institutional use, which we learn when we are taught our language. We are not taught the meaning of one particular speech act but rather something abstract—the "role" or "function" or "grammar." [33] When we learn chess we learn rules rather than memorize particular instances of chess moves. The learning of language is similar except that we sometimes extend the use of words beyond the way it has been taught us.

The third purpose served by the analogy of a game is to emphasize that language, like a game (in most instances), is a *social activity* or institution. "*To obey a rule*, to make a report, to give an order, to play a game of chess, are *customs* (uses, institutions)." (199) [34] As such, language evolves like any other institution. "Commanding, questioning, recounting, chatting, are as much a part of our natural history as walking, eating, drinking, playing." (25) Far from being a fixed matter, new language-games "come into existence, and others become obsolete and get forgotten." (23)

A language-game, in other words, is a part of our culture. "The term 'language-*game*' is meant to bring into prominence the fact that the *speaking* of language is part of an activity, or a *form of life*." (23) [35] This means that our language uses are expressions of culture and, as such, embody attitudes, valuations, perspectives—in short, an organization of experience. A "perspicuous representation" of our grammar [36] "earmarks the form of account we give, the way we look at things." (122) Concepts "are the expression of our interest." (570) Or,

---

[30] "The more abnormal the case, the more doubtful it becomes what we are to say. And . . . if rule became exception and exception rule, or if both became phenomena of roughly equal frequency—this would make our normal language games lose their point." (142.)

[31] (New York: Fordham University Press, 1967.)

[32] *Wittgenstein's Definition of Meaning as Use*, pp. 112-15.

[33] Hallett suggests that this abstract nature of our language as an institution is another reason for concluding that meaning is not something pointed to. (*Ibid.*, p. 115) However, referential theories need simply hold that meaning, at this level of abstraction, concerns the sort of thing referred to.

[34] First italics are mine. In learning a rule we must also learn its application, for a rule may be interpreted in different ways. (185) See also *Remarks on the Foundations of Mathematics*, p. 116, #8.

[35] Last italics are mine.

[36] "Grammar," as Wittgenstein uses the term, "describes . . . the use of signs." (496) That is, it describes our language use.

in a rather different key, Wittgenstein asserts that "grammar tells us what kind of object anything is." (373) The grammar of language about persons, for example, contains an implicit recognition of differences between persons and things. "What has a soul, or pain, to do with a stone? Only of what behaves like a human being can one say that it *has* pains. For one has to say it of a body, or, if you like of a soul which some body *has*." (283)

The analytic philosopher, then, displays our language uses as part of our form of life; [37] but beyond this the philosopher cannot go. "What has to be accepted, the given, is . . . *forms of life.*" (P. 226) "We expect *this*, and are surprised at *that*. But the chain of reasons has an end." (326) "*This is how it strikes me.*" (219) "This is simply what I do." (217) Our final appeal is not to rules, as though these somehow hovered over our form of life and demanded conformity. A language rule is itself simply an agreement in form of life. (241, 224) To ask why we proceed as we do is finally to ask why our way of life is as it is—why we have the agreements that we do. And it is Wittgenstein's contention that we need not have just these agreements; as a matter of fact they change, they have a natural history.[38] But neither are they arbitrary; they reflect our nature and interests and the nature of our world. (P. 56 n.; p. 147 n.; 441) "Our interest certainly includes the correspondence between concepts and very general facts of nature." (P. 230) [39]

It is because language rules are simply well established agreements in our forms of life that we are not completely bound by those rules. That we are able to catch on to the extension of a use is, as Stanley Cavell has so well put it, "a matter of our sharing routes of interest and feeling, modes of response, senses of humor and of significance and of fulfillment, of what is similar to what else, what a rebuke, what forgiveness, of when an utterance is an assertion, when an appeal, when an explanation—all the whirl of what Wittgenstein calls 'forms of life.' " [40] Unlike the logic of language in the *Tractatus*, then, "grammar does not tell us how language must be constructed in order to fulfill its purpose. . . . It only describes and in no way explains the use of signs." (496) Wittgenstein's aim is no longer prescriptive but de-

[37] In the *Blue Book* Wittgenstein speaks of "conventions" in the way he later speaks of "forms of life." Cf. p. 24.

[38] Wittgenstein had not yet come to this view of Rules in the *Philosophische Bemerkungen* ("logic cannot concern itself with the natural history of a word" [p. 59]) or in the lectures reported by Moore (*Mind* [1954], pp. 12-13).

[39] Wittgenstein warns, however, that he is "not saying: if such-and-such facts of nature were different people would have different concepts (in the sense of a hypothesis)." (P. 230)

[40] "The Availability of Wittgenstein's Later Philosophy," *The Philosophical Review*, 1962, reprinted in George Pitcher, *The Philosophy of Wittgenstein*, p. 160.

scriptive. "The aim of grammar is nothing but that of the language." (497) Our language practices simply reflect our forms of life, and no further discussion is open to the philosopher.

As is typical of games, each language-game is played in a particular context or setting and has its own goal, or goals; [41] each performs its own sort of function. A language-game consists both of "language and of the actions into which it is woven." (7) But sometimes when we reflect upon language, rather than simply use it, we concentrate upon the words and overlook the application that we give them and the human activity that is its context. We reflect upon language that is no longer working. It is language on a "holiday." (38) When this happens we are unable to understand the true nature of that language; and so our examination is filled with confusion, meaningless problems are generated, and equally meaningless answers are constructed. *It is this confusion that has produced philosophy.* "When we do philosophy we are like savages, primitive people, who hear the expressions of civilized men, put a false interpretation on them, and then draw the queerest conclusions from it." (194) *Once this confusion is clarified philosophy disappears.* The tools must be returned from the philosophical parlors to the everyday workshops and scientific laboratories where they can be put to work again. In another of Wittgenstein's metaphors, when we philosophize our "language is like an engine idling." (132) It is this conception of philosophy which we must now examine as the third main point in Wittgenstein's position.

When we examine language in abstraction from its applications we are easily deceived by its forms; we fall into "the fascination which the analogy between two similar structures in our language can exert on us." [42] "We remain unconscious of the prodigious diversity of all the everyday language-games because the clothing of our language makes everything alike." (P. 224) In this way we come to see language as quite uniform, and this uniformity suggests that there must be strict rules that underlie it. "The puzzles which we try to remove always spring from just this attitude towards language." [43] Two statements of similar form, then, may be treated as though the rules governing their use were the same. (90) We try to place one statement in the language-game of the other and, so, misinterpret it. (195) Of course, the misplaced statement does not really have a use in that

[41] Our goals change, however, as our form of life changes.

[42] *The Blue Book*, p. 26. The passage continues: "(It is helpful here to remember that it is sometimes almost impossible for a child to believe that one word can have two meanings.)"

[43] *Ibid.* On the same page we read: "This problem about the concept of time asks for an answer given in the form of strict rules." Socrates is then cited as seeking the same sort of answer when he asks "What is knowledge?" See also pp. 17-18 for a discussion of "our craving for generality."

language-game, but this is precisely what we fail to see if we do not ask how the statement is actually used. Whether he is investigating "time" or "meaning" or the "existence of other minds" the philosopher sees the subject too much in terms of its surface grammar—"we predicate of the thing what lies in the method of representing it." (104) Instead we must investigate depth grammar, for it is in this sense of the term that "grammar tells us what kind of object anything is." (373)

This confusion leads the philosopher to ask questions and make statements that do not have a place in any language-game and, so, have no meaning. One might compare them with the question "Is it 5 o'clock on the sun?" (350) or with the command "This—there" when it is made without any accompanying gesture. Such statements are like a switch that has not been connected with a machine. It looks like the other switches that are connected, but unlike them it has no function. The philosopher is led to ask questions and make statements of this sort, because he has become confused about grammar, about the rules governing language use, but does not realize that he is merely dealing with grammar. His statements have the outward appearance of being moves within a language-game, statements that are "empirical" or "experiential," and, consequently, he attempts to interpret them in this way. (295, 360) The philosopher, that is, attempts to use his statements by means of the rules that actually do govern statements about the world we experience and, so, creates the illusion that his statements are meaningful. Rather than being *guided by* the rules of a language-game, his statements are really *about* those rules. Such a statement is one "whose form makes it look like an empirical proposition, but which is really a grammatical one." (251) [44]

This difference between a question asked within a game and one asked about a game can be seen readily in the case of a card game, for example. The question might be asked, within the context of a bridge game, "Is it wise to play my king on his ten?" One might then answer "Yes, because he probably has the ace" or "No, because his partner probably has the ace." The answers make sense in terms of rules governing the relative merit of ace, king, and ten, the taking of tricks, the order of play, the object of the game, some probability rules, etc. Given these rules, the issue is broadly empirical. But if asked "Why does the ace take the king?" one could only answer, "It simply does" or "That is how we play the game." These, of course, are not really answers, but, rather, are refusals of the question. One might be deceived into thinking that it was a genuinely "empirical" question, because, formally, it looks much like the question "Why did he take my king with his ace?" Grammatical questions, of course, may be quite mean-

[44] Cf. *Zettel*, sect. 458; *The Blue Book* p. 35.

ingful when they are recognized to be grammatical and are directed toward a real grammatical uncertainty. One might ask, for example, "Does the ace always take the king?" in order to be sure there are no exceptions to the rule he has learned. It is when they are treated as experiential that they no longer have any use.

This is the sort of mistake that the philosopher makes when he asks, "Do material objects exist?" This looks like the empirical question "Do pink elephants exist?" but it is really grammatical. As a matter of fact, we do play a material object language-game. "Material object" is a grammatical category. When we ask about material objects we are really asking about the rules of use (including the attitudes, valuations, etc. which they embody) of the language-game we play in connection with a certain range of objects, which includes elephant bodies, desks, tables, etc.

Philosophy, then, as Wittgenstein sees it, lies outside of our language-games and is based upon grammatical confusion. But what is the justification for this position? Why should we not rather say that philosophy is itself a language-game with its own special purpose, such as inquiring about the ultimate nature of reality, what sorts of things there are, how we know about them, and so forth? The answer to this lies basically in two themes carried over from the *Tractatus*: (1) the limits of language (with its corollary distinction between what can be said and what shows itself), and, (2) the contrast or exclusion necessary if we are to give sentences an application, interrelating them with our human activities. Let us consider these in order.

The Contrast Principle

First, as we may recall, in the *Tractatus* Wittgenstein viewed the philosopher as attempting to say something about the structure of the world and, consequently, about the structure of language that pictures it. But the philosopher is running his head up against the limits of language, for he must use the structure of language to talk and so cannot talk about it. The structure of language and, so, of the world can be seen only as "showing" itself in the language.

In the *Investigations*, Wittgenstein describes philosophical confusions as the "bumps that the understanding has got by running its head up against the *limits of language*." (119) [45] According to Wittgenstein, "grammar tells what kind of object anything is." (373) The philosopher's mistake is to try to talk about what can only be told or shown by our grammar. The philosopher asks about the essential nature of things, but "*essence* is expressed by grammar." (371)

Furthermore, this distinction between what can be said and what can

[45] Italics mine.

only show itself rests on a principle of contrast which is closely related to the principle of exclusion on which this distinction rested in the *Tractatus*. In both books the essential idea is that to be informative in asserting a proposition we must know under what conditions we would judge that proposition to be false; "It is raining" is informative because it might not be raining and if it were not raining then the assertion "It is raining" would be false. And in both books metaphysical assertions are shown not really to be assertions because there are no conditions under which we would judge them to be false. But this idea is developed in important ways in the *Investigations*.

In the *Tractatus* the assertion of an elementary proposition excludes only its denial. Were it also to exclude certain other propositions it would violate the doctrine of the mutual independence of elementary propositions—the view that the truth or falsity of an elementary proposition is unrelated to the truth or falsity of any other. But trouble begins when we try to find an example of such a proposition. "This is right of that," if it is elementary, must exclude only "It is not the case that this is right of that." Yet it clearly seems also to exclude "This is left of that," "This is on top of that," etc. Similarly, "This is red" apparently excludes "This is blue"; and "This is sharp" apparently excludes "This is dull." Any ascribable property or relation apparently excludes other properties or relations. Because of this problem, by 1929 Wittgenstein concluded that "atomic propositions . . . may exclude one another" [46] and, by 1930, he spoke of "the *system* of propositions." [47]

In the *Investigations*, Wittgenstein holds that propositions are not independent but must be seen in terms of their place in a language-game. The place of a proposition in a game is marked by the range of propositions which it excludes and which therefore provide it with what Wittgenstein now refers to as contrast. "This is red" contrasts with "This is blue," "This is colorless," etc.[48]

The idea of exclusion is also broadened in another important way. Wittgenstein no longer applies it to only one use of language—that of making assertions. In the following passage he applies it to giving commands:

But now it looks as if when someone says "Bring me a slab" he could mean this expression as *one* long word corresponding to the single word "Slab!" . . . We mean the sentence as *four* words when we use it in contrast with

[46] "Some Remarks on Logical Form," p. 168.
[47] *Philosophische Bemerkungen*, pp. 317, 10-11.
[48] It also excludes "This is not red," as in the *Tractatus*. In the *Brown Book* Wittgenstein asks: "Did you say it had a peculiar smell, as opposed to no peculiar smell, or that it had this smell, as opposed to some other smell?" (P. 158)

other sentences such as "*Hand* me a slab", "Bring *him* a slab," "Bring *two* slabs," etc.; that is, in contrast with sentences containing the separate words of our command in other combinations.—But what does using one sentence in contrast with others consist in? . . . We say that we use the command in contrast with other sentences because *our language* contains the possibility of those other sentences. (20)

For each of the words in "Bring me a slab" our language provides a range of possible contrasts. Which of these we are using in giving the command will depend on the situation. In some situations "Bring me a ———" is understood, and so the only contrasts being used are slab, block, pillar, beam—i.e., there is no question of tossing as opposed to bringing, or of bringing two instead of one. In other situations "Bring ——— slab" is understood, and the two sets of contrasts employed are me, him and one, two, three.

It is crucial to notice that when Wittgenstein speaks of using "Bring me a slab" in contrast with "Hand me a slab" this is in contrast with the *use* of "Hand me a slab" and not simply with the words. A word has a range of contrasts in a language-game only if both the word and its contrasts have possible applications. This helps to explain how it may happen that we fail to use a sentence contrastively and yet believe that we are successfully using it in this way; in such cases we have in mind a range of contrasts (learned in other language-games) but we fail to realize that we have not given these contrasts any application. I may judge that "Mumsiroves love sinners" contrasts with "Mumsiroves *hate* sinners" or with "Mumsiroves love the *righteous*" and yet not know how to apply any of these forms of words. In metaphysics I may judge that "Material objects do not exist" contrasts with "Material objects *do* exist" or with "*Mental* objects do not exist," and yet here too there may not be any applications. In theology I may judge that "God loves sinners" contrasts with "God *hates* sinners" or with "God loves the *righteous*" and yet again not know how to apply any of these contrasts.[49]

Once we break away from the idea stressed in the *Tractatus* that contrasts or oppositions are limited to affirmation and denial, the principle of contrasts may be seen, upon reflection, to apply to all language-games—even to nonverbal communication. What we say has sense only because we are saying one thing *rather than* another thing that we might conceivably say—one thing as opposed to another. I ask for the salt rather than the sugar, express joy rather than boredom, frown

[49] We may find this helpful in understanding Wittgenstein's comment on his childhood training in the use of the word "God": " 'Did you understand what this word meant?' I'd say: 'Yes and no. I did learn what it didn't mean. . . . I could answer questions . . . and in that sense could be said to understand.' " (Barrett, *Wittgenstein: Lectures and Conversations* . . . , p. 59)

rather than smile. According to Wittgenstein, the things we say should be seen as moves in a game, and a game provides a set of alternative moves. Wittgenstein comments on his failure to understand someone who says "My idea of death is the separation of the soul from the body" that "If he says this, I won't know yet what consequences he will draw. I don't know what he *opposes* this to." [50] Bearing in mind that, in language, rules often are inexact and concepts often have blurred edges, we may say that the place of a sentence in a language-game is marked by the range of sentences with whose application it contrasts.

In *Wittgenstein's Definition of Meaning as Use*, Garth Hallett rejects this sort of interpretation, arguing that Wittgenstein (1) applies the principle of contrast solely to descriptive uses of words and (2) explicitly accepts certain contrastless uses as meaningful. Concerning the first point, Hallett fails to consider that Wittgenstein's later views on contrast are not identical with those he held in the *Tractatus*,[51] and no mention is made of Wittgenstein's discussion (in section 20 of the *Investigations*) of the contrasts involved in giving commands. The second point refers to the *Brown Book* discussion of intransitive uses that are part of our ordinary language.[52] For example, the word

---

[50] Barrett, *ibid.*, p. 69.

[51] See Hallett, *Wittgenstein's Definition of Meaning as Use*, p. 120. One of Hallett's main arguments is that "some words seem to have no boundaries at all (77)" and so cannot have any contrasts (p. 119). Wittgenstein's "exhortation to bring words back from their metaphysical to their everyday use (116) does not apply to ethical and aesthetical terms, to 'beautiful' and 'good.' For he apparently thought that in their *everyday* use, these terms not only 'merge without a hint of any outline,' but are used without even ill-defined contrast: 'anything—and nothing —is right' (77)." (P. 121) But this is a misinterpretation of section 77. "Anything—and nothing—is right" *if* we try to draw sharp boundaries around concepts whose boundaries are quite blurred—i.e., drawing the boundary here is no more right than drawing it there. In 77 Wittgenstein uses the illustration of a picture "which consists of colour patches with vague contours." (76) "But if the colours in the original merge without a hint of outline won't it become a hopeless task to draw a sharp picture corresponding to the blurred one? . . . 'Here I might just as well draw a circle or heart as a rectangle.' " (77) I may, of course, refer to a patch of color as red (rather than some other color) whether or not it has sharp outlines. Hallett sees support for his view of the non-contrastive use of aesthetical terms on pp. 1-4, 11 of *Lectures and Conversations* where Wittgenstein argues that they are used typically as interjections rather than as descriptions. But even on these pages the contrastive nature of interjections is intimated when Wittgenstein asks, "What *makes* the word ['beautiful'] an interjection of approval?" and then adds in a footnote "and not of disapproval or of surprise, for example?" (p. 2, #5). The vagueness of boundaries does have *this* implication for contrasts: just as a word's applications may not be sharply defined so its range of contrasts may not be either. The listener must catch on to the speaker's new application, and to do this is to catch on to the implied contrasts. The closer the new is to the well established applications the easier it is for the listener to do this, of course.

[52] *The Brown Book*, pp. 158-67.

"mean" is used intransitively in "I said I was sick of it and meant it." [53] Taken transitively its point would be I mean *this* rather than *that* or *that* or *that*. But here its point is to give a kind of emphasis to "I said that I was sick of it." In other words, since "meant" is used intransitively here, "it" is being used non-contrastively.

But this argument misses the point; Wittgenstein's principle of contrast is that a word gets its sense (in any language-game) from the contrasts it *can* be used to make (in that language-game). It retains that sense (in that language-game) even when it is not used to make those contrasts. In Section 20 Wittgenstein shows that for each of the words in "Bring me a slab" our language provides a range of possible contrasts but that which of these we are using in giving a command will depend on the situation. If there were only slabs to be brought I would not be using "slab" contrastively in that situation; even so, I do not give just any word that place in the sentence, and "slab" is the correct one because of the contrasts it *can* be used to make. Similarly, in "I said I was sick of it and meant it" the word "it" is not being used for its possible contrasts, but it has them and that is what makes it the appropriate word here—we could not, for example, just as well use "something else" in place of "it." Notice, incidentally, that "meant" *is* being used here contrastively; we may see it as opposed to something like "didn't really mean it" or "didn't want to make too much of it"—although its sense will vary somewhat with the context.

Occasionally, in certain circumstances, none of the words in a sentence will be used contrastively. *If* "Bring me a slab" were the only order conceivable [54] in the circumstances—say, I am working alone with an assistant, there are only slabs to be brought and only one at a time, the assistant has no other responsibility that requires an order [55] —then I am not using any of these words contrastively.

Here one might just say "Bring" or "Slab" or simply use a gesture or a thumping sound. Or, a more plausible case of no word being used with contrast would be "I am here" [56] in response to another asking "Where are you?" In this case, one might simply say "here" or

---

[53] *Ibid.*, p. 161. The point of Wittgenstein's discussion of this sentence is that "there are many troubles which arise in this way, that a word has a transitive and an intransitive use, and that we regard the latter as a particular case of the former." (P. 160)

[54] Perhaps "reasonably to be expected" is more accurate here. For example, even if one might conceivably say, "Go home, you're not well," we would still not be using "Bring me a slab" in contrast with "Go home" unless the situation presented this alternative as a live possibility.

[55] Perhaps it must also be evident here to the assistant that a slab is now needed; otherwise the present moment seems to be constituted by the "bring"–"don't bring" contrast, so that "bring" contrasts with the otherwise implied "don't bring."

[56] In the *Blue Book*, Wittgenstein discusses "the philosopher who thinks it makes sense to say to himself 'I am here.'" (P. 72)

just whistle. But the point remains that none of these words would have *sense* in this sentence unless they also have contrastive uses in the language-game being played.

Words that do not have contrastive uses are really not words at all; they are not part of language. According to Wittgenstein, the sense of a word is not the way someone reacts to it but rather its place in that (often rather loose) set of alternative applications which Wittgenstein calls a language-game: "A sound is an expression only as it occurs in a particular language-game." (261) I may train my dog to react to the sound "slab" by getting a certain object for me but I do not, in this way, teach my dog the concept of "slab"—I do not teach him what "slab" means in our language, how we use it. His response is not that of following a rule. Wittgenstein's discussion, early in the *Investigations*, of the language-game in which the assistant is to pass the builder a block, pillar, slab, or beam according to the builder's command (2) may seem, at first reading, to contradict our interpretation here. He asks, "Don't you understand the call 'Slab!' if you act upon it in such-and-such a way?" (6) However, he also says that children are taught this game by learning the use of these words, so that they know how to give the commands as well as how to respond to them (6, 7, 9, 10). And this is just what my dog cannot do—use these words. He cannot use barks according to rules; he may give and respond to barks but not as moves in a game. This distinction between language-use and conditioned response has been discussed at length by Rush Rhees,[57] a former student of Wittgenstein's, and also by Dennis O'Brien[58] in distinguishing Wittgenstein's views from the behavioristic theory of meaning.

It is this principle of contrast which is used by Wittgenstein to show that metaphysical statements are meaningless. They are not part of a special metaphysical language-game because it is the very nature

---

[57] "Can There Be a Private Language?" *Proceedings of the Aristotelian Society*, Supplementary Vol. XXVIII (1954); used by permission of the editor. Reprinted in *Wittgenstein*, ed. George Pitcher. Rhees argues that "if people merely carried out orders and made certain utterances when they were ordered . . . they would not be speaking. I suppose people might be trained to do that with Greek sentences without knowing Greek. And the people in our example would not understand what they were saying. They could not do that unless they used the expressions themselves, and using them is not just doing what you are told to do with them." (Pitcher, p. 277.)

[58] "The Unity of Wittgenstein's Thought," *International Philosophical Quarterly* 6, No. 1 (1966), reprinted in K. T. Fann, ed., *Ludwig Wittgenstein: The Man and His Philosophy*. "But if 'Go left!' is meaningful when he goes left or he doesn't go left, then the fact that it is meaningful determines no state of affairs at all. . . . The noise 'Go left' does not have meaning like a conditioned reflex . . . but because it is seen as a move in a game. . . That an order is meaningful determines . . . a range of possible behavior that would be regarded as obeying and disobeying and so on." (P. 402)

of a language-game to provide contrasting applications, and the words found in metaphysical statements have no contrasting application in metaphysics. When philosophers try to talk about material objects, for example, saying they do or do not exist, their statements are compatible with every possible state of affairs. Whatever a philosopher says on this issue, he will not deny that he sees the hand Moore is waving.

Metaphysical statements, then, are not those made by persons that we know in some other way to be metaphysicians. They are statements whose "use" has no contrast, and they are made by all sorts of people. Wittgenstein takes one example from popular science:

We have been told by popular scientists that the floor on which we stand is not solid, as it appears to common sense, as it has been discovered that the wood consists of particles filling space so thinly that it can almost be called empty. This is liable to perplex us, for in a way of course we know that the floor is solid, or that, if it isn't solid, this may be due to the wood being rotten but not to its being composed of electrons. To say, on this latter ground, that the floor is not solid is to misuse language. . . . As in this example the word "solidity" was used wrongly and it seemed that we had shown that nothing really was solid, just in this way, in stating our puzzles about the *general vagueness* of sense-experience, and about the flux of all phenomena, we are using the words "flux" and "vagueness" wrongly, *in a typically metaphysical way, namely without an antithesis;*[59] whereas in their correct and everyday use vagueness is opposed to clearness, flux to stability, inaccuracy to accuracy, and *problem* to *solution.*[60]

Psychoanalysts and mathematicians are others mentioned as sometimes needing philosophical therapy.[61]

Metaphysical statements grow out of a "discontentment with our grammar"[62] for "every particular notation stresses some particular point of view"[63] and "our ordinary language, which of all possible notations is the one which pervades all our life, holds our minds rigidly in one position, as it were, and in this position sometimes it feels cramped."[64] Because of this cramp the metaphysician creates "a new way of speaking" (400), "a new way of looking at things"—

[59] Italics are mine.   [60] *The Blue Book*, pp. 45-46.
[61] "The psychoanalysts . . . were misled by their own way of expression into thinking that they had . . . discovered conscious thoughts which were unconscious." (*Blue Book*, p. 57) "What a mathematician is inclined to say about the objectivity and reality of mathematical facts, is not a philosophy of mathematics, but something for philosophical *treatment.*" (254)
[62] *The Blue Book*, p. 57.   [63] *Ibid.*, p. 28.
[64] *Ibid.*, p. 59. Wittgenstein continues: "Thus we sometimes wish for a notation which stresses a difference more strongly, makes it more obvious, than ordinary language does, or one which in a particular case uses more closely similar forms of expression than our ordinary language. Our mental cramp is loosened when we are shown the notations which fulfill these needs. These needs can be of the greatest variety."

something that is quite similar to inventing "a new way of painting, or, again, a new metre, or a new kind of song." (401) Others then respond by attacking his statements and, in effect, defending the old way of speaking; the dispute really concerns grammar but neither side is aware of this.

For *this* is what disputes between Idealists, Solipsists and Realists look like. The one party attack the normal form of expression as if they were attacking a statement; the others defend it, as if they were stating facts recognized by every reasonable human being. (402)

We shall explore this view at some length in our discussion of its development by John Wisdom.

The metaphysician, then, thinks of his statements as empirical, but they are really grammatical; they do not *say* something about the world but rather *show* us something about either our old grammar or an alternative to it. Here we recall Wittgenstein's statement in the *Tractatus* that its statements did not have empirical sense but were elucidatory, showing something about the logic of our language. This places us on familiar ground when, in the *Investigations*, Wittgenstein says, concerning the proposition "Every rod has a length," that

that means something like: we call something (or *this*) "the length of a rod"—but nothing "the length of a sphere." [65] Now can I imagine 'every rod having a length'? Well, I simply imagine a rod. Only this picture, in connection with this proposition, has a quite different role from the one used in connection with the proposition 'This table has the same length as the one over there.' For here I understand what it means to have a picture of the opposite. . . . But the picture attaching to the *grammatical* proposition could only *show*, say, what is called 'the length of a rod.' And what should the opposite picture be? (251)[66]

Grammatical propositions show something about our grammar; empirical propositions say something about our world. This grammatical-empirical distinction parallels the familiar distinction between analytic and synthetic statements.

But here it may seem that we have located the Achilles heel of the principle of contrast. Surely "A triangle is a three sided plane closed figure" and "Every rod has a length" are sentences whose use is strictly contrastless. We are apt to feel this way if we simply stare at them without remembering to ask how we actually use them. The language-games in which we actually use them, however, do provide contrasting applications.

[65] Compare the *Blue Book*, p. 30: "'The room has length' can be used . . . [to say] that a sentence of the form 'The room is ——— feet long' makes sense."
[66] Italics mine.

"A triangle is a three-sided plane closed figure" has a typical use in teaching the meaning of "triangle." Perhaps in this game the teacher asks Johnny to point to some triangles, and he points rather to rectangles. Here the teacher may say, "But a triangle is *not* a *four*-sided figure." Or perhaps Johnny pointed to a three-sided *open* figure or only to triangles with an interior angle of 90°, and the teacher might say, "A triangle is a *closed* figure" or "A triangle need not have an interior right angle although *some* triangles do."

Wittgenstein treated grammatical propositions in just this way. First, he often pointed out that the metaphysician has failed to provide any contrasting applications for his use of these statements: "Only whom are we informing of this? And on what occasion?" (296)[67] Second, Wittgenstein points out that there are occasions in which grammatical statements have a use, cases "in which we are conversant with" a point of grammar, "but have to be reminded of it." (253) I was looking at our grammar in *that* way but your reminder has brought me to look at it in *this* way. It may be useful, for example, to remind the behaviorist of a difference between the grammar of "He is in pain" and that of "I am in pain." Notice, too, Wittgenstein's contention that "Every rod has a length" "means something like: we call something, (or this) 'the length of a rod'—but nothing 'the length of a sphere.'" (251) The statement has meaning, that is, in a situation in which the contrast rod-sphere is useful. We can imagine a teacher saying, "Every triangle has interior angles but some closed figures do not—circles do not."

Even in the case of grammatical statements, then, words are used meaningfully only in a language-game in which they have contrasting applications. These contrasts constitute the limits of their language-game. What is characteristic of statements made outside the limits of our language-games—whether in philosophy, psychology, mathematics, or religion—is that, since they are compatible with all situations, there are no particular situations in which their use is called for. They have no applications in any of our activities—no role to play. Metaphysical statements make no difference.

This question of application becomes particularly subtle because of the role that pictures play in our thinking and speaking, a role to which Wittgenstein devotes a major part of his considerations. We often use pictures to aid us in applying the rules of our language-

---

[67] Wittgenstein is here discussing the objection, "Yes, but there is something there all the same accompanying my cry of pain." Compare 398: " 'But when I imagine something . . . I have *got* something which my neighbor has not.' . . . What are these words for? They serve no purpose. . . . If as a matter of logic you exclude other people's having something, it loses its sense to say that you have it."

games. "Light travels in a straight line" provides us with a picture that is helpful in dealing with many sorts of light phenomena. Or, the logician speaks of the *in*clusion of one class *in* another class, the spatial metaphor "in" expressing the picture of one circle inside of another which he uses as an aid in working with the rules of his logic. All goes well as long as we are using these pictures or "models," as they are now often referred to, in the language-game in which their use has become customary. But, when we begin to reflect about language, we are in danger of carrying over the picture used in one language-game to another language-game in which it has no application, and, so, this would result in our misinterpretation of that type of language. "What is the meaning of 'justice'?" we may ask. "Well, what is the meaning of 'Jones'?" [68] Perhaps here a picture presents itself of both the word "Jones" and the Jones whom it names. If we carry this picture back to the question about "justice," we may picture an idea subsisting in a realm underlying the world that we see. "When we look into ourselves as we do philosophy," explains Wittgenstein, "we often get to see just such a picture. A full-blown pictorial representation of our grammar." (295) Such a representation, especially under nonphilosophical circumstances, "may indeed safely point a way to further use of a sentence. On the other hand a picture may obtrude itself upon us and be of no use at all." (397)[69] Machine drawings perform a function. Pictures such as we hang on the wall are idle. (291) Wittgenstein's challenge, then, to philosophical picture-gazing is to say: "The picture is there. . . . But *what* is its application?" (424)[70]

Attack on Dualism and Private Language

Wittgenstein applies this challenge to, among other things, the frequent philosophic use of a *picture* of the noetic situation as consisting of one or more ontological realms in which exist the referents of our language. This is a mistake which he believes is shared by monism, both mentalistic and materialistic-behavioristic, but it is to the dualistic version of this error that Wittgenstein devotes a major portion of his attention. In this dualistic version it is supposed that, in addition to a public material world of objects-events-processes, there is a private mental world of objects-events-processes, conceived as closely analo-

---

[68] Strictly speaking, proper names do not have meanings. Their use is not institutionalized as the use of concepts is.

[69] David Pole seems mistaken, then, in saying that "Wittgenstein seems to recognize no positive role at all as belonging to them [i.e., pictures]." (*The Later Philosophy of Wittgenstein* [London: The Athlone Press, 1958], p. 91.) See especially Sect. 144 in the *Investigations*.

[70] See also sects. 352 and 374.

gous to the material. Lying behind my reference to the red book I am holding is my inner experience, whose object is a private entity accessible to no one else, a content of my consciousness and mine alone. If I say "I am in pain," I am reporting a private inner event, a private feeling of pain that occurs in my consciousness. "Understanding" stands for an inner process, and, consequently, the meaning that is understood is something in my mind which underlies its public expression in language. This view or picture of meaning as something separate from its expression in linguistic behavior is, of course, directly opposed to Wittgenstein's view of meaning as use, so that his discussion of it throws considerable light on his own position. It will be helpful, then, for an understanding of Wittgenstein's position, to follow the heart of that discussion.

For a good example of the dualism being opposed, we may turn to John Locke.

Since the mind in all its thoughts and meanings, hath no other immediate object but its own ideas, which it alone does or can contemplate; it is evident, that our knowledge is only conversant about them. Knowledge then seems to me to be nothing but the perception of the connection and agreement or disagreement and repugnance, of any of our ideas.[71]

On the role of language, Locke's view was that

the mind by degrees growing familiar with some of them [particular ideas], they are lodged in the memory, and names got to them. Afterwards the mind, proceeding farther, abstracts them, and by degrees learns to use the general names. In this manner the mind comes to be furnished with ideas and language.[72]

Now, according to Wittgenstein, the basis of metaphysical dualism is the construction of the picture of an inner world by using, as a model, our picture of physical objects, events, and processes. We are "tempted" to take this view by certain analogies at the level of surface grammar—certain similarities in form of expression—such as that between:

"to say something"
"to mean something."

We seem here to be referring to two processes that run side by side.[73]

[71] An Essay Concerning Human Understanding, Bk. IV, Chap. i, in Locke's Philosophical Works, ed. J. A. St. John (London: George Bell and Sons, 1908), II, 179.

[72] Ibid., Bk. I, Chap. ii, in Locke's Philosophical Works, I, 142-43.

[73] The Blue Book, p. 35.

The process of succumbing to this analogy goes like this:

How does the philosophical problem about mental processes and states . . .
arise?—The first step is the one that altogether escapes notice. We talk of
processes and states and leave their nature undecided. Sometime perhaps
we shall know more about them—we think. But that is just what commits
us to a particular way of looking at the matter. For we have a definite
concept of what it means to learn to know a process better. (The decisive
movement in the conjuring trick has been made.) (308)

In this way we come to picture mental processes and states as very
much like physical processes and states, and this picture makes it look
as though the meaning of what we say must somehow be located in the
inner process. The meaning, it then seems, must be something inner,
something underlying its outer expression in words. To borrow from
Gilbert Ryle, it would be silly to ask "Is the tide rising or are your
hopes rising?" or to ask "Did you come home in a car or in a flood of
tears?" We make a similar mistake when we ask, "Is meaning an inner
event or an outer event?" In these cases the questioner fails to see that
two different meanings of "rising," "come home in," and "event" are
involved. That such a picture is inappropriate may be seen from the
fact that it has no application.

First of all, even if we assume that all linguistic behavior is accompanied by some sort of inner event, this picture cannot successfully be
applied as an explanation of the nature of meaning. One may argue,
for example, that the meaning of "red" must be an inner idea, for
only by reference to such an idea could I identify this color in external
objects. But how, then, Wittgenstein asks, are we to identify this inner
idea? (308) Or, one may argue, in learning a numerical series, such as
1, 8, 27, 62, . . . we cannot be said to understand it until we experience
that flash of understanding which makes it possible for us to continue
the series correctly. The inner experience, it is alleged, accounts for
the difference between understanding and not understanding the
series. But it may happen that I have such an experience and exclaim
that I now understand, yet find that my subsequent continuation of
the series is incorrect. Therefore, if this inner "act of understanding"
can take place and be followed by an incorrect response, its occurrence
is not adequate to account for a correct response.

Consider, too, that if I stare at this inner experience I do not see
some sort of label attached to it which reads "flash of understanding." [74]
I am able to call it that because it has often occurred in the context
of a certain sort of activity—e.g., receiving instruction in something

[74] Compare "My kinaesthetic sensations advise me . . ." (P. 185).

and then trying to do it correctly.[75] "What is happening now has significance—in these surroundings. The surroundings give it its importance." (583)

Even the occurrence in my mind of an image does not show understanding, for it is not automatically an image of something—it does not somehow carry with it the necessity of being applied in one particular way. The word "tree" may evoke in my mind the image of a tree, and yet I may take this image as representing an instance of something beautiful, or something tall, or something living, etc. The correct application of a word cannot be determined by an image, for the correct application of an image must itself be learned.[76]

Furthermore, this picture of a separate inner realm has no application or relevance to the activity of communication. Wittgenstein gives the following illustration of this irrelevance in connection with the view that the meaning of the word "pain" is a private inner event to which the word refers:

Now someone tells me that *he* knows what pain is only from his own case!—Suppose everyone had a box with something in it: we call it a "beetle." No one can look into anyone else's box, and everyone says he knows what a beetle is only by looking at *his* beetle.—Here it would be quite possible for everyone to have something different in his box. One might even imagine such a thing constantly changing.—But suppose the word "beetle" had a use in these people's language?—If so it would not be used as the name of a thing. The thing in the box has no place in the language-game at all; not even as a *something:* for the box might even be empty.[77]—No, one can "divide through" by the thing in the box; it cancels out, whatever it is.

This is to say: *if we construe the grammar of the expression of sensation on the model of "object and designation"* the object drops out of consideration as irrelevant. (293)[78]

The last sentence does not say that the experience of pain is irrelevant but only that it would be *if* we attempted to use the word "pain" to refer to something private—or, more accurately, if we attempted to use the word "pain" on the basis of the model or picture of a private inner realm, a private inner room that is furnished by the experiences that our words refer to much as our outer rooms are furnished by

[75] Similarly, of intending or meaning something, Wittgenstein argues: "an intention is embedded in its situation, in human customs and institutions." (337) An inner experience may accompany my meaning something, but the experience does not come labeled. The meaning of "intention" must be taught, and the teacher cannot enter into my mind, as it were, to label experiences. See also 581.

[76] Or an image may have different applications depending on the circumstances: "the same thing can come before our minds when we hear a word and the application still be different." (140)

[77] A habitual use of language not generally accompanied by a particular experience would correspond to the empty box, for example.

[78] Last italics are mine.

various objects to which we may point. In short: "If as a matter of logic you exclude other people's having something, it loses its sense to say that you have it." (398) Language must be pictured rather as a number of tools that have evolved in a *community* to serve its interests and purposes (although putting it this way can also be misleading)[79] We learn pain language in connection with such purposes as giving medical aid or sympathy, purposes that arise in connection with those circumstances in which crying, wincing, and other expressions of pain are appropriate. "What would it be like if human beings showed no outward signs of pain (did not groan, grimace, etc.)? Then it would be impossible to teach a child the use of the word 'tooth-ache.'" (257) Furthermore,

if anyone said "I do not know if what I have got is a pain or something else," we should think something like, he does not know what the English word "pain" means. . . . That expression of doubt has no place in the language-game. (288)[80]

Nor can this picture of meaning as an inner event underlying its outward expression in words be applied to explain why "if a lion could talk, we could not understand him." (P. 223) To explain this we must point out that a lion could not use words as we do for the same reason that a talking machine could not use words as we do: our use of words is interwoven with activities of which neither lions nor machines are capable. The sense of our words is deeply rooted in our form of life.

This picture of inner objects and processes as part of all our speaking also lacks application in that much of our language behavior becomes a matter of habit and, so, is not accompanied by any special inner experience. Speaking, listening, reading, and writing are skills to be mastered. (199) Saying "good morning," though perfectly meaningful, is generally as automatic as tying shoes. In a recent comic strip Blondie asks for a good-night kiss while Dagwood is engrossed in the evening paper. Dagwood's response is to rise and walk off saying, "Yes, yes, dear, I'll get you one."

[79] We must not think here of purpose as something well defined and fixed as it is, for example, in cooking: " 'Cookery' is defined by its end, whereas 'speaking' is not. That is why the use of language is in a certain sense autonomous, as cooking and washing are not. . . . Language is not defined for us as an arrangement fulfilling a definite purpose. Rather 'language' is for us a name for a collection." (*Zettel*, sects. 320, 322) To think of definite, fixed aims, that is, would lead us to think of language too much as a system.

[80] It was failure to realize that meaning could not be separated from community purposes and their circumstances that resulted in the problem of solipsism which we have seen in the case of Russell and which was shared by atomists and positivists alike.

This rejection of the dualistic picture of inner events and processes as very much like outer events and processes and, in the case of language, as underlying the outer should not be construed as expressing a behavioristic theory of meaning. Wittgenstein is not denying the experience of pain, for example, nor is he excluding it as a factor in our use of language about pain. He is rather rejecting the approach to language that uses this particular ontological picture. " 'Are you not really a behaviourist in disguise?' " Wittgenstein asks himself. " 'Aren't you at bottom really saying that everything except human behaviour is a fiction?'—If I do speak of a fiction then it is of a *grammatical* fiction," he replies, using "grammatical fiction" to refer to the *ontological* picture of an inner realm separated from an outer realm. (307) It is a grammatical fiction because it lacks any application. Behaviorism grows out of the dualistic split into separate ontological realms and a subsequent rejection of one of those pictured realms. But this leaves the behaviorist with an ontological picture that leaves out those mental factors to which the dualist had applied an inappropriate picture.

Because this point is central to Wittgenstein's position, it merits further substantiation and elaboration. " 'But you will surely admit that there is a difference between pain-behaviour accompanied by pain and pain-behaviour without any pain?' " Wittgenstein again asks himself. "Admit it?" he exclaims. "What greater difference could there be?—'And yet you again and again reach the conclusion that the sensation itself is a *nothing*.'—Not at all. It is not a *something*, but not a *nothing* either!" (304) To say that pain is not something existing in an alleged mental realm underlying a separate physical world is not to say that pain is unreal. "The conclusion was only that a nothing would serve just as well as a something about which nothing could be said. We have only rejected the grammar which tries to force itself on us here." (304) "Grammar," we remember, refers here to the role that the picture of a separate inner realm allegedly has in guiding our linguistic activity. But, the questioning continues,

"you surely cannot deny that, for example, in remembering, an inner process takes place." . . . The impression that we wanted to deny something arises from our setting our faces against the *picture* of the 'inner process'. What we deny is that the *picture* of the inner process gives us the correct idea of the use of the word "to remember." We say that this *picture* with its ramifications stands in the way of our seeing the use of the word as it is. (305)[81]

When the philosopher, then, contemplates language apart from its actual use, there is nothing to prevent a picture from insinuating itself

[81] Italics mine.

into his thinking which has no application to his subject. Speaking of his earlier work in the *Tractatus*, Wittgenstein remarks, "A *picture* held us captive. And we could not get outside it, for it lay in our language and language seemed to repeat it to us inexorably." (115)

While I am a captive of this sort of picture, I believe, as Wittgenstein did in the *Tractatus*, that the meanings of my inner experience constitute a private language, "*the* language which I alone understand" (*Tractatus* 5.62), because no one else can have my experiences. No one else can enter my inner room. (398)[82] The words of this language have meanings that obviously cannot be taught to me; I give them their meanings by using them to label the various experiences that furnish my inner room. My private meanings of "red" and "pain," then, are entirely independent of anything I can be taught by another who points to red objects and to other persons in pain and, while pointing, explains that this is what *we* call red and that is what *we* call being in pain. "The words of the language are to refer to what can only be known to the person speaking; to his immediate private sensations." (243)

Furthermore, as long as I am a captive of the inner process or inner room sort of picture, I naturally think that I understand such instructions as "that is what we call being in pain" on the basis of my prior knowledge from my own case of what "pain" means. In other words, I can only understand the meanings of our public language on the basis of the meanings of my private language. It is this point of view which lies behind the belief that I can only infer the existence of an external world or of other minds—the belief that I can know other minds only by drawing an analogy from my knowledge of my own mind. This was the point of view, for example, of Descartes and of the classical British empiricists.

Wittgenstein examines the idea of a private language to show that such a thing could not have the characteristics of language at all. We must remember here that by "private" Wittgenstein does not mean a language that no other person happens to share. Since the language refers solely to my experience—the furniture of my inner room—it is a language that no other person could possibly share. Such a "language" could not have any function, for (1) my use of this language would be something that I do privately, (2) there would be then no distinction between thinking I am doing it and really doing it, and (3) there would be then no distinction between doing it correctly and incorrectly. In introducing a word in a private language

---

[82] When we use the inner room picture we may have been misled by the following analogy between surface grammars: "I say, 'I describe my state of mind' and 'I describe my room.'" (290)

"you must inwardly *undertake* to use the word in such-and-such a way. And how do you undertake that? (262) What is it I undertake to do? Suppose, for example, I identify an experience as prain by fixing my attention on it and saying to myself "This is prain." Have I really identified my experience here? Was there, then, something about the experience which I did not know until I told myself? And once I have told this to myself must I also judge whether what I have told myself is true or false? Might I say to myself, I believe this is prain but perhaps I am mistaken? And if I could intelligibly say this, what rules could I have for determining the truth of my belief? Perhaps the rule is that it must be the same experience as the one I had on such and such a date. But what rule determines what is to count as the same? What counts as the same depends upon the purpose to be served in making such a judgment.[83] In public language we have such purposes but in a private language they would be lacking.[84] "And hence also 'obeying a rule' is a practice. And to *think* one is obeying a rule is not to obey a rule. Hence it is not possible to obey a rule 'privately': otherwise thinking one was obeying a rule would be the same thing as obeying it." (202)[85] In such cases "whatever is going to seem right to me is right, and that only means that here we can't talk about 'right.' " (258) We can see what Wittgenstein is driving at here if we ask what difference it would make if my memory of past experiences of prain kept changing so that I identified all sorts of very different things as prain.[86]

There are, then, no meanings that only I can understand, for meaning is use and private use is not an intelligible idea.

Why can't my right hand give my left hand money?—My right hand can put it into my left hand. My right hand can write a deed of gift and my left hand a receipt.—But the further practical consequences would not be those of a gift. When the left hand has taken the money from the right, etc., we shall ask: "Well, and what of it?" And the same could be asked if a person had given himself a private definition of a word; I mean, if he has said the word to himself and at the same time has directed his attention to a sensation. (268)

[83] See 350, 378, 185, 223, 225, 215, 216, 258, 270.
[84] In 258 Wittgenstein introduces the case in which "I want to keep a diary about the recurrence of a certain sensation. To this end I associate it with the sign 'S.' " He then argues at length that "a note has a function, and this 'S' so far has none." (260)
[85] Compare: "A person goes by a sign-post only in so far as there exists a regular use of sign-posts, a custom" (198), and "Are the rules of the private language *impressions* of rules?" (259)
[86] Similarly, Wittgenstein admonishes: "Always get rid of the idea of the private object in this way: assume that it constantly changes, but that you do not notice the change because your memory constantly deceives you." (P. 207)

But neither could something private which I know "only from my own case" be a basis for my knowledge of things outside of myself. When I ascribe pain to another I have only his behavior as my criterion for doing so; I cannot, as it were, get behind his behavior— I cannot see the "beetle" in his box. But what would be the connection between his behavior and what I might mean by "prain" when, in my private language, I refer to my private experience? My own pain behavior can serve as this connection only if I regard it as a criterion by which others may ascribe pain to me; but if I make this connection then what I mean by "prain" in my own case is no longer something private. In other words, if what I mean by "prain" in my private language has nothing to do with the behavior of others then it can play no part in what I mean when I ascribe pain to others;[87] but if what I mean by "prain" is connected with behavior then the meaning is not private.[88]

Similarly, my private meaning for "red" could not be the basis of my public use of it. In our public language I know what the other means by "red" by noticing the objects to which he applies it. If I am in doubt about how he understands it I can ask him to point to several red objects. But what connection would there be between my private "use" of "red" to refer to my private sensation and the activity of the other in pointing to red objects? If I say that I too might point to those objects on the basis of my private knowledge of red and that this forms the connection then my private meaning is no longer private, for another can ask, "Is this what you mean by 'red'?" As Wittgenstein concludes,

The essential thing about private experience is really not that each person possesses his own exemplar, but that nobody knows whether other people also have *this* or something else. The assumption *would* thus be possible— though unverifiable—that one section of mankind had one sensation of red and another section another. (272)[89]

---

[87] This seems to be the point of Wittgenstein's comment that "if one has to imagine someone else's pain on the model of one's own, . . . I have to imagine pain which I *do not feel* on the model of pain which I *do feel*." (302)

[88] Wittgenstein considers the objection, "But if I suppose that someone has a pain, then I am simply supposing that he has just the same as I have so often had." His reply is that I do not understand "It's 5 o'clock on the sun" if I simply think " 'It is just the same time there as it is here when it is 5 o'clock.' . . . What I do not know is in what cases one is to speak of its being the same time here and there. . . . One will say that the stove has the same experience as I, *if* one says: it is in pain and I am in pain." (350)

[89] Second italics are mine. Wittgenstein continues: "What am I to say about the word 'red'?—that it means something 'confronting us all' and that everyone should really have another word, besides this one, to mean his *own* sensation of

When we stop to consider our everyday use of language we do not find any role being played by an allegedly *private* sensation.

Look at the blue sky and say to yourself "How blue the sky is!"—When you do it spontaneously—without philosophical intentions—the idea never crosses your mind that this impression of colour belongs only to *you*. And you have no hesitation in exclaiming that to someone else. And if you point at anything as you say the words you point at the sky. (275)

Or, consider the case of pain. From the private language point of view one will say, "I can only *believe* that someone else is in pain, but I *know* it if I am." (303) But this does not accord with our everyday use of language in either the third person or the first person cases. Often I am sure that the other is in pain and simply say, "He is in pain." "Just try—in a real case," Wittgenstein suggests, "to doubt someone else's fear or pain." (303) But I do not say, "I *know* I am in pain," for the word "know" would have no contrast in this case—it does not contrast, for example, with "I'm not sure, but I may be in pain." I may, in some cases, be in doubt about the other's pain but not about my own. I use criteria in saying, "He is in pain" but not in saying, "I am in pain." Nor do I use criteria when I groan.

The main thrust of Wittgenstein's argument may be put quite simply: first and third person uses must be learned together. Both those who argue "from my own case" and those who argue behavioristically make the mistake of thinking that one of these uses may be learned before the other. The concept "pain," for example, is used in reference to both the sensation and the behavior, for these are two sides of the same coin rather than two different coins. If I say, "I am in pain" and you say of me, "He is in pain," we are referring to the same thing, even though I experience it rather than observe it, and you observe it rather than experience it. Consider the argument that since your pain behavior is in most circumstances a sufficient criterion for me to say, "You are in pain," it follows that I must be referring only to your behavior when I say this; this argument is analogous to the contention that since the shape of the piece is a sufficient criterion for me to say, in a game of chess, "This is the king" it follows that I must be referring only to the shape when I say this. "Pain" has its meaning in a language-game where it is used in both first and third person sentences.

P. F. Strawson has developed this line of argument powerfully in

---

red?" (273) And again, "If I know it only from my own case, then I know only what *I* call that, not what anyone else does." (347)

connection with the concept "person." [90] This is the concept of "something which is both a subject of experiences and a part of the world";[91] in terms of our preceding discussion, "person" is the concept of something that is the subject of both first and third person sentences —the concept in which inner experience and behavior are indissolubly related. Just as first and third person uses must be learned together, so "it is a necessary condition of one's ascribing states of consciousness, experiences, to oneself, in the way one does, that one should ascribe them (or be prepared to ascribe them) to others who are not oneself." [92] I cannot know of your case by first knowing of my case because if I lack the concept of "yours" or "his" I lack the concept of "my." If I knew only of my case, "my" would have no contrast. "The idea of a predicate is correlative with that of a range of distinguishable individuals of which the predicate can be significantly . . . affirmed." [93] Or, as John Wisdom has put it, attributing a property means "marking an affinity between something and other things." [94] If one is to conceive of a private-language, then, one must do so without any reference to the concept of being a self. In their full-length study, The Private-Language Problem, John Saunders and Donald Henze conclude that Wittgenstein's attack on private language becomes decisive when developed in this way.[95]

Curing the Philosopher's Language Confusion

If all this is true, how is the philosopher to be cured of his illusions? How can one "show the fly the way out of the fly-bottle?" (309) Wittgenstein's answer may be seen in his remarks on Augustine's famous expression of puzzlement about the meaning of "time": "Something that we know when no one asks us, but no longer know when we are supposed to give an account of it, is something that we need to remind ourselves of." (89) What we need to do is to remind ourselves "of the kind of statement that we make about phenomena. Thus Augustine recalls to mind the different statements that are made about the duration, past, present, or future, of events." (90) We

---

[90] "Persons," Minnesota Studies in the Philosophy of Science, Vol. II, eds. Herbert Feigl, et al. (Minneapolis: University of Minnesota Press, 1958); reprinted in Wittgenstein and the Problem of Other Minds, ed. Harold Morick (New York: McGraw-Hill, 1967). (A revised and expanded version of this article may be found in P. F. Strawson, Individuals [London: Methuen, 1959], Ch. 3.)

[91] "Persons," p. 128.

[92] Ibid., p. 136. Compare the Investigations (398): "If as a matter of logic you exclude other people's having something, it loses its sense to say that you have it."

[93] Ibid., n.

[94] "The Metamorphosis of Metaphysics," reprinted in Paradox and Discovery (Oxford: Basil Blackwell, 1965), p. 68.

[95] (New York: Random House, 1967), pp. 185-88.

should remind ourselves, in other words, about the way in which a word is used "in the language-game which is its original home." (116) Fundamentally, the idea is to study the use of the word in paradigm cases, helpful examples of its use in our ordinary, nonmetaphysical statements. What Wittgenstein provides is "a number of sketches of landscapes" of some areas of our language which have given rise to philosophic perplexity, sketches in which one of our uses of language is approached from many different directions. (Preface, ix.) Some of the cases used in making these sketches are found in our actual use. Others are invented; these are imagined uses of language which, by comparison and contrast, throw light upon our actual use. (122) These sketches or reminders then *must be arranged* "so that if you looked at them you could get a picture of the landscape." (Preface, ix.) We must come to see the intricate connections between our various uses. (122) It is this clear picture of our use, this "perspicuous representation," which will cure the philosopher of his puzzlement.

This does not mean that there is only one correct view of the workings of our language: "We want to establish an order in our knowledge of the use of language: an order with a particular end in view; one out of many possible orders; not *the* order." (132) To look for *the* order would be to forget that "language is a labyrinth of paths." (203) Since there are many different problems or perplexities to be solved in achieving a clear view of our language, the philosopher will use more than one method for this purpose. (133)

Wittgenstein's methods are, in fact, quite varied. Sometimes intermediary cases are invented:

What makes us use the expression "seeking in our memory," when we try to remember a word? . . . One might say that the case which looking in your memory for something is most similar to is not that of looking for my friend in the park, but, say, that of looking up the spelling of a word in a dictionary.[96]

Sometimes he imagines language in a world different from our own:

Let us imagine the following: The surfaces of the things around us (stones, plants, etc.) have patches and regions which produce pain in our skin when we touch them. . . . In this case we should speak of pain-patches on the leaf of a particular plant just as at present we speak of red patches. (312)

Elsewhere, misunderstanding is "removed by substituting one form of expression for another" (90)—a technique developed particularly by

[96] *The Brown Book,* p. 129. See *Investigations,* 122.

Russell. For example, " 'The room has length' can be used as a grammatical statement. It then says that a sentence of the form 'The room is —— feet long' makes sense." [97] Or Wittgenstein points out that we are trying to talk *"outside* a particular language-game" (47), asks whether there are contrasting applications (251) or in what context we are speaking (117),[98] reveals a picture which is holding us captive (308), shows misleading parallels in surface grammar,[99] asks how the use of the expression is taught (p. 185), etc.

To summarize, we have interpreted the *Investigations* as a profound revision of the *Tractatus.* The concept of the limits of language has been retained in revised form as the concept of the limits of our many language-games; and with this retention has been preserved the distinction between what can be said by our logic or grammar and what must show itself through that grammar. The move from language to language-games is a move from the reductionism, which had so far characterized analytic philosophy, to a recognition that there are many different sorts of meaning. To get clear about the meaning of a term we must study the use to which we actually put it in our everyday or technical language-games. We must see how it is interrelated with a set of human activities—the role that it plays in these activities. When we look at metaphysical language in this way, we discover that it does not play a role in any of our ordinary activities and so is idle, useless, meaningless. It comes into being when, in reflecting on language rather than using it, we ask questions that are really about the grammar of our language-games although we think they are empirical. Questions asked within a language-game are meaningful because they make use of the contrasts (red: non-red) provided by that game and of the rules of that game for using those contrasts. But metaphysical questions are not asked within a language-game; they fail to provide the contrasts that give answers significance in denying one side of the contrast and fail to provide rules to guide our thinking. The person speaking metaphysically fails to see this, because he carries over into this speaking a sense of the rules that his terms have in the language-game that is their home.

It is worth remarking that Wittgenstein's position has significant

---

[97] *The Blue Book,* p. 30.

[98] R. A. Wollheim applies this to Bradley's view that language is too general ever to refer to a particular object or event: "It [Bradley's view] ignores the whole context in which words are used. It treats them not as arrows that we, the marksmen, aim at targets: but as missiles that take themselves there, or fall wide of the mark." ("F. H. Bradley," *The Revolution in Philosophy,* A. J. Ayer, *et al.,* p. 18.)

[99] *The Blue Book,* p. 35.

kinship with Kant's. Compare especially knowledge of grammar with what Kant called transcendental knowledge. According to Kant:

Not every kind of knowledge *a priori* should be called transcendental, but that only by which we know that—and how—certain representations (intuitions or concepts) can be employed or are possible purely *a priori.* The term "transcendental," that is to say, signifies such knowledge as concerns the *a priori* possibility of knowledge or its *a priori* employment.[100]

And according to Wittgenstein, "Our investigation . . . is directed not towards phenomena, but, as one might say, towards the 'possibility' of phenomena." (90)

Four Frequent Criticisms

We shall consider four criticisms of Wittgenstein which have special relevance to our concern with assertions in religion. The first two, we shall argue, are based on mistaken, or at least doubtful, interpretations of Wittgenstein but may properly be directed at a number of his followers. Specifically we shall consider criticisms of (1) Wittgenstein's alleged view that a form of life is beyond criticism, (2) his alleged prejudice against the inner or nonobservable, (3) his definition of meaning as use, and (4) his attack on private language.

Wittgenstein is commonly interpreted to hold that a form of life is beyond rational criticism. And, since ordinary language is part of a form of life, it too is held to be immune from such criticism. At issue here is the nature of man's reflective powers and, consequently, the nature of his philosophical activities. The question is whether reflective reason plays a part in cultural change or whether cultural evolution is a purely nonrational process. Wittgenstein is alleged to deny reflective reason a creative role in cultural change either on the narrow thesis that reason is a rule-bound activity or on the related but broader thesis that reason must presuppose a form of life as the context of its activity and so cannot criticize what it must presuppose. Both theses seem to lean heavily, for their plausibility, on the assumption that a culture or form of life is rather uniform and, so, does not suffer from deeply rooted stresses, strains, and contradictions; both theses also gain plausibility if the history of philosophy is not seriously studied but rather is dismissed as the history of conceptual confusion.

---

[100] *Critique of Pure Reason,* trans. N. Kemp Smith (New York: Macmillan, 1956), p. 96. For a fuller description of this comparison see Stanley Cavell, "The Availability of Wittgenstein's Later Philosophy," pp. 175-77. Cavell points out that Kant also speaks of the "transcendental illusion" that we know what transcends the conditions of possible knowledge.

The narrower thesis that reason is a rule-bound activity is attributed to Wittgenstein by both David Pole and Ernest Gellner.[101] Calculating the sum of 2 and 2 is an example of such rule-bound reasoning. Reasoning must take place in some language-game, and Wittgenstein is alleged to have regarded language-games as "rule-bound activities." [102] We cannot reason about the rules of our language-games for reasoning must presuppose those rules. On Pole's interpretation, "we are to think of two factors in language; on the one hand, particular moves or practices which are assessed by appeal to the rules, and, on the other hand, those rules themselves. Beyond these there is no further appeal." [103] Wittgenstein, then, allegedly pictures our language-games as separate, self-contained, self-sufficient activities—monad-like entities.[104]

We have already presented arguments that Wittgenstein did not regard language as rule-bound. Here we shall simply add two observations. First Wittgenstein does seem to recognize standards for judging new uses of language. They must, we have argued, provide contrasting applications. And in the *Blue Book* Wittgenstein discusses a new use of language by a diviner ("I feel in my hand that the water is three feet under the ground") and refers to one explanation of this new use as a "perfectly good" one.[105] Second, there are passages that suggest that language-games are interrelated. "Our language," for example, "can be seen as an ancient city: a maze of little streets and squares, of old and new houses, and of houses with additions from various periods; and this surrounded by a multitude of new boroughs with straight regular streets and uniform houses." (18) Or, in the *Zettel*, Wittgenstein speaks of "seeing life as a weave" [106] and contends that "one pattern in the weave is interwoven with many others." [107]

Nor does Wittgenstein restrict reasoning to rule-bound activity. In addition to discursive reasoning, as we may call it, Wittgenstein recognizes what we may call intuitive reasoning—our power to grasp a pattern or gestalt. In *Remarks on the Foundations of Mathematics*, for example, he discusses the creation of new systems of mathematics. And, in his preface to the *Investigations* Wittgenstein describes his aim as arranging his "sketches" "so that if you looked at them you could get a picture of the landscape." Drawing our attention to features of this landscape is a form of reasoning; according to G. E. Moore, Wittgenstein contended that reasons in philosophy, like those

---

[101] See David Pole, *The Later Philosophy of Wittgenstein*, and Ernest Gellner, *Words and Things* (Boston: Beacon Press, 1960).
[102] *Words and Things*, p. 150.
[103] *The Later Philosophy of Wittgenstein*, p. 61.
[104] *Ibid.*, p. 95.   [105] P. 10.
[106] Sect. 568.   [107] Sect. 569.

in ethics and aesthetics and law, function to "draw your attention to a thing," to "make another person see what you see." [108] As John Wisdom has suggested, such reasons argue the philosopher's point of view not in the way that links form a chain but rather in the way that legs support a chair.

The *Investigations* is itself an outstanding example of the creative use of reflective reason. In the preface Wittgenstein tells us that he is presenting a new way of thinking and wishes to present it "by contrast with and against the background of my old way of thinking [in the *Tractatus*]." His aim is to change our way of seeing.[109] It is for this purpose that he creates the language-game played in the *Investigations* with its special uses of such terms as "meaning," "rules," "grammar," "language-games," etc. "Every particular notation stresses some particular point of view." [110] Seen in this way, one even finds something of importance in the confusions of metaphysicians: "What you have primarily discovered is a new way of looking at things." (401) "In a certain sense," therefore, "one cannot take too much care in handling philosophical mistakes, they contain so much truth." [111] Our reasoning and other language uses tend to be routine—"it is difficult to deviate from an old line of thought just a little" [112]— but Wittgenstein's interest was in creative rather than routine thought.

Wittgenstein attacks metaphysics not, as Pole and Gellner believe, because it is an attempt to move beyond rule-bound language-games but because its statements are contrastless. Gellner understands the contrast requirement to have the consequence that we cannot use language to examine existing contrasts, for such use, he believes, would be without contrast.[113] Against this alleged consequence, he argues that "the job of philosophy is perhaps to unravel presuppositions of old contrasts or discover contrasts where hitherto none had been perceived" and that "a most important kind of thinking consists of *reassessing* our terms, the norms built into them and the contrasts associated with them." [114] But, the use of language involved here is grammatical, and, as we have argued, Wittgenstein recognized that

---

[108] "Wittgenstein's Lectures in 1930-33," *Mind*, Jan., 1955, p. 19.

[109] In the *Zettel*, for example, Wittgenstein explains: "I wanted to put this picture before your eyes, and your *acceptance* of this picture consists in your being inclined to regard a given case differently; that is to compare it with *this* series of pictures. I have changed your *way of seeing*. (I once read somewhere that a geometrical figure with the words 'Look at this,' serves as a proof for certain Indian mathematicians. This looking too affects an alteration in one's way of seeing.) . . . I cannot illumine the matter by fighting against your words, but only by trying to turn your attention away from certain expressions, illustrations, images, and *towards* the employment of the words." (Sects. 461, 463) Cf. *Investigations*, 144.

[110] *The Blue Book*, p. 28.   [111] *Zettel*, sect. 460.   [112] *Ibid.*, sect. 349.
[113] *Words and Things*, p. 42.   [114] *Ibid.*, pp. 43, 44.

grammatical statements may well be used contrastively; statements of philosophers which are metaphysical (i.e. without contrast) when put forward as empirical, may well express something important (and have contrast) when put forward as grammatical. Although Wittgenstein did not write about the philosophical activity recommended by Gellner, his principle of contrast is entirely consistent with such activity.

According to Pole, Wittgenstein disallowed creative activity at the grammatical level because he discredited "those pictures and analogies that guide or govern the progress of new inquiry." [115] But here, too, we have already argued for a different interpretation. Wittgenstein contended, for example, that "the use of expressions constructed on analogical patterns stresses analogies between cases often far apart. And by doing this these expressions may be extremely useful." [116] And certainly Wittgenstein used the language-game analogy extensively to govern the new enquiry of the *Investigations*.

Wittgenstein is more commonly interpreted to have held that reason must presuppose a form of life as the context of its activity and so cannot critically examine what it must presuppose. Stanley Cavell, for example, in his (surprisingly) caustic criticism of Pole, contends that "Wittgenstein does not discuss whether language-games *ought* to be played for that would amount to discussing either (1) whether human beings ought to behave like the creatures we think of as human; or (2) whether the world ought to be different from what it is." [117] Forms of life, it seems, are beyond rational criticism.

A number of passages in Wittgenstein seem to support this view. First of all, he spoke of a form of life as "what has to be accepted, the given." (P. 226) Second, since language is part of a form of life, the following statements are also relevant: "Philosophy may in no way interfere with the actual use of language; it can in the end only describe it" (124); "we must do away with all *explanation* and description alone must take its place" (109); "every sentence in our language 'is in order as it is'" (98); "is this [everyday] language somehow too coarse and natural for what we want to say? *Then how is another one to be constructed?*" (120); "what we have rather to do is to *accept* the everyday language-game, and to note *false* accounts of the matter *as* false. The primitive language-game which children are taught needs no justification; attempts at justification need to be rejected" (p. 200); "our mistake is to look for an explanation . . . where we ought to have said: *this language-game is played*" (654).

[115] *The Later Philosophy of Wittgenstein*, p. 95.
[116] *The Blue Book*, p. 28.
[117] "The Availability of Wittgenstein's Later Philosophy," pp. 158-59.

But Wittgenstein, after all, writes rather aphoristically, and one aphorism finds its qualification in another. These passages, then, do not necessarily imply that language uses and their forms of life are beyond rational criticism. Against this way of interpreting them we wish to point out (1) they have as their context the limited aims of Wittgenstein's way of doing philosophy, (2) Wittgenstein recognized that "human beings alter their concepts," and (3) there is evidence that Wittgenstein believed deeply in the importance of consciously evaluating one's form of life and deliberately seeking to alter it.

Wittgenstein referred to his activity as simply "one of the heirs of the subject which used to be called 'philosophy.' "[118] His concern was limited to "problems arising through a misinterpretation of our forms of language." (111) When he says, then, that *we* must accept as given a language-game or a form of life, that *we* must do away with explanation, and that *we* ought to say simply "this language-game is played" Wittgenstein is not setting down universal rules. "We," here, does not mean anybody at all no matter what his aims; "we" is anyone seeking therapy for philosophical illness. These "musts" are prescriptions for those who have run their heads against the limits of language.

Even in the activity of philosophical therapy Wittgenstein does not follow these "musts" in any slavish way. Having said, for example, that we must do away with explaining he nonetheless offers the following explanation of our pain language-game:

It is a help here to remember that it is a primitive reaction to tend, to treat, the part that hurts when someone else is in pain. . . . But what is the word "primitive" meant to say here? Presumably that this sort of behaviour is *pre-linguistic*: that a language-game is based *on it*, that it is the prototype of a way of thinking and not the result of thought. . . . Our language-game is an extension of primitive behaviour.[119]

Context is also important in interpreting such statements as "every sentence in our language 'is in order as it is.' " The context here is Wittgenstein's preoccupation with his earlier belief that there is an ideal form for language. He continues after the above statement: "that is to say, we are not *striving after* an ideal, as if our ordinary vague sentences had not yet got a quite unexceptional sense, and a perfect language awaited construction by us." (98) Again and again he returns to this point: "It is not our aim to refine or complete the system of rules for the use of our words in unheard-of ways" (133); "it is wrong to say that in philosophy we consider an ideal language as op-

---

[118] *The Blue Book*, p. 28.
[119] *Zettel*, sects. 540, 541, 545. See also sects. 391, 656.

posed to our ordinary one." [120] It is in this sense that our ordinary language is in order as it is and is not to be interfered with—nor is it necessary for purposes of philosophical therapy to interfere with it. Nothing is said here about never changing ordinary language.

Second, Wittgenstein recognizes that human beings "alter their concepts." He states explicitly that a reform of language "for practical purposes, an improvement in our terminology designed to prevent misunderstandings in practice, is perfectly possible." (132) New facts may also require conceptual revision:

It is a fact of experience that human beings alter their concepts, exchange them for others when they learn new facts; when in this way what was formerly important to them becomes unimportant, and *vice versa*. (It is discovered e.g., that what formerly counted as a difference in kind, is really *only* a difference in degree.[121]

Or, again, through reflection a contradiction may be uncovered and require new rules. Particularly in mathematics "a language-game can lose its sense through a contradiction." [122]

Third, Wittgenstein seems to have believed deeply in the importance of consciously evaluating one's form of life and deliberately seeking to alter it. This finds strong support in certain characteristics of Wittgenstein's Austrian background. The nature of this background finds expression in the following largely neglected passage:

The sickness of a time is cured by an alteration in the mode of life (*Lebensweise*) of human beings, and it was possible for the sickness of philosophical problems to get cured only through a changed mode of thought and of life. . . .

Suppose the use of the motor-car produces and encourages certain illnesses, and mankind is plagued by such illness until . . . it abandons the habit of driving.[123]

In seeking, then, to cure philosophical sickness, Wittgenstein sees himself in this passage to be encouraging a change in form of life.

[120] *The Blue Book*, p. 28. It is instructive that Wittgenstein's disciple John Wisdom says of metaphysical statements, "They are needed where ordinary language fails, though it must not be supposed that they are or should be in some perfect language." ("Philosophical Perplexity," *Proceedings of the Aristotelian Society*, 1936; reprinted in *Philosophy and Psycho-Analysis*, p. 50.)

[121] *Zettel*, sect. 352.

[122] *Remarks on the Foundations of Mathematics*, part II, sect. 80; see also sects. 77, 78.

[123] *Ibid.*, Part I, App. II, No. 4.

He was in fact deeply alienated from much of the university life of his time.[124]

This passage reflects the situation in Austria at the end of the Austrian monarchy—a background that Wittgenstein shared with Freud [125] and Kafka. A sense of dissolution—of the illness of the time—was widespread in Wittgenstein's Austria and was expressed in a widely read book of the period entitled *Lebensformen*.[126] Erich Heller tells us that Wittgenstein especially admired Karl Kraus, a contemporary Austrian poet and the author of a volume entitled *Language*, who "suspected that institutions could not be but corrupt if the idiom of the race was confused, presumptuous and vacuous, a fabric of nonsense, untruth, and self-deception." [127] Against this background we see better the man who regarded Kierkegaard as "by far the greatest philosopher of the nineteenth century." [128] Far from regarding forms of life as beyond rational criticism, Wittgenstein was obsessed with the problems of curing the sickness of a time. This he was attempting for philosophy, for "the philosopher is the man who has to cure himself of many sicknesses of the understanding before he can arrive at the notions of sound human understanding." [129] And in the Preface to his *Investigations* Wittgenstein expresses the hope that his work "in the darkness of this time . . . [might] bring light to one brain or another." Forms of language and life may well require a therapy in which reflective reason plays a key role.

It should be noted, too, that Wittgenstein was quite sensitive to conflict between divergent cultural practices. Karl Britton reports, for example, concerning a walk with Wittgenstein, that "as we passed Swansea's immense new Guildhall, Wittgenstein expressed horror and

[124] Cf. Karl Britton, "Portrait of a Philosopher," *The Listener*, June 16, 1955; reprinted in Fann, *Ludwig Wittgenstein: The Man and His Philosophy*, pp. 59, 62. Britton reports that Wittgenstein was "horrified" at the "clever conversation of the dons" because they "talked like that only to score."

[125] Stanley Cavell finds significant parallels between Wittgenstein and Freud in "their discovery that knowing oneself is something for which there are methods" (p. 178) and in their wish "to prevent understanding which is unaccompanied by inner change. Both of them are intent upon unmasking the defeat of our real need in the face of self-impositions which we have not assessed (sect. 108), or fantasies ('pictures') which we cannot escape (sect. 115)." (P. 184)

[126] Reported by Stephen Toulmin in an unpublished lecture. The author was Eduard Spranger.

[127] E. Heller, M. O'C. Drury, N. Malcolm, and Rush Rhees, "Ludwig Wittgenstein: A Symposium," *The Listener* (Jan. 28 and Feb. 4, 1960); reprinted in Fann, *Ludwig Wittgenstein*, p. 65. Among other Austrians, Heller also mentions the composer Schönberg and the architect Loos ("whose teaching and example is clearly discernible in the mansion that Wittgenstein designed and built in Vienna") who sought a renewed integrity in their disciplines, fighting against the merely sentimental and ornamental. (Pp. 65-66.)

[128] Reported by M. O'C. Drury in "Ludwig Wittgenstein: A Symposium," p. 70.

[129] *Remarks on the Foundations of Mathematics*, part IV, sect. 53.

disgust. . . . He said it was the architecture of a religion which nobody now professed." [130]

Whatever be the correct interpretation of Wittgenstein, however, the relativistic belief that forms of life are not properly open to critical evaluation is, I believe, quite mistaken. Cultural relativism thrives in the context of the classical empiricist view of man as a blank slate on which experience writes out a form of life. The question, we might say, is whether mind is simply a tool in the service of needs and interests as these are shaped by experience or whether mind contributes needs of its own to our life as persons—the need for some kind of conceptual unity, for example. From the point of view of the natural law tradition a man's greatest need is to develop and exercise his distinctively human potentialities—e.g. the potentiality for meaning and freedom through self-chosen goals. If there is truth in this view, then forms of life may be judged by how well they contribute to the realization of our potentialities. It is in this way that reflective reason may play a significant role in cultural change.

Reason is effective, however, only in conjunction with other forces of cultural change, particularly those of science and technology. Its role in such change is to discern the new possibilities that these forces create, bringing them to conscious articulation and shaping the form of their future realization.

Now in the course of undergoing change a culture or form of life is subject to deeply rooted stresses, strains, and contradictions. Language becomes more and more confused as old uses come into increasing conflict with new uses. The history of philosophy, I believe, is above all the history of man's reflective response to these conflicts, his attempts to clarify them and to regain a conceptual and valuational coherence that is firmly rooted in present realities—and all of this informed by his sense of himself and of what it means to be human. In view of the enormity of this enterprise it is not surprising that the philosopher has often been confused and muddled, and one can only welcome the insights of a Wittgenstein into the sources of these confusions. But those who deny that reflective reason has a significant role to play in the transformations of our forms of life seem to be inattentive to the serious study of the history of philosophy and to the conceptual stresses and strains that mark cultural change.

There are also other sources of confusion—and indeed of distortion —in our language practices and their forms of life. We have learned much about these sources from Marx, Freud, Nietzsche, Kierkegaard, and the like. It is notable in this connection that, in addition to his

[130] "Portrait of a Philosopher," p. 60.

high regard for Kierkegaard, Wittgenstein was also much interested in Freud.

But particularly important to our concerns with religious language is the question whether the uses of one language-game may conflict with those of another. I believe that they may because our language-games are not separate and self-contained practices. Helpful as it is in drawing our attention to the plurality of our language functions, Wittgenstein's model of language-games becomes misleading when it blinds us to the sense in which language is also a unity—the games significantly interrelated.

First of all, the organization of our experiences, purposes, concerns, sensitivities, and the like with which a particular language use is bound up is part of a wider organization of these factors; for our form of life does not divide into neatly separable components. Consider, for example, that our value experience does not belong to a special compartment of life but pervades all our activities; consequently, we give expression to value in all our language-games. It is, in fact, not the exception but the rule that a single speech act functions in two or more ways at once. "John! Do you realize the speed limit here is 55?" may function simultaneously to express feeling, to convey information, and to command to slow down. Language is bound up with a continuous range of richly variegated and complexly interrelated experience and activity.

Second, and closely related, is Pole's point that language-games "do not break away from their common origin" and consequently that "language is unitary by reason of certain structural concepts that appear constantly throughout the plurality of its parts." [131] As we have discussed in connection with G. E. Moore, our language activities have a common foundation in the basic fund of meanings or uses common to all who speak that language. For example, in defining the basic concepts of a technical language such as psychology, physics, philosophy, or theology one must use the language of everyday. (Cf. 120) And through these different uses run such concepts as "cause," "truth," "knowledge," and "time."

Further, if "grammar tells us what kind of object anything is" then grammars may be significantly interrelated because they deal with the same object. A case in point is the fruitful discussions between existentialism, psychotherapy, theology, and other disciplines on the nature of man.

I am contending that conceptual revision is a legitimate and important activity, and that, although Wittgenstein reserves the term "phi

---

[131] *The Later Philosophy of Wittgenstein*, pp. 92-3.

losophy" for his own therapeutic aims, still his point of view is consistant with conceptual revision. It is simply in terms of its function in clearing up conceptual confusion that Wittgenstein contends that philosophy simply describes, assembles reminders, puts everything before us. (124, 126, 127) There are, however, several critical points to be made about this account of therapeutic philosophy.

First of all, Wittgenstein saw traditional philosophy too much in terms of linguistic confusion. By his own admission he had read comparatively little philosophy[132] and seemed to look at all philosophy in terms of his own *Tractatus* and the confusions he saw there.

Second, description is by no means the only thing that Wittgenstein does in the *Investigations*. He contends that his philosophy "neither explains nor deduces anything" (126), advances no theses,[133] and makes no generalizations about language (there being nothing common to all we call language) (65). Yet in fact he does all these things. We have already noted Wittgenstein's explanation of our pain language-game as "an extension of primitive behaviour." [134] We have seen, too, that Wittgenstein argues *deductively* that something private cannot be a language.[135]

That Wittgenstein does put forward important and controversial theses even though this was not his purpose is commonly recognized by his interpreters.[136] Wittgenstein's important argument that there cannot be a private language is based on his theses or generalizations about language that "the meaning of a word is its use in the language" (43) and that a language use is an agreement in practice. Were these not meant as generalizations about language, then showing that we cannot give sense to the idea of a private agreement (202) would not establish the conclusion that there cannot be a private language. Consider, too, that Wittgenstein's attack on metaphysical statements as meaningless stands or falls on the thesis or generalization that a word

---

[132] See Karl Britton, "Portrait of a Philosopher," pp. 60-61.

[133] Wittgenstein maintained that "if one tried to advance *theses* in philosophy . . . everyone would agree to them." (128)

[134] *Zettel*, sect. 545.

[135] For similar interpretations see Malcolm, "Wittgenstein's *Philosophical Investigations*" (1954), reprinted in Pitcher, ed., *Wittgenstein: The Philosophical Investigations*, p. 75; Moreland Perkins, "Two Arguments Against a Private Language" (1965), reprinted in Morick, ed., *Wittgenstein and the Problem of Other Minds*, p. 98; Pole, *The Later Philosophy of Wittgenstein*, p. 19, n.

[136] See George Pitcher, *The Philosophy of Wittgenstein* (Englewood Cliffs, N.J.: Prentice-Hall, 1964), p. 323; Carl Wellman, "Wittgenstein's Conception of a Criterion" (1962), reprinted in Morick, *Wittgenstein and the Problem of Other Minds*, pp. 162-63; Paul Feyerabend, "Wittgenstein's *Philosophical Investigations*" (1955), reprinted in Pitcher, p. 104; P. F. Strawson, "Review of Wittgenstein's *Philosophical Investigations*" (1954), reprinted in Pitcher, p. 64; Perkins, "Two Arguments Against a Private Language," p. 98; Charlesworth, *Philosophy and Linguistic Analysis*, p. 124; Pole, *The Later Philosophy of Wittgenstein*, pp. 79-80.

has meaning only if its application contrasts with the application of other words. And, among other generalizations, we may mention the contentions that our final criteria for the correct application of a term are publicly observable characteristics of the thing referred to rather than an allegedly private sensation or mental picture, that "the speaking of language is part of . . . a form of life," (23) and that ways of speaking "are as much a part of our natural history as walking, eating, drinking, playing." (25)

Wittgenstein is criticized by P. F. Strawson for his alleged prejudice against the inner—"his hostility to the idea of what is not observed (seen, heard, smelt, touched, tasted)." [137] Wittgenstein is alleged to hold that "no words name sensations" and that "all there is to be said about the descriptive meaning of a word is said when it is indicated what *criteria* people can use for employing it." [138] Contrary to Strawson's view, we find Wittgenstein saying: "A person [can] write down or give vocal expression to his inner experiences—his feelings, moods, and the rest—for his private use" (243); [139] "we talk about sensations everyday, and give them names" (244); "think how many different kinds of things are called 'description': . . . description of a sensation of touch; of a mood" (24); "describing my state of mind (of fear, say) is something I do in a particular context" (p. 188); "nor do I ever have the feeling of an invisible presence; other people do, and I can question them about their experiences" (p. 184); "the question whether the dreamer's memory deceives him when he reports the dream after waking cannot arise" (p. 222); "someone later reveals his inmost heart to me by a confession." [140] We must remember, however, about the use of names in connection with the inner that "we call very different things 'names.'" (38)

George Pitcher understands Wittgenstein to hold that sensations have names and that these names "may be used to describe one's inner state." [141] The purpose of such a description may be any one of a number of things. It may be to tell one's doctor the source of the trouble or to decline an invitation. But the purpose cannot be to tell the hearer what the sensation feels like, Pitcher contends, for "everyone acknowledges that sensations are private," [142] and private sensations "do not enter into pain language-games, any more than the contents of a pictured pot 'enter into' the picture." [143] "What

[137] "Review of Wittgenstein's *Philosophical Investigations*," p. 52.

[138] *Ibid.*, p. 42.

[139] See also *Zettel*, sect. 329: "I make a plan not merely so as to make myself understood but also in order to get clear about the matter myself (i.e., language is not merely a means of communication)"

[140] *Zettel*, sect. 558.   [141] *The Philosophy of Wittgenstein*, p. 303.

[142] *Ibid.*, p. 297.   [143] *Ibid.*, p. 299.

does play a part in pain language-games is pain behavior . . . and pain–comforting behavior . . . —in short, the external circumstances in which the word 'pain' is used." [144] When we see someone's pain behavior "we have no idea what he might be feeling—what the beetle in his box might be like." [145] Concluding his account, Pitcher contends that "there are certainly powerful objections which could be urged against some of [Wittgenstein's] arguments.[146]

Against Pitcher's interpretation it must be urged that Wittgenstein rejects the idea that sensations are private; he does not draw the conclusion attributed to him by Pitcher that since I cannot experience another's feelings I can have no idea what those feelings are.[147] Pitcher misinterprets the key passages. First of all, in quoting the beetle in the box passage, Pitcher ends with "the thing in the box . . . cancels out, whatever it is." But the next sentence is crucial: "*If we construe the grammar of the expression of sensation on the model of 'object and designation' the object drops out.*" (293) [148] Wittgenstein's point is that this grammar should be construed differently.

Second, Pitcher finds support from section 297 in which Wittgenstein asks, "What if one insisted on saying that there must also be something boiling in the picture of the pot." But Wittgenstein continues, "The image (*Vorstellung*) of pain certainly enters into the language-game in a sense; only not as a picture (*Bild*)." (300) [149] This image, Pitcher argues, "enters in . . . by a reference to the *circumstances* . . . of the present pain behavior." [150] But this contradicts Wittgenstein's contention that "this image is not replaceable in the language-game by anything we should call a picture." (300) Circumstances surely can be pictured just as pain behavior can. And elsewhere Wittgenstein says:

I can perhaps imagine (*Vorstellen*) (though it is not easy) that each of the people whom I see in the street is in frightful pain, but is artfully concealing it. And it is important that I have to imagine an artful concealment here. . . . *Perhaps I look at one and think: "It must be difficult to laugh when one is in such pain."* (391)[151] . . . "So *what* do I imagine?"—I have already said what. And I do not necessarily imagine *my* being in pain. (393)

---

[144] *Ibid.*
[145] *Ibid.*
[146] *Ibid.*, p. 313.
[147] *Ibid.*, pp. 297-98.
[148] Italics are mine.
[149] Pitcher translates "*Vorstellung*" as "representation" (p. 307), while the translator reserves this term to translate "*Darstellung.*" See sections 397, 366, 367. Alan Donagan suggests that "*Vorstellung*" be translated as "imaginative representation." ("Wittgenstein on Sensation," in Pitcher, *Wittgenstein,* p. 330, n.).
[150] *The Philosophy of Wittgenstein,* p. 307.
[151] Italics mine. See also *Zettel,* sects. 544, 546.

Third, Pitcher finds support [152] from section 272 in which Wittgenstein asserts:

The essential thing about *private* experience is . . . that nobody knows whether other people also have this or something else. The assumption *would* thus be possible—though unverifiable—that one section of mankind had one sensation of red and another section another.[153]

But Wittgenstein is here drawing implications that would follow from a grammar that construed experiences as private objects—i.e., as having no essential connection with behavior. Far from concluding, as Pitcher contends, that our grammar allows this assumption that another's experience may be "something altogether different" [154] than mine, Wittgenstein's point is that we do not entertain this as a possibility when we are not doing philosophy: "Just try—in a real case—to doubt someone else's fear or pain" (303); "the idea never crosses your mind that this impression of colour belongs only to you." (275)

Pitcher's interpretation would saddle Wittgenstein with the dubious view that to believe that another is in pain or has any experiences at all is simply to take an attitude toward him, to behave toward him in a certain way. Against such a view one must argue that my attitude is not directed toward an object with a certain kind of behavior; it is directed toward a person who is in pain, and talk of attitudes leaves the concept of person unexplained. Furthermore, belief that the other is in pain may be accompanied by a wide range of attitudes (e.g., sympathy, indifference, sadism) many of which also accompany other beliefs. Wittgenstein, Pitcher contends, would concede that "of course we cannot help thinking that the other fellow . . . is feeling something," but he would reduce this to "we treat people in a certain way. . . . We just *do* treat people differently from automata, and people we believe to be in pain differently from people we believe to be shamming." [155] But this, in turn seems to reduce to "we treat differently those people whom we treat differently." Attitudes are not beliefs; they are determined by beliefs.

In everyday affairs we have no difficulty with the idea that we know what the other is experiencing. We say, "I've felt the same way as you do now" or, "I've never had quite that experience but something rather like it." On some occasions we also say, "I have no idea what he is experiencing," but we do not say this when the other is groaning

[152] *The Philosophy of Wittgenstein*, pp. 297-98. On page 299 Pitcher misinterprets section 271 in the same way.

[153] Italics mine.

[154] *The Philosophy of Wittgenstein*, p. 298.

[155] *Ibid.*, pp. 311-12.

and writhing in pain. In the *Zettel* Wittgenstein speaks of something as showing us *"what we go by* in determining whether something that takes place 'in another' is different from or the same as in ourselves. This shews us what we go by in judging inner processes." [156] It is not unintelligible to ask whether we can ever really know what the other feels,[157] but in everyday affairs such doubts are idle. We do not necessarily have doubts wherever it is "possible for us to *imagine* a doubt." (84) "Doubting has an end." (P. 180)

The idea that we have no notion of what the other feels is plausible only when we are captive to the private inner room picture or to something like it. It seems to us then that the behavior of others simply cannot be the criterion of their feelings; at best it can be a symptom, and since we lack a criterion it turns out that we really have no idea what the behavior is a symptom of. But, for Wittgenstein, the feelings of others are neither private nor reducible to behavior. "If I see someone writhing in pain with evident cause I do not think: all the same, his feelings are hidden from me." (P. 223) [158] " 'I cannot know what is going on in him' is above all a *picture."* (P. 223)

The charge that Wittgenstein is prejudiced against the inner fails, especially, to take full account of his view that language-games are part of a form of life. "Only in the stream of thought and life do words have meaning." [159] "What belongs to a language-game is a whole culture." [160] This is particularly important to our concerns with religious assertions. It is true that, according to Wittgenstein, meaning is use and use is something that can be described. But if use is inseparable from a form of life, then any description of use must either presuppose an understanding of that form of life or must describe that form of life.[161] "In order to get clear about aesthetic words you have to describe ways of living." [162] "To describe [aesthetic words'] use . . . you have to describe a culture." [163] If we fail to understand the form of life we cannot understand the meaning of the language. If we are in a strange country then "even given a mastery of the

---

[156] Sect. 340.

[157] In the final chapter we shall discuss this sort of question in terms of what Stephen Toulmin has called "limiting questions."

[158] And on the same page we find: " 'What is *internal* is hidden from us.'—The future is hidden from us. But does the astronomer think like this when he calculates an eclipse of the sun?"; and also, "I am putting a jig-saw puzzle together; the other person . . . guesses my thoughts and utters them."

[159] *Zettel*, sect. 173.

[160] *Lectures and Conversations*, p. 8. sect. 26.

[161] What this description of a form of life will include will vary from case to case: "Whether this or that belongs to a complete description will depend on the purpose of the description." (*Zettel*, sect. 311)

[162] *Lectures and Conversations*, p. 8, sect. 26.

[163] *Ibid.*, p. 8, sect. 25.

country's language, we do not *understand* the people. 'We cannot find our feet with them.'" (P. 223) Or in speaking of music "you say 'I experienced that passage quite differently.' But still this expression tells you 'what happened' only if you are at home in the special conceptual world that belongs to these situations. (Analogy: 'I won the match.')" [164] This inseparability of language and form of life is dramatically illustrated in the case of a judge in a court of law, for "if the being that he is to judge is quite deviant from ordinary human beings, then e.g., the decision whether he has done a deed with evil intent will become not difficult but (simply) impossible." [165]

That we understand the use of words only as we are able to participate in a form of life is further evident in Wittgenstein's account of the teaching and learning of words. "If someone is brought up in a particular culture—and then reacts to music in such-and-such a way, you can teach him the use of the phrase 'expressive playing.'" [166] "By being educated in a technique, we are also educated to have a way of looking at the matter which is just as firmly rooted as that technique." [167]

It follows that description of use may well involve reference to inner experience, for understanding a culture includes understanding inner experience. For example, "whether a word of the language of our tribe is rightly translated into a word of the English language depends upon the role this word plays in the whole life of the tribe; the occasions on which it is used, the expressions of emotion by which it is generally accompanied, the ideas which it generally awakens [168] or which prompt its saying, etc., etc." [169] In speaking, say, of "something that gives meaning to a configuration of chess pieces" I may have in mind "the special experiences that we associate with such positions in a game." [170] Or, in describing the meaning of words in poetry Wittgenstein refers to inner experiences that accompany our hearing of these words. (530-534) [171] And in section 6 Wittgenstein speaks of a language-game the entire use of which might be to evoke pictures of objects in the mind of the hearer. In short, "how words are understood is not told by words alone. (Theology)" [172]

Wittgenstein's definition of the meaning of a word as its use in the

---

[164] *Zettel*, sect. 165.   [165] *Ibid.*, sect. 350.   [166] *Ibid.*, sect. 164.
[167] *Remarks on the Foundations of Mathematics*, part III, sect. 35.
[168] In the *Investigations*, for example, Wittgenstein points out that "when children play at trains their game is connected with their knowledge of trains. It would nevertheless be possible for the children of a tribe unacquainted with trains to learn this game from others. . . . One might say that the game did not make the same sense to them as to us." (282)
[169] *The Brown Book*, p. 103.   [170] *Zettel*, sect. 143.
[171] Also *Zettel*, sects. 155, 170.   [172] *Zettel*, sect. 144.

language has received much critical attention.[173] We must limit ourselves to some fairly representative criticisms in two of the most widely
read accounts of the *Investigations*.

According to Strawson "the *natural* place of the word 'meaning'
and its derivatives in ordinary use" is in the language-game in which
one learns the reference of particular words.[174] Consequently, Wittgenstein surely cannot have meant to say, "Look at the use, for *that*
is the meaning." [175] To avoid this impression he might better have
said, "In doing philosophy, it can't be that you are ignorant of the
meaning: what you want to know is the use." [176] And Pitcher says
similarly that "what Wittgenstein might better have said is that it is
not the job of the philosopher to give us the meaning of philosophically difficult words, but rather to give us their uses." [177]

These comments, however, fail to consider that by "use" Wittgenstein meant the semantic aspect of meaning as well as its syntactic and
pragmatic aspects. He says, for example, "In the use of words one might
distinguish 'surface grammar' from 'depth grammar' " (664), "surface"
referring to the syntactic dimension of grammar and "depth" to its
semantic and pragmatic dimensions. Questions about meaning sometimes concern the semantic dimension, but at other times—especially
but not only in doing philosophy—they concern the pragmatic
dimension.[178] The two are distinguishable but not separable. Wittgenstein points out that only someone who knows how to put a
word to work can meaningfully ask its definition. In defining "meaning"
in separation from its pragmatic aspect, Strawson simply fails to consider part of its family of uses.

In support of his criticism of Wittgenstein's identification of meaning
and use, George Pitcher contends that "it is quite possible to know
the meaning of a word yet not know its use and to know the use
without knowing the meaning." [179] For example, "if someone tells
me, a non-Latin speaker, that 'ultus' means revenge in Latin, I thereby
know the meaning of that word but I have no idea how or when
to use it." [180] Conversely I may know how to use "Amen" or "Q.E.D."
without knowing their meaning. Then, too, although Wittgenstein
speaks of the meaning of proper names (40, 79) they really have not

[173] See Hallett, *Wittgenstein's Definition of Meaning as Use*, Ch. 5, for an
extensive consideration of these criticisms.
[174] "Review of Wittgenstein's *Philosophical Investigations*," p. 24.
[175] *Ibid.*   [176] *Ibid.*
[177] *The Philosophy of Wittgenstein*, p. 253.
[178] Questions about meaning may also, of course, concern the syntactic dimension.
[179] *The Philosophy of Wittgenstein*, p. 252.
[180] *Ibid.*

meaning but only use. "One cannot ask 'What is the meaning of John Paul Jones?' but only 'Who is John Paul Jones?' " [181]

None of the examples, however, shows Wittgenstein's definition to be in error. First of all, when we are told "ultus" means revenge we know the meaning of "ultus" because we do know how to use "revenge," and the implication is that "ultus" has a similar use in Latin. If the use in Latin is not similar then it is false that "ultus" means revenge. Second, if I really understand fully the use of "Amen" and "Q.E.D." in the sense that I grasp all the rules involved at least well enough to converse in full accordance with them, then I do in fact know their meaning. For example, if asked "What does 'Q.E.D.' mean?" one might perfectly well reply without giving either the Latin words or a strict translation of them, e.g., "which was the thing to be proved"; on the other hand, if some uses required a knowledge of the Latin then one would not know the full use if one lacked this knowledge. Finally, Wittgenstein was no doubt mistaken in speaking of the meaning of proper names. But he was mistaken not because proper names have only a use but because they do not have a use in the institutional sense of use. Wittgenstein, we must remember, defined meaning in terms of institutional use. The fact that each of us is ignorant of the names of millions of English-speaking people does not mean that our knowledge of the English language is incomplete.

Pitcher's criticisms are typical of many others that charge that Wittgenstein's definition is too narrow or too broad or too vague. Not infrequently, the critic fails to distinguish institutional use and particular speech acts. The charge of vagueness, however, does seem well supported; but in assessing it we must remember that the definition cannot be understood apart from the way its terms are actually used in the *Investigations*. Then, too, clarity is a relative matter, and, as Strawson and Hallett suggest,[182] Wittgenstein apparently framed this definition with only the therapeutic purposes of the *Investigations* in mind.

Finally, we may consider a frequent criticism of Wittgenstein's argument against the logical possibility of a private language. A language use that I alone could understand would be by that very fact a use for which there could be no independent criteria of correctness. Therefore, Wittgenstein contended, in a private use there would be no distinction between correct and incorrect use. "Justification consists in appealing to something independent." (265) Against this contention

[181] *Ibid.*
[182] Strawson, "Review of Wittgenstein's *Philosophical Investigations*," p. 27; Hallett, *Wittgenstein's Definition of Meaning as Use*, p. 143.

A. J. Ayer asks us to consider a Robinson Crusoe who is left alone on an island as an infant and is raised by a wolf.

He will certainly be able to recognize many things upon the island, in the sense that he adapts his behaviour to them. Is it inconceivable that he should also name them? . . . But if we allow that . . . why not allow that he could also invent words to describe his sensations. . . . His knowing how to use these words will be a matter of his remembering what objects they are meant to stand for. . . . Unless something is recognized, without being referred to a further test, nothing can be tested.[183]

The same criticism is made by Carl Wellman and P. F. Strawson.[184] Even in the case of public language we must finally trust our memory concerning the reference of our words; therefore, in the case of private language as well, memory can serve as an adequate check of correct use.

These criticisms, however, misunderstand Wittgenstein's argument. His point is not that memory is unreliable but that in the case of private use there would be no distinction between remembering rightly and remembering wrongly.[185] Consider the sensation we call pain. Suppose I attempt to create a private meaning by saying to myself of an instance A of pain, "This I will call 'prain.'" Later I experience something else, experience B. Am I to call B prain or not? How and in what respects must B be similar to A for me to classify it under the same concept? In our public language what we call pain is determined finally by the purposes served by the pain language-game. But in a private language these purposes would be lacking. "Why can't my right hand give my left hand money?" Well, "the practical consequences would not be those of a gift." (268)

It is worth noting here that Rush Rhees argues against Ayer that language must not only be shareable but must actually be shared.[186] His argument seems to me to be important and correct, but we shall not consider it here since I do not find Wittgenstein to take a clear position on this.[187]

---

[183] "Can There Be a Private Language?" *The Concept of a Person and Other Essays* (London: Macmillan, 1963); reprinted in Morick, *Wittgenstein and the Problem of Other Minds*, pp. 89-91.

[184] Wellman, "Wittgenstein's Conception of a Criterion," p. 169; Strawson, "Review . . . ," p. 44.

[185] Wittgenstein asks himself, for example, about checking one's memory of a departure time by calling to mind the appropriate time-table: 'If the mental image of the time-table *could not* itself be *tested* for correctness, how could it confirm the correctness of the first memory?" (265) (First italics are mine.) The point to notice is that he says not that the time-table must be tested but only that it must be testable.

[186] "Can There Be a Private Language?" pp. 267-85.

[187] Compare, for example, Rhees, p. 277 with sect. 2 of the *Investigations*. See also sects. 199, 378, 380 and *Remarks on the Foundations of Mathematics*,

Some Applications to Talk of God

In his brief account of Wittgenstein's life and character, George Pitcher comments that

he understood what Kierkegaard meant by despair and agreed with his view that man by himself is in an utterly hopeless situation. . . . It must have distressed Wittgenstein that although wanting and needing to believe in God, he was nevertheless unable to do so.[188]

In addition to Kierkegaard he was deeply impressed by Plato, Augustine, Dostoievsky, Tolstoy, and William James (*The Varieties of Religious Experience*). A man of exceptional seriousness, integrity, and concern for being truly human, Wittgenstein abhorred dishonesty and superficiality. He seemed to admire religious faith that was genuine regardless of his inability to share it. Norman Malcolm tells us, for example, that Wittgenstein

had read an account by Dickens of a visit to a shipload of Mormons about to emigrate from England to America, and Wittgenstein was much impressed by the picture of the simple resolution of those people in the face of hardship. He thought they were an excellent illustration of what religious faith can do. But he went on to remark to a friend that in order to understand them (I think he meant to understand their religious conceptions) one must have a certain "obtuseness." Then came this simile: like needing big shoes to walk across a bridge that has holes in the flooring! [189]

Wittgenstein was once prompted to say, "Of course, that is where the great problems of philosophy lie, space, time and Deity." [190] In his writings, though, we find little attention to Deity. In his account of "Wittgenstein's Lectures in 1930-33," Moore reports that

about "God" his main point seemed to be that this word is used in many grammatically different senses. He said, for instance, that many controversies about God could be settled by saying, "I'm not using the word in such a sense that you can say . . . "; and that different religions treat things as making sense which others treat as nonsense, and don't merely deny some proposition which another religion affirms.[191]

---

p. 94, #66 and #67. Moreland Perkins contends that sect. 243 of the *Investigations* provides an example of an unshared language because it concerns "human beings who spoke only in monologue." (P. 103) Perkins fails to consider, however, the implications of the fact that they all spoke the same language.

[188] *The Philosophy of Wittgenstein*, p. 11. On Wittgenstein the man see Norman Malcolm, *Ludwig Wittgenstein; A Memoir* (New York: Oxford University Press, 1958) and many of the essays in Fann, *Ludwig Wittgenstein: The Man and His Philosophy.*

[189] "Ludwig Wittgenstein: A Symposium," in *Ludwig Wittgenstein: The Man and His Philosophy*, pp. 72-73.

[190] M. O'C. Drury, *ibid.*, p. 68.   [191] *Mind*, Jan., 1955, p. 16.

And G. E. M. Anscombe indicates that Wittgenstein said of his later work, "Its advantage is that if you believe, say, Spinoza or Kant, this interferes with what you believe in religion; but if you believe me, nothing of the sort." [192]

The most extensive account available of Wittgenstein's ideas on religious belief is from notes that three students took of a few lectures in 1938.[193] Here he emphasized particularly how different religious beliefs were from other sorts of belief both in their relation to the evidence for them and in the believer's use of them as a basis for regulating his entire life. One who does not share another's religious beliefs may very often be said not to contradict them but simply not to look at things that way at all—not to have any sense of himself in terms of that form of life.

> Why shouldn't one form of life culminate in an utterance of belief in a Last Judgement? But I couldn't say "Yes" or "No" to the statement that there will be such a thing. Nor "Perhaps," nor "I'm not sure." . . . In one sense, I understand all [this believer] says—the English words "God," "separate," etc. I understand.[194] I could say: "I don't believe in this," and this would be true, meaning I haven't got these thoughts or anything that hangs together with them. But not that I could contradict the thing.[195]

The major consequences, however, of Wittgenstein's work for the problem of assertions about God must be drawn by implication from his general position. Most of these points we shall treat very briefly in order to avoid repeating arguments we have already considered. In the case, though, of Wittgenstein's attack on the dualistic picture of mind and body and on the possibility of a private language which it entails we shall study at some length its implications for those pictures which guide our talk of God.

Of fundamental importance is Wittgenstein's emphasis on the great variety of our language uses and on the differences between them. From this perspective we may look at each religious language-game on its own terms, freed from the demand that it be shown to follow the logic of, say, a scientific language-game.

Moreover, since a language-game is part of a form of life, Wittgen-

---

[192] "What Wittgenstein Really Said," *The Tablet*, April 17, 1954, p. 373.

[193] *Ludwig Wittgenstein: Lectures and Conversations*, ed. Cyril Barrett.

[194] In his next lecture Wittgenstein explains concerning the word "God," "I did learn what it didn't mean. . . . I could answer questions . . . and in that sense could be said to understand." P. 59. And in his final lecture Wittgenstein notes that a nonbeliever may achieve a degree of understanding of a statement by a believer by discovering "what consequences he will draw, . . . what he opposes this to." P. 69.

[195] *Ludwig Wittgenstein: Lectures and Conversations*, pp. 58, 55.

stein's emphasis on the variety of language-games and the possibilities for the creation of new ones is at the same time an insistence that there are many forms of life available to us as human beings and many more that we may yet create. Among these are a variety of religious forms of life. To see that language is part of a form of life is also, for Wittgenstein, to see that language-use neither requires nor can be given a justification by some principle or principles of reason. Always our reasons come to an end, for human understanding in any of its forms ultimately presupposes participation in or standing under a form of life. Always the participant is the final expert in any assessment of a religious language-use and its form of life.

On the other hand, Wittgenstein's emphasis on the variety of different language-games and forms of life does not support a fideistic view of religious language-games. We have argued at length that Wittgenstein does not place language-uses and their forms of life beyond critical assessment, but says rather that he is attempting to clear the ground on which language stands. He is particularly critical of his own earlier analytic practices as well as those of G. E. Moore. And in his lecture on religious belief he calls one account "unreasonable": "I would say, if this is religious belief, then it's all superstition. . . . I would say: here is a man who is cheating himself." [196] Let us apply some of Wittgenstein's critical tools to assertions about God.

Wittgenstein has emphasized how readily similarities in the surface grammar of two sentences may mislead us into thinking that their depth grammar or use is also similar. The similarities between "God loves Mary" and "John loves Mary" may encourage us to assume that our talk of God is more like our talk of John than it really is, particularly when placed in the service of those motives for self-deception to which Freud, Marx, Kierkegaard, and others have called attention. It may even be that a sentence that has no application seems to us to have one because its surface grammar is similar to that of sentences that do have an application.

The basic criterion for distinguishing talk that only seems to have an application and talk that really does is the principle of contrast. If our theological language-game is genuine it will provide us with a set of alternative moves or contrasting applications. What we say about God has sense only if we are saying one thing *rather than* another thing that we might conceivably say. However, "saying something" must be understood to mean not just uttering words but applying them. We could reason that "God forgives the repentant" contrasts with "God *ignores* the repentant" or with "God forgives the *un-*

[196] Barrett, *Ludwig Wittgenstein: Lectures and Conversations*, p. 59. See also p. 57.

repentant" and yet not know how to apply any of these contrasts, just as we could reason that "All Mumsiroves are *tall*" contrasts with "All Mumsiroves are *short*." In these cases we would have in mind a range of contrasts which we have learned in other games where they do have applications.

An important sort of talk which either distorts or entirely lacks contrasting application is that which psychologists call projection. When John says "Smith hates me" and yet Smith's behavior is clearly not the sort that justifies his saying this, we conclude that John is projecting his feeling into Smith. His use of "hates" in this case lacks the contrasting application that gives it its normal sense. Perhaps John would say this no matter how Smith behaved toward him. Perhaps he would not say this if, say, Smith's behavior were more decisively friendly or caring—in which case John is simply distorting the normal range of our application of "hates." On the other hand, perhaps John would say this regardless of how Smith behaved toward him so that what he says lacks any contrasting application at all; that is, he is not applying it to one sort of behavior on Smith's part in contrast with another. In either case we see the intimate logical connection between projection and the principle of contrast. Similarly, when the believer is prepared to make his affirmations about God regardless of anything that could conceivably happen, so that what he says lacks any contrasting application, Freud concludes that the believer is simply projecting, reading into whatever happens certain infantile feelings.[197]

Wittgenstein's attack on dualistic pictures of the self, including his attack on the idea of a private language, has far-reaching consequence for the logic of God.

A clear example of the dualistic picture attacked by Wittgenstein is that used by Michael Novak in *Belief and Unbelief*.[198] According to Novak, "the chief virtue in taking intelligent consciousness as a model for conceiving of God is that it does not require a corporeal body for its referent," [199] and "the 'world' of subjects in which God and I live is the more radically real; the world of objects passes." [200] It is precisely this belief that there is no necessary connection between the inner and the outer, between mental process and physical behavior, which I believe that Wittgenstein has refuted. Our very concept of self, Strawson has shown, is the concept of "something which is both a subject of experiences and a part of the world."

It will be helpful if we distinguish two aspects of the logic of God,

---

[197] John Wisdom makes somewhat related comments about what we may call the tendency in metaphysics toward loss of contrast. See "Philosophy, Metaphysics and Psycho-Analysis," in *Philosophy and Psycho-Analysis*, pp. 281-82.

[198] (New York: Macmillan, 1965).

[199] *Belief and Unbelief*, p. 119.   [200] *Ibid.*, p. 122.

namely, the use of "God" as the subject of religious affirmations and the use of such words as "calls," "delivers," "judges," and "forgives" as the predicates of these affirmations. Since our shared language could not be derived from a private language even if there were such a thing, our use of the term "God" could not be based on any sort of private experience or private innate idea. By "private" Wittgenstein meant something inner which has no essential relation with something publicly observable. If our experience of pain were not essentially related to pain behavior then the use of the word "pain" could not be taught and we could not know that someone else was in pain. We would have the experience and it would have an effect on us, but it would have no meaning for we would not have the concept "pain." A pet dog may be conditioned by pain, but he does not know that it is pain. Like the beetle in each man's private box—private in the sense that only he can see its contents—the experience could not enter into human communication. Similarly, private experience of God could not enter into human communication. We would lack the concept "God," and the experience would not have any meaning. Religious communities are able to teach their meaning of "God" only because it is rooted in the observable. Like the concept "beauty" or the concept "obligation" the concept "God" is essentially related to the sensory. For example, if a man says, "Oh yes, I know there is a God who watches over us but what of it" and then yawns and turns to the sports pages we know that he does not understand what "God" means. We know this, in part, by what we see and hear.

It is well to remind ourselves that Wittgenstein is not a behaviorist. A man who never experienced pain could not learn the full meaning of pain by observing pain behavior. Similarly the full meaning of "God" cannot be learned simply from what is observable. Indeed, Wittgenstein insisted that a language-game is part of a form of life and so cannot be played by those who are not participants in that form of life. The language-game of a religious community, then, cannot be fully understood by those who are not participants in the form of life of that community. And when a form of life undergoes significant change its language game or games may well become disrupted and confused and its participants may be especially tempted by the illusory security of utterances that lack contrasting application, or, as we might say, of behavior that lacks meaning.

The predicates that religious affirmations apply to God are, for the most part at least, those which we first learn to use about human beings. For the same reason that we could not apply them to another person if they were not essentially related to observable behavior, we could not apply them to God if they were not essentially related to something we can observe. We can meaningfully say "John has forgiven Smith" because we know the sort of behavior which is indicative of forgiveness and the sort which is not. Similarly we can speak of God's forgiveness only if we know to what sort of situation such talk is applicable and to what sort it is not applicable. If God's forgiveness had no publicly observable dimensions it would have the same status for us as the beetle in the other's private box. We could not meaningfully talk about it. We would have no idea what it was.

As we have seen, we must beware of the temptation here to say, "Well, even though God's forgiveness has no essential relation to anything observable still I know what human forgiveness is and so I can think of God's forgiveness as in some sense essentially the same." The concept "same" is, like any other concept, one that is governed by rules we have learned, and in a statement of the sort we have just considered the problem we are trying to escape from reappears when we ask what "the same" means in this case—how we are able to apply it. Could we give "It is five o'clock on the sun" a meaning by saying simply that it means the same as "It is five o'clock here" means? We could not, Wittgenstein contended, for "what I do not know is in what cases one is to speak of its being the same time here and there." (350)

Put in its simplest terms, Wittgenstein's argument is that the dualistic picture of man has no application. One way of putting the point of our discussion of religious predicates is to say that this sort of picture also has no application in talking of God. It will be helpful if we examine at some length this question of theological pictures. To echo Wittgenstein's comment on philosophy, when we look into ourselves as we do theology we often get to see a picture that plays a central role in our theological grammar. Our ordinary language supplies us with an anthropological picture, a picture of human actions and relations, by which to think about God and his actions. The crucial question, then, becomes *whether this picture has an application.* May it be that the believer is simply misled into thinking that he gives this picture a use, because this picture carries over with it some of the grammatical rules that govern our talk about observable human beings but that do not work in connection with an unobservable God?

As we have said, we first learn to use predicates such as "forgiving" and "delivering" in our ordinary language about human beings. We then modify their ordinary meanings in using them about God. If their theological use did not, in this way, remain significantly related to their original meaning we would simply not be using the same concepts at all and we would have no reason for using the same words. Furthermore, since God has no body, if the theological use of these concepts were too far separated from their use about human beings it would lose the all-essential tie with observable behavior. As Ian Ramsey has put it:

theological assertions must have a logical context which extends to, and is continuous with, those assertions of ordinary language for which sense experience is directly relevant. From such straight-forward assertions, theological assertions must not be logically segregated: for that would mean they were pointless and, in contrast to the only language which has an agreed meaning, meaningless.[201]

The meaningfulness of religious use, then, depends upon what traditionally has been explained as an analogical relation with the meanings that its terms have in ordinary language. Let us see, then, whether the traditional analogical approach can provide an application in talk about God of a picture of human actions and relations.

We may take the work of E. L. Mascall [202] as fairly representative of the modern dress in which the traditional doctrine of analogical predication is being clothed. If we are to talk about God intelligibly, it is argued, we require an analogical use of our ordinary terms which would lie someplace in between univocal and equivocal use. If one applies such terms univocally, asserting their meanings of God *"in the same sense* in which you assert them of finite beings, you are rendering God incapable of fulfilling the very function for whose performance you alleged him to be necessary." [203] God becomes merely a part of the universe rather than its sustaining source. Yet if one applies these terms equivocally, predicating their meanings of God "in an *altogether different sense* from that in which you assert them of finite beings, you are making statements about God to which you can, *ex hypothesi*, assign no intelligible content." [204] To use Wittgensteinian terms, if we simply retain the rules governing ordinary use, then our terms are applicable only to finite objects. We have not given them a religious use at all. There is nothing named "God" to which they can be applied in this way, and such an entity, in any event, would not be the God meant by Christians. But, if no rules are carried over from their ordinary use to the use of these terms in connection with "God," then they simply have not been given the rules necessary for their use.

Mascall seeks to find middle ground between these poles of anthropomorphism and agnosticism by an inseparably interrelated use of the doctrines of the analogy of proportionality and of the analogy

[201] "Contemporary Empiricism," p. 181.
[202] *Existence and Analogy* (London: Longmans, Green & Co., 1949).
[203] *Ibid.*, p. 87. Italics mine.   [204] *Ibid.*

of attribution or proportion. When we predicate of God a characteristic found in man, such as goodness, we do so, first of all, by the analogy of proportionality in which we say that the different senses or "modes" in which God and man possess goodness are determined by the difference in their natures. We get the "proportion" that God's goodness is to the nature of God as man's goodness is to the nature of man.[205] But so far this is of little help, since God is still an unknown. We have simply said that there is some sort of relation between the goodness of an unknown and the nature of an unknown. Nor do we have any idea of the nature of that relation, for it is itself merely *analogous* to the relation of man's goodness to his nature. Man's nature determines how his goodness is related to his nature, and God's nature determines how his goodness is related to his nature. Austin Farrer expresses this by saying that the proportion merely asserts that "divine intelligence is appropriate to divine existence as creaturely to creaturely." [206] And even here we apparently have two different senses of "appropriate," the sense of "appropriate" which is appropriate to God and that appropriate to man, and so on in infinite regress. As Mascall bluntly states, "we have denied that our equal signs [between these relations] really stand for equality and we have not indicated anything definite that they do stand for." [207]

This proportion, then, must be "held together by that analogy of attribution which asserts, not merely in the conceptual but in the existential order, that finite being can exist only in dependence on God." [208] Analogical predication, that is, must be based on the real relation of creative causality between God and his creation. God must have the characteristics of his creatures in whatever way is necessary in order to create those characteristics in his creatures.[209] That God has these characteristics, then, means simply that he is able to produce them. In other words, since God is able to produce an effect, we may say of him that he is able to produce that effect.

But this seems to be entirely redundant. We still do not know what it means to say this of God—that he can produce an effect. We know only one term of the "causal" relation, namely, the effect. The other term, "God" or "Divine Cause," remains an unknown, as does the causal relation itself. We still have no idea, that is, what sense the term "cause" has when it is predicated of God. We still do not know the analogical meaning that we allegedly are able to give to the terms that we apply to God.

[205] *Ibid.*, p. 104.   [206] *Finite and Infinite*, p. 53.
[207] *Existence and Analogy*, p. 108.
[208] *Ibid.*, p. 120.   [209] *Ibid.*, p. 102.

Mascall admits, concerning any effect that is caused by God that

the concept which we form of this effect can in no case be transformed for us into the concept of God which we lack, but we can attribute to God, by our affirmative judgment, the *name* that denotes the perfection corresponding to this effect. To proceed in this way is not to posit God as similar to the creature, it is to ground oneself on the *certitude* that, since every effect resembles its cause, the creature from which we start certainly resembles God.[210]

The believer's certainty is about an unknown resemblance. On this account the believer is able to "attribute" terms to God, because he knows what these terms refer to when applied to man and he feels certain that they do have an application to God. In other words, we know one use and feel certain there must be another use that stands in some unknown relation to the first. We feel certain that there is a religious use, but do not know what it is. The doctrine of analogy, then, cannot provide the foundation for a religious language-game. We are given a picture of finite entities, with their qualities and relations, but the alleged *application of this picture* is one that human beings so far do not know how to make. It should be noted that this problem of meaning is not a question of belief versus unbelief. There can be no belief unless one is presented something to believe in. We cannot commit ourselves to something unknown. Let us examine in more detail this failure to provide an application of the theistic picture.

Austin Farrer suggests that our difficulties here arise

only in the (finite) terms with which we are bound to express the unique Divinity if we are to have any discourse about Him at all. That which originally comes to bear on the mind is not the scheme of proportionality, but God as active in us, a reality which drives the mind to such straits as these in the effort to comment on it.[211]

But the question is whether the experience or "direct awareness" that we have of God's activity in us [212] can be thought and spoken about as religious people attempt to do. Can we think about it or (meaningfully) speak about it as "God's activity," for example? Can we give this experience a coherent place in the system by which we organize our experience? What the doctrine of analogy has failed to do is to enable us to relate this experience significantly to the rest of our experience.

[210] *Ibid.*, p. 118. Italics mine.
[211] *Finite and Infinite*, p. 54.
[212] *Ibid.*, p. 61.

To put the matter another way, the analogical approach does not enable us to apply the theistic picture cognitively. "In religious contemplation, the believer must suppose, there is through and with all images some noesis of the supreme noumenon, God himself." [213] Yet, Farrer maintains, one cannot hope "to reduce analogies to true images." [214] But what can be meant by "true images"? The question is whether our images can be applied successfully to our experiences. It is not a question of "supposing" that our images have a noetic use. A noetic use is one by which we make assertions that are subject to some sort of test. In the absence of a test it does not make sense to talk about knowledge.

Not only are we left ignorant concerning *how* to use terms in connection with God, but we also do not find any guidance from this doctrine about *which* terms to use. According to the analogy of attribution, we can say that God is four-legged, green, bald, capable of becoming soggy, and so on, because he has created these things. To know which terms are appropriate seems to require some knowledge about the nature of God, some placement of religious experience in our total account of things.

The analogical approach, then, lifts up the theistic picture of God active in the world and denies that this picture may be applied by means of the grammatical rules of our language about human activity. It affirms that this picture is to be applied but does not explain how we can apply it. If, as Wittgenstein has argued, to know the meaning is to know the use, then this approach does not establish that our ordinary terms do have analogical meaning when applied to God. This question of the application of the theistic picture is of such crucial importance that it will be good for us to pursue it at greater length.

Austin Farrer argues that "to think of the divine perfection," of which we are dimly aware when we apprehend the imperfection or finitude of the finite, "is always to have taken our start from various and impure finitude and to be in the process of purifying and simplifying it in the direction of the absolute and the one." [215] We do not, in this way, redraw the picture that we have taken from the finite world, but "we mark certain aspects as unworthy of God, without being able to abstract them and leave the remainder." [216] For example, although "if we wish to conceive the divine activity, we must undoubtedly conceive it as temporal," yet, since temporality is a mark of finitude, the doctrine of proportionality warns us "that

[213] *Ibid.*, p. 56.   [214] *Ibid.*
[215] *Ibid.*, p. 60.   [216] *Ibid.*, p. 54.

in our conceived image it is the activity and not the temporality that represents God." [217]

This is another way of saying that in giving words a theological application we lose all the rules governing their nontheological use which depend upon our temporal, overt behavior—which depend, that is, upon the fact that man has a physical body locating him in space and time. But, does thinking away this aspect of their ordinary application leave us with a meaningful theological application? Are we left with a residue of rules from our ordinary use of these terms sufficient to establish our theological use?

William P. Alston has given a lucid account of this problem in his essay, "The Elucidation of Religious Statements." [218] According to the rules of ordinary language, when may I say that a human being has spoken or has forgiven? When I say someone has spoken to me, I convey the fact of the bodily activity of producing audible sounds on the part of that person. Similarly, when I say someone has forgiven me, I imply that some appropriate observable action has been performed by him, such as saying "I forgive you," or shaking my hand, or flashing a friendly smile. (One can conceive of possible exceptions to this, unusual cases in which the other has some reason not to communicate his forgiveness but has forgiven me "in his heart." But even in such cases it makes sense to talk about the sort of acts which the other would perform were it not for reasons to the contrary.) But "when we apply such predicates to God," notes Alston,

> no such implications [of appropriate physical expression] hold. I can say "God has forgiven my sins" without being prepared to specify any utterance, embrace, or smile equally perceivable by all bystanders; I may say "God has spoken to me" and stubbornly hold onto it in the face of a failure by others in the vicinity to hear anything.[219]

Are there, then, other components of meaning that are not lost in this way when such words are applied to God? Perhaps these components may be found in the mental states that frequently accompany our observable actions. "Thus 'God has forgiven my sins' would mean something like 'God has said to Himself, "I forgive Alston's sins,"' feels compassion toward me, and does not feel grudges or resentments against me.'" God speaking to me would mean that "God privately rehearses [a] command" or certain thoughts.[220] Alston calls this procedure of removing certain aspects of meaning and working with those

[217] *Ibid.*, p. 56.
[218] *Process and Divinity*, ed. William Reese and Eugene Freeman (LaSalle, Ill.: Open Court Publishing Co., 1964).
[219] *Ibid.*, p. 433.   [220] *Ibid.*, p. 436.

that are left the "whittle-down method," a phrase also used by Ian Crombie.[221]

By itself, however, such a meaning component would prove inadequate. An "act" that was nothing more than a private mental occurrence would not be religiously relevant, because it would not involve any contact with the worshiper. But suppose that we also carry over to their theological use a second component of the meaning that these words ordinarily have, the impact of the act on the person to whom it is directed?

Thus "God has forgiven me" means . . . also that I have feelings of release from guilt, of being accepted, of a profound peace, etc., i.e., feelings like those I have when a man has forgiven me. And part of what is meant by "God has spoken to me" will be that I have experiences something like those I typically have when a man for whom I have a very high regard speaks to me, e.g., hearing a voice speak with authority, being seized with a sudden conviction, having a sudden sense of illumination, etc.[222]

Does not the introduction of this rule give us sufficient guidance in using statements about God acting?

To answer this question Alston selects the statement "God forgives the sins of those who truly turn unto Him." If the whittle-down method has been successful in establishing a theological use of statements like this one, then it should enable us to answer questions such as the following:

(1) "How can I know whether this is true?"
(2) "How can I tell whether I really believe this?"
(3) "How do I go about truly turning unto Him?"
(4) "Why should I truly turn unto Him? Why should I care whether God has forgiven my sins?" [223]

How, then, can we tell whether this statement is true once we have whittled-down the ordinary meaning of "forgives"? Suppose that I have feelings of having been forgiven—"a sense of cosmic acceptance." Does this establish the sentence as true or does the statement assert something more? What about the private mental occurrence in which God says to himself, "I forgive"? Well, am I to interpret this description as fiction or fact? Does this description simply function as a kind of story by which I give expression to my feelings, or is God objectively real? The whittle-down method gives us no guidance here. The situation is similar to that in which a description has been given of King Arthur without any accompanying indication as to whether the account is fictional or historical in reference. If "God" is

[221] "Theology and Falsification," *New Essays in Philosophical Theology*, p. 122.
[222] "The Elucidation of Religious Statements," p. 437.
[223] *Ibid.*, p. 438.

to be used as merely fictional in reference, then "God forgives" will mean "feelings of cosmic acceptance occur." "God has forgiven me" is then logically similar to "I have a headache," and there is no point in asking how I know this is true. But, if "God" is to be used as having objective reference, then the occurrence of certain feelings is not enough. Indeed, as Alston points out, believers commonly continue to assert God's forgiveness even in cases where feelings of having been forgiven are absent. They might say, for example, "I know that God has forgiven me, for the Bible promises that He will forgive those who truly turn unto him, but I still feel dreadfully oppressed and guilty. What is wrong?" As this example suggests, for some, at least, the criterion of truth is the authority of the Bible. For others, the claim will be that the experience of God's forgiveness is somehow self-authenticating. The direct experience does not, it is alleged, leave room for doubt. Still others may say, "If you humbly confess your sins now, and then lead a blissful existence after death, that will show that this statement is true." But none of these verification rules is supplied by the whittle-down method. Nor does this method enable us to choose between them. In each case the whittled-down description could also be accepted.[224]

If, then, the whittle-down explanation does not enable us to decide whether statements such as "God forgives those who truly turn unto him" are true, it obviously can fare little better with respect to the question "How can I tell whether I believe this?" Insofar as believing involves intellectual assent, the questions of truth and of belief become identical and the problems considered above repeat themselves. One cannot simply give assent to the "emasculated concept" of "forgives" as a private event in the mind of God, because assenting to it as a fiction is a very different matter from assenting to it as having objective reference. Assenting to it as a fiction expressing certain subjective feelings reduces "God forgives" to something like "feelings of cosmic acceptance occur." On the other hand, one cannot assent to it as having objective reference without knowing how it is to be used in this way, because this use is an essential part of the meaning. But the inadequacy of the whittle-down explanation is even further compounded when it is taken into account that the believer typically understands belief to include more than intellectual assent. Belief commonly is used to include an orientaion of the will, a commitment to certain types of response or way of life, such that a person who did not "turn to God" could not be said to believe that "God forgives the sins of those who truly turn unto him." Does our proposed explanation of "God forgives" enable us to know what is involved in this turning or com-

224 *Ibid.*, pp. 438-39.

mitment'? Just at this point we have come to see that the question of belief is inseparable from the third of our questions.[225]

"How do I go about truly turning unto him?" Here we confront the same problem in slightly altered form. Instead of asking whether and in what sense intellectual assent to "God forgives" has objective reference, we now enquire whether and in what sense an act that is commonly understood to be necessarily connected with this intellectual assent is directed to an objective reality. As Alston puts the matter, "How does one address an immaterial being," and "however we do it, what constitutes it an address *to God*, rather than talking to ourselves or an imaginary conversation?" [226] For one who interprets "God forgives" as merely a verbal means of expressing feelings of "cosmic acceptance," "turning" would mean inculcating or making oneself receptive to this subjective state. The whittled-down meaning is equally compatible both with this account and with an account that uses "God" as having objective reference. Talk about private occurrences in the mind of God leaves untouched the question whether and in what way there is contact between God and believer. Interaction between persons involves physical activity, and simply to whittle-away all reference to such activity from our explanation of an act of God without replacing it by another sort of explanation is to leave interaction between God and man unexplained. We are not helped here by pointing to certain feelings that are a concomitant of God's activity toward man, for this does not explain the meaning of our reference to this activity itself. This method, then, "fails to connect sentences about God to the religious activities which they both guide and reflect." [227]

Another inadequacy in the attempt to explain the theological use of words by merely whittling-down or negatively qualifying their ordinary use is revealed when we ask, "Why should I truly turn unto him?" One may or may not be interested in golf or in art exhibits, but it is typical of the believer's understanding of "God" that the possibility of indifference toward God, his forgiveness, will, etc. is ruled out. Kierkegaard speaks of "passionate interest," Tillich of "ultimate concern," Farrer of "aspiration" toward the infinite. As Alston puts the point, "A man who says, 'Oh yes, I know God made and sustains me, judges me, and died for my sins to save me,' then yawns and turns to the sports page . . . is exhibiting . . . a misunderstanding of 'God.' " [228] But in what sense could the "set of disembodied conscious states" with which the whittle-down method leaves us command unconditional interest? Such an object would

[225] *Ibid.*, p. 439.
[227] *Ibid.*, p. 440.
[226] *Ibid.*
[228] *Ibid.*

fail not only to necessitate interest but even to arouse it in any but a handful of speculators such as Aristotle and the Deists. From this point of view, then, the whittle-down explanation commits a fallacy analogous to what G. E. Moore called the naturalistic fallacy in ethics, the fallacy of defining "good" in such a way that moral obligation is left out of account. Nor is the difficulty remedied by bringing into consideration the feelings of cosmic acceptance in the believer. It is true, of course, that such feelings are a matter of interest. But the method we are considering does not enable us to determine whether more is involved than the subjective state of the speaker. Is the interest rather in God's forgiveness? Does this concern, that is, extend beyond the subjective feeling to an objectively real God—to a relationship of which the feeling is but a component? As we have noted earlier, some believers assert God's forgiveness even on occasions when feelings of having been forgiven are absent.[229]

We see, then, that the whittle-down explanation of statements about God's activity supplies us with a *picture* of this activity, albeit a very ghostly one, but does not give us rules that enable us to use it. To understand "God forgives the sins of those who truly turn unto him," we are invited to picture a human act of forgiveness and then to omit from that picture all physical activity. But in making this negative qualification

we have taken away an essential condition of the literal use of "forgives" without indicating what is to be put in its place. At this point we have but a fragment of a meaning. We don't yet know . . . what would count for or against its truth, what sort of implications it has, or what to do about it.[230]

To speak of God as acting implies that he makes contact with some-one, but in the whittle-down account we have not contact but a private mental state. To be sure, this method does leave us with the additional factor of feelings of having been forgiven, but it does not help us to understand in what way, if any, these feelings are related to the alleged private mental state. We are not, that is, enabled to understand in what sense the feelings are a concomitant of some sort of interaction between God and believer. It does not help simply to assert that the private mental occurrence in God must, in some way, be the cause of the feelings in the believer, for this would not enable us to answer the questions we posed: "How do I know whether this is true?" "How do I 'turn unto him'?" etc. Perhaps, for example, the one causes the other in the sense that a fictitious story about a for-giving God evokes feelings of forgiveness, or perhaps "God" is to be

[229] *Ibid.*   [230] *Ibid.*, p. 441.

given an objective reference and "causes" will have a quite different meaning. The whittle-down method does not enable us to decide. We are led to agree, then, with the judgment of I. M. Crombie concerning the results of the whittle-down method that "such ghostly and evacuated concepts are clearly too tenuous and elusive to be called the meanings of the words we use." [231]

Wittgenstein's point that *a language-game may give us a picture without providing adequate rules for its application* is illustrated by Alston with an example drawn from psychoanalytic theory. From Freud's *The Ego and the Id* Alston selects the following statements:

At the very beginning all the libido is accumulated in the id, while the ego is still in process of formation or far from robust. Part of the libido is sent out by the id into erotic object-cathexes, whereupon the ego, now growing stronger, attempts to obtain possession of the object-libido and to force itself upon the id as a love-object. [232]

As is the case in theological language so here, too, words are borrowed from our ordinary language about human beings and given a new use. Obviously one is not to think of the ego as one person who is flirting with another named "Id," say, by making eyes at him. If we follow our previous method of whittling away the meanings that no longer apply, we might say that "the id is like a lustful brute, but without a body and not even a glimmer of reason, etc; the ego is like a prudent business man, except for analogous restrictions." [233] This would give us a picture, but we would not know how to use it. To add rules for its use "we must make explicit the sort of behavior which is to be expected in particular cases when this attraction does or does not take place; we must specify some way of (at least roughly) measuring the amount of energy possessed by the ego or id at a particular time." [234]

From the perspective provided by Wittgenstein, then, we have examined at length the attempt to indicate an analogical meaning for religious language—a meaning that will avoid anthropomorphism, on the one hand, and an empty equivocation, on the other. We have argued that the analogical approach does not enable us to apply our religious language. We are given a picture without adequate guide for using it.

[231] "Theology and Falsification," p. 122.
[232] "The Elucidation of Religious Statements," p. 441. Even more graphically, Freud continues: "When the ego assumes the features of the object, it fixes itself, so to speak, upon the id as a love-object and tries to make good the loss of the object by saying, 'look, I am so like the object, you can love me as well.'"
[233] *Ibid.*   [234] *Ibid.*, pp. 441-42.

An alternative picture is provided by Hartshorne, Ogden, and others who think of the entire universe as the body of God. God's relation to man, it is contended, is analogous to man's relation to his body. God may then be seen to be immediately aware of man in much the sense that man is directly aware of his body.

This analogy is fundamentally deficient, however, as a guide to talk of God acting in history. When we speak of God as calling, judging, delivering, reconciling, forgiving, and the like our predicates are taken from man's relation with his world rather than from his relation with his body; and the rules governing talk of our inter-personal relations are far different from the rules governing talk of our awareness of our bodies. Consider, for example, "My elbow hurts," "My foot has fallen asleep," "I feel great." Such talk has much less in common with talk of God acting than does talk of John acting. The picture is there, but what is its application?

Before concluding our account of Wittgenstein we may at least mention two further points of relevance to religious-use. First, Wittgenstein warned that the range of application of many of our concepts will not be defined by one particular characteristic. Instead of this, the phenomena to which a concept applies may be related in terms of "family resemblances." As William James pointed out in *Varieties of Religious Experience* the various things that are called religion share no essential characteristic. We may well find this to be true of many other concepts that find an important place in our religious language-games.

Secondly, we may recall Wittgenstein's belief that "it was possible for the sickness of philosophical problems to get cured only through a changed mode of thought and of life." Whether or not one chooses to use the word "sickness," the application to religious problems is evident.

Our account finds an apt conclusion in these words by M. O'C. Drury:

[Kierkegaard once wrote] "Let the understanding condemn what is transitory, let it clear the ground, then wonder comes in the right place, in ground that is cleared in the changed man." . . . That was the secret of Wittgenstein. . . . No one had such power to awaken again that primitive wonder from which all great philosophy begins. . . . One evening not long before his death Wittgenstein quoted to me the inscription that Bach wrote on the title page of his *Little Organ Book.* "To the glory of the most high God, and that my neighbor may be benefitted thereby." Pointing to his own pile of manuscript, he said: "That is what I would have liked to have been able to say about my own work." . . . I think that wish was granted him.[235]

[235] "Ludwig Wittgenstein: A Symposium," pp. 70-71.

PART THREE: *Subsequent Developments*

JOHN WISDOM: *Paradox, Platitude, & Discovery*

Chapter Seven

The most significant development of Wittgenstein's point of view by linguistic philosophers is their more constructive view of metaphysical language-use. There have been two main lines of development among these philosophers, one having its center at Oxford, the other at Cambridge. Oxford philosophers have been especially concerned with ordinary language, although in recent years they have given increasing attention to metaphysics. Cambridge philosophers follow Wittgenstein more closely in practicing philosophy as a "therapy" for the mental cramp that is characteristic of metaphysics. John Wisdom is the leading figure in the Cambridge line of development and is fairly representative.

As early as 1936, Wisdom wrote that Wittgenstein "too much represents [philosophical statements] as merely symptoms of linguistic confusion. I wish to represent them as also symptoms of linguistic penetration." [1] Wittgenstein held that ordinary grammar "tells us what kind of object anything is." But, according to Wisdom, our ordinary grammar only tells us part of the story, for between one sort of object and another there are "likenesses and differences concealed by ordinary language." [2] This is because "with every name we apply we compare

---

[1] "Philosophical Perplexity," *Philosophy and Psycho-Analysis*, p. 41. Originally published in *Proceedings of the Aristotelian Society*, 1936. Used by permission of the editor. Urmson speaks of this article as "the first which throughout embodied the new philosophical outlook." (*Philosophical Analysis*, p. 173.)

[2] "Philosophical Perplexity," p. 41.

one thing with another, with many others." [3] If we call something a desk we compare it with many other things that we also call desks. When, in this way, we classify one thing with a second rather than with a third, we draw attention to the likenesses and away from the differences it has with the second, and we draw attention to the differences and away from the likenesses it has with the third. If we say "creativity is work" we draw attention to the likenesses of creativity to work and to the differences of creativity from play. But if we say "creativity is play" we draw attention to the differences of creativity from work and the likenesses of creativity to play. Everything is at least a little like and a little unlike everything else, and no matter how we group things we tend to lose sight of how richly varied these things are. Wisdom emphasizes that "any classificatory system is a net spread on the blessed manifold of the individual and blinding us not to all but to too many of its varieties and continuities." [4]

It is the function of metaphysical theories to point up some of these likenesses and differences which ordinarily go unnoticed—likenesses and differences between various sorts of knowledge and between various types of things known. They do this by presenting a grammar that shows some of the features that ordinary grammar conceals; they really function as "penetrating suggestions as to how [language] might be used so as to reveal what, by the actual use of language, is hidden." [5] Metaphysical sentences that have this use express "metaphysical paradoxes," so called because they are contrary to what we ordinarily or conventionally say—hence para-conventional. But these statements conceal what was brought out by ordinary grammar, so they must be balanced by "metaphysical platitudes," "timely reminders of what is revealed by the actual use of language and would be hidden by the new." [6] One metaphysician may argue paradoxically that we cannot really have knowledge of the future. Another may reply platitudinously that we obviously do have knowledge of the future; no one really, sanely, doubts that the sun will rise tomorrow. G. E. Moore, we may recall, made devastating use of such platitudes. Wittgenstein's reminders about the grammar of ordinary language are also metaphysically platitudinous, while Wisdom contends that "philosophers should be continually trying to say what cannot be said." [7]

There are important insights in metaphysical theories, then, but

[3] "Philosophy, Metaphysics and Psycho-Analysis," *Philosophy and Psycho-Analysis*, p. 274.

[4] "Philosophy, Anxiety, and Novelty" (1944), reprinted in *Philosophy and Psycho-Analysis*, p. 119.

[5] "Metaphysics and Verification," *ibid.*, p. 100.

[6] *Ibid.*, pp. 100-101.

[7] "Philosophical Perplexity," p. 50.

metaphysicians have been confused about these insights. Like Wittgenstein, Wisdom seeks to "remove the wrong idea that [the metaphysician's point concerns] a question of fact whether natural or logical." [8] Because his questions look as if they are in some sense questions of fact, the philosopher sees his theory about them as incompatible with the theories of other philosophers and, perhaps, with the conventional point of view of common sense. But each of these approaches may be useful, for each may bring out a point about the subject matter that the others conceal. Since any classificatory system, any grammar, will blind us to some features of a thing, it is "in accepting *all* systems [that] their blinding power is broken, their revealing power becomes acceptable; the individual is restored to us, not isolated as before we used language, not in a box as when language mastered us, but in 'creation's chorus.' " [9] The more comparisons and contrasts we make between things the more we come to see each for what it is.

To understand Wisdom's procedure in removing metaphysical confusion and clarifying metaphysical insight, it will be helpful to consider at some length a subject to which he has devoted particular attention, namely, metaphysical reflection on our knowledge of other people's feelings. Ordinarily if someone acts in an angry way, we feel that this justifies our saying that we *know* he is angry. But the philosophic skeptic tells us that we do not really know (and can never know) what we think we know (paradox!), because the other person may be deceiving us (and may continue to do so). More than that, we have never once got behind these behavioral signs to discover, by direct experience, that there is a corresponding inward state or, indeed, any sort of consciousness. We are entitled to say that we *think* he is angry or that he appears to be angry but not that we *know* he is angry. Asked to justify our claim to know the other's inward state by other than our ordinary reasons, such as what one says and how one acts, "we are as helpless," suggests Wisdom, "as an electrician if he is asked to make sure that a battery is charged, without connecting it to a tram, an electric light bulb, a clock or a bell." [10]

Using this model, the positivist tries to rescue us by insisting that the skeptic's doubts are pointless; they are pseudo-doubts, since to know that a man is angry just is to know that he behaves in certain ways. The meaning just is the method of verification, and, as we have seen in our chapter on positivism, this means that evidence must be just the same sort of thing as that for which it is evidence. Since

[8] "Metaphysics and Verification," p. 100.
[9] "Philosophy, Anxiety and Novelty," p. 119.
[10] "Philosophy, Metaphysics and Psycho-Analysis," p. 256.

our alleged knowledge of another's mind is supported solely by observations of his behavior this knowledge must really be knowledge of his behavior.

But this positivistic answer breaks down, because the way that we know consciousness is not just like the way that we know behavior or the way that we know electricity. Anger is more than angry behavior in ways that electricity is not more than electrical phenomena. The experience of our own anger is more than our experience of our own angry behavior, and our experience of own anger plays a part in what we mean when we say that we know that someone else is angry. If one is color-blind, he does not know about someone else's experience of red in just the way that someone who is not color-blind does. And then, too, people can practice deception—electricity cannot.[11] Meaning and verification, then, are not identical. There is more than one sort of relation between knowledge and evidence.

Both the skeptic and the positivist are making the same mistake. They are treating our knowledge of other people's minds as though it were something other than it is. When the skeptic says that we cannot know that someone else is angry, he is not using "know" to mean what we ordinarily mean by it in speaking of another's anger. He is using it to mean what it does mean when we say that we know our own anger or, perhaps, that we know that so-and-so is acting in an angry way. In other words, he is not using "know" in its "literal" or "strict" sense,[12] that is, in the sense that it ordinarily or conventionally has in statements about other people's minds. This is what Wisdom means in concluding that the skeptic's statement is not true if taken literally.[13]

But the statement makes a point rather obliquely in calling attention to certain features of our knowledge about other people's minds, namely, how different this is from our knowledge of their behavior or of our own minds. The statement makes a point because it is just these differences which our ordinary grammars conceal when we speak of our knowledge in each of these cases as certain.

The defect in the positivist's defense is similar in that he wrongly believes he is defending the literal or conventional meaning of "know" when it is used in this context, and is actually using it in the sense that it has when we say that we know someone else's behavior. It is not true that the literal, conventional meaning of "know" in these two contexts is identical, and it is just those differences in the two

[11] *Ibid.*, pp. 257-58.
[12] See Wisdom's use of these terms in *ibid.*, p. 273, and in "Philosophical Perplexity," p. 44.
[13] "Philosophy, Metaphysics and Psycho-Analysis," pp. 258-59.

uses of "know" that the skeptic has complained about, and has obliquely drawn attention to, to begin with.[14] This is the error of any reductionist; he confuses and wrongly equates the way in which we know one sort of statement with the way in which we know another sort of statement. In other words, as Wisdom has put it, "the reductionist says statements of class C^1 are in the end verifiable in the same way as statements of class C^2 when this is not the case." It was the defect which may be seen, for example, in the atomist's program (which Wisdom formerly shared) of analysis as (reductive) translation.[15] And this is what Wisdom and the other language philosophers are pointing to when they insist that a philosopher cannot reduce anything to anything else, that he leaves everything as it is, and, to borrow from Butler via Moore, that everything is what it is and not another thing (often called "the idiosyncrasy platitude" when cast in the form that every type of expression has its own peculiar logic).

But there is a point to the positivist's reductionistic move, just as there is to the skeptic's. The skeptic draws attention to the difference between these uses of "know"—these ways of knowing; the positivist reminds us of their similarities. The moves of both are useful as devices by which we may come to see our knowledge of other minds more clearly—see it in terms of its similarities to and differences from other sorts of knowledge. By means of these devices, we simply must come to see and accept this knowledge for what it is. There are, in effect, no problems about it. If we come to see this by following Wisdom's therapeutic method of interpreting these philosophic statements as intuitive devices, the therapy is successful. We are cured of the grammatical illusion that there are philosophic problems, in this case a problem about our knowledge of other minds. We come to see that doubts about the possibility of such knowledge are idle but that we could understand the nature of such knowledge clearly only by tracing these doubts to the grammatical insight that is their source.

Once we trace these doubts to their source we *see* the comparison we were making of our knowledge of other people's minds with our knowledge of their behavior, a comparison which, since we were not aware of making it, led us into the trap of rejecting one sort of knowledge because it is not just like another sort. We were trapped, that is, by the unexamined tyranny of a subconsciously favored language

---

[14] *Ibid.*, pp. 258-60.

[15] Urmson remarks of the atomists that "they did not see that their own reclassificatory moves, such as their thesis that physical objects were logical constructions and not genuine particulars, because physical objects did not answer to their justified notion of a particular, were not so different from the reclassificatory moves of those who said that time was *unreal* because it did not answer to their *requirements for a genuine substance*." (*Philosophical Analysis*, p. 196. Italics mine.)

use or type of knowledge. Without fully realizing it, we assumed that all relations of knowledge to evidence must be of the sort that it is in our knowledge of behavior or of electricity. Our knowledge of other minds simply is what we think it is when we do not allow our grammar to suggest nonexistent similarities and to conceal real differences.[16]

This is the therapeutic task of the philosopher, the task of removing the metaphysician's confusions and clarifying his insight. Wisdom is trying simply to lay our grammars before us so that we can see them as they are. What we come to see is something that we have always known but have not been clear about, and, so, we have been vulnerable to the danger that linguistic habit will allow our grammars to mislead us.

Wittgenstein's cure for linguistic confusions, then, is incomplete. His goal was to show what the confusion is, namely, an attempt to use a grammar for a subject matter to which it is not suited, a subject matter that is outside the scope of the language-game that that grammar defines. The positivist, for example, tries to apply to our talk of knowing another's mind the grammar that governs our talk of knowing another's behavior. But Wittgenstein gave too little attention to the way in which this wrong application of a grammar may also be *illuminating;* in looking at, say, our knowledge of another's mind from the point of view of the grammar we ordinarily apply to another's behavior we may notice features of our knowledge of another's mind which are concealed by our conventional grammar for that knowledge.[17] This wrong application provides this illumination by forcing a comparision of the two sorts of knowledge or types of statement, in effect asking the question "Do X sentences mean the same as Y sentences?" [18] "Do other-mind sentences mean the same as behavior sentences?" By asking this we may notice differences between our knowledge of another's mind and our knowledge of his behavior, differences that our ordinary grammars conceal in using the same word, "know," in both cases. According to Wisdom, then, "the philosopher's purpose is to gain a grasp of the relations between different categories of being [e.g., mind and body], between expressions used in *different manners,*" [19] between what Wittgenstein called different language-games. "Only such

---

[16] "Philosophy, Metaphysics and Psycho-Analysis," pp. 259-60.

[17] We may recall that Wittgenstein did say such things as: "What [the metaphysicians] have primarily discovered is a new way of looking at things" (*Philosophical Investigations,* 401); "philosophical mistakes contain so much truth" (*Zettel,* 460); "the use of expressions constructed on analogical patterns stresses analogies between cases often far apart. And by doing this these expressions may be extremely useful" (*Blue Book,* p. 28).

[18] "Metaphysics and Verification," p. 100.

[19] "Philosophical Perplexity," p. 42.

treatment of the puzzles as increases a grasp of the relations between different categories of being is philosophical"—i.e. constitutes "philosophical progress." [20]

The metaphysician, then, would not be satisfied with Wittgenstein's treatment, for he would insist that he really was making a point. Wisdom attempts to draw out his point, to show him how he has been confused about it, and to show him the contribution he really makes with it. In this way the metaphysician may be cured of his doubt and puzzlement about our ordinary grammar, and may come to see how his insight can be reconciled with other points of view.

According to Wisdom, then, this method is therapeutic. He even suggests that this therapy has similarities with psychoanalytic therapy: "When we consider the obstinate doubts of the metaphysician 'Can one ever know what's right or wrong?' 'Can one ever know what others think or feel?' they readily remind us of the chronic doubts of the neurotic and psychotic 'Have I committed the unpardonable sin?' 'Aren't they all against me really?' " [21] The impasses of metaphysical dispute make us wonder "whether the forces at work in this curiously unsatisfactory struggle which never ends in success nor in failure aren't *in part* the same as those at work in those other struggles" [22]—those dealt with in psychoanalysis. The analysis of these "forces at work" is too vague to be much more than suggestive, although Wisdom does carry it one step further in saying that the philosopher's doubt differs from the neurotic's because there is genuine insight at the bottom of it.[23] Somewhat clearer, however, is his contention that the two therapies are somewhat alike in treatment. In psychoanalysis the analyst encourages the patient "to describe his own case, not in 'septic' general terms . . . but in 'aseptic' story language." [24] Similarly the metaphysician must be encouraged to

describe fully the sort of question or statement he is considering. By the time he has done this . . . he has set it in the language map with regard to all other questions. And thus he has answered his own question.[25]

In this way, Wisdom offers an explanation as to why metaphysical problems have proved insoluble, all attempts at solution leading to

[20] *Ibid.*

[21] "Philosophy, Metaphysics and Psycho-Analysis," pp. 218-82.

[22] *Ibid.*, p. 281. (Italics mine.)

[23] "Philosophy and Psycho-Analysis" (1946), reprinted in *Philosophy and Psycho-Analysis*, p. 174. Recently, however, Wisdom said to me, "What I say about the difference is unsatisfactory. The neurotic and the psychotic may show insight."

[24] "Other Minds I," reprinted in John Wisdom, *Other Minds*, 2nd ed. (Oxford: Basil Blackwell, 1965), p. 1, n.

[25] *Ibid.*

a deadlock between opposing theories. This would be difficult to understand had the issues really been ones of fact, whether empirical or logical. Conflicting attempts to solve these problems have resulted in an impasse because there are no such metaphysical problems in the first place; attempts at their solution must be reinterpreted as the employment of rather ingenious linguistic "devices" that provide, not new facts, but new insight into facts. By these devices we are able to see for the first time ways in which facts of sort A are similar to facts of sort B and different from facts of sort C. These relations between different sorts of facts Wisdom at one time called the "ultimate structure of facts." The point of philosophical statements "is the illumination of the ultimate structure of facts, i.e. the relations between different categories of being." [26]

Reasoning About Patterns

Wisdom's discussion of our knowledge of other minds illustrates his important ideas on the nature of rational procedures. Both the skeptic and the reductionist are worried about the apparent logical jump in going from premises about angry behavior to a conclusion not about behavior but about an angry state of mind. Propositions about behavior are of a different logical type than propositions about states of mind. On the other hand, yet another sort of metaphysician, the transcendentalist, rightly sees that we do know about other minds, yet shares the worry about the difference in logical types involved in the relation of knowledge and evidence if behavior is our only evidence. The evidence that we seemingly must use to close the gap between our knowledge of another's mind and the evidence that supports it, he concludes, must be found in some sort of intellectual intuition of the other's mind. The mind must be a special sort of entity about which we can know a special sort of fact.[27] But, talk of such transcendent, metaphysical entities fares no better than talk of invisible leprechauns who run watches. The transcendentalist's mistake is to share with the skeptic and the reductionist the belief that meaning and verification are identical, or to put it more helpfully, that a deductive argument is valid only if an analytic relation exists between evidence or premises and conclusion so that it is logically contradictory to affirm the truth of the premises while denying the truth of the conclusion.

Most of our everyday argument, in fact, is not this analytic sort but is rather of a sort that Stephen Toulmin calls substantial. Typically our conclusions involve more than the evidence of our premises. We

---

[26] "Philosophical Perplexity," p. 37.
[27] "Metaphysics and Verification," p. 85; "Gods," p. 151.

draw conclusions about anger from angry behavior, about the future from the past, about beauty from visible features of a painting, about God from patterns in nature and events in history.[28] Acknowledging a special indebtedness to Wisdom, Toulmin criticizes formal logicians for their preoccupation with analytic arguments, for this leaves much of our everyday reasoning unclarified and encourages the deeply entrenched tendency to identify valid deductive argument with analytic argument.[29] A further example of this tendency is the following:

Christian moral judgments are decisions, not conclusions. From the point of view of "pure reason" it must be confessed that the "practical reason" (Kant's moral faculty) works in a style quite as arbitrary and absurd as the leap of faith. . . . We cannot build a logical bridge from facts to values, from is-ness to ought-ness. Indeed this applies as much to aesthetics as to ethics. . . . This elementary truth [has] its classical form in Hume's argument. . . . Both ethics and jurisprudence are evaluating and choosing; science and logic are only auxiliary.[30]

The limited usefulness of analytic argument may be seen if we take an example from one of the most popular texts on formal logic.

All times when Bill wears a sweater are times when Bill does not go to work.
This morning is a time when Bill wore a sweater.
∴ This morning is a time when Bill did not go to work.

This argument is analytic only if the "all times" referred to in the first or major premise includes this morning, for otherwise there would be no contradiction if the premises were true and the conclusion false. But if "all times" includes this morning then the conclusion merely restates part of the information contained in the major premise and such restating, one can readily see, is of rather limited usefulness.[31]

Closely related is Wisdom's insistence that much valid reasoning is neither of the inductive nor of the deductive types described in textbooks of formal logic. A doctor reasons inductively when he makes a diagnosis in light of certain symptoms. Perhaps he says "duodenal

[28] Cf. *Other Minds*, Preface; "Metaphysics and Verification," p. 51.
[29] *The Uses of Argument* (Cambridge: The University Press, 1958), Chap. 3 (esp. p. 145).
[30] Joseph Fletcher, "Six Propositions: The New Look in Christian Ethics," *Harvard Divinity Bulletin*, Oct., 1959, pp. 8-9.
[31] Toulmin proposes that the major premise be understood not as a premise but as a statement of the warrant or justification for going from the minor premise to the conclusion. As a warrant it would read "If any time is a time when Bill wears a sweater it may (certainly, almost certainly, with some probability, or etc.) be taken to be a time when Bill does not go to work." If the warrant is justified it will have adequate reasons to serve as its backing. An argument will be analytic if and only if the conclusion is already contained in the backing. (Cf. pp. 97-125.)

ulcer." Here there is an element of prophecy, for the future course of the disease and perhaps further testing and examination will confirm or disconfirm the diagnosis. Finally, when the disease has run its course and all the facts are in, the diagnosis may be completely confirmed and the doctor can say, "There you are, it was duodenal ulcer." At this point the reasoning is deductive, for it would be contradictory to accept the facts that are evidence and yet deny the conclusion "duodenal ulcer." Wisdom contrasts these cases with the very different type of case in a court of law in which the facts of the case are agreed upon and yet opposing counsels present arguments concerning, for example, whether reasonable care was exercised. Here the conclusions have neither the element of prophecy present in a diagnosis nor the demonstrative completeness of a diagnosis fully confirmed.[32] The reasoning is neither inductive nor deductive but is that of tracing patterns in the relationships between the various facts of the case, comparing one pattern with another and with yet another, contrasting it with still others.

In such cases we notice that the process of argument is not a *chain* of demonstrative reasoning. It is a presenting and representing of those features of the case which *severally cooperate* in favour . . . of calling the situation by the name by which he wishes to call it. The reasons are like the legs of a chair, not the links of a chain.[33]

To call the situation by the name "negligence" is to classify or connect it with others of that sort, while to call it "reasonable care" is to make a contrasting classification. Similar examples may be found, say, in aesthetics, in ethics, in medical diagnosis, in literary criticism; or we may consider Newton's work in connecting the fall of an apple with the orbit of a planet, Freud's work in connecting adult and childhood experience, and, as we have seen, Wisdom's own work in metaphysics. Wisdom departs radically, then, from the analytic-synthetic dichotomy so powerfully employed in the positivistic tradition from Hume to Ayer and Braithwaite. Statements that give us new insight, drawing attention to patterns we have missed, are cognitive also.

This process of connecting and comparing is, in fact, the most fundamental of our ways of reasoning, for simply in using a concept we are comparing one thing with others, and in predicating, say, a quality of something we are comparing it with other things of which we predicate this quality. If, for example, I call a decision unjust

---

[32] "Philosophy, Metaphysics and Psycho-Analysis," pp. 267-68.
[33] "Gods," p. 157. Originally published in *Proceedings of the Aristotelian Society*, 1944. Used by permission of the editor.

I am, implicitly at least, comparing it with other decisions that I have regarded as unjust.[34] According to Wisdom, then,

> examples are the final food for thought. Principles and laws . . . can help us bring to bear on what is now in question what is not now in question. They help us connect one thing with another and another. But at the bar of reason, always the final appeal is to cases.[35]

To ask what a thing is is to ask for comparisons and contrasts with other things, and it is here that reason does its most basic work.

Successful explanation relates the unfamiliar to the familiar and, with typical consistency, Wisdom shows the nature of metaphysical statements by showing how they are like and how they are unlike other sorts of statement with which we are quite familiar. In his early article "Philosophical Perplexity," [36] Wisdom argues both paradoxically that "philosophical [i.e., metaphysical] statements are really verbal" [37] and platitudinously that "philosophical statements are not verbal." [38] It is the word "really" that gives us the tip we are dealing with paradox, although the paradox-platitude distinction—paradox suggesting how language might be used, platitude reminding us how it actually is used—is not clearly made until two years later in "Metaphysics and Verification." [39] Unfortunately, however, the meaning of "verbal" is somewhat confused, for "verbal" is used sometimes in the sense of "verbal recommendation" [40]—a recommendation about how words are to be used—and sometimes in the sense of a statement conveying facts about words.[41] When "verbal" is taken in the sense of "verbal recommendation," by "not verbal" Wisdom makes the correction that a philosophical sentence is a statement—an assertion of fact—and so the correction draws attention to the similarities of philosophical and factual statements. But when "verbal" is taken in the sense of "statement about words," by "not verbal" Wisdom makes the correction that the philosopher's statement has a different point than a factual statement has. A philosophical statement is used to show something about the structure of a fact—its relation to other sorts

[34] In "The Metamorphosis of Metaphysics," *Paradox and Discovery* (Oxford: Basil Blackwell, 1965), p. 68, we read that attributing a property means "marking an affinity between something and other things."

[35] "A Feature of Wittgenstein's Technique," in *Paradox and Discovery*, p. 102. Compare J. S. Mill, *A System of Logic*, Book II, Chapter III, Section 4.

[36] Urmson notes that "this article was the first which throughout embodied the new philosophical outlook." (*Philosophical Analysis*, p. 173.)

[37] "Philosophical Perplexity," p. 36.   [38] *Ibid.*, p. 37.

[39] In his first paragraph, in fact, Wisdom mixes instances of paradoxical and platitudinous statements, while his subsequent talk about verbal recommendation is, of course, applicable only to the former.

[40] "Philosophical Perplexity," p. 36.

[41] *Ibid.*, p. 37.

of fact—and only incidentally reports a fact. An ordinary statement is used to report a fact and only incidentally shows something about the structure of that fact.[42] For example, philosophical statements about our knowledge of other minds show something of the relation of that knowledge to other sorts of knowledge, whereas the ordinary statement "I happen to know that John is quite angry about this" reports a fact about John while rather obliquely suggesting the similarity of this knowledge with other types of knowledge.

Wisdom notes that G. E. Moore criticizes the verbal recommendation interpretation of (paradoxical) philosophical statements on ground that when one literally *recommends* a change in verbal behavior he "means by this that we ought to do this as a regular thing. Moore then says that philosophers don't do all that. Undoubtedly he is right." [43] We might say the recommendation is that we consider a way that language *might be* used so that we come to see more clearly how it *is* used.[44] And yet the danger in putting it like this is that we may fail to take the paradox seriously enough really to get its point.[45] Just as in psychoanalysis insight comes not in stating a truth in general terms but in working through in detail the actual events concerned, so in metaphysics we do not really see the point until we have done the detailed comparing and contrasting of particular cases and so have brought out all the reasons for and all the reasons against accepting the recommendation.

When Wisdom says, then, that "a philosophical answer is really a verbal recommendation" he is himself *really* making a verbal recommendation, and then this statement is in turn *really* a verbal recommendation, and so on. But, as Wisdom points out, the problem is in "trying to say what cannot be said." [46] For there is no adequate paraphrase for the detailed comparing and contrasting with which Wisdom's writings abound and which by their omission make any general account of his work so inadequate.

Once again the purpose of philosophical statements is "the illumina-

[42] When the fact it reports is true, the philosophical statement is platitudinous, since it merely reminds us of what our ordinary grammar reveals about the structure of the facts. When the fact that it reports is false the philosophical statement is paradoxical, revealing something about the structure of facts that ordinary grammar conceals. If the point of a paradox were to report a fact, then it would be rejected because false. But since its point is to reveal something about the structure of a fact, it is accepted as illuminating.

[43] "Philosophy, Anxiety and Novelty," p. 116.

[44] "Thus the metaphysical paradoxes appear no longer as crude falsehoods about how language is actually used, but as penetrating suggestions as to how it might be used so as to reveal what, by the actual use of language, is hidden." "Metaphysics and Verification," p. 100.

[45] "Philosophy, Anxiety and Novelty," p. 116.

[46] "Philosophical Perplexity," p. 50.

tion of the ultimate structure of facts,[47] i.e. the relations between different categories of being or . . . the relations between different sub-languages within a language." [48] "What is wanted," Wisdom explains, "is some device for bringing out the relations between the manner in which [sentences of one type] are used and the manners in which others are used—so as to give their place on the language map." [49]

Limitations of the Paradox-Platitude Classification

We may be helped to see more adequately this process of mapping statements if we consider a possible criticism of this process as we have so far described it. It may be asked whether we can really come to see the *ultimate* structure of facts, whether we can really get this all placed on a language map deserving to be called *the* language map. Perhaps we can say that this is simply an unobtainable ideal to be borne in mind as we go about the unending task of describing similarities and differences. But notice what happens if we allow the descriptive method to be tied to Wisdom's classifications of paradox and platitude. Paradoxical views, those differing from our actual use of language as described in platitudinous views, are allowed the power to illuminate but not to eliminate or significantly to alter our language uses. We must take such paradoxes seriously enough so that we do not castrate their power to reveal something about the use they challenge [50] but not so seriously that we fail to castrate their power to call into question the adequacy of that use—fail to reduce these paradoxes from a recommendation to a device. The paradoxical assertion that "we cannot really know another's mind" is a helpful device to draw attention to differences between our knowledge of another's mind and our knowledge of his behavior, but we surely would not seriously consider dropping our ordinary talk about another's mind—e.g., about his anger or his pain. Yet the resulting eternal recurrence of the platitude as the correct view of things has the effect of placing beyond challenge our present language uses. It has the effect of making our present uses infallible guides to the ultimate structure of the facts, or, as Wisdom more commonly says, to the relations between different categories of being. It seems, too, to neglect the fact that language uses change and that they may well vary from one speech community to another.

The paradox-platitude scheme is most plausible in those tried and

---

[47] Compare this with the statement made in his logical atomism period that "the philosopher's intention is increased clearness in the apprehension of the ultimate structure of facts." ("Ostentation" [1933], reprinted in *Philosophy and Psycho-Analysis*, p. 8.)

[48] "Philosophical Perplexity," p. 37.

[49] *Ibid.*, p. 50.

[50] "Philosophy, Metaphysics and Psycho-Analysis," p. 273.

true areas of language use to which Wisdom has devoted particular attention, e.g., talk of knowing that there is cheese on the table or, especially, of knowing that John is angry. Uses in these areas seem to change little, if any. In fact, it is difficult to see how they could change significantly unless the conditions of human life undergo radical change. How, for example, could we make applicable a doubt whether we ever really know there is cheese on the table? This sort of doubt turns to dust when we try to give it an everyday employment. We might, for example, say "probably there is cheese on the table" in those cases where we now say "there is cheese on the table" but if we were to make this change, Wisdom points out, we should have to find some new way of indicating the practical differences in certainty which we now mark by the use of "probably." Consequently we would have changed only the form of words. The use of "probably" would become quite idle as did the warning calls of the boy who cried "wolf" too often.[51]

But Wisdom has also given attention to more unsettled and varied areas of language, particularly that of religion, and subsequent developments in his thought lend support to what seem evident conclusions in any event, namely, (1) that the use of his method of comparing and contrasting particular cases has no necessary tie to the paradox-platitude classification and (2) that the sort of rational reflection carried on by this method may and does lead to helpful changes in language.

Although in his early essays in the thirties [52] Wisdom speaks very broadly about finding the place of sentences on the language map by comparing and contrasting uses, by 1944 [53] he speaks more precisely about comparing the ways in which sentences may be supported, the sort of reasons which may be given to justify them. And a few years later we are told that "epistemology—puzzles of the form 'Do we really know?' 'How do we really know?'—and ontology—puzzles of the form 'What is it that we claim to know?'—are one." [54] To say that two things are of a different nature, then, is really to say that they are known in different ways.[55]

With this clarification we are in a position to see that the determina-

[51] "Philosophical Perplexity," pp. 42 ff.
[52] "Philosophical Perplexity" (1936), and "Metaphysics and Verification" (1938).
[53] "Philosophy, Anxiety and Novelty," "Moore's Technique," "Gods."
[54] "Note on the New Edition of Professor Ayer's Language, Truth and Logic," p. 229.
[55] However, as we have seen in the case of our knowledge of other minds, the way that we know something may include more than the procedure we use for verifying a belief about it. Justification of talk about other minds must finally include reference to experience of our own minds.

tion of the place of a type of statement on the language map of statements is a critical process in which we may find sufficient reason for
saying that a statement has no place on the map at all or that it
has a place that is different from the place it is commonly thought
to have—i.e., the place it would have to have if certain inferences that
are sometimes drawn from it were truly justified. Wisdom distinguishes, for example, between disputes that are "practical and settleable"
and those which are "academic and idle." [56] "The dispute as to whether
it is a leprechaun or a brownie who makes my watch sing . . . becomes
[academic and idle] when not only every tested but every testable consequence of the two hypotheses is the same." [57] We are able to
enquire whether a dispute is settleable or idle, or settleable in some
respects but idle in others, because we know the meaning of "settleable
and idle." We know, that is, some particular cases that are settleable
and some particular cases that are idle, cases about which everyone
agrees. Everyone agrees, for example, that disputes about who will
win the race are settleable, whereas disputes as to whether an invisible
leprechaun rides on the shoulders of every winning horse are idle. Unless
we do know about some cases we could not enquire about others because the enquiry must proceed by comparison and contrast of the
doubtful and unclear with the certain and clear. Our terms of classification, in other words, must be understood. They must have their
paradigm cases.

Placing a type of statement on the statement-map, then, is not
prescriptive but descriptive. If we believe that a dispute is mistakenly
being taken as settleable and we wish by rational persuasion to bring
the disputants to see this and to withdraw their bets as misplaced we
will compare their case with others that they agree are idle and contrast
their case with those they understand to be the betting type. If they,
in turn, point to comparisons we had not understood we may then
see that their dispute is more of the betting sort than first appeared.

We see, then, that the critical process of finding a statement's place
on the map, describing its relation to other sorts of statement, must
finally be rooted in some language uses about which we all agree.
There must be some platitudes as points of reference for our reasoning.
But this does not at all mean that anything that people do with words
is by that very fact beyond rational criticism and simply to be accepted
as platitudinous.

This becomes especially clear in Wisdom's discussion of religious
language use. We shall soon see something of his efforts to map a
logic of religious use which retains essential features of traditional
and biblical use while withstanding comparison with the logics of

---

[56] "Other Minds I," p. 12.   [57] Ibid.

statements of science and psychoanalysis. For now we are concerned only with Wisdom's view that present religious uses are generally unclear and confused. To become more clear about religious beliefs, however, we must do more than compare and contrast the way we support these beliefs with the ways we support beliefs in other more settled areas. We must first come to distinguish more clearly the reasons for these beliefs from the causes of these beliefs. In criticizing certain beliefs

we have not only to ascertain what reasons there are for them but also to decide what things are reasons and how much. This latter process of sifting reasons from causes is part of the critical process for every belief, but in some spheres it has been done pretty fully already. In these spheres we don't need to examine the actual processes to belief and distil from them a logic. But in other spheres this remains to be done.[58]

The logic of a type of belief is not a psychological question. It is not a question of the causes for a person's holding the belief. Rather, it is a philosophical question. It is a question of how the belief is supported by evidence. It is a question of what reasons may properly be appealed to for its justification.[59] After all, any beliefs that people hold will have causes, and the same sort of cause may well be operative both in those beliefs for which adequate rational justification may be given and in those for which no adequate rational justification may be given. To get clear about the sort of support there is for a belief we must come to see as fully as possible all the sources of that belief, reasons and causes alike; for if some sources are undetected we will not know whether they are in the nature of further sorts of reasons which must be taken into account if we are not to give a distorted account of the logic in question.

Clearly, then, in cases such as those of certain religious uses in which a logic has not yet adequately been distilled there can be no question of designating such uses as platitudinous. In fact, we could not even know quite what it would mean to call them platitudinous since platitudes are reminders of the logic of our uses. And it may well be that we will find some present religious uses to be without adequate forms of rational justification and come to see them, say, as mere psychological projections.

That Wisdom's method of comparing and contrasting particular cases has no necessary tie to the paradox-platitude classification receives

---

[58] "Gods," p. 163.

[59] Here, too, we must have our paradigms of reasons and of causes, and proceed by the method of comparing and contrasting. What in some cases we will then come to see is "how near to reasons are some causes which aren't reasons and how beside the point are many reasons." ("Other Minds I," p. 1., n.).

further support from the fact that, as Wisdom recognizes, the sort of rational reflection carried on by this method may and does lead to helpful changes in language. Wisdom tells us that one of the aims of his work in *Philosophy and Psycho-Analysis* "is a better recognition of our power to form new concepts, new habits of thought, when those we have already are inadequate." [60] In the concluding chapter of that book, for example, Wisdom states that

in describing people, though our language serves us well enough up to a point, we are often concerned with likenesses and differences which it not only fails to reveal but in so far as we rely upon it conceals. Consequently for any minute understanding of people's spiritual states laws such as "If he loves he doesn't hate," "He can't think this and also not think it" become as much a menace as a help.[61]

And in the same essay Wisdom points out that

unlike one who uses a pattern ready made for him Newton had to cut out a pattern in order to show the connections in a whole which no one had ever apprehended as a whole. We now are given the conceptions of gravity and of energy. Newton developed the conception of attraction and with it presented the power of the distant. Freud developed the conception of the unconscious and with it presented the power of the past. Each introduced a word and from it bred a notation which encourages us towards new experience and also enables us to co-ordinate old experience.[62]

Again, in a later book, *Paradox and Discovery*, Wisdom speaks of "that power to place on the manifold of nature those phenomena which seem anomalous, which a changing conception may give us." [63] And, in an essay on "Tolerance," Wisdom notes "an important group of occasions when someone asks a 'What is . . . ?' question because he is on the point of modifying an old concept or of developing a related but new concept." [64] For example, "we may imagine Einstein asking himself 'What is simultaneity?' when on the point of developing that concept of simultaneity which permitted him to think of events as being simultaneous with respect to one observer and not with respect to another." [65]

Perhaps, on balance, it is fairest to Wisdom's position to say that,

[60] *Other Minds*, Preface.

[61] "Philosophy, Metaphysics and Psycho-Analysis," p. 277, n.

[62] *Ibid.*, p. 253.

[63] "Paradox and Discovery," in *Paradox and Discovery*, p. 126.

[64] "Tolerance," in *Paradox and Discovery*, p. 145.

[65] *Ibid.* Here Wisdom notes, too, our frequent resistance to such conceptional change: "We often fear, resent, find intolerable, anyone's tampering with our old well-tried ideas." (P. 146.)

although our uses may sometimes be changed, if we carefully examine
their logic then very often we will find no need for change. In any
event, it is not, in his mind, the business of the metaphysical philosopher to use this method to bring about change. The metaphysician's
aim is to compare and contrast the epistemologies of our various
language uses or, as we may also say, to map the relations between
different sorts of being. To be sure, he may find it useful to invent
cases by which to make further comparisons and contrasts. Wisdom
frequently does this, as did Wittgenstein. We have already alluded to
Wisdom's example of the singing watch. But the metaphysician's purpose in this sort of invention is not that we should come to adopt
its logic but that we might use it to see better the logic we now use. It
is in this sense that we may say not of philosophy in all its outreaches
but of metaphysical philosophy that its aims result in the eternal
recurrence of the platitude. But if we say this we must remember these
points. First, the platitude does not express simply whatever is in fact
done with words. Rather the platitude expresses the logic of a use
—its true epistemology—which has been distilled by careful rational
reflection. Second, Wisdom frequently points out that his method
of reflection on the pattern of relations between things has led to
highly significant change in our language use. Third, Wisdom warns
repeatedly about the dangers of generalization and the consequent need
to work with particular cases. We have suggested, in turn, that this
warning be applied to generalization about metaphysical use and that
careful comparison of the metaphysicians' work concerning cheese on
the table with their work concerning religious uses will show that the
platitude-paradox classification is far more fitting for the former for
the latter.

In addition to the metaphysical philosopher, Wisdom also refers to
other sorts of philosopher, e.g., the "psychoanalytic philosopher" [66]
and the "philosophical scientist." [67] In these cases, the concern to
advance our knowledge in a particular area, e.g., psychology or physical
science, leads to philosophical reflection on, say, the nature of mind
or the nature of simultaneity with the result that conceptual changes
are achieved which are needed for progress in the area. Often but
not always this philosophical reflection will be prompted by the discovery of new empirical facts that are not readily assimilable to the
old systems of connecting things. Renford Bambrough, in his helpful
and sympathetic treatment of Wisdom's work on religious use, suggests
that we think of these as applied philosophy to distinguish them
from the pure philosophy of the metaphysician. We may then contrast

[66] "Philosophy, Metaphysics, and Psycho-Analysis," p. 274.
[67] Ibid., p. 254.

philosophical science, philosophical psychology, philosophical theology, etc. with philosophy of science, philosophy of psychology, philosophy of theology, etc., the latter designating the work of the pure philosopher or metaphysician.[68]

What must be noted in all this is that language changes through philosophical reflection, through the discovery of new facts, and through technologically based changes in the human environment, and that as language changes there is new work for the metaphysician. This is beautifully expressed in Wisdom's review, "Bertrand Russell and Modern Philosophy":

Russell has presented us not with photographs but with sketches which for all their multiplicity are united into a moving picture of successive generations of men trying to make an outline *map of where they are* and trying to gain such a grasp of their own methods of projection that these will not muddle or fossilize their apprehension of the world. Their endeavours, their energy, ability, integrity and dishonesty in these endeavours have not been unconnected with their hopes and fears, their sense of sin and desire of salvation.[69]

Wisdom, in fact, places his work and that of this fellow analysts directly in the line of traditional metaphysics: "If we look at what traditional philosophers said about philosophy, not at the forms of words . . . but at the procedure they adopted, . . . then we see that what they did was after all different only in air and in guise from what is done by their logico-analytic successors." [70] Here again we see Wisdom's contention that the method he uses is really fundamental to human rationality. That it is and always has been the basic procedure of metaphysics will be seen if we follow that method and compare the logic of what has been done with the logic of his own procedure. "I believe that if, faced with the extraordinary pronouncements of metaphysicians, we avoid asking them to define their terms, but instead press them to present us with instances of what they refer to contrasted with instances of what they do not refer to" then their pronouncements will appear "as often confusingly presented attempts to bring before our attention certain not fully recognized and yet familiar features of how in the end questions of different types are met." [71] Even the skeptical metaphysician and those skeptical of metaphysics have failed to notice that while their skepticism is of reasoning that is neither inductive nor

[68] *Reason, Truth and God* (London: Methuen, 1969), p. 9.
[69] Pp. 208-9. (Italics mine.)
[70] "The Metamorphosis of Metaphysics," p. 75.
[71] "A Feature of Wittgenstein's Technique," in *Paradox and Discovery*, pp. 101-2. Cf. "Moore's Technique," p. 123.

deductive, nonetheless their own skeptical reasoning has also failed to fit either of these patterns.[72]

Unlike those considered in preceding chapters, Wisdom has done important work on the logic of religious use. Consequently it will be in order to turn directly to this subject before attempting a critical evaluation of his general position.

The Logic of God

Religion, we may recall, is seen by Wisdom as one of the spheres in which we have yet to "examine the actual processes to belief and distill from them a logic" by "sifting reasons from causes." Wisdom begins this process in his essay "Gods" by noting that disputes about the existence of God are now generally much less of an experimental or betting sort than they used to be, as for example they were for Elijah on Mount Carmel, and that "this is due in part, if not wholly, to our better knowledge of why things happen as they do." [73] However, disputes that gradually cease to be experimental, disputes that gradually cease to be a matter of one disputant expecting something of future experience which the other does not, do not necessarily cease to be genuine disputes open to rational argument. To bring this out Wisdom presents his famous parable of the invisible gardener:

Two people return to their long neglected garden and find among the weeds a few of the old plants surprisingly vigorous. One says to the other "It must be that a gardener has been coming and doing something about these plants." Upon inquiry they find that no neighbour has ever seen anyone at work in their garden. The first man says to the other "He must have worked while people slept." The other says "No, someone would have heard him and besides, anybody who cared about the plants would have kept down these weeds." The first man says "Look at the way these are arranged. There is purpose and a feeling for beauty here. I believe that someone comes, someone invisible to mortal eyes. I believe that the more carefully we look the more we shall find confirmation of this." They examine the garden ever so carefully and sometimes they come on new things suggesting that a gardener comes and sometimes they come on new things suggesting the contrary and even that a malicious person has been at work. Besides examining the garden carefully they also study what happens to gardens left without attention. Each learns all the other learns about this and about the garden. Consequently, when after all this, one says "I still believe a gardener comes" while the other says "I don't" their different words now reflect no difference as to what they have found in the garden, no difference as to what they would find in the garden if they looked further and no difference about how fast untended gardens fall into dis-

[72] "Philosophy, Metaphysics and Psycho-Analysis," pp. 268-69; "Note on the New Edition. . . ," pp. 245-46.
[73] "Gods," p. 149.

order. At this stage, in this context, the gardener hypothesis has ceased to be experimental, the difference between one who accepts and one who rejects it is now not a matter of the one expecting something the other does not expect.[74]

At this point the dispute is still genuine, still rational, and may well be continued, "each presenting and representing the features of the garden favouring his hypothesis, that is, fitting his model for describing the accepted fact; each emphasizing the pattern he wishes to to emphasize." [75] The point is, then, that discerning and reasoning about patterns is cognitive, for the pattern of relations between facts is itself a kind of fact and one of fundamental importance in human understanding. And here Wisdom again emphasizes that even in scientific hypotheses the discernment of patterns occupies an important place alongside predictive power.[76]

Wisdom's idea, we see, is that talk of God has more and more become talk of patterns in the flow of events and, if so, then talk of God remains highly cognitive and rational.[77] The question now becomes the sort of model which is appropriate to the discernment of this pattern. God has often been spoken of in personal terms, and persons are complex patterns.[78] Perhaps, therefore, we may use the logic of belief in animal and human minds as a kind of analogy by which to "get the hang of" the logic of God. Are there, then, "facts in nature which support claims about divine minds in the way facts in nature support our claims about human minds"? [79] And if there are, "we may still ask 'But are these things sufficiently striking to be called a mind-pattern? Can we fairly call them manifestations of a divine being?' " [80] Wisdom's position is that there are "in human reactions" what may be called mind-patterns that are additional to those we normally think of as manifesting human-minds and that these are easily overlooked, but that there are not mind-patterns such that we can "fairly call them manifestations of a divine being."

The argument begins with a critical evaluation of religious experience as evidence of a divine being, experience of the sort typified by Words-

[74] *Ibid.*, pp. 154-55.   [75] *Ibid.*, p. 159.

[76] *Ibid.* Wisdom elsewhere notes that "Einstein, when astronomers were hurrying to check his theory, remarked to Bertrand Russell 'Whatever they find, it's a damn good theory.' Further observation was not irrelevant to the theories of Newton and Einstein, but we are apt to forget how much they called for thought, for reflection on phenomena which had already been observed." ("A Feature of Wittgenstein's Technique," p. 96. See also "Things and Persons," p. 228.)

[77] "Gods," p. 154.

[78] "Things and Persons" (1948), reprinted in Wisdom, *Paradox and Discovery,* p. 225.

[79] "Gods," p. 151.   [80] *Ibid.*, p. 152.

worth's famous line: "I have felt a presence that disturbs me with the joy of elevated thoughts." This feeling, Wisdom says, is "misplaced like the feeling in a house that has long been empty that someone secretly lives there still. Wordsworth's feeling *is* the feeling that the world is haunted." [81] Such belief in a transcendent God, Wisdom believes, is the result of "bad unconscious reasoning" in which one is "influenced by connections which should not influence him." [82] Wisdom brings out these connections in the following passage:

What are our feelings when we believe in God? They are feelings of awe before power, dread of the thunderbolts of Zeus, confidence in the ever-lasting arms, unease beneath the all-seeing eye. They are feelings of guilt and inescapable vengeance, of smothered hate and of a security we can hardly do without. We have only to remind ourselves of these feelings and the stories of the gods and goddesses and heroes in which these feelings find expression, to be reminded of how we felt as children to our parents and the big people of our childhood. [83]

The false connection is in believing that our present religious feelings are directed to a big-person in the present, i.e., God. Once we, therefore, following Freud and others, turn "the light of reason" on them, "we can recognize systems of superhuman, sub-human, elusive, beings for what they are—the persistent projections of infantile phantasies." [84]

Assertions of the existence of God do have an important point, however, insofar as they speak of God as within us and, so, refer to certain patterns that are easily neglected, namely, those "patterns in human reactions which are well described by saying that we are as if there were hidden within us powers, persons, not ourselves and stronger than ourselves." [85] The purpose of theological reference to these patterns is to bring out their significance for salvation, the "release from human bondage into freedom." [86] "One thing not sufficiently realized," Wisdom explains, "is that some of the things shut within us are not bad but good." [87] There are many, such as artists like Proust and Manet or psychologists like Freud, who "have tried to find ways of salvation," and even though their reports are apt to be misleading "they are by no means useless; and not the worst of them are those which speak of oneness with God"—by which Wisdom means "oneness with one another." [88]

Wisdom concludes by saying of this power for oneness that "sometimes it momentarily gains strength. Hate and the Devil do too. And what is oneness without otherness?" [89] Here the question "Does God

[81] *Ibid.*, 164.
[82] *Ibid.*, pp. 162, 161.
[83] *Ibid.*, pp. 164-65.
[84] *Ibid.*, pp. 162, 166.
[85] *Ibid.*, p. 166.
[86] *Ibid.*, p. 168.
[87] *Ibid.*, p. 166.
[88] *Ibid.*, p. 168.
[89] *Ibid.*

exist?" is placed on a logical par with the question "Does the Devil exist?" They each have the same sort of function, the one asking whether there are powers in nature which make for evil, the other whether these powers are "matched" by others making for good. "The old question 'Does God exist?' 'Does the Devil exist?' aren't senseless, aren't beyond the scope of thought and reason," [90] Wisdom argues. "On the contrary they call for new awareness of what has so long been about us, in case knowing nature so well we never know her." [91] Wisdom takes an example from Tolstoy's *War and Peace*. Hearing of Natasha's grave illness:

Prince André laughed evilly—again reminding one of his father. Here I feel the presence of evil, evil that has flowed from the father to the son. . . . But then when we come to the father it doesn't seem to lie altogether in him either. . . . [In the words of Freud] dark, unfeeling, unloving powers determine human destiny.[92]

The logic of God, then, is not like that of an elusive gardener or watchmaker. As an alternative model for this logic, Wisdom, in a later essay, "The Logic of God," examines the logic of our talk about energy. When we say that a machine is electrical our evidence is not simply that its behavior is orderly but that its order is of a certain character. Similarly when we say that energy is indestructible our evidence is not simply that nature is orderly but that its order is of a certain character. Analogously, talk of God draws attention to a certain kind of order in nature. It expresses the belief that this order is not, as it might conceivably have been, "of a character which would make it fair to say, 'It is all in the hands of someone who made it and then fell asleep' or, 'It's all in the hands of someone who arranges the little ironies of fate' " [93] or "that life can be won only by overcoming 'the will to live.' " [94] At least part of what is meant is, as we have seen, the experience of power for good which is not entirely the power of the person who manifests it in his actions, for it has flowed to him from others, and although he shows it at times in his behavior it does not seem to be entirely his to command. It is the experience of a power to bring what has variously been called salvation or eternal life or the kingdom of God.

The logic of energy, we see, is a helpful model, but it is not entirely adequate, for "people have spoken of knowing the presence of God not from looking around them but from their own hearts." [95] In this way our knowledge of God may helpfully be compared with our

[90] "The Logic of God," in *Paradox and Discovery*, p. 22.
[91] *Ibid.*   [92] *Ibid.*, p. 19.   [93] *Ibid.*, p. 14.
[94] "Tolerance," p. 142.   [95] "The Logic of God," p. 15.

knowledge of the mind of another person. Here, too, we understand what we see around us partly from experience of our own minds.[96]

For Wisdom, in fact, a growing self-knowledge is an important aspect of the way to salvation. The reader may have noticed how, unlike Wittgenstein, Wisdom speaks of knowledge of our own minds.[97] Wisdom gave me as an example of their difference about this Wittgenstein's contention that to say of someone "unconsciously he's contemptuous of me" is equivalent to saying "he says that he isn't but he acts as though he is." Against the adequacy of this account, Wisdom, among other things, expressed his agreement with Susan Isaacs that in psychotherapy the patient must be the final judge of the correctness of the diagnosis for, although his judgments may at times be mistaken, he is in a unique position with regard to knowledge of his own mind.[98] The importance of this for Wisdom's understanding of our religious uses of language is suggested in the following passage:

[Christ] increased our insight into ourselves and our demands upon ourselves. For . . . since he spoke we have felt that we have no true picture of ourselves until we have looked within, searched our hearts. . . . Freud carried the process still further. For before Freud spoke, most of us trusted the appearances in our own hearts, but after he spoke we were obliged to recognize how deceptive these too may be.[99]

Wisdom presents all this as no more than the beginning of an account of the logic of God as we see it in the talk of many for whom salvation or the kingdom of God is a matter not of life in another world or life to come but a matter of this present life. It is only a very partial account in two ways. First of all, it is true for all who speak of these things that our grasp of what we are trying to say is really quite feeble. This is due partly to the exceeding complexity of the pattern, partly to the anxiety connected with this quest and partly, perhaps especially, to the fact that here as elsewhere we are responding to connections that we only dimly or half-consciously or even unconsciously discern and that we have been unable to put into words.[100] Part of the explanation may also lie in that possibility which is

---

[96] *Ibid.*

[97] For example, "when it is said that no one but Joan really knows how Joan feels what is meant is that no one knows this like Joan does." ("Philosophy, Metaphysics and Psycho-Analysis," p. 258).

[98] Cf. "Paradox and Discovery," pp. 117-18; "The Logic of God," p. 18; and "Other Minds I," p. 2.

[99] "Tolerance," pp. 146-47.

[100] In "Gods," for instance, Wisdom speaks of "connections operative but not presented in language, or only hinted at." (P. 162.)

cryptically expressed as "a contradiction in perfection." [101] In these respects our situation is something like that of the artist who only gradually comes to see what he is trying to do;[102] or it may be compared to that of a child who, having grasped the pattern of a simple play, asks about the meaning of a play too complex for him to be able yet to understand. Just as his question has sense to it so ours has sense when we ask about the meaning of the drama of Time.[103]

The second and closely related source of Wisdom's sense of the essential incompleteness of his description of the logic of our increasingly this-worldly talk of God is that his emphasis on patterns in the drama of Time has left an essential aspect of this logic unaccounted for. This is the way in which many speak of God's unfailing love, of his absolute power and perfect goodness, no matter what evil they see in the world. Yet "asked the reason for what they assert they seem to point to nothing which isn't known to everyone, and—a different point—to nothing which justifies their confidence." [104] Wisdom wrestles hard with this problem in "Religious Belief" and especially in his recent article "Eternal Life," and there is one aspect of his struggle to which we may profitably give special attention.

Wisdom cites Helmut Kuhn's account [105] of the Existentialists' view of despair that in answer to the question "What do you will with unwavering devotion, so that everything else is willed and lived only for the sake of this first objective and greatest good?" they present a string of negations: "not wife, children, friends; not wealth, learning or power; not high living standards for all men; not . . ." Here, Wisdom remarks, "we are reminded of St. Augustine's words, 'the chief good— that which will leave us nothing further to seek in order to be blessed, if only we will make all our actions refer to it.'" [106] His reply is that even if no one of these things taken separately can give life meaning "it does not follow that life hasn't a meaning nor even that it isn't these things which give it its meaning." [107] One is reminded of

[101] "The Logic of God," p. 16. Elsewhere he asks, "Does the contradiction in the philosopher's quest for perfect knowledge of others reflect a conflict in the human heart which dreads and yet demands the otherness of others?" ("Symposium: Other Minds," in *Other Minds*, p. 229.)

[102] "The Logic of God," p. 16.

[103] "The Meanings of the Questions of Life," in *Paradox and Discovery*, p. 41.

[104] "Religious Belief," in *Paradox and Discovery*, p. 49. Originally published in *Cambridge Review*.

[105] *Encounter with Nothingness*.

[106] "Existentialism," in *Paradox and Discovery*, p. 36. The reference is to *City of God*, Bk. viii., 8.

[107] "Existentialism," p. 37. "To win a set of tennis," he continues, "is not the *summum bonum* but this doesn't prove that it is not *part* of what makes a life good." In "Gods," p. 153, Wisdom quotes from John P. Marquand's

Philip's discovery in Somerset Maugham's *Of Human Bondage* that

as the weaver elaborated his pattern . . . so might a man live his life, or . . . look at his life, that it made a pattern. . . . Whatever happened to him now would be one more motive to add to the complexity of the pattern, and when the end approached he would rejoice in its completion.[108]

But Wisdom seems to sense a profound limitation in this point of view. For example, he cites a passage from Virginia Woolf:

as we lift the cup, shake the hand, express the hope, something whispers, Is this all? Can I ever know, share, be certain? Am I doomed all my days to write letters, send voices, which fall upon the tea-table, fade upon the passage, making appointments, while life dwindles, to come and dine? [109]

This theme is echoed in "Eternal Life" where Wisdom asserts that those who say "there is a way to eternal life" . . . are seeking a remedy against a sort of despair which comes . . . from a disappointment with life together with the thought that it ends in death." [110] Ecclesiastes, for example, "has tried many things and has found some pleasure but never the contentment he was looking for. He no longer expects to find it." [111] At least part of the logic of talk of eternal life, even for those who do not mean by such talk that life endures forever, involves "presenting a view of things which they regard as a truer view than any which generates despair, and also brings with it a sort of happiness which even the disappointments of life and the thought of death cannot take from us." [112] Taking Spinoza as an example, Wisdom notes that some sort of mystical experience seems to underly his philosophy, but he then struggles in vain to discover what it is that this experience conveyed. Rather, with William James, he concludes, "We recognize the passwords to the mystical religion as we hear them but we cannot use them ourselves." [113] Such words do seem somehow to convey something, but the nearest Wisdom can get to saying what they convey is to point out that experiences do sometimes come to us with revelatory power: "What happens in a dream, what happens in a play presented on the stage, what happens

---

H. M. Pulham, Esq.: "Of course, Kay and I do quarrel sometimes but when you add it all together, all of it isn't as bad as the parts of it seem. I mean maybe that's all there is to anybody's life."

[108] Chap. 106.

[109] "Symposium: Other Minds," pp. 228-29. The quotation is from *Jacob's Room.*

[110] In *Talk of God,* G. N. A. Vesey, *et al.* (New York: St. Martin's Press, Inc.; Macmillan & Co., Ltd., 1969), p. 239.

[111] *Ibid.*   [112] *Ibid.,* p. 240.   [113] *Ibid.,* p. 246.

in real life, sometimes is such that for the rest of one's life one sees things differently." [114]

Some, then, talk of God to express a sense of meaning which cannot be undercut by despair. It is not simply a question of finding a pattern to one's life, for of some life-patterns one may merely say that "when you add it all together, all of it isn't as bad as the parts of it seem." [115] Talk of God seems to concern a kind of life which is rooted in a special sort of experience. Among other things we must "consider what it is about human beings which is referred to by one who says that they are not one with God but could become so." [116] Perhaps we will then see more clearly why "in Christ there was, for all his knowledge of human beings, still a love of them, and a hope that many, a confidence that some, would achieve what He called 'eternal life.' " [117]

This, at least, is one way of piecing together the present stage of Wisdom's thought on the logic of God. Wisdom seems to be searching for further clues, clues that will take us beyond Spinoza, who himself surely was unclear about what he was trying to say. Whatever the pattern he glimpsed he was surely mistaken in describing it in terms of a mathematical deductive model.[118] And even apart from this, there remains for Wisdom the problem that Spinoza described the totality of things as splendid, while, as Wisdom expressed it in a conversation, "to me it does not look splendid." How, Wisdom seems to be asking, can monotheism or pantheism make sense unless one is in some way blind to the evil in the world? Are not good and evil related in a more fundamentally dualistic way? If the theist sees the meaning of life finally in terms of triumph, Wisdom, at this point, sees it as "a mixture in which sweet and bitter are forever mixed" [119]—mixed "in the infinite dialectic of good and evil." [120]

Critical Evaluation of Wisdom's General Position

Criticism of Wisdom's basic position has revolved around his belief that "every philosophical question . . . when it is fully asked, answers itself," [121] if, by "fully asked" we mean describing it fully through comparison and contrast with other sorts of statement and so setting

---

[114] *Ibid.*, p. 250. Cf. "Religious Belief," p. 50; "Things and Persons," p. 228; "Philosophy, Metaphysics and Psycho-Analysis," pp. 270-71.

[115] Quoted from Marquand in "Gods," p. 153.

[116] "Paradox and Discovery," p. 124.

[117] "Tolerance," p. 241.

[118] "Eternal Life," p. 242.

[119] "The Meanings of the Questions of Life," p. 42.

[120] "Religious Belief," p. 46.

[121] "Other Minds I," p. 2.

it "in its place on the language map with regard to all other questions." [122] In one form or another these criticisms ask whether Wisdom has not suppressed the philosophical question about the truth of his belief that every philosophical question when fully described answers itself. In other words, may we not dispute philosophically Wisdom's view of the procedure by which philosophical disputes may, in principle, be settled?

The correct reply, I believe, is that for Wisdom the nature of metaphysics is certainly a metaphysical question and so may be reasoned about like any other metaphysical question. It is true that he sometimes refers to this question as meta-metaphysical, but we should not take him to mean that its logic is not the same as the logic of any other metaphysical question, for, as we have seen, he discusses the nature of metaphysical knowledge by the same procedure as that by which he discusses the nature of any other sort of knowledge.

One of the critics to whom I refer is David Pole. According to Pole, Wisdom's method is "to do no more than to describe . . . the actual workings of ordinary language" [123]—to describe actual "usage." [124] But metaphysicians present alternative systems of language classification, and "some will conflict with others, and disputes as to their relative merits will arise." [125] How could mere description of actual usage settle such conflicts? And how could mere description allow Wisdom to distinguish "between questions that are 'practical and settleable' and questions that are 'academic and idle' "? [126] Clearly, some unstated assumptions must underly Wisdom's use of his method. According to Pole, then, Wisdom's way of settling metaphysical disputes really presupposes the correctness both of the "traditional analytic-synthetic dichotomy" and of "his own categorization of forms of factual statement." [127]

Against this account several objections may be raised. First we have seen that, although Wisdom at first spoke of comparing uses, by 1944 he talked rather of comparing the ways in which statements may be supported, the sorts of reasons which justify them. Second, far from presupposing the traditional analytic-synthetic dichotomy, Wisdom's method, we have seen, is based upon his repeated and explicit rejection of this dichotomy. Third, what Pole refers to as "mere description" is said by Wisdom to be rational argument of the most fundamental sort, comparable, for example, to the sort of argument that often takes place in a court of law after all the particular

---

[122] Ibid.
[124] Ibid., p. 110.
[126] Ibid., p. 126.

[123] The Later Philosophy of Wittgenstein, p. 125.
[125] Ibid., p. 127.
[127] Ibid., p. 127.

"facts" are agreed upon. Pole charges that "it seems to be supposed that the use of theories . . . is not only characteristically but exclusively the procedure of scientists," [128] but Wisdom has pointed out in many places how extensively argument about scientific theories involves the same sort of rational procedure that he is using. Fourth, since the mere use of a method does not guarantee the correctness of the results, Wisdom's actual mapping of language categories, his comparison of their logics, is open to criticism by the very method he uses. Far from aiming at "the circumvention of disputes," as Pole alleges,[129] Wisdom's method is rather a rational procedure for conducting such disputes, a procedure whereby in principle they are settleable. Notice that we must say in principle, for to say that full description will settle such a dispute is not to say that such full description is necessarily within our grasp. On the contrary, we have seen that Wisdom believes we are very far from achieving this concerning the logic of God.

Pole's final criticism of Wisdom's method is that, while it will undoubtedly be helpful at certain times, "at other times we shall need new ideas, not a re-examination of the old; not retrenchment but rather creativeness." [130] Again, to the contrary, we have cited Wisdom's recognition of the need for new ideas, but this side of his thought is so often missed that perhaps one further reference will be in order:

When I look back on all that has been said about God then I feel though much of it has been false or doubtful or obscure, still the words "There is a God above" may yet with further thought guide us to some truth which is still of great importance for our lives.[131]

Charlesworth is another critic who sees Wisdom and his fellow "therapeutic analysts" as attempting to settle philosophical disputes without themselves entering the philosophical arena. According to Charlesworth, for Wisdom and the others "any systematic formulation of the method of therapeutic analysis is impossible" [132] for they would otherwise repeat the mistake of the positivists who charged that metaphysics is pure muddle and yet, as Wisdom remarked, have "pretended that their own meta-metaphysical conclusion is an exception." [133] But the therapeutic analysts, too, "are concerned to tell us that things are not in *reality* as they *appear* at first sight—that for

---

[128] *Ibid.*, p. 126.   [129] *Ibid.*, p. 127.   [130] *Ibid.*, p. 129.
[131] "Eternal Life," p. 244. Unlike the earlier references this was written after Pole's book appeared.
[132] *Philosophy and Linguistic Analysis*, p. 165.
[133] "Philosophy, Metaphysics and Psycho-Analysis," p. 269.

example, metaphysical statements are not as they seem, directly factual—so they cannot pretend that their view is self-evident." [134] They, too, must enter the arena and argue the case. And when they do this, one of the problems they must face is the apparent contradiction in asserting, on the one hand, that metaphysical statements are really linguistic proposals and yet denying, on the other hand, that there is any such thing as "a special kind of philosophical knowledge." [135] They must explain what kind of philosophical knowledge our knowledge of the nature of metaphysical statements is.

Here again what is too little recognized is that Wisdom's method is essentially a method of reasoning and argument, and in this sense he does enter the arena. Unlike the positivists he is not claiming to make non-metaphysical statements about metaphysical statements; rather he explicitly recognizes that his statements are included among the metaphysical statements to which they refer—they are, we have seen, self-referential. His point about the positivists was that they failed to see that the method by which they arrived at their anti-metaphysical conclusions is fundamentally akin to that which they were attacking. Concerning his own method, however, Wisdom argues its fundamental kinship with that which he contends his metaphysical predecessors were really using, although they were doing so in a very unclear way.

As to the sort of knowledge which philosophical knowledge is, Wisdom says explicitly that it is knowledge of the relations between epistemologies of different types of statement.

The rational justification of Wisdom's metaphysical position concerning the nature of metaphysical method and metaphysical knowledge—it comes to the same thing since epistemology and ontology are finally identical—has two aspects. First, it involves locating his sort of metaphysical statement on the language map by comparing and contrasting it with other sorts of statement. Second, it involves comparing his procedure with that of the traditional metaphysicians in an effort to show a fundamental similarity. This comparison, if we are careful to look at what is actually done rather than at what is said about what is done, will show that "what they did was after all different only in air and in guise" [136] from what Wisdom is doing.

But we may ask whether there is not a danger that Wisdom will simply read his own views into the arguments presented by more traditional metaphysicians and their followers, especially when it must be contended that they were rather confused about what they were

---

[134] *Philosophy and Linguistic Analysis*, p. 167.
[135] *Ibid.*, pp. 162-63.
[136] "The Metamorphosis of Metaphysics," p. 75.

doing. Here I think that Wisdom will concede that the status of the assertions of other metaphysicians must finally be determined in dialogue with them for, just as in psychoanalysis the patient is the final authority, so in metaphysics each metaphysician is the final authority about what he intends. Wisdom says, for example, that in psychoanalysis "the explaining to the patient what is wrong with him consists in allowing the patient to describe his own case" and that "in like way a philosophical difficulty such as 'What then, do you say that philosophical questions are meaningless?' . . . may be removed by getting the patient to . . . describe fully the sort of question or statement he is considering." [137] And here Wisdom concludes that "it appears that the man who asked the question was best placed for answering it." [138]

The dialogue will be possible only if both parties agree about the logic of some sorts of statement, for, as we have seen, we can map a statement about whose logic we are unclear only by comparing and contrasting it with statements about whose logic we are clear—statements that we know how to map and by whose positions on the map we determine the meaning of other positions. We cannot, for example, meaningfully ask whether a question is idle unless we know other questions that are idle. Nor can we ask whether a statement is straight-forwardly factual unless we know statements of this sort.

It seems, then, that there may be some difficulty as to the basic reference points of the dialogue. May there not also be some question about the rules of the dialogue in the sense that Wisdom is entering the arena only after insisting that the weapons be of his own choosing? In other words, is not the use of Wisdom's method to argue the correctness of its use as the metaphysical method in a sense question-begging?

There is a circularity here, but it would be vicious and question-begging only if the use of Wisdom's method necessitated his particular conclusions. But there is no reason why Wisdom's partner in the dialogue may not surprise him in the comparisons he makes, in the sorts of reasons he gives as support to his statements. If this happens then either Wisdom will have come by rational persuasion to see the statements of the other differently, or he may argue in turn that the comparisons are not accurately drawn, that the reasons given are not really reasons, or he may simply not be sure what judgment to make.[139] Indeed, "the problem 'What is rationality?' like the prob-

---

[137] "Other Minds I," p. 2.
[138] Ibid. Cf. "Paradox and Discovery," p. 124.
[139] For example, in "Paradox and Discovery" (p. 125) Wisdom says of such a case that "the speaker himself may insist that he is speaking absolutely literally and not with license. . . . We cannot deny that that which he says is of a certain

lem . . . 'What is meaning?' . . . is involved in every philosophical problem and is consequently involved twice over in itself. Thus we ask 'What is the meaning of "meaning"?' 'What reasons are there for saying that a procedure is rational?' " [140] Here again we cannot meaningfully ask whether some things are reasons unless we know other things that are reasons; but here, too, there may be some disagreement about these fundamental terms of discussion. Wisdom's procedure, however, remains relevant even to this sort of disagreement.

It might still be argued that the procedure is viciously circular if the traditionalist were to claim that the logic of his statements was so idiosyncratic, so utterly remote from the logic of any other sort of statement, that it cannot be mapped by this method of comparison. But this seems untenable for, first of all, severed from the language of both our everyday and our technical concerns such utterances lose all relevance to these concerns, and, second, if such utterances are so remote from the rest of what we call language then they lack the family resemblance that would make it meaningful even to refer to them as language.

But just here we come to another potential source of trouble for the Wisdom-traditionalist dialogue. For when we have given the fullest possible comparison and contrast between a doubtful statement and one the logic of which we grasp clearly we may yet be faced with a decision[141] whether to say it has the same logic. Concerning the statement that "Christ was one with God," for example, the speaker may offer a surprising account of his statement as more conventional in its logic than we had expected. We might then say of this account that "the affinity it unfolds is so profound that we cannot but take it seriously and yet the difference it ignores is so enormous to seem to take from the words of the statement not merely some of their usual sense but all of it and even to render the statement no longer of the family to which it purports to belong." [142] In other words, there may be disagreement about when a statement no longer belongs to a certain family, about how far on the map it may be from statements that are clearly of that family or category before it may be said to lie outside the boundaries of that category. The dialogue partner may, for example, dispute Wisdom's judgment that "some belief as to the nature of the world is of the essence of religion" [143] and consequently

---

sort has indeed a whole assembly of the characteristic features of things of that sort. It's only that it lacks some and that the lack of these seems fatal to his claims. Hasn't he overlooked this? No he has not. That's what beats us."

[140] "Note on the New Edition . . . ," p. 229.
[141] Wisdom uses this term in this connection very frequently.
[142] "Paradox and Discovery," p. 125.
[143] "Religious Belief," p. 54.

may call sentences essentially religious which simply express commitment to a way of life.

However, another sort of dialogue is involved, for the metaphysician aims to map knowledge of every type—metaphysical, mathematical, psychological, ethical, religious, and that of any other area in which we use the word "know" seriously.[144] What, then, of the dialogue between what we have called the pure and the applied philosophers? On Bambrough's interpretation of Wisdom, "pure philosophy is neutral on all questions that do not belong to pure philosophy: it has nothing to tell us about the world or life or man or God," [145] for "to know *how to verify* a proposition is quite different from knowing *that it is* verified or falsified." [146] Consequently pure and applied philosophy are "logically independent" of each other in the sense that results of the one count neither for nor against any results achieved by the other.[147] In light of this interpretation Bambrough later launches his major criticism of Wisdom by commenting, "It is significant that Wisdom's treatment, which is offered as a neutral account of the logic of theological disputes, has found more favour among atheists and agnostics than among their theological opponents." [148]

But whether a purely philosophical account of the logic of God will entirely avoid all substantive issues such as whether in fact God exists or was incarnate in Jesus requires careful examination. Since, in philosophy as elsewhere, the appeal is ultimately to examples, formal and substantive issues are not ultimately separable. Our ability to inquire how we know the truth of statements of a certain type does not depend upon our knowing the truth of any particular statement of that type but does depend upon our knowing the truth of at least one statement of that type. And conversely, any assertion implies a particular logic that governs that assertion.[149] Both Bambrough and Wisdom recognize these points. In connection with the former point, Bambrough, for example, begins with a description of the logic of Homer's belief in the existence of the gods of Olympus because modern knowledge has placed its falsity beyond dispute.[150] Similarly, Wisdom argues that we have at least some idea of the logic of "In Jesus God

[144] "Seriously" here means that reasons for and against knowledge claims can be given.

[145] *Reason, Truth and God*, p. 10.   [146] *Ibid.*, p. 9.

[147] *Ibid.*   [148] *Ibid.*, p. 65.

[149] In making an assertion, that is, the speaker implies that he has sufficient evidence of a sort that justifies his making the assertion and also that the assertion may be used in an argument of a certain sort.

[150] *Reason, Truth, and God*, p. 26.

was incarnate" because we know the unquestionable falsity of "In Nero God was incarnate." [151]

The philosopher's elucidation of the logic of a certain kind of dispute, then, may—and, if we are to avoid needless confusion, should—be neutral concerning substantive issues provided he can assume agreement concerning some substantive issues of that type. Whether there is cheese on the table or whether John is angry are questions that we do very often agree about in answering.

But the philosopher's situation is far different in those less settled areas of language, such as the religious, which have long been undergoing change and which are being deeply affected by forces of cultural change. For here we find little agreement either about what is true and what is false or about the logic that governs such judgments.

Concerning the logic of God, Bambrough recommends that here as elsewhere we start with cases of substantive agreement, for "when we are dealing with epistemological questions . . . it is convenient not to have to engage at the same time in non-philosophical controversy." [152] But after we have discussed the logic of Homer's beliefs and come with Wisdom to the assertions, say, of Spinoza, substantive and logical discussion becomes mixed, for here we are unclear about either the truth or the logic of what is said. In fact, concerning the logic of God in contemporary usage substantive and formal issues are necessarily mixed not only for the pure but for the applied philosopher as well. Because he cannot assume a long-settled logic, the substantive work of the applied philosopher will often involve significant development at that primary, largely subconscious level of reflection by which, for the most part, we achieve our epistemological principles—principles that we then attempt to elucidate by our more critical and self-conscious mode of secondary, philosophical reflection.

In such an area, even though the final concern of the pure philosopher is with formal questions while that of the applied philosopher is with substantive questions, because formal and substantive matters are at present so deeply mixed the results of the pure and applied philosophers will be more intertwined logically than they need be in more settled areas. To insist upon the degree of neutrality appropriate to other philosophic tasks is to ask the philosopher to withhold his skills until a time when the logical situation is more settled and those skills are less needed.

We must treat carefully, then, Bambrough's statement that the pure philosopher tells us nothing about the nature of man or of God. Since epistemology and ontology are one and grammar tells us what kind

[151] "The Logic of God," p. 20.
[152] *Reason, Truth, and God*, p. 24.

of object anything is, Bambrough does not mean that the philosopher does not describe the general nature of man or of God. It is rather, as Wisdom repeatedly says, that the philosopher does not tell us anything we do not in some sense already know. And the point of our discussion has been to show how in the area of religion, among others, even this must be modified.

What all this means is that dialogue between pure and applied philosophers is particularly essential in the area of religion. By asking the right question the pure philosopher may help the applied philosopher toward the fuller description of his logic that we seek. At the same time, however, the pure philosopher must also judge the credibility of those truth claims which he finds the applied philosopher using as his reference points in the dialogue.

And just here we come to another problem to which dialogue is so essential, namely, the fact that our ability to understand the epistemology of a type of language use depends finally on our ability to understand both the other sorts of rules governing that use and also the form of life of which that use is a part. This may easily be overlooked in describing talk of cheese or of anger, but it becomes a frequent obstacle to successful dialogue on the logic of God. Wisdom gives recognition to the point when, for example, he notes: "Mr. Williams [p. 206] [153] remarks that it is very difficult for anyone to describe the character of religious statements who has never felt much need to make them." [154] And elsewhere he argues that "a man, a god, who had never felt pain could not know that another was in pain, only that he groaned." [155]

Just what Wisdom's reaction would be to this discussion of the relation between formal and substantive issues in contemporary religion is something for which I find no clear evidence in his writing. He does say, however, that the work of the metaphysician is "less superfluous" to our substantive concerns in the area of religion than it usually is in other areas.[156]

From this discussion we conclude, then, that by the very nature of the method of rational discussion which he uses Wisdom's views are entirely open to rational argument. He has hence given rational support to his views, including those on the nature of metaphysics and the nature of God. Furthermore, when he says that philosophical questions answer themselves once their relations with other sorts of questions

[153] The reference is to Flew and MacIntyre, *New Essays in Philosophical Theology.*

[154] "Religious Belief," p. 47.

[155] "Philosophy, Metaphysics and Psycho-Analysis," p. 275. Cf. "The Logic of God," p. 15.

[156] "Religious Belief," pp. 44-49.

are fully described, Wisdom is indicating the nature of philosophical questions rather than prophesying their speedy demise, for he recognizes how exceedingly difficult this task may become—especially in the less settled areas of language. If, at times, he seems to underestimate the difficulty of settling philosophical disputes—especially in dialogue with those less empiricist in their orientation—nonetheless one must be impressed both with his great concern to be completely fair to what another is trying to say and with the exceedingly careful and painstaking attention to particular cases which typifies his work. Finally, the use of Wisdom's method seems not to beg substantive philosophical issues but rather to open a way for rational discussion across philosophic lines.

Critical Evaluation of Wisdom's Philosophy of Religion

Criticism of Wisdom's treatment of the logic of God centers in the charge that he fails to show that this logic has any distinctively theological function. According to Frederick Ferré, Wisdom joins Braithewaite, Hepburn, Hare, and others in seeking "to understand the logic of theological discourse exhaustively in terms of functions which language may serve outside the strictly theological context." [157] And Renford Bambrough suggests that Wisdom makes "of Christian theology one among many possible sets of terms for conducting a kind of reflection that need not be conducted in *theological* categories at all." [158]

According to Ferré, Wisdom maintains both that "the function[159] of theological discourse . . . is to *direct our attention* to patterns in 'the facts' " [160] and that "language is used in its 'attention-directing' role . . . also in aesthetic and other discussions." [161] This criticism, however, seems less well placed than Bambrough's. First of all, in his essay "Gods," [162] Wisdom's concern with talk of God was not with its functions in general but with its epistemology. Second, and more important, Wisdom concludes the essay by saying that talk of God points a way to "salvation," to "oneness with God," to release "from human bondage into human freedom." This function is clearly different from the attention-directing use of language in disputes about the

---

[157] *Language, Logic and God*, p. 134.   [158] *Reason, Truth and God*, p. 67.

[159] Later Ferré speaks not of *the* function but rather of "the subtle interweaving of several functions in the 'attention-directing' interpretation" (p. 134) for he has earlier recognized that according to Wisdom "There is a God" also "evinces an attitude to the familiar." ("Gods," p. 156.)

[160] *Language, Logic and God*, p. 133.   [161] *Ibid.*, p. 135.

[162] Ferré was writing before "The Logic of God" and "Eternal Life" were published.

beauty of a painting or about the question of negligence in a court of law.

Nonetheless it must be asked whether Wisdom's focus on the logic of theological *disputes* has not led him to speak of the relation between talk of God and the "achievement" of salvation too much in terms of the attention-directing use of such talk. We may recall that Wisdom distinguished between statements that are indirectly attention-directing, yet function primarily to convey information, and metaphysical statements that incidentally convey information, yet function primarily to direct our attention. What Wisdom has not made sufficiently clear is the continuum in which the attention-directing aspect of talk of God gradually becomes less and less the primary function of the utterance and more and more something that operates only indirectly or obliquely in the service of other aims such as to convey information, evince an attitude, or undergird and renew one's courage and one's acceptance of self and others and life as a whole. But he does recognize that talk of God may function to bring salvation even though our grasp of the patterns involved is rather feeble, and this suggests that in these cases the attention-directing function is secondary and indirect.

More to the point than criticism of the attention-directing role would be the criticism Ferré levels at those who analyze the logic of God simply in terms of the function of existential affirmation: "What is the difference between affirming one's situation in existence by means of theological language, with Marcel, and by means of self-consciously atheistic language, with Sartre?" [163] For Wisdom contends that Proust, Manet, Freud, and others who are not theologians are also seeking ways to salvation.[164]

It is this line of criticism which Bambrough develops in saying that the logic of God as described by Wisdom does not require theological categories at all. For Bambrough, as for Wisdom, uses of the term "God" are united by what Wittgenstein called family resemblances. Analyzing the logic of this term for Homer, Aeschylus, and Sophocles, Bambrough finds for it three basic features. When they speak of the gods (1) they are making assertions, (2) these assertions have their basis in our familiar, everyday world, and (3) these assertions refer not only to features of our familiar world but also to something that transcends these features.[165] The logic described by Wisdom retains the first two of these features but loses the third. Homer thought of Poseidon as one who dramatically intervened in human life.[166] Wisdom, however, does not think of God in this way, and in failing to describe a logic of transcendence, Bambrough charges,

---

[163] *Language, Logic and God*, p. 134.   [164] "Gods," pp. 167-68.
[165] *Reason, Truth and God*, p. 40.   [166] *Ibid.*, p. 30.

he loses an essential feature of the logic of God. His logic does not belong to the family we rightly call theological, for, with the loss of transcendence, the differences between his logic and that of theology proper "count for more" than the resemblances between them.[167] In evaluating this criticism we shall consider, first, the all-important question of transcendence and, second, the problem of judging those features which are essential for membership in the family of uses of the concept "god" which are properly called theological.

Consider three of the important senses in which we may speak of transcendence. We may say, first, that the thief is more than missing jewels, fingerprints, and a broken lock, or second, that the book is more than its manifestations, or third, that Jones is more than his behavior. Clearly Poseidon's transcendence of the evidences of his intervention is closest to the transcendence of the thief.

In its pure form, in fact, Bambrough apparently thinks of the logic of intervention as exactly that of the thief. As our knowledge of the material world increases, however, this logic evolves by degrees into that of a metaphysical substance which, although manifested in our experience, exists quite independently of those manifestations. Though no longer up there, God is somehow out there. Here a picture has been carried over which, like the everlastingly elusive gardener, no longer has an application. Uprooted from all means of verification the bloom fades from the meaning of our statements about God. Their logic is now identical with that of transcendent material and mental substances except that, as we have seen, "in all these other fields a belief in transcendent entities has arisen from a misunderstanding of the nature of knowledge and its ultimate grounds." [168] The dilemma is familiar. Statements about God are either false or meaningless—meaningless, at least, in their function as statements.

Now Wisdom's logic does not include reference to a "something over and above" what we can experience in either the interventionist or the transcendentalist senses of these metaphors. And yet, as Bambrough recognizes, Wisdom's logic does not reduce the nature of God to features of our experience, for it does not identify meaning and verification. God is seen to be something more than those features of experience in something of the senses in which a book or energy or another's mind is more than our experiences of them, more than their manifestations, more than the evidence by which we support our statements about them. The question, then, is whether the logic of this sort of talk of "something more" is not also a logic of transcendence, or, if it is not, whether transcendence in its more restricted meaning really is, as Bambrough alleges, basic to the logic of God.

[167] Ibid., pp. 66, 40.   [168] Ibid., p. 51.

"Something more," in Wisdom's sense, concerns our way of grouping phenomena according to certain patterns in our experience which are important to our concerns, which make possible certain inferences beyond those immediate experiences, and which keep us open to the possibility of new inferences and of a grasp of still other patterns of significance. In "Gods," for example, Wisdom refers to those "unseen worlds which some philosophers 'believe in' and others 'deny,' while non-philosophers unconsciously 'accept' them by *using them as models with which to 'get the hang of' the patterns* in the flux of experience." [169] When the reductionist, then, in his fight against the skeptic and the transcendentalist, insists that "a book is nothing but sensations and possibilities of more" or that "a mind is nothing but a pattern of behavior" he fails to take into account the models involved in our talk of books and minds by which we (1) bring to mind the way certain experiences hang together—the kind of hanging together this is—and (2) license certain kinds of inference from our statements about these things.

The model of material substance is our way of grouping certain patterns such as those of trees, chairs, and animal bodies and so of emphasizing their similarities. The model of mental substance groups other patterns according to the way in which these "things" behave so cunningly all by themselves unlike even the most ingenious machines." [170] Those who say paradoxically that all is mind or all is matter want to call attention to certain similarities between mind patterns and matter patterns which our ordinary models obscure. And so on.

Concerning the existence of God, the question becomes whether we can here follow the reductionist in equating meaning and verification or whether "God" is used in ways that are not served by talk about the evidences of God. Do we employ a substance model or some other model in our talk about God which makes possible a use to which we do not put talk about the manifestations of God, so that it becomes meaningful to say, "I mean God himself and not just religious phenomena"? Or, rather, can any statement about God be reduced to a set of corresponding statements about religious phenomena— reduced in the sense that this set of sentences serves, if less efficiently, the same purposes as the statement about God? To argue that statements about God are ultimate and irreducible is really to argue that religious-phenomena statements do not serve all the same functions as statements about God. The reductionist argues that they do. But if we use Wisdom's method of comparison and contrast we can come to see that in some ways the same functions are served and in some

[169] "Gods," p. 151. (Italics mine.)   [170] *Ibid.*

ways this is not the case. As Wisdom puts it, "Are X facts or propositions reducible to Y facts or propositions?" may be reformulated "When
we have an X sentence used in that way with which you are familiar,
is there some combination of Y sentences used in that manner with
which you are familiar, which serves the same purpose?" [171] Settling
this is frequently like settling the question "Which of the purposes
served by a bridle does the strip of hide serve?" [172]

When we ask, then, whether the relation of God to the evidence
for God is closer to the relation of books or minds to the evidence
for them than it is to the relation of the clever thief or elusive
gardener to the evidence for them, we are asking about the relative appropriateness of these models in enabling us to "get the hang of"
religious patterns in our experience. Here we may recall our discussion
in the chapter on Bertrand Russell of models adequate to our talk
of books and chairs. According to Wisdom, Russell

substituted for an old and muddling model of the connection between
realities and appearances a new model. For to say that a chair is a logical
construction out of appearances of a chair is to say that a chair is related
to its appearances *not* as a thing is related to the images of it in a mirror,[173]
not as a member of parliament to his constituents, but as the average
plumber to plumbers, as a family to its members, *as energy to its manifestations*, as electrons to the evidence for electrons.[174]

The application of the model of logical constructions provides us with
comparisons by which we are helped to see that it is silly to lament,
"Confined as we are to our sensations how can we claim knowledge
of spades?" [175] The use of this model also throws doubt upon the
appropriateness of the question "Confined as we are to the manifestations of God in our experience of the finite world how can we claim
knowledge of God?" Wisdom has argued accordingly that the relation
of God to his manifestations in finite events is more like the relation of
energy to its manifestations than it is to the relation of objects to their
shadows on the wall of a cave or to the relation of the watchmaker to
his watches. Of course, the logic of God must also be compared with the
logic of mind, and so we see finally that no one of these models is
entirely adequate.

But should these relations of God to the evidence for God be

---

[171] "Metaphysics and Verification," pp. 94-95.
[172] *Ibid.*, p. 95.
[173] Wisdom has earlier noted that "philosophers had often represented us
as seated sadly guessing from the images in the mirrors of our minds at what
was happening in reality." ("Bertrand Russell and Modern Philosophy," p. 204.)
[174] "Bertrand Russell and Modern Philosophy," p. 205. Italics mine.
[175] *Ibid.*, p. 207.

classified in terms of transcendence? If Wisdom's argument is sound that the transcendentalists were attempting in a confused way to provide us with models adequate both to the uses of our various sorts of statements and to the ways in which we justify them, then what is essential about their accounts is not their models but what they were trying to do with their models. Consequently, if transcendence is an essential feature of their logic it must refer not to their models but to what they were confusedly trying to do with them.

Let us suppose that other considerations lead us to conclude with Bambrough that the family of logics to which the term "transcendence" may properly be applied is limited to those of the interventionist and the transcendentalist. Since the pure transcendentalist is the victim of a picture that lacks any application, transcendence turns out to mean the interventionist logic that is typified by the relation of the thief to evidence of his visit. No doubt we must also include here the logic of the halfway house between interventionism and trancendentalism which may be compared to belief in a gardener who, although himself not directly discernible in human experience, causes certain alterations in the garden—sometimes, perhaps, in response to the believer's supplications. But how clear is it, we must ask, that transcendence in the sense of an elusive or invisible gardener who nonetheless tends his garden is essential to the logic of God?

Theologians such as Bultmann and Tillich have frankly rejected interventionist and transcendentalist models not only as inessential but also as inadequate to our existential concerns, to our modern knowledge of the physical universe, and to our epistemological insight. As a consequence, Bambrough suggests that their "use of traditional words has now been carried so far away from the original and basic use that an element of deception or at least of self-deception is involved in the use of the old words for the expression of new belief." [176] But several points must be made in reply here. First, Bambrough neglects entirely both the arguments of Tillich, Bultmann, and others that an existential dimension is essential to the logic of God and their extensive efforts to show this for the entire history of the Christian church.[177] Second, he neglects the emphasis given by phenomenologists, including Tillich, to the experience of the holy as basic to the meaning of "God." Third, judgments about what is essential to the meaning of a word are made within the context of a particular mode of life and so may well change in the course of cultural evolution. We cannot here

[176] *Reason, Truth and God*, p. 36. See also p. 34.
[177] In his analysis of the Greek theologians Bambrough touches on their existential dimension and its value in understanding our own experience but then simply waves this off as beside the point for theological matters. (*Ibid.*, p. 34.)

do full justice to Bambrough's argument that some form of the interventionist model is logically essential to the meaning of "God," but I think these considerations considerably weaken it.

Unlike Bambrough, Wisdom has recognized from the start that existential concern is an essential aspect of the meaning of "God." It is, I think, partly as a result of this that he takes the following position about replacing interventionist models:

The demythologized beliefs were latent in the old beliefs, and at least the new beliefs are still beliefs as to what in fact is so. Because of these affinities in content and in general character . . . we may say perhaps that both systems of beliefs are "in essence religious." [178]

It does remain true, however, that Wisdom has not yet succeeded in showing that the concept "god" has an irreplaceable function in religious thought and activity. By our use of a concept, we remember, we compare one thing with many others. Our question, then, is whether by the concept "god" we make comparisons not made by any other concept. In concluding our discussion of Wisdom we shall consider three factors that are either latent in his thought or entirely compatible with it which not only would provide an answer to this problem but would also bring his position surprisingly close to that of Paul Tillich as we shall interpret it in our final chapter.

First, as we have seen, Wisdom has not remained content with his Freudian treatment of mystical experience in "Gods." In his unfinished essay "Eternal Life" he discusses the way in which for Spinoza and others a kind of mystical experience has provided an answer to "a sort of despair which comes . . . from a disappointment with life together with the thought that it ends in death." [179] This is at least comparable to Tillich's pairing of existential questions and their theological answers—answers rooted in religious experience. Furthermore, in Tillich's phenomenological analysis, it is this experience of the holy which is fundamental to the concept of "God." Wisdom says repeatedly that the words by which Spinoza and others describe their experience and its answer to despair seem to convey something to him but that he cannot say what. From a Tillichian perspective, at least, it is the location of a mystical element in one's experience, an ultimate concern, which provides the key to unlock this meaning. In other words, the key is in moving from a cosmological to an ontological approach to the logic of God, with its stress on an immediate awareness of a dimension of ultimacy in human experience. The concept "god" in this

[178] "Religious Belief," pp. 52-53.
[179] "Eternal Life," p. 239. See also p. 244.

approach is seen to group experiences marked by a sense of the holy, a sense of something ultimate.

Second, Wisdom is giving considerable thought to the kind of affirmation we find Paul making in Romans 8:39 that "nothing can separate us from the love of God." For example, in his discussion of the connection between religious experience and the struggle against despair, Wisdom concludes a paragraph on Augustine with, "Those who have said 'There is a way to eternal life' . . . have sought to combat despair by presenting a view of things which . . . brings with it a sort of happiness which even the disappointments of life and the thought of death cannot take from us"; [180] "in spite of all the wretchedness of the world," [181] in spite of regrets for the past or fears for the future,[182] in spite of "the distress of guilt and of disappointment with ourselves and with others" [183] in spite of anything that may happen, "they speak still with undiminished confidence." [184] Here, then, is recognition of a despair that involves disappointment with ourselves, with others, and with life as a whole. Here, too, is at least some recognition of a connection between this disappointment and the "distress of guilt," [185] on the one hand, and its answer in a distinctively religious awareness, on the other. Wisdom has further talked of guilt both in terms of the problems of self-acceptance and of reconciling warring elements within the self [186] and also in terms of a hope that seems to be conveyed by the promise of forgiveness.[187] Yet in spite of all this Wisdom has never quite considered whether the happiness or eternal life of which Spinoza, Tillich, and others speak is not precisely the experience of self-acceptance or self-affirmation and with it that affirmation of the other and of life as a whole from which self-affirmation is inseparable. For Spinoza speaks of eternal life not as something passive but as an *active* state that is rooted in a love for God or for life as a whole. These considerations might lead in turn to reflection on the relation between mystical experience of the sort that underlies Spinoza's thought and the fact, which Wisdom recognizes, that we have a relation to, an attitude or stance toward, life as a whole. The final link in the structure of this logic of God would then lie in connecting Wisdom's talk of God as "a power for good from which we may turn, on which we may draw" [188] with the

---

[180] *Ibid*, p. 240.   [181] "Religious Belief," p. 49.   [182] "Eternal Life," p. 248.
[183] "Religious Belief," p. 50.   [184] *Ibid.*, p. 51.
[185] In his reference to Ecclesiastes Wisdom also makes a connection with meaninglessness. For an analysis of the relation of meaninglessness and guilt see Paul Tillich, *The Courage to Be* (New Haven: Yale University Press, 1959), Chap. 2.
[186] "A Critical Notice: *Science and Ethics* (C. H. Waddington and Others)" (1943), reprinted in Wisdom, *Philosophy and Psycho-Analysis*, pp. 107-8.
[187] "Religious Belief," p. 56.   [188] *Ibid.*, p. 51.

experience of being accepted—an acceptance from which we may turn but which, if we accept it, unlocks in turn our own powers of affirmation and reconciliation.

Wisdom's occasional attention to the existential philosophers shows no grasp of their distinction between the active and the passive self. The existential elements in his own thought seem to derive largely from the influence of Freud,[189] whose own sense of the active-passive distinction is greatly overshadowed by the deterministic framework of his thought. In any event, when Wisdom considers the existential-ists' treatment of finding meaning in life he criticizes them for failing to consider that the sense of meaning may be basically the sense of a pattern in one's life and yet fails himself to see their point about the active selfhood necessary to meaning.

This same preoccupation with pattern leads him to wonder whether those who profess complete and unshakable confidence in the love of God are not somehow blind to so much in life that is far from good.[190] "It's their confidence which seems so unamenable to reason, so insensitive to what is so, that puts into mind the suggestion that their words express no claim as to what is or is not the case." [191] But the question that is latent in Wisdom's own thought is whether acceptance of self, of other, and of life is possible in spite of all that is negative about life, including guilt and the divisions within the self;[192] if so, the question is then in what conditions is this possibility rooted. Wisdom touches on our need for the other in connection with our quest for salvation.[193] What is not clear is, first, the nature of salvation and, second, whether in our relations with others there is also involved our relation with life as a whole.

The logic of God which I am suggesting as a possible development of Wisdom's thought will be more fully presented in the concluding chapter. What I wish to emphasize here is that there are elements of this logic latent in Wisdom's work and that Wisdom has already provided a means of connecting his emphasis on pattern with Tillich's emphasis on the liberating experience of acceptance when he notes that "what happens in real life sometimes is such that for the rest of one's life one sees things differently." [194]

---

[189] One should also mention the influence of others such as Dostoevsky, Tolstoy, Kafka, and Chirico.

[190] "Religious Belief," p. 49.   [191] Ibid., p. 51.

[192] In what sense, for example, may we "defeat" the isolation that we "cannot vanquish"? ("Symposium: Other Minds," p. 229.)

[193] For example, "we can hardly do this by ourselves. But there are those who will go with us, and, however terrifying the way, not desert us." ("Philosophy, Metaphysics, and Psycho-Analysis," p. 282.)

[194] "Eternal Life," p. 250.

The third factor in Wisdom's thought about the logic of God to which he has himself given too little attention is what we may call the element of prophecy. Wisdom has been so concerned to argue the cognitive nature of our grasp of patterns that his frequent references to the forward-looking side of talk of God are usually missed completely.[195] In "Gods" Wisdom asserts that "it is sometimes felt that a lover's attitude is somewhat crazy even when this is not a matter of his having false hopes about how the person he is in love with will act." [196] And yet he then notes how

we may draw the lover's attention to certain things done by her he is in love with and trace for him a path to these from things done by others at other times which have disgusted and infuriated him. And by this means we may weaken his admiration and confidence.[197]

What goes unnoticed here is the element of prophecy involved in the word "confidence." Clearly if the lover's confidence is weakened he will not be surprised about future behavior that otherwise would have surprised him. The expectations may be much less well defined than some we would call "having false hopes about how the person he is in love with will act," but they are expectations and rather important ones. Coming to see a pattern, then, may well involve a change in expectations concerning future experience.

It is this sort of intimate relation between pattern and prophecy in the case of religious assertions which is not brought out by comparing disagreement about the existence of God with those disagreements about negligence or about an invisible gardener which take place after all the facts are in. But when Wisdom is arguing that "some belief as to what the world is like is of the essence of religion" he uses examples in which the element of prophecy is clearly present.

When St. Paul said "The wages of sin is death" . . . it involved moral judgment and it involved also an assertion as to what happens. . . . The words "If ye forgive not men their trespasses, neither will your Father forgive your trespasses" (Matt. vi, 15) seem to convey a warning. The words "If ye forgive men their trespasses your heavenly Father will also forgive you" seem to convey a hope.[198]

It often seems that Wisdom's account of the logic of God omits this dimension of hope entirely and retains only that discernment of a pattern in time with which it is connected. But an element of hope is

[195] See, for example, Ferré, *Language, Logic and God*, pp. 131-32 and Bambrough, *Reason, Truth and God*, Chap. 4.
   [196] "Gods," p. 160.   [197] *Ibid.*, p. 161.   [198] "Religious Belief," pp. 55-56.

clearly present in much that Wisdom says in presenting his account of this logic. Consider, for example, the following: "Many have tried to find ways to salvation";[199] "For they, too, work to release us from human bondage into human freedom";[200] "We may then consider what it is about human beings which is referred to by one who says that they are not one with God but could become so." [201] And the element of hope is also central in Wisdom's recent efforts to find yet another key to the complexities of the logic of God. "Those who have said 'There is a way to eternal life' . . . have sought to combat despair by presenting a view of things which . . . brings with it a sort of happiness which even the disappointments of life and the thought of death cannot take from us";[202] "In Christ there was . . . a hope that many, a confidence that some, would achieve what He called 'eternal life' ";[203] "No matter what happens . . . those who speak of God and a power for good from which we may turn, on which we may draw, speak still with undiminished confidence." [204] Then, too, we may notice the reference to future experience in the following statements from "The Logic of God." "We don't know what would be heaven and this shows itself . . . in our feeble grasp of what it is we want to do with the words, 'Will the kingdom of heaven come?' 'Does God exist?' " [205] "The statement 'There is someone who feeds the cattle upon a thousand hills . . .' is not one to which what is still hidden from us in space and time is all irrelevant." [206]

It is one of the strengths of Wisdom's work on the logic of God that he gives at least some account of its existential dimension and has returned to it again in his latest efforts. And by its very nature the existential concerns not only the past but the past, present, and future in indissoluble unity.

The demythologizing of religious belief, in other words, omits some strands of hope but may well retain others. It omits those strands which are bound up with the old "mythological" picture of the world—the old interventionist model. But it may retain existential strands of hope, entwining them with modern knowledge and sensibility by utilizing new models. It may also, as Wisdom has been showing us, retain reference to those patterns in human experience which were basic to the old form of hope. Further still, Wisdom has shown that statements about God in their demythologized use will retain their paradoxical nature when approached from the perspective

[199] "Gods," p. 168.
[200] Ibid.
[201] "Paradox and Discovery," p. 124.
[202] "Eternal Life," p. 240.
[203] "Tolerance," p. 141.
[204] "Religious Belief," p. 51.
[205] "Logic of God," p. 16.
[206] Ibid., p. 21.

of patterns other than those to which they refer.[207] Whether a demythologized use of sentences about God retains the element of hope and of paradox depends at the very least upon whether these sentences continue to function as assertions involving patterns in time easily missed. This insight, surely, is a contribution of major importance.

In the course of Western culture the basic sense of what it means to understand and to explain has varied. In the classical Greek era to understand something meant finally to see its place in the pattern of things; in the Middle Ages it meant to see it in relation to the divine ground and source of its being; in the modern West it means to place it under a predictive law. We may think of these respectively as the aesthetic, religious, and scientific modes of understanding. Concerning the logic of God, then, we may say of Wisdom, first, that he has emphasized the aesthetic dimension of this logic; second, that he has not omitted but has paid too little attention to and wavered somewhat concerning the orientation toward future experience which this logic shares, however distantly, with the scientific; third, that he is now giving renewed attention to the religious awareness that Tillich and so many others have emphasized as basic to the uniquely religious dimensions of this logic. In our final chapter we shall present a view complementary to Wisdom's, giving particular attention to the second and third of these dimensions.

[207] From the point of view of our more commonplace and conventional ways of organizing experience, that is, one may say of this sort of demythologizing theologian that "no familiar facts could be conventionally described by his words." ("Philosophy, Metaphysics and Psycho-Analysis," p. 273.)

OXFORD PHILOSOPHY: *Ordinary Language & Paradigm-Cases*

Chapter Eight

Wittgenstein had said of ordinary language that it is in order just as it is. Wisdom took the modified view that, although ordinary language is indeed not to be replaced by some sort of ideal language, it nonetheless reveals only part of the truth about the nature of things and actually conceals or even distorts other aspects of this truth. Believing that Wittgenstein overemphasized the extent to which philosophy is based on confusion about ordinary language, Wisdom maintained that the philosopher is concerned to reveal something of that truth which is ordinarily hidden, although his language will also conceal and distort.

In recent years, however, the center of interest has shifted from Cambridge to Oxford, where, under the leadership of Gilbert Ryle and John Austin, a different line of development has been followed; at Oxford the primary concern has been not with metaphysics but with the examination and defense of the logic of ordinary language. This group[1] is very much in the tradition of G. E. Moore and what they take to be his insistence on the ordinary meaning of words: ordinary use is regarded as correct use. Indeed, Ryle is representative in seeing the value of Wittgenstein's work as that of creating a "rationale" for Moore's *ad hoc* analytic practices.[2] Because of their interest

---

[1] We must enter the warning here that these philosophers do not wish to be regarded as a school, for there are many differences between them. They do, however, share enough in common to justify grouping.

[2] "Ludwig Wittgenstein," *Analysis*, 1951. Much in the *Investigations*, however, is a direct attack on Moore's approach. As a member of the Cambridge "school" points out, Wittgenstein "follows Moore in the defence of common sense and

in ordinary language for its own sake and often quite apart from traditional philosophical problems, Wittgenstein is said to have regarded Oxonians as "more linguists than philosophers." [3] The shift from Cambridge to Oxford is comparable to a shift from Plato to Aristotle. Wittgenstein, for example, read much of Plato but nothing of Aristotle.[4] As was true of Plato, Wittgenstein's quest was for therapy, for vision, for insight. They shared poetical and mystical strains that were entirely absent in Austin and Aristotle. Wittgenstein said to the metaphysician, "What you have primarily discovered is a new way of looking at things. As if you had invented a new way of painting." (401) But for Austin and Aristotle philosophy is closer to scientific discovery than it is to artistic vision. Concerning this difference, John Wisdom mentioned to me the way in which John Austin had once responded to a comment of his by saying that he (Austin) was concerned not with what one is inclined to say or might say but with what one does in fact say.

Despite their differences in emphasis and aim, however, the Oxonians are fundamentally Wittgensteinian so that any extensive presentation of their general position would involve much repetition of ground covered in our discussion of Wittgenstein's later work. Consequently we shall presuppose a familiarity with Wittgenstein and confine our consideration of Oxford philosophers largely to their work on religious assertions. We shall limit our more general discussion to a review of the main features of the Wittgensteinian approach, an examination of the paradigm-case argument, a brief look at some aspects of the work of Ryle and Austin, and a note of some recent developments at Oxford.

The basic principle of the Wittgensteinian approach is that the meaning of a word is the rules for its use. As Ryle put it, "If I know the meaning of a word or phrase I know something like a body of unwritten rules or . . . general recipe. I have learned to use the word correctly in an unlimited variety of different settings." [5] For the most

---

in a regard for our ordinary language; but criticizes the notion of *analysis* in a way that has quite changed philosophy." (G. A. Paul, "Wittgenstein," *The Revolution in Philosophy*, p. 88.) Wittgenstein has Moore in mind when he says, for example, that some philosophers "see in the essence [of language] not something that already lies open to view and that becomes surveyable by a rearrangement, but something that lies *beneath* the surface. Something . . . which an analysis digs out." (*Philosophical Investigations*, par. 92.)

[3] D. Gasking and A. Jackson, "Ludwig Wittgenstein," *The Australasian Journal of Philosophy*, 1951, p. 80.

[4] Karl Britton, "Portrait of a Philosopher," p. 61.

[5] "Ordinary Language," *The Philosophical Review*, 1953, p. 179. As we have seen in our discussion of the later Wittgenstein, some of this group wish to distinguish meaning and use, but this does not involve a significant departure from Wittgenstein in practice.

part, these rules are inexact in the sense that the correct use of a concept is not neatly circumscribed by them. Our concepts have "blurred edges" or, as Friedrich Waismann put it, they have "open texture." [6]

Furthermore, our words have use only in particular contexts. To take Kurt Baier's example, "it is all right to say 'It looks like a horse' (1) when it is far away, or in a mist, (2) when one knows it is a mule, or (3) when it is a representation of a horse which is difficult to recognize, but not when it is standing in front of one in the stable and when one can see quite clearly that it is a horse." [7] Failure to take context into consideration may generate pseudo-problems; typical are the paradoxes we have seen Russell find concerning definite descriptions such as "The present King of France is bald." One does not describe a king in contexts in which it is clear that none exists just as one does not say "Please shut the door" when climbing a mountain.

More broadly, language-use is part of a way of life. As S. N. Hampshire puts it, "The significance of any statement whatever . . . presupposes some constant background of ordinary human interests and purposes and of ordinary human experience." [8]

Language loses meaning when we try to use words outside those natural contexts in which their use has evolved. To continue Hampshire's statement, "If we try to use ordinary forms of words in some context where this background of ordinary experience is lacking, we find ourselves merely playing with words in a void." [9] Taken out of its natural context, our language only *seems* to have a use; it lacks meaning in this circumstance because it no longer provides those contrasts by which when we say one thing we exclude other things we might have said. According to G. J. Warnock,

the Positivist shows us *that* metaphysical doctrines are not susceptible of ordinary confirmation and falsification; Kant suggests an answer to the question *why* not. To put it roughly, the metaphysician takes some concept which is ordinarily applied, rightly or wrongly, within a particular field, and proceeds to apply it to the whole of that field; but since the contrast between right and wrong application lies *within* this field, its application to the *whole* field abolishes the possibility of contrast.[10]

To say that there are no material objects or that nothing is solid does not convey information, because these utterances are compatible with every possible state of affairs.

---

[6] "Verifiability" (1945), reprinted in *Language and Logic*, ed. Antony Flew, First Series (Oxford: Basil Blackwell, 1960), pp. 125-27.
[7] "The Ordinary Use of Words," *Proceedings of the Aristotelian Society*, N. S., III (1951-52), 55.
[8] "Metaphysical Systems," *The Nature of Metaphysics*, ed. D. F. Pears, p. 27.
[9] *Ibid.*
[10] "Criticisms of Metaphysics," *The Nature of Metaphysics*, p. 138.

In defining meaning in terms of use, Oxford philosophers are anti-reductionistic. They reject the belief of the atomists and positivists that language is basically a rather uniform system in which, aside from mathematics and logic, the sole function is to describe—or, if not quite the sole function, at least the only function of interest to the philosopher. Against this "descriptive fallacy," as Austin called it,[11] the Oxonians unfurled their twin banners, "Every statement has its own logic" and "Don't ask for the meaning [i.e. analysis], ask for the use." These banners or slogans functioned, in the early stages of this revolution, as warnings against expecting all sentences to function in pretty much the same way and against expecting all non-simple statements to be reducible to or analyzable into statements conforming to certain preconceptions.

The source not only of this but also of many other philosophical confusions is held to be the misleading nature of our surface grammar or syntactical form. When sentences look pretty much alike it is easy to fall into the assumption that they must have the same sort of meaning.

Philosophical Issues and Ordinary Language Use

Many or even most of the traditional philosophical problems are believed to derive from this confusion. Misled by surface resemblances the philosopher treats the logic of one expression as more like that of another than it actually is; in his very posing of the problem he distorts the ordinary use or meaning of that expression. Gilbert Ryle, for example, argues that philosophical confusions about the concept of mind have arisen from the mistaken belief that statements about mind are of the same logical category as statements about matter. "The belief that there is a polar opposition between Mind and Matter," he explains, "is the belief that they are terms of the same logical type."[12] It is this and similar "category mistakes"—mistakes about the ways concepts are properly used [13]—which are held to generate at least most philosophical confusions. This means that at least many or most philosophic issues are to be settled by an appeal to the meaning that ordinary use gives to the concepts in question. A typical case is

[11] "Other Minds" (1946), reprinted in Austin, *Philosophical Papers* (Oxford: The Clarendon Press, 1961), p. 71.

[12] *The Concept of Mind* (London: Hutchinson and Co., 1949), p. 22.

[13] Ryle explains that "the logical type or category to which a concept belongs is the set of ways in which it is logically legitimate to operate with it." (*Ibid.*, p. 8.) We will be misled by Ryle's terminology, however, if we take the terms "category" and "logical type" too seriously. Ryle does not mean that the ways we use concepts fall into neat groupings to which we can attach various names for purposes of classifying. See Ryle, *Dilemmas* (Cambridge: The University Press, 1954), p. 9.

Ryle's appeal to ordinary use to prove that "both Idealism and Materialism are answers to an improper question." [14] His argument is that "the 'reduction' of the material world to mental states and processes, as well as the 'reduction' of mental states and processes to physical states and processes, presupposes the legitimacy of the *disjunction* 'Either there exist minds or there exist bodies (but not both).'" [15] But, in ordinary use, "the phrase 'there occur mental processes' does not mean the same sort of thing as 'there occur physical processes,' and, *therefore*, . . . it makes no sense to conjoin or disjoin the two." [16] The disjunction "mind or matter" involves the same sort of mistake as that in saying "She came home either in a taxi or in a flood of tears."

Another sort of appeal to ordinary use to settle philosophical issues is the paradigm-case argument. According to Antony Flew, this sort of argument now seems to be "the clue to the whole business" [17] of replying to metaphysical criticisms of ordinary use. He contends that "if there is any word the meaning of which can be taught by reference to paradigm-cases, then no argument whatever could ever prove that there are no cases whatever of whatever it is." [18] As Wittgenstein maintained, statements without a conceivable antithesis are meaningless because in excluding nothing they tell us nothing. We cannot meaningfully say that nothing is real or that nothing is solid or that we can never know what is true, for if the terms "real," "solid," and "true" have no possible applications then they have no meaning. To use a term meaningfully is to recognize standard or paradigm-cases of its application so that the metaphysician must assume paradigm-cases for the terms he uses and he contradicts himself if he uses those terms to deny that they have paradigm-cases or applications. It makes sense to say that something is unreal only if it makes sense to say that something else is real. The paradigm-case argument settles the philosophic issue as to whether anything is an X by presenting a paradigm-case for the application of "X" in our ordinary language. Or, in John Wisdom's terminology, the paradoxical [19] statement that nothing is an X may be replied to by the platitudinous statement that as a matter of fact we do call a certain thing an X.

The paradigm-case way of arguing, however, has an ambiguity that, in one form or another, has been widely discussed. This ambiguity

---

[14] *The Concept of Mind*, p. 22.   [15] *Ibid.*   [16] *Ibid.*

[17] "Philosophy and Language" (1955), reprinted in Antony Flew, ed., *Essays in Conceptual Analysis* (New York: St. Martin's Press, 1963), p. 19.

[18] *Ibid.*

[19] This statement is paradoxical if the term "X" has a place in our ordinary grammar.

lies close to the heart of Oxford philosophy and merits our careful attention. An example of this ambiguity appears in A. G. N. Flew's attack on the argument that it would be a logical contradiction to say that "God might have made people so that they always in fact freely chose the right." [20] Flew attempts to show that there is no contradiction in saying that an act is free and yet fully determined, so that God could logically have made men free and yet determined them always to choose the right. In condensed form, his argument is that "since the meaning of 'of his own freewill' can be taught by reference to such paradigm-cases as that in which a man, under no social pressure, marries the girl he wants to marry (how else *could* it be taught?): it cannot be right, on any grounds whatsoever, to say that no one *ever* acts of his own freewill." [21] There can therefore be no contradiction in saying an act is free yet fully determined for, if there were, *then* grounds for saying all acts are fully determined would be grounds for saying no one ever acts of his own freewill. "Anyone who tells us that science shows or could show us that there is no such thing as acting freely, etc. is: *either* just wrong, because there certainly are cases such as our paradigms; *or* misleadingly using the expressions in some new sense needing to be explained." [22] To say that no action is free is analogous to saying that nothing is real or solid; such statements either equivocate on the meaning of the key term or else fall into the contradiction of assuming the contrasting applications that give this term ("free," "real," "solid") its actual use in order to deny it really has these applications.

The ambiguity in Flew's way of arguing is that "paradigm-case" may mean *conceivable* case or it may mean actually existing case. Wittgenstein dismissed, as metaphysical, statements that lacked any conceivable application. Flew's argument equivocates between this sense and the sense of actually existing case. We may get at this by considering J. W. N. Watkins' attack on Flew's argument.

In his well-known essay, "Farewell to the Paradigm-Case Argument," [23] Watkins argues that there is a fatal mistake in Flew's argument, namely, the falsity of the implied "denotative theory of the meaning[24] of descriptive terms." [25] This is the theory that "simple descriptive terms must be defined *ostensibly* by pointing to paradigm

[20] "Divine Omnipotence and Human Freedom" (1955), reprinted and expanded in *New Essays in Philosophical Theology*, ed. Flew and MacIntyre, p. 149.
[21] "Philosophy and Language," p. 19.
[22] "Divine Omnipotence and Human Freedom," p. 151.
[23] *Analysis*, December, 1957.
[24] "The meaning" here refers to the semantic aspect of a term's meaning—what it can be used to refer to—but not to the pragmatic and syntactic aspects of its meaning.
[25] "Farewell to the Paradigm-Case Argument," p. 29.

instances";[26] their paradigm-cases, that is, must be actually existing cases. Flew contends that "acting freely" and related expressions can be taught denotatively because the paradigm-cases he gives for them are

those by reference to which the expression . . . *ultimately always has to be explained*. . . . We are not dealing with some compound descriptive expression . . . which like "the first man to run a four minute mile" might or might not have found an application.[27]

In other words, such expressions not only can but must be explained denotatively; "How else *could* it be taught?" [28] Flew asks. Furthermore, "a moment's reflection will show that analogous arguments can be deployed against many philosophical paradoxes," [29] the stated exception being those involving not descriptive terms but value terms. Against this theory Watkins argues that "the meaning of most descriptive terms (including most of those which figure in philosophical controversies) cannot be taught merely by pointing to paradigm instances." [30] Descriptive terms such as "yellow" and "wet" have to be taught ostensively, but descriptive terms such as "miracle," "vacuum," "spy," "freewill," and "unpredictable" do not have to be and, in fact, cannot be taught in this way. The (semantic) meaning of "spy," for example, cannot be taught by pointing to one or more instances of a convicted spy since any or all of these instances might be mistaken convictions and the people involved might be innocent victims. Theoretically, in fact, there might be no spies at all. Even were this the case, though, the descriptive term "spy" would be meaningful, for we understand its objective connotations—rules or criteria for its application—and so we would know how to apply it and might conceivably do so in the future. For convenience we may refer to those descriptive terms which can be taught ostensively as simple descriptive terms and to those which cannot as complex, although the distinction is not precise and certainly not absolute.

To put this another way, the question of human freedom which Flew is debating is what Wittgenstein called a grammatical question: "Does the concept 'freedom' have a correct place in our language-game about human actions?" The implication of Flew's argument is that since this is a grammatical question the findings of science could not logically affect the correct answer because that would mean it was an empirical question; that there is an *actual* paradigm-case of the use of this concept is, the argument implies, not an empirical fact

---

[26] *Ibid.*
[27] "Divine Omnipotence and Human Freedom," pp. 150-51. Italics are mine.
[28] "Philosophy and Language," p. 19.   [29] *Ibid.*
[30] "Farewell to the Paradigm-Case Argument," p. 31.

but a grammatical one. If it were an empirical fact then the case pointed to conceivably might not be a case of acting freely; but since the case pointed to *defines* the meaning of "acting freely" it logically must be a case of acting freely. Just as "Every rod has a length" states a grammatical fact, so "Every case in which a man, under no social pressure, marries the girl he wants to marry is a case of acting freely" states a grammatical fact. Now Flew's contention that this grammatical fact presents us not just with a conceivable case of acting freely but with an actual case is correct only if "acting freely" *has to be* defined by pointing to an actual instance. On the other hand, if "acting freely" is not defined denotatively then a description of grammar can tell us the sort of thing to which that expression may correctly be applied but cannot tell us whether in fact such things actually exist. The ambiguity in the term "paradigm-case" is whether it refers to an actually existing case or to a conceivable case.

This ambiguity is especially evident when, having described a case of acting freely, Flew asks, "If this is not a case of Murdo deciding then what is?" [31] If "this" referred to an actual case by means of which "decides" is defined then Flew's question would seem sound enough. But in asking this question, and indeed throughout his article, "this case" actually refers to a complex description that Flew has given—a conceivable rather than an actual case. Flew's complex description obviously cannot be taught simply by pointing to an actual case, yet he insists that the meaning of the expression whose application he is describing *must be* taught by pointing.

Regardless of what is true of *his* use of "free," though, Flew's argument against those who use "free" and "completely determined" as mutually contradictory collapses. It collapses because it depends on the false assumption that "free" must be defined denotatively.

The rule governing all descriptive terms, then, is that they have meaning only if we conceive of paradigm-cases of their applications. Simple descriptive terms are a special case under this rule; we can conceive of paradigm-cases for simple terms such as "yellow" and "wet" only if we have experienced instances of them. To generalize that because some descriptive terms can only be defined denotatively this must be true of all descriptive terms is to commit what we may call the "denotative fallacy."

The findings of science may be relevant to the grammar of complex descriptive terms, because our grammar is related to our beliefs about the nature of things. As Wittgenstein pointed out, new knowledge may lead and has led to changes in our grammar.[32] We know the meaning of a term if we know the rules for its use; we need not

---

[31] "Divine Omnipotence and Human Freedom," p. 153.   [32] *Zettel*, sect. 352.

necessarily know or even believe that actual applications of the term are correct. Consequently a people may commonly apply a term to certain actual cases in light of their knowledge of and beliefs about those cases, yet that application may gradually come to be modified or discarded at a later time in light of new knowledge and changed beliefs. If, for example, men believe that some human actions are fully determined by physical, psychological, and sociological causes and that other actions are not, one of their rules for the application of "acted freely" may be that the action is believed to be not fully determined. Eventually science may show them that all actions are fully determined, and they will then either abandon the use of "acted freely" or modify its meaning by dropping the rule about not being fully determined. When "free" is taken in this sense of not fully determined, then, questions about human freedom may be either grammatical or empirical. Wittgenstein had pictured language "as an ancient city: a maze of little streets and squares . . . surrounded by a multitude of new boroughs with strait regular streets." Sometimes, we are now saying, with the addition of a new street old streets are blocked off or fall into relative disuse or take on a somewhat different use. The findings of science, then, may be relevant to the grammar of complex descriptive terms; such terms are often governed by complex rules and so their use may be complexly related to factual belief.

According to Watkins, in failing to recognize that the complexity of connotations and other rules governing the application of a descriptive term often makes denotative definition impossible, Flew argues in a way that, if valid, would prove the existence of at least some instances of the things connoted by every descriptive term that men have ever used. For example, men have applied such terms as "miracle," "demon," and "witch"; if these terms are defined by certain cases to which they have actually been applied then miracles have actually happened and demons and witches have actually existed. But the argument can prove none of these things. As Watkins points out, "If 'p' has been defined by pointing to a, b, c then 'a is p' is a tautology and 'a is not p' is a self contradiction." [33] Neither statement, therefore, can tell us anything empirical. If I define "witch" by pointing to Mrs. Smith, I cannot tell you anything about Mrs. Smith by saying "Mrs. Smith is a witch." Similarly if I define "acted of his own free will" by pointing to Murdo's action in marrying Mairi, I cannot tell you anything about Murdo's action by saying "Murdo acted of his own free will when he married Mairi."

That most descriptive terms must be defined in terms of their objective connotations points to the fact that the uses of our terms

---

[33] "Farewell to the Paradigm-Case Argument," p. 30.

are complexly interrelated. The connotations of a term are conditions that must hold if that term is to be applied correctly. I can apply that term to a situation only if I can also apply the terms for those conditions to that situation. And this means there are also contrasting terms that cannot properly be applied to that situation. If I call something a square I must also be able to say of it that it is four-sided, its sides are equal in length, it is not a circle, and so on. The ways in which we use "square" and "circle" are such that we cannot properly ask "Is it a square and a circle?" Similarly, Ryle argues that the ways we use "mind" and "body" are such that we cannot properly say "Either there exist minds or there exist bodies (but not both)." And Flew himself, as we have noted, gives the paradigm-case of "acting freely" not by pointing to an actual event but by presenting a number of conditions: the actor was "of an age to know his own mind," he acted "without being under any pressure to act in this way," "there were alternatives, within the capacities of one of his . . . I. Q., with his knowledge, and open to a person in his situation." [34] Furthermore, having maintained that "free" and "determined" are not used in mutually exclusive ways, Flew discusses an implication of this for the way in which "motive" and "cause" are related;[35] clearly there are implications for many other terms as well. Such is the interrelationship of our terms that the grammar of a paradigm-case is often quite complex; consequently in describing grammar it seems necessary to follow Wittgenstein in making and arranging a good number of sketches.

A related ambiguity is found in the application of the paradigm-case argument to questions of value. When we ask whether something is good there is an ambiguity that lies in the distinction between what is called good in prevailing practice and what really is good. To argue that something is good because we ordinarily say that it is good is a version of the naturalistic fallacy of arguing from fact to value—i.e., from what is the case to what ought to be the case.[36] Matters of value cannot be established by paradigm-case arguments and yet, Flew confesses, "almost everyone who has used them, certainly the present writer, must plead guilty to having from time to time failed to see this." [37]

This criticism relates to questions of any sort of value including questions about whether reasons given in support of a certain sort of

[34] "Divine Omnipotence and Human Freedom," p. 150.
[35] *Ibid.*, p. 152.
[36] The naturalistic fallacy is discussed in Chap. II. In *The Language of Morals* (Oxford: The Clarendon Press, 1961), pp. 91-93, R. M. Hare criticizes this sort of argument in much the same way that Watkins criticizes Flew's.
[37] "Philosophy and Language," p. 19.

inference are really good reasons. Granted that we call certain reasons good the question remains whether there are good reasons for calling these reasons good. This question may express a genuine doubt or only intellectual curiosity but in either case it cannot be answered simply by reference to what we do in fact say.[38]

But if the paradigm-case argument is to be restricted to descriptive terms the further difficulty presents itself that descriptive and valuational functions are not neatly separable. The belief that they are was attacked by John Austin as "the value/fact fetish." [39] Our values find expression throughout our language uses. In defending ordinary language, then, great care must be taken to distinguish descriptive and valuational aspects. When G. E. Moore, for example, defended the reality of time he did so in the descriptive sense, whereas many who have contended that time is unreal were thinking mainly in terms of value.

Even our use of language to describe the paradigms and other aspects of the logic of our language expresses values implicit in the point of view of the describer. According to Strawson, for example, such descriptions are done "in an impermanent idiom, which reflects both the age's climate of thought and the individual philosopher's personal style of thinking." [40] We may recall here Foster's argument, which we have considered in connection with Moore, that the proper concern of philosophical analysis is with that aspect of language use which involves the adoption of a basic attitude, the commitment to a convictional point of view, on the part of the user. To use moral language correctly one must

be initiated into the basic moral attitudes by which the use of the language is determined. What a man needs to learn in order to use words correctly in *this* sense (not purely linguistic facility)—this is what provides the basis of philosophical analysis.[41]

When the philosopher, therefore, talks about how "we" use a word, "we" means those who share with him the attitude or commitment expressed in that use. "The correct use, that is the philosophically important use, for him is that which he can adopt." [42] Analysis, then, results in making "clearer what the initial affirmation involved." [43] One might say that analysis was commitment seeking understanding. Descriptions of the logic of our language, although they cannot settle

[38] For a helpful discussion of this, see J. O. Urmson, "Some Questions Concerning Validity" (1953), reprinted in Antony Flew, ed. *Essays in Conceptual Analysis.*

[39] *How to Do Things with Words,* p. 150.

[40] *Individuals* (London: Methuen, 1959), p. 11.

[41] " 'We' in Modern Philosophy," *Faith and Logic,* p. 199.

[42] *Ibid.,* p. 201.   [43] *Ibid.*

value issues, may reveal us to ourselves by articulating some of the things to which our point of view commits us.

In the use of ordinary language to settle philosophical disputes, then, another ambiguity concerns whether the ordinary language philosopher argues from the same convictional point of view as that taken by his opponent. Those against whom Flew is arguing, for example, take quite a different view of human freedom and so of human nature than Flew does.

Descriptions of the logic of ordinary language, in other words, may get at characteristics of the language-use of all speech communities or characteristics of the language use of only those taking a particular convictional point of view. In her article "Metaphysics and Ethics," Iris Murdoch offers a case in point. Concerning the description of the ethical use of language, she summarizes "our present position" in this way: "A man's morality is seen in his conduct and a moral statement is a prescription or rule uttered to guide a choice, and the descriptive meaning of the moral word which it contains is made specific by reference to factual criteria of application." [44] This is a position that "might be described as the elimination of metaphysics from ethics." [45] But here, Miss Murdoch points out, the language philosopher has merely produced "a model of his own morality"—"the morality most commonly held in England." [46] The description of moral use has been in terms of the "liberal" view in which "we picture the individual as able to attain by reflection to complete consciousness of his situation. He is entirely free to choose and responsible for his choice." [47] It is in this choice that he expresses his morality and shows what he finds to be of value. The philosophical background for this, she points out, is the empiricist tradition and especially the position of Hume from whom "we have derived a philosophical tendency, which is still with us, to see the world in terms of contingently conjoined simples, to see it as a totality of ultimate simple facts which have no necessary connection with each other." [48] Any idea that these simple elements are joined by real connections is merely due to habit and custom. A moral attitude was viewed by Hume as a habit of this sort.

In contrast to the liberal picture, which is assumed in the typical Oxford description of moral language, is the position of the "Natural Law Moralists—Thomists, Hegelians, Marxists."

Here the individual is seen as moving tentatively *vis-à-vis* a reality which transcends him. To discover what is morally good is to discover that reality, and to become good is to integrate himself with it. He is ruled by laws which he can only partly understand. He is not fully conscious of what he is. His

---

[44] In *The Nature of Metaphysics*, p. 104.   [45] "Metaphysics and Ethics," p. 105.
[46] *Ibid.*, pp. 112, 111.   [47] *Ibid.*, p. 115.   [48] *Ibid.*, p. 113.

freedom is not an open freedom of choice in a clear situation; it lies rather in an increasing knowledge of his own real being, and in the conduct which naturally springs from such knowledge.[49]

This leads Miss Murdoch to the basic criticism of Oxford analysis that

we have been led to adopt a method of describing morality in terms of which all moral agents are seen as inhabiting the same world of facts, and where we are unable to discriminate between different types of morality, except in terms of differences of act and choice. Whereas, I am arguing, it is possible for differences to exist also as total differences of moral vision and perspective.[50]

Our values find expression throughout our language-uses, including our use of language to describe the logic of language.

Use, Usage, and Metaphysics

The potential ambiguities in appealing to paradigm-cases are closely related to the ambiguity that may be involved when we ask about the meaning of a word by asking how it is used, for "use" may refer simply to usage—anything that is in fact said—or "use" may refer to correct usage. What we say is not meaningful simply because we say it. Gilbert Ryle, for example, warns that

the appeal to prevalence is philosophically pointless, besides being philosophically risky. What is wanted is, perhaps, the extraction of the logical rules implicitly governing a concept, i.e., a way of operating with an expression.[51]

The way in which we are to determine the logical rules, Ryle suggests, is analogous to the way in which we could determine how to operate with a given tool—trying it this way and that to see the sort of use that its structure makes possible. "A way of operating with a razor-blade, a word, a traveller's cheque or a canoe-paddle is a *technique*, knack or method. Learning it is learning how to do the thing." [52]

This approach is open to two main criticisms. The first we have just been considering: language-use rests on a convictional point of view. As Wittgenstein argued, the use of a word is part of a form of life and so its use involves much more than knowing a technique.

Let us assume, however, an adequate familiarity with or description of the form of life involved. A second criticism remains: "The use of a tool is to some extent dictated by the structure of the tool itself, but words or expressions in themselves have no use in this way; it is we

[49] *Ibid.*, p. 115.
[51] "Ordinary Language," p. 177.
[50] *Ibid.*, p. 116.
[52] *Ibid.*, p. 175.

who *give* them a use." [53] In reply it can be said that a word of the sort philosophers investigate does have a structure in the sense that its use is complexly interrelated with that of many other terms. The philosopher examining a word already knows how to use that term in relation to the others and is trying to make this knowledge explicit.

The rules constituting proper or correct use, then, are extracted from usage. But how are we to distinguish usage which correctly embodies the rules from that which does not? If we are not simply to select whatever usage is dominant or "prevalent" it seems that we must finally determine correct use in terms of consistency of the rules and semantic adequacy of the rules. Let us examine these criteria briefly.

It was really to consistency of rules that Ryle appealed in rejecting Idealism and Materialism. A rule that would make meaningful the disjunction "Either there exist minds or there exist bodies," he argued in effect, would be inconsistent with many of the rules governing our use of "mind" and "body."

We may take as another example our use of "see." Two features of this use are that we speak of seeing things at a distance and we speak of seeing things happen when they happen. Bertrand Russell has argued in effect that these two rules must be held to be inconsistent with each other in light of our knowledge that it takes time for light from the object to reach the eye and more time for the message to travel from the eye to the brain. Only when the message reaches the brain does the experience of seeing take place, and so we do not see things at a distance when they happen.[54] Whether there really is an inconsistency depends finally on whether the time factor Russell brings up plays any part in the purposes served by our ordinary talk about seeing things happen. But we need not pursue the question further, for this will at least illustrate the sort of thing meant by the question of the consistency of rules of use.

The second criterion, the semantic adequacy of the rules, concerns whether the rules enable us to know under what conditions we are to apply the term and under what conditions we are not to apply it. William Alston provides a succinct formulation: "A sentence is meaningful only if its utterance is governed by at least one rule that requires that certain conditions hold such that for each of those conditions the claim that the condition holds is empirically confirmable or discon-

---

[53] Charlesworth, *Philosophy and Linguistic Analysis*, p. 181.

[54] For a critical discussion of Russell's argument see Richard G. Henson, "Ordinary Language, Common Sense and the Time-Lag Argument" (1967), reprinted in Jerry H. Gill, ed., *Philosophy Today No. 2* (London: Collier-Macmillan, 1969).

firmable." [55] For example, if "The Holy Ghost descended upon us" is meaningful we must know under what conditions this would be true and under what conditions it would be false. Similarly, if the petition "Come, Holy Ghost, descend upon us" is meaningful we must know under what conditions the petition could be said to have been granted and under what conditions not. In Chapter VI we have discussed this requirement at some length in terms of Wittgenstein's contrast principle.

That ordinary use may often be appealed to in one way or another to settle philosophic disputes is generally what the Oxford philosophers mean by their contention that ordinary language is correct language. They defend ordinary language against the metaphysician's charge that its rules are inconsistent. Their contention that ordinary language is correct is also used as a protest against the reductionist's view that ordinary language really is or ought to be replaced by some sort of logical calculus. Some Oxford philosophers, however, mean by this that ordinary use is extremely likely to be correct, whereas others mean that ordinary use must be correct.

Norman Malcolm, for example, contends that "the proposition that no ordinary expression is self-contradictory is a tautology." [56] This is because an ordinary expression is one "which is ordinarily used to describe a certain sort of situation," [57] and "a self-contradictory expression . . . would *never* be used to describe *any* sort of situation." [58] From this Malcolm concludes that the belief of some metaphysicians that "an ordinary expression *can* be self-contradictory" is false.[59] But this conclusion is surely not correct. Since self-contradictory things do not exist (what could it mean to say that?) the metaphysician is obviously not saying that terms which do describe existing things may be self-contradictory. Rather the metaphysician is saying that sometimes when people think they are describing something they are mistaken because they are saying something that is self-contradictory—i.e. governed by inconsistent rules. All that can be concluded from Malcolm's tautology is that if the metaphysician succeeded in showing an inconsistency in the rules governing our use of an expression then this expression would not be what Malcolm means by "ordinary expression."

Others put the contention that ordinary language is correct in more guarded form. G. J. Warnock, for example, argues that "language does not develop in a random or inexplicable fashion. . . . It is at the very least unlikely that it should contain either much more, or much less,

---

[55] *The Philosophy of Language* (Englewood Cliffs, N. J.: Prentice-Hall, 1964), p. 75.

[56] "Moore and Ordinary Language," p. 359.

[57] *Ibid.*, p. 358.   [58] *Ibid.*, p. 359.   [59] *Ibid.*, p. 358.

than [its] purposes require." [60] And in his study of Berkeley he allows that it is "always possible that any system of language may contain more or less latent contradictions and obscurities" although "a language in constant daily use is far less likely to be thus unsatisfactory than a technical vocabulary, devised rather *ad hoc*, which has in fact never been tested and shaped and modified by actual use." [61] Now one may share a respect for the richness and complexity of ordinary language without having quite this confidence in the consistency and adequacy of its rules—especially in an age of rapid cultural change and its attendant confusions. Nonetheless I believe that the defenders of ordinary language are successful more often than not, and the important thing is that questions of its adequacy be answered by careful examination.

Oxford philosophers not only defend ordinary language against its metaphysical detractors but also study ordinary language for its own sake and quite apart from its relation to traditional philosophic issues. Among those who do the latter, John L. Austin has been especially influential and has developed his views independently of Wittgenstein.

By 1939 Austin had created the category of performatory utterances or performatives. A performative is contrasted with a constantive such as "The cat is on the mat" in that in a performative utterance we are *doing* something rather than simply saying something.[62] Performatives include such things as making a promise, making a bet, saying "I do" as part of a marriage ceremony, expressing thanks or sympathy, making a diagnosis, issuing an order, making a concession.[63] In making a promise, for example, I do not so much refer to something as perform, by means of language, the act of promising—an act that might have been performed without words, simply by a nod of my head or a handshake.

In the course of his investigation, though, Austin finds that the distinction between performative and constantive breaks down, for stating something is also doing something. One might perfectly well remark, "In saying that it was raining, I was not betting or arguing or warning: I was simply stating it as a fact," [64] and this remark places stating, betting, arguing, and warning on the same level. Consequently, Austin turns from the performative/constantive distinction to a theory of speech-acts in which he distinguishes some of the different senses

[60] *English Philosophy Since 1900*, p. 150.
[61] *Berkeley* (Baltimore: Penguin Books, 1953), p. 239.
[62] John Austin, *How to Do Things with Words*, pp. 5-7. See also John Austin, "Other Minds."
[63] *How to Do Things with Words*, pp. 152-62.
[64] *Ibid.*, p. 133.

in which saying something is doing something. First of all, in saying something I utter a sentence, e.g. "Close the door" or "You can't do that." This kind of doing Austin calls a locutionary act. Second, I utter a sentence for some reason or intent, e.g. in uttering it I give a command or protest your doing something. This sort of doing Austin terms an *il*locutionary act, using "il" for "in" to indicate that I do this *in* uttering a sentence. Third, very often in uttering a sentence I seek to bring something about which is not accomplished simply in the utterance itself, e.g., I want to get you to close the door or I want to stop you from doing something. This type of doing Austin refers to as a *per*locutionary act, using "per" for "by" to indicate that I do this—e.g. stop you—*by* the locutionary act of uttering a sentence.[65] In saying, therefore, with Wittgenstein, that the meaning of a word is its use, "use" refers to the sort of illocutionary act which can be performed with that word.

This stress on performing or doing does not mean that everything we say is meaningful just because we say it. What makes an utterance a genuine illocutionary act is the conventions or rules that govern it. Austin lists the following as necessary for the successful or "happy" performance of an illocutionary act:

(A.1)   There must exist an accepted conventional procedure having a certain conventional effect, . . . and further,
(A.2)   the particular persons and circumstances in a given case must be appropriate for the invocation of the particular procedure invoked.
(B.1)   The procedure must be executed by all participants both correctly and
(B.2)   completely.
(C.1)   Where, as often, the procedure is designed for use by persons having certain thoughts or feelings, or for the inauguration of certain consequential conduct on the part of any participant, then a person participating in and so invoking the procedure must in fact have those thoughts or feelings, and the participants must intend so to conduct themselves, and further
(C.2)   must actually so conduct themselves subsequently.[66]

If, for example, I make a promise, I use the meaning that "promise" has in the existing language-game (A.1), I must be in a position to keep that promise (A.2), and I must intend to do so (C.1). If I state "The cat is on the mat" I do so in accordance with existing rules for determining the truth of this sort of statement (A.1), I must be in a position to know or have good reason to believe the truth of what I say (A.2), and I must believe that what I say is true (C.1).

Austin's emphasis on speaking as doing calls attention to the fact

[65] *Ibid.*, pp. 98-107.   [66] *Ibid.*, pp. 14-15.

that we speak not as spectators but as participants. Our speaking is part of the way we involve ourselves in the stream of life. That we are involved in what we say is, obviously, of particular importance to an understanding of religious language use.

Oxford philosophers differ from Wittgenstein not only in their interest in pure research into the logic of ordinary language but also in their renewed interest in recent years in continuing the work of metaphysics. Wittgenstein saw his work as a radical departure from traditional philosophy, "one of the heirs of the subject that used to be called philosophy," as he put it.[67] Oxford philosophers see their work as a continuation of perennial philosophy, albeit with significant differences in perspective and method.

First of all, important work has been done on descriptive metaphysics. In this work the concern is not with just one area of language but with the entire structure of language. P. F. Strawson, for example, subtitles his book *Individuals* as "An Essay in Descriptive Metaphysics," an attempt to describe something of "the actual structure of our thought about the world." [68] Although "up to a point, the reliance upon a close examination of the actual use of words is the best, and indeed the only sure way in philosophy," this procedure is too limited "to meet the full metaphysical demand for understanding. For when we ask how we use this or that expression, our answers . . . are apt to assume, and not to expose, those general elements of structure which the metaphysician wants revealed." [69] Stuart Hampshire is also concerned with the general structure of ordinary language in the introductory portions of his ethical study *Thought and Action*,[70] although unlike Strawson, who contends that "there is a massive core of human thinking which has no history," [71] Hampshire believes that even our most basic concepts undergo change. Then, too, as we have noted in our discussion of Wisdom, Stephen Toulmin seeks to "build from scratch a pattern of analysis which will do justice to" the nature of inference in any area of language.[72] We may note further that Austin's descriptions of performatives are applicable to at least a very wide range of language.

Closely related to this task of descriptive metaphysics is what Strawson describes as "the explanatory work of the philosophical imagination." [73] In this work the philosopher seeks to determine "how the nature of our thinking is rooted in the nature of the world and in our own natures." [74]

[67] *The Blue Book*, p. 28.

[68] *Individuals*, p. 9.

[69] *Ibid.*, pp. 9-10.

[70] (New York: Viking Press, 1960.)

[71] *Individuals*, p. 10.

[72] *The Uses of Argument*, p. 97.

[73] "Construction and Analysis," *The Revolution in Philosophy*, p. 107.

[74] *Ibid.*

In addition to descriptive metaphysics Oxford philosophers show renewed interest in revisionary metaphysics. According to Strawson, in his "creative or constructive work" the philosopher considers how we might view the world "through the medium of a different conceptual apparatus." [75] And Anthony Quinton maintains "that the real point of constructing a metaphysical system is the recommendation of a conceptual framework, a set of concepts, that is, that can be applied to the whole of our experience and will do full justice to it." [76] This aim is especially important in view of the conflict that results from the fact that "we describe and explain what happens in the world with a number of partly independent, partly overlapping systems of concepts—physical, biological, psychological." [77]

On the whole, though, Oxford philosophers are more definite about what is to be rejected in traditional metaphysics than about what method metaphysics—especially revisionist metaphysics—should pursue. For one thing, they reject the deductive method because it cannot take into account the specific contexts of human life in which statements are understood.[78] Although it is argued that "exploring the relations between these most general notions—existence, truth, identity and so on—will provide us with the outlines of the map of human knowledge," nonetheless, "as Kant and Wittgenstein suggested, we have to start on this explanation from the actual human situation which conditions all our thought and language, the situation, that is, of men observing and acting from a particular position in time and space, referring to particular things." [79] Second, since deduction is out, "ontologizing is out" [80]—"ontologizing" being taken to mean the assertion of "the existence or occurrence of things unseen" on the basis of "purely philosophical or conceptual reasons." [81] Third, even though "Kant was right in looking for some few categories, or elements of grammar, which are the most fundamental of all, and in trying to show some systematic connection between them, perhaps no one would now claim that there is just one, finally correct way of exhibiting this systematic connection." [82]

With the "Wittgensteinian spade" some digging is underway to discover the many roots of metaphysics. The attitude of many seems to be that "digging is the proper philosophical activity at this time." [83] As Gilbert Ryle puts it,

[75] *Ibid.* See also the succeeding article by G. J. Warnock, "Analysis and Imagination."
[76] "Final Discussion," *The Nature of Metaphysics*, p. 142.   [77] *Ibid.*
[78] Hampshire, "Metaphysical Systems," *The Nature of Metaphysics*, p. 34.
[79] *Ibid.*, p. 31.   [80] Gilbert Ryle, "Final Discussion," p. 149.
[81] *Ibid.*, p. 144.   [82] Hampshire, "Metaphysical Systems," p. 35.
[83] B. A. O. Williams, "Metaphysical Arguments," *The Nature of Metaphysics*, p. 60.

the time is not yet ripe for new global syntheses. For forty years the canons and apparatus of philosophical reasoning have been undergoing a continuous transformation, the culmination of which is still in the future. In the meantime, we do well to educate ourselves by tactical, rather than strategic enterprises.[84]

This much is clear, though: for Oxford philosophers, metaphysics will deal not with entities transcending human experience but with general structures wholly within our experience.

Assertions About God

The Question of Logical Segregation

With this brief account of the Oxford philosophers' approach to the logic of language we may now turn directly to their discussion of the logic of assertions about God. Two general principles guide this discussion. On the one hand, the logic of religious assertions is not to be reduced to the logic of some other sort of assertion but is to be studied on its own terms. On the other hand, the logic of religious assertions must have significant similarities with that of other sorts of assertion, for we would otherwise simply be equivocating on the meaning of "assertion" in applying that term to religious utterances. The crucial issue in the religious crisis of our time is whether conceptions of divine transcendence are meaningful. Expressed in linguistic terms, the crucial issue is not whether talk of God performs useful functions but whether it performs a function that is significantly similar to that of assertions in other areas of language.

The insistence that the logic of religious assertions is to be studied on its own terms finds its strongest expression in the use of the paradigm-case type of argument. We shall consider two such arguments.

The first of these paradigm-case arguments is that presented by John Hick in his *Philosophy of Religion*. As I understand this argument, it is that the revelatory events of the Bible are the paradigm-cases of God's manifestations in human experience. The meaning of "God," for the believer, is *defined by* these events, and consequently the question of God's existence cannot arise. Because of the introductory nature of this book, however, Hick does not state the argument very rigorously, so that it will be good to have before us the passages on which my interpretation is based.

Hick begins with a paradigm-case argument for the reality of our material environment. It is simply meaningless to doubt whether anything whatever is real,

[84] "Final Discussion," p. 156.

for if nothing is real, there is no longer any sense in which anything can be said to be *un*real. . . . If the word "real" has any meaning for us, we must acknowledge standard or paradigm cases of its correct use. . . . But if tables and chairs and houses and people, etc. are accepted as paradigm cases of real objects, it becomes self-contradictory to suggest that the whole world of tables and houses and people may possibly be unreal. *By definition*, they are not unreal.[85]

Hick then draws a parallel to the question of the existence of God: "Just as our knowledge of the physical world is ultimately based upon sense perception, so any religious knowledge must ultimately be based upon aspects of human experience which are received as revelatory." [86] These paradigm cases or "facts of faith" define the meaning of "God": "The 'facts of faith' upon which a given religion is based define that religion." [87] Consequently, for the believer, the question of God's existence cannot arise.

The biblical writers were (sometimes, though doubtless not at all times) as vividly conscious of being in God's presence as they were of living in a material environment. . . . It would be as sensible for a husband to desire a philosophical proof of the existence of the wife and family who contribute so much to the meaning in his life as for the man of faith to seek a proof of the existence of the God within whose purpose he is conscious that he lives and moves and has his being.[88]

In this use of the paradigm-case approach, if I have correctly represented it, Hick makes the same mistake as I have tried to show that Flew does. Both assume that the descriptive term under consideration can only be defined denotatively; in other words, the term can have meaning only if an actual case can be pointed to. But if the meaning of a term is the rules governing its use, then a descriptive term will have meaning if we know how to apply it, and we may know how to apply it even if there are no cases of its actual application to which we can point.

Much of what Hick says is true only of simple descriptive terms. He contends that "when doubt becomes universal in its scope, it becomes meaningless," [89] but, unlike doubting whether anything is red, it is hardly meaningless to doubt whether anything is a spy or a witch or a miracle. Similarly, Hick maintains (1) that "if nothing is real, there is no longer any sense in which anything can be said to be unreal" or, in other words (2) that "if the word 'real' has any meaning for us, we must acknowledge standard or paradigm cases of its correct use";[90] but this holds only if "real" is a simple descriptive term. If "real" is a complex descriptive term it is correct to say only (1)

---

[85] *Philosophy of Religion*, p. 60. Last italics are mine.
[86] *Ibid.*, p. 76.   [87] *Ibid.*, p. 77.   [88] *Ibid.*, p. 61.
[89] *Ibid.*, p. 60.   [90] *Ibid.*

that "if it is *inconceivable* that anything is real, there is no longer any sense in which anything can be said to be unreal" or, in other words, (2) that if the word "real" has any meaning for us we must *conceive* of a paradigm case of its correct use.

Whether or not "real" is a simple descriptive term, "God" is not a simple descriptive term, and so Hick commits what we have termed the denotative fallacy when he contends that the meaning of "God" is defined by certain historical events. Hick describes God as infinite, self-existent, holy, creator, personal, loving, and good and explains that his use of the last four of these terms is an adaptation of their secular use.[91] We cannot, then, say of an event that it is a manifestation of God unless we know with respect to that event that certain conditions hold—conditions that are indicated by this way of describing God. But if we must know these conditions to be able to identify that event we cannot define these conditions by pointing to that event. If we were to define "God" or "infinite, loving being" by pointing to an event then it would be a non-informative tautology to say that that event is a manifestation of God or infinite, loving being.

To know the meaning of "God" we must conceive of a paradigm-case, and this means we must know what conditions must hold if it is correct to say of any given event that it is a manifestation of God. Furthermore, these conditions must be open to experience so that the belief that they hold in any given case is experientially confirmable or disconfirmable. But if, as Hick explains, God is outside of human experience because he is infinite, it is difficult to see how conditions we can experience can serve as adequate criteria for our talk of God. We shall explore this problem at some length, but our point for the present is that it cannot be met by simply pointing to certain events. In other words, that the believer affirms certain events as revelatory —paradigm-cases of the meaning of "God"—is not sufficient to establish that he uses the term "God" meaningfully. What we must know is what conditions hold which are the experiential basis in those events for calling them revelatory.

Another application of the paradigm-case argument to the existence of God is presented by Norman Malcolm in his discussion of Anselm's second argument for the existence of God. Anselm's conception of God is the conception of a being that cannot be conceived not to exist. God's existence is necessary existence. So conceived, the grammar of "God" is such that "the conjunction 'God necessarily exists but it is possible that he does not exist' is . . . as plainly self-contradictory as the conjunction 'A square necessarily has four sides but it is possible

---

[91] *Ibid.*, pp. 6-14, 79.

for a square not to have four sides." [92] Consequently, either God exists or there is something wrong with the concept itself; Anselm can be rebutted only by arguing that the conception of necessary existence is either self-contradictory or nonsensical. This conclusion seems to me to be correct.

It is to show that the conception of a necessary being is not non-sensical that Malcolm uses the paradigm-case argument:

In the Ninetieth Psalm it is said: "Before the mountains were brought forth, or ever thou hadst formed the earth and the world, even from ever-lasting to everlasting, thou art God." Here is expressed the idea of the necessary existence and eternity of God, an idea that is essential to the Jewish and Christian religions. In those complex systems of thought, those "language-games," God has the status of a necessary being. . . . Here we must say with Wittgenstein, "This language-game is played!" I believe we may rightly take the existence of those religious systems of thought . . . to be a disproof of the dogma . . . that no existential proposition can be necessary.[93]

The concept of a necessary being is meaningful because it has long been applied. It has its paradigm-cases.

This appeal to paradigm-cases, however, seems to me to fail to establish the meaningfulness of Anselm's concept of necessary being. First of all, to point to the ninetieth psalm or to other references to God's being as necessary, eternal, unlimited, and the like is not the same thing as describing the logic or sense of these terms. Malcolm rightly insists that a good way of getting at the sense of "necessary being" is to see how it is supported or proved by those who use it.[94] But there is and always has been wide disagreement in Christian systems of thought as to whether "necessary being" is to be supported in the way that Anselm supports it. Malcolm in fact refers to several Christian thinkers who argue against Anselm's position—his interpretation of the logic that "necessary being" has in the Christian religion. If we cannot tell whether the conjunction "God is necessary being but it is possible for him not to exist" is self-contradictory without seeing how "necessary being" is actually used in a language-game then are we to take Anselm's use or that of his Christian opponents as the correct use? Or is Anselm's argument valid for the way in which some Christians use the concept "God" and not for the way others use it? These questions are not answered by pointing to a line from the psalmist as a paradigm-case.

Second, and more important, that a complex descriptive term has been given a meaningful use cannot be established by simply pointing

[92] "Anselm's Ontological Arguments" (1960), reprinted in Malcolm, *Knowledge and Certainty*, p. 158.
[93] *Ibid.*, p. 156.   [94] *Ibid.*, p. 153.

to something that is said—an instance of its usage. What we must know is whether there are adequate rules to govern the term's application or, as we put it in discussing the later Wittgenstein, whether the term has contrasting application so that in using it to say one thing we exclude other things that we might conceivably have said. We must know not just that the term is used but what there is about a situation that makes the term applicable.

There are, we have said, two questions to be raised about the concept of "necessary being" or about any other concept for that matter: are the rules that govern its use (a) adequate to determine when it can and when it cannot properly be applied, and (b) consistent with each other? We are arguing that simply pointing to a paradigm-case does not establish requirement A—although it does establish the need for careful examination before concluding that the rules are not adequate. Concerning requirement B, however, Malcolm makes the important point that "there are as many kinds of existential propositions as there are kinds of subjects of discourse" [95] and consequently that we cannot judge the assertion of the necessary existence of God contradictory before we examine the sense that "existence" has in talk about God. There is, in fact, "no more of a presumption that it is self-contradictory than is the concept of seeing a material thing. Both concepts have a place in the thinking and the lives of human beings." [96]

But here again we must emphasize that the question of this concept's consistency is left unanswered by pointing to paradigm-cases of its use. Paul Tillich, for example, places himself in the tradition of Augustine and Anselm in holding that the concept of God's necessary being excludes the possibility of his nonexistence: "The question of the existence of God . . . implicitly denies the nature of God." [97] Yet Tillich contends that both Augustine and Anselm use this concept in a contradictory way; [98] one of Tillich's main concerns, in fact, was to present a consistent grammar for its use. For those of the Tillich-Anselm-Augustine tradition, the connotation of "God" as eternal, necessary, infinite and the like is based on an immediate awareness; it is a part of the meaning of "God" which must be defined denotatively: "The question of God [i.e. not of God's existence but of his nature] is possible because an awareness of God is present in the question of God. This awareness precedes the question." [99] Tillich contends that Augustine and Anselm fall into contradiction by using this connotation to establish the existence of a highest or "uncondi-

[95] Ibid.   [96] Ibid., p. 160.   [97] Systematic Theology, I, 237.
[98] Ibid., p. 207; "The Two Types of Philosophy of Religion," p. 15.
[99] Systematic Theology, I, 206.

tioned being within reality." [100] In Wittgensteinian terms, they present, as part of the grammar of "God," rules taken from talk of finite beings which are inconsistent with rules connected with God's eternal or necessary being. One conceives of God as a highest being within reality when one speaks of God as acting in addition to or along side of the actions of finite beings. Since it is conceivable that any particular actions might not have occurred, it is conceivable that the doer of particular actions might not have existed. The contradiction is that our immediate awareness of God's necessary, infinite being, which is concomitant with our awareness of the contingency and fini- tude of the being of everything that exists, makes nonsense of the idea that God might not have existed. It is one thing for Malcolm to argue against simply presuming that the concept "necessary being" must be self-contradictory; it is quite another thing for him to contend that "here we must say with Wittgenstein, 'This language-game is played!'" and to take this as a disproof of the view that Anselm's concept is self-contradictory.

We shall discuss the grammar presented by Tillich in our final chapter; our present point is simply that the meaningfulness of talk of God's eternal being cannot be established by the fact of paradigm- cases of such talk. "Eternal being" or "necessary being" must be under- stood in the context of an entire language-game about God, and the fact that a language-game was or is played establishes neither the consistency of its rules nor the adequacy of those rules in providing an application of its concepts. We need simply to remind ourselves of the concept "witch" or the concept "miracle." Malcolm makes the important point concerning "necessary being" that "there cannot be a deep understanding of that concept without an understanding of the phenomena of human life that give rise to it" [101] and suggests as one such phenomenon the experience of guilt such that one requires "a forgiving mercy that is limitless, beyond all measure." [102] This has some parallel to the "anxiety of guilt" which plays such an important part in Tillich's grammar. But is the experience of such forgiving mercy a subjective experience or is it the experience of an objective reality (which is indicated by referring to God as necessary *being*)? Such a question is answered not by the fact that there is an experience but by the place of that experience in a language-game.

The insistence that religious assertions have their own logic, we have said, is balanced by the requirement that this logic have significant similarity with that of other sorts of assertion. The basic reason is that if these similarities were lacking we could not speak of religious asser-

---

[100] *Ibid.*, p. 207.
[101] "Anselm's Ontological Arguments," p. 160.   [102] *Ibid.*

tions without simply equivocating on the term "assertion," which would be misleading at best. There are, however, two additional reasons for this requirement.

The first of these reasons is that unless religion "condemns itself to triviality and irrelevance . . . it will need a language in which it may relate itself intelligibly and pertinently to the different areas and interests of culture." [103] But a religious language cannot be relevant to its culture unless it maintains significant contact with the language of that culture. For this reason Ian Ramsey, for example, rejects the attempt to "explicate religious language within the charmed circle of the discourse peculiar to and distinctive of some Confession or Church: language knit inextricably with that distinctive kind of behavior called 'Church-going,' 'Kneeling for prayer,' perhaps 'Worship.' " [104] "It is plain," he argues,

that this logical segregation of theology makes theology utterly irrelevant, its words having no relation to ordinary discourse. It is "pointless" for the same reason that Wittgenstein considered much traditional metaphysics "pointless," viz., that it had no association with men's ordinary behavior. [105]

This is a considerable part of the force behind the skeptical linguist's insistence that "if the theologian is to communicate at all, he must establish some sort of contact-points between his special senses of the words he uses and the ordinary senses of these words." [106] Indeed, as Basil Mitchell makes clear, the believer who feels deeply the analytic philosopher's concern over how these two sorts of language are related sees in this concern an expression of the religious crisis in Western culture:

We often hear that the old beliefs have "lost their meaning" and that people today no longer find them relevant to the rest of their thought and practice. Christians are accused of a kind of "doublethink" by which they contrive to talk two entirely independent languages with no way of relating what is said in one to what is said in another. [107]

The second additional reason why the meaning of religious assertions must maintain significant contact with the meaning of ordinary non-religious assertions is that when we make statements about God's actions, or about attributes he is alleged to have in virtue of those actions, we borrow our words from the language we use in talking about men. When we speak of God as calling, loving, judging, forgiving,

---

[103] Hutchison, *Faith, Reason, and Existence*, p. 131.
[104] "Contemporary Empiricism," p. 182.   [105] *Ibid*.
[106] Ronald Hepburn, *Christianity and Paradox* (London: C. A. Watts, 1958), pp. 6-7.
[107] "Introduction," *Faith and Logic*, pp. 7-8.

delivering, etc., the meaning that these predicates have is derived, at least in part, from their ordinary, nonreligious meaning. As MacIntyre explains, religion does not

confer on such expressions a new and esoteric meaning. That this is so is shown by the insistence of theologians that certain particular expressions should be used in religious utterance, and others not. God is our Father, but not our Mother; loves us, but does not hate us; we are bound to obey him, not defy him, and so on.[108]

We first learn to use these terms in speaking about men, and then modify this use to extend it to speaking about God. If their ordinary, nonreligious use be designated as their literal meaning, then, when applied to God, they are said to be used nonliterally, that is, analogically or symbolically. Applied to God, their meaning shifts away from their original, literal meaning but not completely away from it. If their theological meaning were entirely different it would be at best pointless to use the same terms and very likely quite misleading to do so. But if the meaning of statements about God acting must retain significant contact with the meaning of corresponding statements about a man acting, the way in which religious statements are verified must retain some relationship with the way in which their nonreligious counterparts are verified. In other words, there must be a significant relationship between the expectations embodied in these two types of assertions.

The religious skeptic believes that this relationship gets stretched too far for religious assertions to function meaningfully. As Ronald Hepburn has put it concerning the statement "God is outside the universe, outside space and time,"

the word "outside" gets its central meaning from relating item to item *within* the universe. It too is being stretched to breaking-point in being applied to the whole universe as related to some being that is not-the-universe: its sense is being extended to the point where we may easily come to speak nonsense without noticing it, since the phrases "cause of the universe" and "outside the universe" are certainly still *grammatically*, though perhaps no longer logically, in order.[109]

Our familiarity with the grammatical form of these words, that is, may be obscuring an actual breakdown in meaning in which the term "outside" has "lost touch with its normal range of uses." [110]

If religious assertions are to be meaningful, then, their predicates must retain a significant part of the meaning they have when used

---

[108] "The Logical Status of Religious Belief," *Metaphysical Beliefs*, p. 175.
[109] *Christianity and Paradox*, p. 5.
[110] Hepburn, "Poetry and Religious Belief," *Metaphysical Beliefs*, pp. 149-50.

in ordinary language about human beings. One who takes this approach to religious meaning, therefore, will argue against those who rule out either the importance or even the possibility of a philosophic examination of religious statements. As Hepburn states it,

no theology can ultimately escape those questions of meaning and verification with which we have been concerned—even those theologies which set their faces against natural religion, arguments for God's existence, or apologetics *in toto*. In so far as they use words at all, questions about the *use* of those words can and must be asked.[111]

One concerned particularly with Protestant theology will think here of Karl Barth and his followers. Let us explore briefly some of the analytic reaction to this type of theology.

Typical of the Barthian approach is what Hepburn labels "strict Christology," by which he means the "belief that all statements about God are analysable without reminder into statements about Jesus." [112] In other words, statements about Jesus are to be taken at the same time as statements about God. The basic problem, as Hepburn argues, is that as long as the "strict" Christologist deals with these strictly (without remainder) as statements about Jesus, it would seem logically impossible for him to give any content whatsoever to the claim that they are somehow also statements about God. To put it another way, certain expectations concerning human behavior are attendant upon the use of these statements as assertions about a human being. To say, for example, that Jesus was a loving person is to expect that his life was characterized by loving actions. Were this not the case the expectation would be frustrated and, so, the assertion falsified. But if statements about Jesus are *also* taken as assertions about God, then *additional* expectations must be attendant upon their use, the frustration of which would falsify them. And it is just these additional expectations with which the "strict" Christologist refuses to deal. One can scarcely avoid the conclusion, therefore, that, whenever he uses the term "God," the "strict" Christologist is implicitly supplying his unstated, hence unexamined, conception of this "more." Hepburn sees this as the "strict" Christologist's "chief hazard," "the temptation upon the theologian to supplement illicitly his knowledge of God by what has *not* been strictly derived from knowledge of Jesus." [113] One finds further support for this conclusion in the closely related problem posed by Hepburn:

[111] *Christianity and Paradox*, p. 187.
[112] *Ibid.*, p. 64. Strict Christology is here distinguished from a "free" Christology which compromises a bit on the "without remainder." It is only the strict Christologists "who can say with some plausibility that they rely on no metaphysics." (*Ibid.*, p. 65.)
[113] *Ibid.*, p. 68.

With his characteristic boldness, Barth has claimed that Jesus is not particularly impressive as a historical figure. . . . Yet presumably God *is* particularly impressive, even though Jesus is not. Here then is the riddle: How can one at once *both* make Jesus one's sole guide to what can be affirmed about God, *and* insist that many things we say about Jesus may *not* properly be said about God also? [114]

The Barthian's rejoinder to all this would be to remind us of his view that man's greatest problem is his rebelliousness against God and that philosophy is often an expression of sinful pride. Concerning those offering skeptical analyses of the meaning of religious language, T. F. Torrance would say, "They cannot think otherwise until there is a fundamental change in their makeup." [115] One should not, then, be surprised that religious language seems meaningless in the face of philosophical criticism, for revelation "will not yield its secret to analytical and logical investigation.[116] Indeed, as W. F. Camfield has said:

These words of ours are, in themselves, quite meaningless as applied to God, but they are the only words we have, and God may use them as a medium to convey to us the truth about Himself. These human words of ours can become charged with new and divine content. While in themselves meaningless they can be made meaningful. Or, better, we shall say that while in themselves they convey positive untruth, they can be so laid hold of by God as to yield real illumination.[117]

To attempt to evaluate a position in which the possibility of evaluation is ruled out in advance is like attempting to gain a footing in a frictionless world. But we do not live in a frictionless world, and, applied to itself, such a position seems to fall into a *reductio ad absurdum*—quite appropriately, a reduction to soundlessness. Thus, Camfield's own words become meaningless. And, in saying that words about God "in themselves" convey positive untruth, his words "in themselves" convey positive untruth, and so on.[118] Why then does Camfield choose to say these particular things at all? Surely he cannot know in advance that God will act to make them meaningful. But surely, on the other hand, what he writes is not pure chance, a sort of random trial and error method to see whether God will in fact use what he writes. His religious positivism would seem to limit him merely to reporting those sentences which he and/or others believe that God has used to illuminate their minds. There is no ground for

[114] *Ibid.*, p. 67.   [115] *The Hibbert Journal*, p. 241.
[116] T. F. Torrance, Review of *The Inspiration and Authority of the Bible*, by Warfield, *The Scottish Journal of Theology*, 1954, p. 107.
[117] *The Collapse of Doubt* (London: Butterworth Press, 1945), pp. 45-46.
[118] One cannot logically have it both ways, however. If these words are meaningless, they cannot convey anything, even untruth. Moreover, if untruth is conveyed, if the wrong expectations are expressed, it seems logically inconsistent to claim that truth cannot be conveyed, the correct expectations expressed.

moving from these sentences to others, since the ordinary logic of language which makes this possible has been rejected. And even in reporting that God has used certain sentences one would be saying something that was "in itself" without meaning.

Such an account seems further inconsistent in that, if all words are held to be equally meaningless as applied to God, it can give no reason why the religious man should say one thing rather than another, no reason why the preacher should read from Scripture rather than from a joke book, no reason why revealed theology should be preferred to natural theology or Christian theology to that of some other religion. As Hepburn asks of Barth, "What would have to happen for him to change his mind about his affirmation that Christianity and no other is the God-adopted faith?" [119] Their Christological emphasis affords no reply, since words about Jesus' relation to God, etc., are "in themselves" as meaningless as any others.

To show that some words are more appropriate than others is to show that their ordinary meanings are more appropriate. But then we are back to our original problem. In other words, if the word "meaning" is to retain any of its ordinary nontheological meaning when it is said that God makes certain sentences meaningful, then the theologian must indicate the nature of this connection between ordinary and, shall we say, inspired meaning. As John A. Passmore has put it, "Not even God can 'give a meaning' to a meaningless expression without giving it a meaning; we must recognize that the expression has a meaning—is not, then, intrinsically meaningless—before we can ask the question, 'Who gave it this meaning?'" [120] We must not lose sight of the fact that, in this position, the inspired use of "meaning" has no relation whatsoever with our ordinary use of the term. One possibility raised by Ferré is that perhaps that inspired use of the term "meaning" has something to do with the sense of importance or momentousness that accompanies inspired communication.[121] But if "meaning" is reduced to mean simply important, then "what of the 'truth' which is supposedly given 'from without' by God's miraculous gift of his Word? Meaning is a logical prerequisite for truth and falsity." [122] Hepburn also raises the question whether this sense of momentousness does not create the illusion that the language somehow manages to have something like cognitive meaning in the ordinary sense of the term.[123]

Perhaps the reply will be that statements about God do express certain expectations and hence are meaningful in the ordinary sense

[119] *Christianity and Paradox*, pp. 81-82.

[120] "Christianity and Positivism," *The Australasian Journal of Philosophy*, 1957, p. 128.

[121] *Language, Logic and God*, pp. 90-91.

[122] *Ibid.*, p. 91.   [123] "Poetry and Religious Belief," pp. 155 ff.

of the word, but these possibilities can only be seen from the Christian perspective. We may recall, for example, Wisdom's work in showing how new language perspectives give us new insights into old facts. However, insofar as "inspired" language is dealing with old facts, i.e., the same realities that our ordinary language perspectives deal with, it retains something of this ordinary meaning. And the problem remains of giving an account of why the "inspired" language uses just those terms from our ordinary language that it does. What, for example, is the relation between the expectations normally attendant upon our use of the word "love" and those expectations which its inspired meaning expresses?

A further criticism to be made of this "logic of obedience" is that offered by Ferré in calling it a "logical docetism." As he argues, "the value of the human is minimized, denied, and deplored ostensibly to glorify the miraculous inspiration of the divine; but such a policy can never lead to a genuine theory of incarnation, only to a violation of the debased human by the divine which, instead of 'inspiring' the human, assaults and replaces it." [124] Then, too, such a position invites use as a covert expression of hostility toward the human.

Then, too, the rejection of ordinary rational criticism opens the way for any sort of superstition, fanaticism, and the like. It is well to be reminded that, especially in religious matters, one cannot properly divorce thinking from the condition and situation of the thinker. But this can scarcely be used as a ground for attacking philosophy of religion. Surely the work of the theologian is not more immune from being an expression of sinful pride than is that of the skeptical philosopher. To reject any discussion of the logic of language on grounds of wrong motives is to be guilty of the *ad hominem* fallacy.

The chief contribution of the "logic of obedience" school, it seems to me, is the attention it draws to the difference between thinking about something in a detached, impersonal manner and thinking about it with respect to its personal meaning for oneself. The danger is that the difference between objectivity and personal involvement will be overdrawn. Surely the decision to give an alleged truth personal application to oneself becomes possible only if one objectively grasps something of its meaning. The very charge that skeptical philosophy is an expression of rebelliousness seems logically to presuppose that the skeptical philosopher has grasped enough of the meaning of the subject matter to have something against which to rebel. It seems rather that vagueness and ambiguity in the logic of religious language often seriously obscure the decision between faith and unfaith.

Because of the importance in religious language use of the way in

[124] *Language, Logic and God*, p. 89.

which the speaker involves himself in what he is saying, Austin's concept of performatory utterances provides a helpful tool for the study of this use. In *The Logic of Self-Involvement*,[125] Donald Evans has pioneered the application of Austin's concept to biblical language. Of relevance to our study is (1) Evans' contention that biblical assertions are typically self-involving for the speaker, (2) his recognition that other sorts of performatory utterances have factual presuppositions, and (3) the radical dependence of his analyses upon an adequate account of the informative function of religious assertions.

First of all, then, Evans argues that, although not all statements imply value judgments, biblical statements about the actions of God do entail such judgments—do commit the speaker to certain values. For example, "When Jones says, 'God is my Creator,' his utterance is self-involving if it occurs in the biblical context." [126] This utterance involves Jones in a certain attitude to God and in a commitment to a certain way of life.[127] Jones would violate the logic of biblical language if he were to say, "Oh, I suppose God is my Creator but I don't see that it really matters very much."

Second, Evans recognizes that other sorts of performatory utterances such as thanking or asking for help have factual presuppositions. In thanking or asking for help I presuppose the existence of the other and also an understanding of that for which I am giving thanks or of the sort of thing which would constitute giving help.[128]

Third, Evans' analyses of biblical performatory utterances involve constant references to God and so would be in large measure unintelligible if these references were unintelligible. According to Evans, for example, "In the biblical context, if I say, 'God is my Creator,' I acknowledge my status as God's obedient servant, . . . I acknowledge God's gift of existence, and I acknowledge God's self-commitment to me." [129] But to perform an acknowledgment of these things I must know what I mean by them, and to know this I must know what would count for and what against my belief that these things really are the case. The account that Evans gives of this factual aspect seems very similar to that of I. M. Crombie [130] which we shall evaluate in this chapter. The point to be made in our present discussion is that the application of Austin's concept of performatory utterances to talk of God does not enable us to bypass the problem of whether assertions about God can be meaningful.

The Oxford approach to religious language use, we have been saying, typically involves the rejection of any logical segregation of that meaning. But some who practice the Oxford type of philosophy play upon

---

[125] (London: SCM Press, 1963.)   [126] *The Logic of Self-Involvement*, p. 162.
[127] *Ibid.*, pp. 225, 251.   [128] *Ibid.*, pp. 252-56.
[129] *Ibid.*, p. 158.   [130] See, for example, *ibid.*, pp. 199, 133, 224-25.

the ambiguity in "meaning is use" in such a way as to interpret religious language as having just such a logically segregated meaning. If "use" is taken in the sense of actual usage, rather than correct use, then, of course, religious language is meaningful because people actually do use it. Wittgenstein, we may recall, insisted that language is meaningful only if it is interwoven with our human activities. It is tempting for some to regard the activity of worship as fulfilling this requirement in the case of religious language. We read, for example, that "I don't decide whether a man is my co-religionist by seeing how he argues, but by whether I find him kneeling beside me at church."[131] In effect, this not only isolates religious language from the rest of language but it also isolates religious activity from the rest of our activity, and so makes religion irrelevant to life as a whole. One must then either ignore or somehow explain away the fact that the language of worship makes much reference to our everyday living. This account not only makes religion irrelevant to everyday life, then, but also fails to explain why worship should use just the terms that it does.

In order to show that religious language is meaningful, one must show that its terms retain part of the meaning that they have when used in our ordinary language about human beings. The attempt to deal with this problem has resulted in the doctrines of analogical and symbolic predication. The doctrine of analogy has been discussed in the chapter on the later work of Wittgenstein, where we concluded that this doctrine fails to show that in attempting to apply terms to God we do retain part of their ordinary meaning. Religious language provides us with a picture of human actions and relations by which we are to think about God and his actions, but the doctrine of analogy does not show that this picture has an application. As we may recall from our examination of Alston's use of this approach, the problem in applying this picture to God is that the rules governing the ordinary application of the terms involved depend upon the existence of the human body. If these terms are to be applied to an immaterial being, these rules must somehow be replaced by others sufficient to guide this application. As Alston concluded, "By drawing analogies we get a

---

[131] A. M. Quinton, "Philosophy and Belief," *The Twentieth Century*, June, 1955, p. 519. Gellner comments that, "given the activity theory of mind, one can see how Quinton and others have been tempted to give an account of conviction in terms of kneeling, etc., and not of believing (partly, of course, because *believing* itself is turned into a kind of doing)." (*Words and Things*, p. 221, n.) He also notes here the fallacious belief that form and content can be separated: "The fact that a 'verbal behaviour' account of religion, for instance, is in conflict with the transcendental claims found *within* religions, which is obvious, only illustrates the point which is ignored by linguistic philosophers, namely, that formal and substantive doctrines are so mixed up in human life through a long history of intermixture that it is quite impossible to treat one without the others." (*Ibid.*, p. 156.)

picture with taboos against using it in familiar ways. What is needed is a positive description of the ways in which it is to be used." [132]

The problem of establishing an analogical or a symbolic meaning for the terms borrowed from ordinary language is, in large measure at least, the problem of reformulating the rules governing the verification and falsification of the ordinary statements in which they are used. Religious assertions are assertions only insofar as they are governed by such rules. It is this problem which seems to be the focal point of the discussion among Oxford philosophers, particularly in terms of the falsifiability of assertions about God.

As William T. Blackstone puts it, "One of the mild forms in which positivism has survived is found in the principle of falsifiability, first clearly formulated, so far as I know, by Karl Popper." [133] According to Popper, "the *empirical content* of a statement increases with its degree of falsifiability: The more a statement forbids the more it says about the world of experience." [134] To assert something, in other words, is equivalent to denying its opposite, and should this opposite turn out to be the case, then the assertion is falsified. If it is logically impossible for a statement to be falsified, then it denies nothing and, so, asserts nothing.

This principle is applied to religious language in the famous discussion concerning "Theology and Falsification." [135] The question dealt with is whether statements about an alleged divine being named "God" could, under any circumstances, be counted as false. The statement that John is loving carries with it certain expectations, namely, that at least some of his actions will be of the sort that we designate "loving" *and*, so, that the opposite will not be the case, i.e., that the loving actions fail to materialize and that his actions, rather, are predominantly indifferent or hostile. If, then, one believes that there exists a being named "God" who is loving, one entertains expectations concerning particular actions on the part of that being. If, furthermore, this divine being is believed to be omnipotent, in the sense that nothing can prevent him from intervening in any situation in which he chooses, the expectation is that he will intervene whenever human welfare could be advanced by his doing so. At this point there arises, in one of its forms, what traditionally has been called the problem of evil. Situations arise in which it seems that divine intervention would further human

---

[132] "The Elucidation of Religious Statements," p. 442.

[133] *The Problem of Religious Knowledge* (Englewood Cliffs, N.J.: Prentice-Hall, 1963), p. 73.

[134] *The Logic of Scientific Discovery* (New York: Basic Books, 1959), p. 119.

[135] Antony Flew, R. M. Hare, Basil Mitchell, and I. M. Crombie (1950-51), reprinted in *New Essays . . . ,* pp. 96-130. Crombie's contribution was originally published separately from the rest in Volume V of *Socratic Digest*.

well-being, and yet this intervention is not forthcoming. The believer learns that he cannot be very definite in his expectations concerning the love of God. God's love is, at least at times, mysterious and inscrutable. But the question is, do not the believer's expectations become so vague that they do not deserve to be called expectations at all? His assertion that God is love does not seem to deny that anything will take place—it does not seem to contradict any of the expectations of the non-believer—and so it does not seem to assert anything.

Antony Flew presents this point in the following parable, which is based upon the somewhat similar parable in Wisdom's "Gods":

Once upon a time two explorers came upon a clearing in the jungle. In the clearing were growing many flowers and many weeds. One explorer says, "Some gardener must tend this plot." The other disagrees, "There is no gardener." So they pitch their tents and set a watch. No gardener is ever seen. "But perhaps he is an invisible gardener." So they set up a barbed-wire fence. They electrify it. They patrol with bloodhounds. (For they remember how H. G. Wells' *The Invisible Man* could be both smelt and touched though he could not be seen.) But no shrieks ever suggest that some intruder has received a shock. No movements of the wire ever betray an invisible climber. The bloodhounds never give a cry. Yet still the Believer is not convinced. "But there is a gardener, invisible, intangible, insensible to electric shocks, a gardener who has no scent and makes no sound, a gardener who comes secretly to look after the garden which he loves." At last the Sceptic despairs, "But what remains of your original assertion? Just how does what you call an invisible, intangible, eternally elusive gardener differ from an imaginary gardener or even from no gardener at all?" [136]

In his last question the Sceptic, in effect, "was suggesting that the Believer's earlier statement has been so eroded by qualification that it was no longer an assertion at all." [137] The *difference in expectations* that at first appeared to define the issue gradually has been dissipated, and so its status as an assertion has been "killed by inches, the death by a thousand qualifications." [138] For the believer to continue to insist that his utterance is an assertion without treating it according to the rules that govern the making of assertions is, Flew suggests, akin to the concept of *doublethink* in George Orwell's *1984*, "the power of holding two contradictory beliefs simultaneously." [139] "Perhaps religious intellectuals," Flew concludes, "are sometimes driven to double-think in

---

[136] "Theology and Falsification," p. 96. The point of Wisdom's parable is quite different from Flew's.

[137] *Ibid.*, p. 98.   [138] *Ibid.*, p. 97.   [139] *Ibid.*, p. 108.

order to retain their faith in a loving God in the face of a heartless and indifferent world." [140]

R. M. Hare's response to this problem is that "on the ground marked out by Flew, he seems to me to be completely victorious." [141] Belief in God, Hare maintains, is on a different logical level from belief about a particular matter-of-fact. The believer's talk about a gardener or a providential God is not an assertion—in the sense of being "some sort of *explanation*, as scientists are accustomed to use the word" [142]—but is rather the expression of a "blik" or way of looking at something—the garden or the world. The lunatic, for example, who is convinced that all dons want to murder him has a blik about dons. Since nothing that the dons do dissuades him, falsifies his blik, his expressions of this fear do not have the status of assertions, yet do express a significantly different way of thinking about dons. Bliks are not assertions or explanations, but, "as Hume saw, without a *blik* there can be no explanation; for it is by our *bliks* that we decide what is and what is not an explanation." [143] We see, then, that "our whole commerce with the world depends upon our *blik* about the world." [144]

Religion, then, is fundamentally a matter of adopting a blik. Religious bliks are distinguished from other bliks in that by means of them "our whole way of living is organized." [145] Really to believe in God, then, is to have a certain blik about the world which is not shared by those who do not really believe in God. Hare suggests "very tentatively" that belief in divine creation is "worshipping assent to principles for discriminating between fact and illusion," [146] and says elsewhere that belief in God is the "*blik* about the world which makes me put my confidence in the future reliability of steel joints; . . . in

[140] *Ibid*. "Heartless and indifferent world" apparently is offered here as more than a picture preference. It seems to be put forward as a metaphysical assertion about the ultimate nature of things. One would like to know just how much is being asserted here, i.e., what would have to happen to falsify Flew's statement. Perhaps he means simply that some things happen which are, at least if judged from our finite perspective, contrary to the expectations embodied in the belief in a loving and all-powerful divine being. But this is not something that at least most believers would deny. Or perhaps it is the more substantial assertion that these expectations are frustrated as often or more often than they are realized—in Wisdom's terms, that the order of things is such that one might appropriately say, "It is all in the hands of someone who arranges the little ironies of fate." If so, and if it is to carry weight, Flew must argue the case rather than merely insinuate it.

[141] *Ibid.*, p. 99.   [142] *Ibid.*, p. 101.

[143] *Ibid.* Hume spoke of "opinions" which "we embrace by a kind of instinct or natural impulse, on account of their suitability and conformity to the mind." (David Hume, *A Treatise of Human Nature*, ed. T. H. Green and T. H. Grose, I [London: Longmans, Green & Co., 1898], 501.) According to Hume, it is just such a natural belief which gives "a foundation to all the articles of religion." (*A Treatise* . . . , p. 456.)

[144] Hare, p. 101.

[145] Hare, "Religion and Morals," *Faith and Logic*, p. 189.   [146] *Ibid.*, p. 192.

the general non-homicidal tendencies of dons; in my continued well-being (in some sense of that word that I may not now fully understand) if I continue to do what is right according to my lights; in the general likelihood of people like Hitler coming to a bad end." [147] This distinction between religious statements as assertions and as expressions of my fundamental blik about the world is Hare's way of interpreting Plato's distinction when he "said of the idea of the Good, which was his name for God, that it was not itself a being, but the source or cause of being." [148]

But, at this point, Hare's account of the logic of bliks becomes inconsistent. On the one hand, he maintains that "differences between bliks about the world cannot be settled by observation of what happens in the world." [149] As he sees it, a *"blik* is compatible with any finite number of such tests." [150] Yet, on the other hand, Hare makes a distinction between "insane" and "sane" bliks or between "right" and "wrong" bliks.[151] Surely such a judgment must be based on some sort of tests. But if there are tests that count toward verifying or falsifying our bliks, then they are closer in function to assertions than Hare allows. Concerning the lunatic, Hare asserts that "there is no behaviour of dons that can be enacted which he will accept as counting against his theory; and therefore his theory, on this [falsifiability] test, asserts nothing." [152] But surely it is mistaken to say that his claim that all dons want to murder him asserts nothing. We do not judge a blik insane because it differs from the blik held by most people, but because of the way in which it differs. The lunatic's blik is insane because on its basis he puts forward an assertion—entertains certain expectations—yet will allow nothing to count against that assertion. As we may recall Wisdom saying,

When a man has an attitude which it seems to us he should not have or lacks one which it seems to us he should have then, not only do we suspect that he is not influenced by connections which we feel should influence him and draw his attention to these, but also we suspect he is influenced by connections which should not influence him and draw his attention to these.[153]

That the lunatic will not allow present experience to count against his assertion is what leads us to believe that there *must* be experiences of the past, such as severe hurt in past relationships with those important to him, that are unconsciously operating as compelling reasons in support of his blik. The lunatic, we say, is deluded. "But what is he

[147] "Theology and Falsification," *New Essays . . .* , p. 101.
[148] "Religion and Morals," p. 192. The reference is to Plato's *Republic,* 509 b.
[149] "Theology and Falsification," p. 101.   [150] *Ibid.*
[151] *Ibid.,* p. 100.   [152] *Ibid.*   [153] "Gods," p. 161.

deluded about?" [154] asks Hare. "About the expectations embodied in his *assertion* about dons," we must reply.

It is precisely, then, when a person will not "listen to reason" in a discussion of bliks, but clings to his position compulsively that we stop taking his assertions seriously as assertions and begin to look for the psychological pressures that are operative. In short, the distinction between sane and insane bliks depends upon the fact that the experiences to which we apply a blik do logically count for or against it.

We must further argue that the distinction between right and wrong bliks is really not the same as that between bliks held sanely and those held insanely, but that it, too, depends upon the ability of experience to frustrate or confirm our bliks. Whether we hold a blik sanely is a matter of whether we allow our experiences to count for or against the expectations that we have of our experience. Whether a blik is right is a matter of whether our experiences turn out to be what, holding that blik, we expect them to be. One thinks, for example, of Job's blik concerning God's rewarding of the righteous with prosperity, a blik that he gave up in the face of his experience to the contrary. Indeed, does not the process of maturing as a person involve a continuous modification [155] of one's bliks as things happen which are *contrary* to one's expectations or *opinions* (para-doxa)? One may, then, sanely hold a (relatively) wrong blik, modifying it as experience tells against it, or one may hold a right blik in such a way that nothing would be allowed to count against it—i.e., insanely.

If we recall the things that Hare indicated as part of his own blik, two points become evident. First of all, they express *expectations* about future experience. He stated his confidence, for example, "in my own continued well-being (in some sense of that word that I may not now fully understand) if I continue to do what is right according to my lights" [156] Second, the expectations expressed are *far less definite* than are those embodied in straightforward assertions, such as "The cat is on the mat," but they are nonetheless of *importance* to Hare—some of considerable or even ultimate importance. It is insofar as Hare's position draws attention to the relative indefiniteness of the expectations embodied in our bliks that it is of value in clarifying the logical difference between the expression of a blik and an ordinary assertion about a particular matter-of-fact. It is this that Blackstone fails to see when he argues against Hare that right bliks "turn out not to be bliks at all, but falsifiable assertions" and so with the "notion of a right blik

---

[154] "Theology and Falsification," p. 100.

[155] Sometimes, of course, the change in blik is less a modification than it is a radical upheaval or conversion, as in the case of Job. We may take, as another example, Paul's change of blik from justification by works to justification by faith.

[156] "Theology and Falsification," p. 101.

[Hare] reverts to the grounds on which Flew is admittedly victorious." [157]
When Hare speaks of "the ground marked out by Flew," he means the
interpretation of any statement about God as an explanation in the
scientific sense.[158] He interprets Flew, that is, as demanding a quite
definite specification concerning "what would have to occur or to have
occurred to constitute for you a disproof of the love of, or of the
existence of, God." [159] Clearly bliks do not have this degree of specificity; nor does the distinction between right and wrong bliks require it.
And here we should add that Flew, in fact, seems to be demanding
a greater degree of specificity than that typically found in the sciences
or in many everyday conversations.

Even though the tests for our bliks are less definite than those for
our ordinary assertions about particular matters-of-fact, they are tests
nonetheless. To be sure, if the cognitive value of a statement is the
guidance it gives us concerning future expectations, then, as the expectations expressed become less definite, the cognitive value is less. It
is the worry of the religious skeptic that the expectations embodied
in religious statements become so vague that the guidance they offer
becomes virtually worthless because indecipherable. Like the Cheshire
cat, the expectations may vanish to the point that nothing remains
except a smile toward life. But, however legitimate this worry, if
bliks are an indispensable part of the human posture, then the criticism
of a blik that it embodies less definite expectations than do our ordinary
assertions is irrelevant—indeed, it is itself made from the perspective
of a blik.

Hare's account, then, of bliks as attitudes on which assertions depend
but which are themselves "compatible with any finite number of . . .
tests" is neither an adequate account of the logic of the perspectives
from which we experience things nor consistent with his own distinction
between sane and right bliks, on the one hand, and insane and wrong
bliks, on the other. Taken at face value, Hare's account leaves him
open to the criticism leveled by Flew that, on this account, statements
that religious people commonly make, such as "You ought to *because* it
is God's will" and "My soul must be immortal *because* God loves his
children," reduce to "You ought to" and "My soul must be
immortal," [160] except that the addition of the word "God" expresses
the attitude of the speaker. But there is more to be brought out about
taking an attitude toward things than this. As John Hick points out, what
we also need to know is "whether the way the believer feels and acts
is appropriate to the actual character of the universe." [161]

---

[157] *The Problem of Religious Knowledge*, p. 78.
[158] "Theology and Falsification," p. 101.   [159] *Ibid.*, p. 99.
[160] *Ibid.*, p. 108.   [161] *Philosophy of Religion*, p. 99.

As we may recall Wisdom arguing, if we say "that when a difference as to the existence of a God is not one as to future happenings then it is not experimental and therefore not as to the facts, we must not forthwith assume that there is no right and wrong about it, no rationality or irrationality, no appropriateness or inappropriateness, no procedure which tends to settle it, not even that this procedure is in no sense a discovery of new facts." [162] According to Hare, it may well be that we are tempted to call certain ordinary empirical facts supernatural facts "because our whole way of living is organized around them" and that this temptation "could be said to be the result of failing to distinguish in logic what cannot be distinguished in practice, namely, facts, and our attitudes to them." [163] But Hare wrongly separates what he rightly distinguishes. Surely we take up a certain attitude because of what we believe about the nature of the facts, so that if further experience and reflection convince us that this belief is in error, we change our attitude—a matter on which Hare wavers inconsistently, as we have seen. If it were the taking of a certain attitude toward the facts that made them religious, there would seem to be no justification in Hare's distinction between right and wrong bliks. Is it not rather something about the facts that evokes a religious attitude? This need not be a question as to whether there is a special realm of supernatural facts underlying the realm of natural facts. One may ask, instead, whether ordinary facts have some sort of religious dimension.

From our discussion there emerges the point made by Alasdair MacIntyre: "The essential crux that the Verification Principle raises for theistic assertions is not that they are unfalsifiable but that they are either unfalsifiable or false." [164] If they assert, for example, that nothing will happen which contradicts what we would expect if the world were controlled by a loving God, then they are false. Blackstone seeks to impale Hare on one horn of this dilemma. Flew seeks to throw him entirely on the other—if unfalsifiable, then neither right nor wrong. We have pushed Hare's discussion toward a third option, namely, that bliks are falsifiable even though the point at which the evidence becomes sufficiently conclusive logically to warrant this judgment must remain, to some degree, indefinite.

Hepburn argues against Hare that the believer not only has a special "slant" upon the world but also assents "to certain belief-propositions— [propositions] of different logical types, but some of which are irreducibly *historical*" and so are logically falsifiable.[165] But this overlooks the way in which bliks grow out of certain personal and historical ex-

---

[162] "Gods," p. 159.
[163] "Religion and Morals," *Faith and Logic*, pp. 189, 190.
[164] "The Logical Status of Religious Belief," p. 182.
[165] "Poetry and Religious Belief," *Metaphysical Beliefs*, p. 128.

periences. Hare says, for example, that "taking up an attitude of worship to an object considered as a person is not quite like adopting a purely factual belief; nor is it simply subscribing to certain principles of conduct; but it involves both these things."[166] This relation between our basic beliefs and particular personal and historical events is developed by Basil Mitchell in his reply to Flew.

To bring out this important dimension of the logic of faith which Flew has not recognized, Mitchell offers his own parable:

> In time of war in an occupied country, a member of the resistance meets one night a stranger who deeply impresses him. They spend that night together in conversation. The Stranger tells the partisan that he himself is on the side of the resistance—indeed that he is in command of it, and urges the partisan to have faith in him no matter what happens. The partisan is utterly convinced at that meeting of the Stranger's sincerity and constancy and undertakes to trust him.[167]

Subsequently, the Stranger is sometimes seen helping members of the resistance, but at other times betraying them. The partisan's friends begin to regard the Stranger as a traitor, but the partisan continues to trust him even though he "recognizes that the Stranger's ambiguous behavior *does* count against what he believes about him. It is precisely this situation which constitutes the trial of his faith."[168] The believer, then, does have expectations that distinguish him from the nonbeliever, and certain occurrences do frustrate these expectations. He does not doublethink but honestly recognizes the contradictory nature of the evidence. According to Mitchell,

> The theologian surely would not deny that the fact of pain counts against the assertion that God loves men. This very incompatibility generates the most intractable of theological problems—the problem of evil.[169]

So far there are two points to be noted. First, the believer's metaphysical picture or blik grows out of certain historical events which he regards as revelatory of the nature of God. As Mitchell puts it in discussing religious experiences,

> We have, in fact, to master a conceptual apparatus which will make sense of the experiences in question and relate them significantly to each other and to further facts. It is part of the function of a religious tradition to provide us with such an apparatus, and *part of the verification of a religious revelation lies in its capacity to do this.*[170]

Second, in the account given so far, the logic of assertions about God is similar to the logic of ordinary assertions. But some ordinary asser-

[166] "Religion and Morals," p. 189.
[167] "Theology and Falsification," p. 103.
[168] *Ibid.*, p. 104.   [169] *Ibid.*, p. 103.
[170] "The Grace of God," *Faith and Logic*, ed. Basil Mitchell, p. 164.

tions, such as "The Stranger is on our side," are not "conclusively falsifiable" [171] and religious assertions share this characteristic too. Because of this and because of his faith the believer not only need not but will not allow anything "to count decisively against [his assertions about God]; for he is committed by his faith to trust in God. His attitude is not that of the detached observer, but of the believer." [172] To open his assertions to the possibility of falsification would be a failure in faith: "Thou shalt not tempt the Lord thy God." [173] To refuse to allow any experience to count against (or for) his assertions would be "a failure in faith as well as in logic." [174] To enter into a trusting relationship with God is to embrace and hold fast to certain expectations.

Now, although some of our ordinary assertions are not conclusively falsifiable, in that the evidence against them could never provide more than a very high degree of probability, the point may be reached where it becomes reasonable to decide against them. Concerning the partisan's position of faith in the Stranger, Mitchell asks, "How long can he uphold [this] position without its becoming just silly?" [175] This, he replies, we cannot determine in advance, for it will depend on "the impression created by the Stranger." [176] The rules governing the falsification of such beliefs, then, are characterized by a certain indefiniteness, but they do provide a rational basis for judgment, and so we may come rationally to discard a belief of this sort. Faith, though, requires the suspension of such judgment in the case of religious beliefs. Frederick Ferré interprets this to mean that "any abandonment of religious belief will not be on the basis of evidence but will in every case be due to a 'failure of faith.' " [177] But this way of putting it neglects the logical bearing that evidence has on belief. According to Mitchell, to refuse to recognize the force of the evidence would be a failure of faith; it is not that the tests of experience might not lead to the abandonment of faith on logical grounds, but that one cannot be committed to God and allow his commitment to be tested in that sense.

Mitchell's interpretation of religious beliefs as assertions that experiences may count for or against, and his suggestions concerning the indefiniteness that to some degree is a characteristic of their logic seem to me to be sound. What must be questioned, however, is the sort

---

[171] "Theology and Falsification," p. 105.
[172] Ibid., p. 103.   [173] Ibid., p. 105.
[174] Ibid.   [175] Ibid., p. 104.
[176] Ibid. It will also depend on how the Stranger's behavior is taken, in the sense that if the partisan does not regard it as counting for or against his belief about the Stranger one must assume that he is "thoughtless or insane." (Ibid.)
[177] Language, Logic and God, p. 51.

of bearing that he sees faith to have upon the logic that we give
to these assertions, namely, that faith is incompatible with any genuine
testing of them. Certain experiences, that is, are contrary to the (somewhat indefinite) set of expectations around which the believer organizes
his life, but he must not regard them as a test.[178] There is one
difference between the situation of the believer and that of the partisan
which is of crucial importance in evaluating this aspect of Mitchell's
position. The believer's understanding of God's nature is problematic
in a way that the partisan's understanding of human nature is not,
or, to put the matter linguistically, the rules governing our talk about
finite persons are relatively well established and clear, while the rules
that we attempt to derive from them to govern religious language use
are not. Indeed, these rules are so far from being well established and
clear that religious statements are faced with the charge of meaninglessness with which we are fundamentally concerned. Now, since it
is in terms of our language rules that we understand what it means to
trust another, the partisan's understanding of what it means to trust
the Stranger is relatively clear, while the believer's understanding of
what it means to trust God is relatively lacking in clarity. The question
which this raises is how closely we can identify what is and what is not
a trusting relationship with God with any one set of rules by which
we attempt to understand that relationship. Although to enter into
a relationship includes, as an important factor, the way we understand
its meaning, it is also, of course, much more than this. When our
understanding of a relationship is altered, then, has the relationship
necessarily been broken or may it not simply have been altered—perhaps
for the better? What we must ask of Mitchell's position is whether
the believer could not allow experience to test his understanding of
God without this constituting a test of his trust in God. Indeed, does
not trust in God require that we refuse to treat as an absolute anything
that is the product of our finite minds, including the most central
of our assertions about God? If we refuse to test the images of God
which are expressed in our articles of faith, do we not turn these
images into idols? Mitchell's view seems sound, that to use religious
language meaningfully we must "master a conceptual apparatus" which
is the interpretation that a religious tradition has placed upon the
revelatory events recorded in the Bible.[179] The question is whether
testing and changing that interpretation must be regarded as a failure
in faith. The other side to this question is whether it is not idolatrous
to refuse to test a religious tradition.

[178] One does not test something unless he is prepared to draw conclusions
from that test, should they seem warranted.
[179] "The Grace of God," *Faith and Logic*, p. 164.

In elaborating this question, let us begin with the encounter with the Stranger. The believer points to the person of Jesus and interprets the encounter with this person as, at the same time, an encounter with God. He trusts in God's love, because he has seen that love in the life of Jesus. It is around this event and related events that the believer organizes his life. He does this by deriving from this event a life-shaping picture and interpretive rules for the application of this picture to the entire range of our experience. It is these rules that give sense to our religious assertions. Now the rules followed by both Mitchell and, doubtless, a majority of Christians belong to the conception of God as *a being* in the sense that he is subject to the causal structure of the universe and, so, performs particular actions—actions which constitute a special form of causality. God's omnipotence, consequently, is taken to mean that nothing can prevent him from doing what he wills, and, so, we have the problem as to why we experience evils that are contrary to what we *expect* of an omnipotent and loving divine being.

In contrast is another set of rules—in many respects a modification of the first—in which God is conceived of as the divine depth in every particular being. In this view, "the symbol of omnipotence expresses the religious experience that no structure of reality and no event in nature and history has the power of removing us from community with the infinite and inexhaustible ground of meaning and being." [180] The expectation is not that a divine being will act in such a way that no lasting evil will occur—no evil, that is, which is not somehow necessary to a greater good—but that there is a source of courage which can enable a man to face creatively any negativity, a source of benediction which leads one to affirm life in-spite-of the evils suffered.

This alternative will be further developed in the next chapter. We touch on it here to emphasize that there is nothing self-evidently correct about any one interpretation of the revelatory events in response to which faith is founded, and so it is not clear why a faithful relation with God must be identified exclusively with the interpretation that Mitchell uses. How are we to determine what interpretation constitutes the most reliable and fruitful application of the theistic picture to the whole of our experience if not by the test of experience?

Does not Mitchell's position, then (and, indeed, the entire discussion of religious propositions among Oxford philosophers), suffer from a failure to distinguish clearly enough challenges to faith as a relationship with God and challenges to a way of conceiving God? The issue with which the discussion in "Theology and Falsification" is dealing concerns

---

[180] Tillich, "Science and Theology," *Theology of Culture*, p. 128.

the adequacy of the conception of God as *a being*. It is the question as to whether the logic of our language about God is similar in certain ways to the logic of our language about particular beings. To reach a negative conclusion about some of these alleged similarities need not be a turning away from a relationship with God. It may be only a turning away from a doubtful way of conceiving that relationship. Or, to put it a little differently, such a negative conclusion may be only a judgment that to conceive of God as a being prevents one from adequately grasping the relation of religious experience to other areas of experience—a point which we shall explore in Chapter X. In matters of doubt as well as of guilt the believer is justified by faith. Healing relationship with God, that is, surely is not bound to any one interpretation achieved by the human mind. If relationship with God is offered unconditionally, then it must include the courage to call into question concepts fundamental to one's way of life.

Relationship, however, if it includes the whole person, includes the mind, so that an alteration in our understanding of a relationship is an alteration in the relationship itself. But it seems characteristic of genuine relationships that encounter brings new insight and change in understanding. Still, it may be argued that a given interpretation or way of speaking is essential for the proper expression of the biblical view of God. But how is one to determine what is essential? This surely is always an open question, subject to continuous re-examination— especially in view of the admittedly serious difficulties in getting clear about the meaning of "God." Job decided against a conception of God which his friends clung to as beyond challenge, namely, that God materially rewards the righteous and punishes the wicked. Paul fought vigorously against the belief, which he himself had held, that the Law is essential to true faith.[181] Faith, he argued, is not a matter of circumcision or uncircumcision. Belief in an earth-centered universe has been bitterly defended as essential. In case after case man's understanding of his relation with God has been changed as the expectations embodied in that understanding have been frustrated by experience. When one says, then, that a given interpretation is essential, this seems to mean simply that it is that interpretation which, for him, carries

---

[181] In arguing that we must give up, as inadequate to our day, the interpretation of God as a being, John A. T. Robinson says that "it may be easier for us to recognize this if we look first not at our own situation but at one which, though not strictly parallel (since it involved the preaching of a new gospel altogether), has sufficient similarities to be instructive," and he proceeds to note that, although Paul regarded the Law as "holy and just and good" (Rom. 7:12), he yet believed that the time had come when it was proving to be "the stumbling-block to knowing the very God whose truth it existed to shape." (*Honest to God* [Philadelphia: Westminster Press, 1963], p. 123.)

conviction.[182] Yet for many believers today the interpretation of God as a being is lacking in conviction, and they are joined by still others in believing that this interpretation constitutes a needless stumbling block for many nonbelievers for their discovery of the reality of God. As the Anglican Bishop of Woolwich, John A. T. Robinson, has said,

What looks like being required of us, reluctant as we may be for the effort involved, is a radically new mould, or *meta-morphosis*, of Christian belief and practice. Such a recasting will, I am convinced, leave the fundamental truth of the Gospel unaffected. But it means that we have to be prepared for *everything* to go into the melting—even our most cherished religious categories and moral absolutes. And the first thing we must be ready to let go is our image of God himself.[183]

To let go of the image of God as a being is, he recognizes, a far reaching reinterpretation, and yet one that he feels has become necessary:

It will doubtless seem to some that I have by implication abandoned the Christian faith and practice altogether. On the contrary, I believe that *unless* we are prepared for the kind of revolution of which I have spoken it *will come* to be abandoned. And that will be because it is moulded in the form we know it, by a cast of thought that belongs to a past age—the cast of thought which, with their different emphases, Bultmann describes as "mythological," Tillich as "supranaturalist," and Bonhoeffer as "religious." [184]

When Flew replies to Mitchell, then, that his interpretation of God as omnipotent rules out the "plausible excuses for ambiguous behaviour" [185] that present themselves in the case of the finite Stranger, this need not be construed as a challenge to faith in a loving God. It may rather be understood as a challenge to the adequacy of Mitchell's concept of omnipotence for the application of the theistic picture to the whole of our experience.

Let us look more closely at Mitchell's defense of this conception of an omnipotent being. Against Flew's charge that such a conception is empty (or Tillich's that it is absurd) [186] Mitchell has argued that there are expectations embodied in the Christian's religious assertions about a loving, all-powerful God—expectations that are not entertained by the religious skeptic. But there is something peculiar about these expectations. The believer expects certain things not to happen which he knows do happen. He holds side by side conflicting expectations—the expectations of his religious belief and certain expectations based on

---

[182] It is, however, the faith community that, in the final analysis, determines the norms of belief.

[183] *Honest to God*, p. 124.   [184] *Ibid.*, p. 123.

[185] "Theology and Falsification," *New Essays . . .* , p. 107.

[186] "Science and Theology," p. 129.

everyday experience. According to his faith, certain things should not happen which experience teaches him do happen. Concerning the occurrence of evil, then, around which the present discussion is organized, the expectations of believer and skeptic concerning what actually will happen do not seem to differ. But *genuine* assertions *are* about the kind of world this is, which means they *are* about what our experience will *actually* be like. Do the religious assertions in question really function in any way as a guide concerning what we may expect *actually* to happen?

In view of this difficulty, it seems necessary to Mitchell's position to maintain that the believer does expect something different of experience in the long run. It is after the war that the Stranger's ambiguous behavior will be clarified, and the partisan differs from his friends concerning what the result of that clarification will be. Similarly the believer traditionally has entertained expectations that the ambiguities of his experience in this life will be clarified in the life to come. The claim might be, then, that it is here that the differences in expectation between believer and skeptic become real.

It is John Hick who has most vigorously pursued this idea of "eschatological verification." According to him, "to postulate the divine Kingdom, in which God's will is wholly fulfilled, as the final end-state of human existence, is to postulate a sphere in which the evidence for God's reality, instead of being systematically ambiguous, is wholly indicative of the divine presence and activity." [187] By "indicative of the divine presence" Hick means that "the human mind will see all things as God sees them";[188] we will "see his loving purpose universally at work." [189] The believer, then, sees the world as "an intended *process* leading to a conclusion," rather than, as in the parables of Flew and (in a sense) [190] of Wisdom, as a "universal garden in which we may expect to find traces of a divine Gardener." [191] In an alternative parable Hick likens the believer and skeptic to two men who must travel the same road, one of whom believes that its destination is a "Celestial City," the other that it goes nowhere. Yet as long as they are in the process of their travel "the issue between them is not an experimental one. They do not entertain different expectations about the coming details of the road, but only about its ultimate destination." [192]

Hick considers the following objections to this position:

---

[187] *Faith and Knowledge* (Ithaca: Cornell University Press, 1957), p. 160.
[188] *Ibid.*   [189] *Ibid.*, p. 161.
[190] Hick's way of putting Wisdom's view here is apt to be misleading since "traces of a divine Gardener" suggests a concept of divine transcendence which is entirely foreign to Wisdom's position.
[191] *Faith and Knowledge*, p. 150.   [192] *Ibid.*, p. 151.

Surely, it may be said, theism makes a difference in this present life. . . . The power of Christianity is the power of what Paul Tillich calls the New Being; and this is a potent present experience, not merely a future hope. . . . Belief in God has radically changed [the believer's] inner life.[193]

To this Hick replies that "the fact that belief in the proposition 'God exists' operates in this way" does not make "God exists" a factual statement.[194] It is instructive that Hick understands this experience in terms of believing in a proposition while Tillich understands it in terms of being grasped by God. This points to the fundamental difference that for Hick our awareness of God is always a mediated, indirect awareness while for Tillich our awareness of God is an immediate, direct awareness.[195] In our final chapter we shall explore the logical implications of this difference.

Blackstone objects to Hick's account that "there is as much problem with . . . the notion of the Kingdom of Heaven as there is with that of an all-powerful, wholly good, loving heavenly father." [196] Although Blackstone does not state the problem that he sees here, its general nature can probably be discerned in his subsequent contention that "the question of according any . . . sentences some degree of the attitude of belief cannot even arise unless they are *given some clear meaning.*" [197] Somewhat more pointedly, James A. Martin, Jr. asks whether experiences in an after-life can be regarded as evidence; for those analysts who reject the cognitive status of talk about God accept as evidence "only what can be experienced under publicly available, specifiable conditions of space and time." [198] Nothing after death could qualify as evidence in this sense because, Martin argues, death means an end to space and time as we know them.[199] But Hick indicates

---

[193] *Ibid.*, pp. 152-53.   [194] *Ibid.*, p. 153.   [195] Cf. *Systematic Theology*, II, 166-67.
[196] Blackstone, *The Problem of Religious Knowledge*, p. 114.
[197] *Ibid.*, p. 167 (Italics mine).
[198] *The New Dialogue Between Philosophy and Theology* (New York: Seabury Press, 1966), p. 96.
[199] Martin adds the criticism that no "post-mortem" experience could verify the belief in question to the point of "excluding rational doubt," as Hick contends, for doubt "might return with some future eruption of contrary evidence." (*The New Dialogue* . . . , p. 98) But two points must be made in reply to this criticism. First, Martin sees Hick as identifying the *single experience* of the "Beatific Vision" with the "Kingdom of God"; but Hick states that "we have not seen any reason to adopt the doctrine of the Beatific Vision" (in the sense of a single experience) (*Faith and Knowledge*, pp. 159-60), and that the Kingdom of God refers not to a single experience but to our total experience. Second, by excluding rational doubt Hick means having "as good ground . . . as it is possible for us to have." (P. 158) But we can never have grounds for ruling out as a logical possibility "some future eruption of contrary evidence," and so this possibility does not mean that rational doubt in Hick's sense cannot be excluded. Martin also earlier misrepresents Hick as maintaining that "the theistic interpretation of the world . . . appeals to all facts of experience . . . for its validity." (*The New Dialogue* . . . , p. 92.) The attempt

that the believer expects a next life that will be characterized by time as we now know it and by space that will be like space as we know it in all respects crucial to the logic of informative language: "Suppose that after death we find ourselves surviving as personalities endowed with spiritual bodies in a spirit world, inhabiting a new environment which is as real to us as our present world, and still subject to the passage of time." [200] "Body" and "environment" clearly imply space, and this implication is made explicit in his article "Theology and Verification." [201] That he means by "space" at least whatever is necessary to make applicable the logic of cognitive language is clear when, in discussing the possibility of experiences in the afterlife which are contrary to the believer's expectations, he contends that "once again there is no ascertainable point at which in logic [faith] ought to succumb." [202] Hick does, then, give *some* specification of the conditions he has in mind, and to this extent at least he has shown the believer's eschatological expectations to have content. Some may decline to play a language-game in which conditions are not more clearly specified or more readily available, but this is not the issue. The question is not what one is prepared to accept as evidence but what qualifies logically as evidence.

One may say, of course, that afterlife experiences do not qualify as evidence and, in this way, call attention to the differences in clarity and availability demanded by the logic of Hick's language-game and that demanded by the logic of the scientist's language-game. But, in light of what Wisdom has shown us, we must then *also* say afterlife experiences do qualify as evidence and, in this way, call attention to the similarity between these two logics, namely, that both require the expression of expectations concerning future experience. Moreoever, it is the latter statement that is platitudinous, the former that is paradoxical.[203] At least, this is so if the real is simply that which "makes a difference" (Hick) [204] rather than that which makes the sort of difference which can be articulated with, say, a fairly high degree of clarity. Or, to put it somewhat differently, Hick's language-game is cognitive if cognition has to do simply with expectations rather than with the sort of expectation that can be articulated with a fairly high degree of clarity. To decide otherwise is to believe that reality—or at least significant reality—is such that if it can be grasped at all it can

---

to *interpret* all facts is not the same thing as *appealing* to all facts for the validity of that interpretation, for, as Hick states, the theistic interpretation "is clearly focussed in some situations and imperceptible in others." (*Faith and Knowledge,* p. 131.)

[200] *Faith and Knowledge,* p. 155.   [201] *Theology Today,* 1960, pp. 12-31.

[202] *Faith and Knowledge,* p. 156.

[203] To say Hick's expected experiences do not qualify as evidence would be platitudinous only if they are not classified as evidence in that language-game.

[204] *Philosophy of Religion,* p. 106.

be grasped with clarity. It seems to me that the degree of clarity to be required should be determined by the subject matter in question. As Whitehead is reported to have said: "You may always be sure that when an idea is clear and distinct you have left out something."

Another critic, Kai Nielsen, charges that in Hick's argument "there is the assumption that these words ["non-physical space"] have a use or a sense, but they do not and Hick does not provide us with one." [205] The reply, however, is simply that Hick does in fact use them to express his admittedly vague expectations concerning future experience.

The basic problem we find in Hick's position is that of showing the grounds we presently have for these future expectations. Hick himself points out that "the alleged future experience cannot, of course, be appealed to as evidence for theism as a present interpretation of our experience; but it does suffice to render the choice between theism and atheism a real and not merely an empty or verbal choice." [206] Hick's appeal is to the authority of Christ which will be confirmed (all rational doubt excluded) when, in the life to come, "the person of Christ will be manifestly exalted." [207] There are many senses, though, in which Jesus might be regarded as authoritative. The skeptic, for example, might find the example of his life morally compelling. But what is there in our knowledge of Jesus that indicates his authority with respect to the logical problems that we are considering? Surely his mind was subject to the limitations of human finitude and his experience of God shared the ambiguities of our experience of God. Hick goes so far as to make Jesus' teachings the authority for our belief that God's nature is infinite, even though this is a concept that the human mind neither can understand nor, even in the life after, ever will understand.[208] But how could the finite Jesus be an authority for something that he himself could not understand? [209] And how could we believe something without knowing what it means?

Concerning Hick's account of the reality of God we may now put the question: if grammar tells us the kind of reality we conceive our language to be concerned with, what does Hick's account of the grammar or logic of theistic language show his conception of the reality of God to be? He agrees with John Wisdom that "the theistic assertion serves to bring out characteristics of the world and of human experience which are concealed by the contrary assertion." [210] In

[205] "Eschatological Verification," *Canadian Journal of Theology*, 1963; reprinted in *Philosophy of Religion*, eds. G. L. Abernethy and T. A. Langford (2nd ed.; New York: Macmillan, 1968), pp. 291-92.

[206] *Philosophy of Religion*, p. 102.   [207] *Ibid.*, p. 104.   [208] *Ibid.*

[209] Appeal here to some sort of miraculous inspiration of Jesus' mind raises the question of verification all over again.

[210] *Faith and Knowledge*, p. 187.

addition, the believer expects these characteristics to become dominant in his post-resurrection experiences. So far the rules can serve to show the nature of God in terms of patterns and of expectations which are expressed in talk of these patterns. Yet Hick maintains that he means something more—an "extra person . . . in addition to the world" [211] whose activity is mediated by the things that happen in the world. It is reference to this more that seems not to have been given a use by Hick's account.

It is true that when we experience the behavior patterns of another person we understand them as expressions of a human consciousness. But this is based partly on our experience of our own behavior and of our own consciousness as embodied in it. What basis is there in our experience for us to understand a certain pattern or order of the world as a whole as indicative of something mediated by it? As John Wisdom has argued, the world pattern pointed to by the theist is not sufficiently analogous to patterns of human behavior to be mind-proving, as human behavior is mind-proving.

Perhaps a better analogy could be found in the way that employees of a corporation might understand a large number of things to be manifestations of the activity of an executive whom they have never seen or heard. But the difficulty here is that the employees know what it would be like to experience the executive directly while, on Hick's account, we do not know this in the case of God. Unless we can go beyond this account the world order pointed to by the theist must mean to us simply its manifestations for the same reason that electricity must mean to us simply its manifestations.

We have not mentioned the sense of the presence of God which the believer has, according to Hick, when he interprets his experience of the world as mediating the activities of an unseen Person. But the fact that this sort of experience results when such a picture is carried over from our interpersonal relations does not seem to say anything about what sort of reality behind our experienced-world this picture might be used by the believer to refer to. Primitive peoples and small children have a similar sense of presence in, say, the tree that slapped them with its branch. Wisdom sees this sense which the believer has of presence in the world as misplaced in the way that one's feelings are misplaced when an empty house seems to him to be haunted. We see the picture: only what is its application?

Ian Crombie, in his contribution to the "Theology and Falsification" discussion and in a subsequent article on "The Possibility of Theological Statements," [212] combines many of the points already considered. When we apply our ordinary terms to God we know that

---

[211] *Ibid.*   [212] In *Faith and Logic,* ed. Basil Mitchell.

their meaning changes, but, because we cannot conceive God's nature, we do not know what their new meaning is. Therefore, when we apply words to God we continue to mean by them what we ordinarily mean by them, and, by means of this speaking in "parables," we at least are able to form some idea of the sort of world that one who believes in God will expect this world to be.[213] Certain experiences, such as suffering, then, do run contrary to the believer's expectations and, so, count against his beliefs. But the believer will not allow anything to count decisively against his beliefs, because he believes that in the life to come they will be confirmed.[214] Our selection of certain terms and of the images they convey for application to God—such as the image of God as creator—is based on two things: "firstly on the fact that we find ourselves impelled to regard the events recorded in the Bible and found in the life of the Church as the communication of a transcendent being, and that the image is an essential part of this communication; secondly on the fact that the more we try to understand the world in the light of this image, the better our understanding of the world becomes." [215] Particularly we are impelled to regard the Christ event as a reliable image. Obviously the first of these bases, that of sheer commitment, leaves our problem untouched. The second, however, requires examination.

Crombie does not develop this second point, but at least a central part of what he has in mind seems to be suggested by the third "fortress" of faith which he adds to the compelling authority of Christ and the expected confirmation in the life to come, namely, "that in the religious life, of others, if not as yet in [one's] own, the divine love may be encountered." [216] This is not elaborated by Crombie, but he does refer the reader to Basil Mitchell's article on "The Grace of God." [217] According to Mitchell, God's activity "issues in discernible differences," and yet "we cannot with confidence predict what these will be." [218] He argues that, "if in certain people there appears a quality of life which is out of scale with its natural antecedents, and if such people move us in an unaccountably profound and yet not morbid fashion, and if we ourselves from time to time are aware, or seem to be aware, of an unsuspected power, informing but not distorting our natural faculties, then we may see in these things the grace of God perfecting nature." [219] If, as we have maintained, expectations need not be very definite to play a significant role in our orientation toward things as a whole, then here, surely, we find a

---

[213] "The Possibility of Theological Statements," pp. 69-71.
[214] *Ibid.*   [215] *Ibid.*, p. 81.   [216] "Theology and Falsification," p. 129.
[217] *Faith and Logic.*   [218] "The Grace of God," p. 170.   [219] *Ibid.*, p. 173.

significant difference between the expectations of believer and skeptic concerning experience in this life.

It must be noted, though, that these expectations concerning "the grace of God perfecting nature" are not distinctive of the interpretation of God as a being. One may agree that conscious relation with the "object" of religious awareness involves this sort of difference without interpreting this relationship in terms of particular actions on the part of God.

Then, too, as Crombie recognizes concerning the believer's interpretation of things, "success, even supreme success, in interpreting life could only confirm it as an interpretation of life." [220] The power of the believer's images of God to illuminate experience is not all that is meant by calling them images of God. To accept the doctrines that spell out this interpretation "is not only to believe that they illuminate the facts which come within our view, but also to believe that they do so because they are revelatory of facts which lie outside our view." [221] Our entire discussion of falsification has focused on the *effects* of God's actions. What indication can be given of the sort of reference "*God*" has?

According to Crombie, we do not know "to what to refer our parables; we know merely that we are to refer them out of experience, and out of it *in which direction*." [222] This direction is given by certain elements of religious awareness which are a part of our experience. Among these elements

perhaps the most powerful is what I shall call a sense of contingency. Others are moral experience, and the beauty and order of nature. Others may be actual abnormal experiences of the type called religious or mystical. There are those to whom conscience appears in the form of an unconditional demand; to whom the obligation to one's neighbor seems to be something imposed on him and on me by a third party who is set over us both. There are those to whom the beauty and order of nature appears as the intrusion into nature of a realm of beauty and order beyond it.[223]

This sense of the finitude of the world, and so of a contrasting infinite over against it, is the basis of the believer's concept of a divine being, the "undifferentiated theism" to which he gives content by applying the parables of his faith. The believer knows that these

[220] "The Possibility of Theological Statements," p. 79.   [221] *Ibid.*
[222] "Theology and Falsification," p. 124. This "reference range" of theological statements—a reference outside of present experience—is fixed by their paradoxical nature or logical "oddness" in that the latter prevents us from taking anything finite as their reference ("The Possibility of Theological Statements," p. 50). On the other hand, it is just this paradoxical nature of statements that are put forward about a particular being and yet not allowed to follow the logic of statements about particular beings which constitutes the problem of meaning with which we are concerned.
[223] "Theology and Falsification," pp. 111-12.

elements can be interpreted in other ways, but he feels that he is "bringing out more of what they contain or involve." [224]

The theist can go still a little further in indicating the reference range of religious statements. He can point out that these statements have affinities with other sorts of statements, namely, those of ethics, cosmology, history, and psychology.[225] Second, he can point to the dissatisfactions that we feel with the finite world, "certain deficiencies in our experience," [226] and say that, whatever the divine is like, these imperfections are absent from it.

Crombie's starting point here seems sound. If we are to give meaning to the subject term of religious assertions, we must surely refer it to elements of religious awareness in our experience. What must be questioned, however, is whether Crombie's account has marked out a genuine difference between regarding the world *as if* it were in the hands of a divine being and really believing that such a being exists. What is the difference between believing and not believing "facts which lie outside our view"—that is, outside of all experience in this life? Surely the difference must lie in certain expectations concerning future experience of those facts, for if the believer, in asserting that there are such facts, does not entertain expectations not shared by the skeptic, then he is not really making an assertion at all. Really to believe is really to have expectations concerning experiences. But, unlike Hick, Crombie does not work out his views about experience in the next life.

Furthermore, although the expectation that one will be brought back to life after one dies does itself mark out a real difference in belief, neither this expectation nor the expectation that this future existence will be unambiguously good is identical with the belief in a divine being. As Hick points out, "an actual experience of survival [would not] necessarily serve to verify theism. It might be taken as just a surprising natural fact." [227] Then, too, even in "an experienced situation which points unambiguously to the reality of God," Hick admits, one's "consciousness of God will still be, formally, a matter of faith in that it will continue to involve an activity of interpretation." [228] Once again we must ask what would be the difference in expectations, in such a future existence, between believing and not believing that a divine being had something to do with all this. What is it to believe that these are effects of divine actions? If religious awareness is necessary to give non-reductionistic meaning to the subject term of religious beliefs, then (1) expectations attendant upon the use of the term "God" must concern the occurrence of religious experience and its

[224] *Ibid.*, p. 122.   [225] "The Possibility of Theological Statements," pp. 51-52.
[226] *Ibid.*, p. 56.   [227] *Philosophy of Religion*, p. 102.   [228] *Ibid.*, p. 103.

significance for the whole of one's existence, and (2) these expectations together with the model by which we organize them constitute the content of belief in God. Let us turn, then, to consider an approach to religious meaning in which the experience of "encounter" with God is emphasized.

Encounter with God

A large number of theologians and philosophers of religion—Buber, Brunner, Farmer, and Donald Baillie, to name only a few—give central importance to an immediate experience of God as personal, often referred to as an encounter with the divine Thou. These terms are drawn from the distinction, which is so much stressed by the existentialists and to which Martin Buber has contributed so signally, between our experience of another when we approach him in an impersonal, external, detached manner, and our experience of him when we empathize into his life as he personally lives it from within. On the one hand, we experience the other, and indeed anything else in the world, merely as an object or an "It" that can be observed, conceptualized, measured, even manipulated as, say, a consumer, or unit of productive force, or means to one's own prestige, or sex object. On the other hand, we experience the one who has the observed characteristics, the one who wears the mask, the person to whom these things happen, the agent of decision, the personal source of resistance to our efforts, the "Thou" we encounter only as we become a person for the other. As Paul Tournier expresses it,

the person always eludes our grasp; it is never static. It refuses to be confined within concepts, formulae and definitions. It is not a thing to be encompassed, but a point of attraction . . . which demands from us [an] . . . attitude, which moves us to action and commits us.[229]

The "encounter" theologian emphasizes that our experience of God is always personal, always similar, that is, to our personal experience of other human beings. We can never experience God as an "It," because there is nothing about God that can be objectified.

Those who take this approach typically make two main points with respect to the falsification problem. First of all, although everyone experiences the impersonal dimensions of reality, the ability to experience the world in a personal way is not something that one automatically grows into. It is an achievement, something that one may or may not become very capable of. Hence, failure to experience God as personal may be due simply to one's impersonal manner of relating. Second, encounter with the divine Thou is an experience

[229] *The Meaning of Persons* (New York: Harper, 1957), p. 179.

that is not open to doubt. It is the very nature of the experience of encounter that one is immediately aware of being confronted by another Thou, a limiting presence. That the experience has objective reference is "self-authenticating." The whole issue of verification and falsification pertains only to the world as we objectively experience it, the world of "It," those aspects of reality which may be conceptualized. God, however, may not be objectified; he transcends the split between subject and object and, so, may not be approached by means of a language whose logic pertains to the objective world—i.e., one whose logic includes verification rules.

This assertion that an objective reference is part of what is immediately given in experience presents a logic radically different from the logic governing our assertions about the existence of particular entities. This latter logic takes into account the fact that my experience is subject to error, that I may see a red book that turns out to be an orange box, or I may see water on the road ahead of the car which turns out to be nothing more than the visual effects of heat waves. The belief that I experience a finite object is formulated in a system of language rules that include public testing procedures—procedures for verifying or falsifying that statement which, in principle at least, anyone may follow. If this belief is falsified, my experience is not, of course, changed. It simply was what it was. It could, in this sense, perhaps, be said to be self-authenticating. But this would have to do with the subjective experience and not with the objective reference of that experience. As C. G. Martin concludes, "Because 'having direct Experience of God' does not admit the relevance of a society of tests and checking procedures it places itself in the company of other ways of knowing which preserve their self-sufficiency, 'uniqueness' and 'incommunicability' by making a psychological and not an existential claim." [230] But the encounter theologian will reply that Martin's requirements are inapplicable to personal knowledge; the "sense of meeting a Thou" is taken from our experience of the other not as an object, our statements about which are susceptible to verification procedures, but as a person who, as Tournier puts it, "refuses to be confined within concepts, formulae and definitions." As a "Thou" the other can be named and addressed, but not described and observed.[231] Our knowledge of the "Thou" of the other is simply

[230] "A Religious Way of Knowing," *New Essays in Philosophical Theology*, p. 85.

[231] For a helpful discussion of our problem in terms of naming and describing see Hepburn, *Christianity and Paradox*, pp. 56 ff. His challenge to the theologian's claims to immediacy for his judgments about God is that the latter merely gives "an illusion of immediacy through oscillating between descriptive and proper-name uses of the word 'God.'" (P. 57.)

given in our immediate personal encounter with him, and this is also true of our knowledge of God.

The difficulty with this reply is that, although our experience of the other as personal is quite different from our objective experience of him, the former is not separable from the latter. Our experience of the other "Thou" is made possible only by means of our objective experience of him. As Tournier puts it:

The person pure and simple does not exist. The real inner encounter . . . is enveloped in the external dialogue which expresses it. Even when this communication is felt in silence . . . this silence is itself charged with the words that have been exchanged before it began.[232]

Let us take an example from the existential psychotherapists who give this distinction between the personal and objective a central place in their work, for the significance of such a distinction must prove itself to them by aiding in their efforts to help their patients regain health:

Obviously a knowledge of the drives and mechanisms which are in operation in the other person's behavior is useful; a familiarity with his patterns of interpersonal relationships is highly relevant . . . and so on *ad infinitum.* But *all these fall on to a quite different level* when we confront . . . the immediate living person himself. When we find that all our voluminous knowledge about the person suddenly forms itself into a new pattern in this confrontation, the implication is not that the knowledge was wrong; it is rather that it takes its meaning . . . from the reality of the person of whom these specific things are expressions.[233]

When we encounter another as "Thou," the objective facts about him are not left behind but are seen now as expressions of that person. In this way our personal knowledge of the other retains its connection with falsification rules. As Tillich has put it:

When we encounter a person, we receive an impression. But often if we act accordingly, we are disappointed by his actual behavior. We pierce a deeper level of his character, and for some time experience less disappointment. But soon he may do something which is contrary to all our expectations, and we realize that what we know about him is still superficial. Again we dig more deeply into his true being.[234]

Indeed, apart from the availability of objective tests, the sense of personal encounter may itself be illusory insofar as we interpret it as

[232] *The Meaning of Persons,* p. 130.
[233] May, "Contributions of Existential Psychotherapy," *Existence,* p. 38. (Italics mine.)
[234] *The Shaking of the Foundations,* pp. 53-54.

an experience of the personal presence of another. Perhaps one learns this lesson from the sort of experience suggested by Hepburn: "I may speak to John, 'sensing' his presence with me, although unknown to me John may have quietly slipped out of the room, thinking that I had fallen asleep." [235] John's absence does not necessarily make my "response" of no significance to our relationship, but the fact remains that the "sense of presence" was unreliable.

Checking procedures for our knowledge of another person will differ, though, from those of our knowledge of an object. Tests of our personal knowledge will generally be less specific than those of our impersonal knowledge. Moreover, these judgments of personal knowledge are possible only for those who have empathically entered into the point of view of the person known, for this is what it means to know the other. My expectations about future experience of the other are not that he will respond this way to this stimulus (for I have observed that he always responds this way). Rather my expectations are that one with his point of view will respond in some such way as this or this or this but not that or that or that; taking what I believe to be his point of view enables me to understand or stand under or find myself in the former sort of actions but not in the latter. In other words, my personal knowledge of another is tested not by how well I can foresee or predict just what he will do but by how well I can understand his actions as truly *his* actions.

Checking procedures, then, do accompany our talk about the existence of another "Thou." Our personal experience of another is inseparable from our objective experience of him. But it is this objective aspect which is not a part of our experience of God, the encounter theologians have insisted. Concerning the analogy, then, between our experience of a finite "Thou" and our sense of a divine "Thou," we must ask with Hepburn whether we can "allow experiences of encountering God to elude absolutely every checking procedure, without a grave risk of eroding away the original analogy altogether." [236]

The encounter theologian does make an important point in distinguishing personal and impersonal forms of knowledge. Then, too, as we have argued, specific checking procedures are not the only sort of test that an assertion may have. The expectations embodied in assertions about God concern the whole of life and, so, are tested by the entire life-process. But, after this much has been said against the arguments of Martin and Hepburn, the general point remains that the existence of *some sort* of test is basic to what is meant by saying that a statement has objective reference. The claim of the encounter

[235] *Christianity and Paradox*, p. 34.
[236] *Ibid.*, p. 58.

theologian is not simply that he has certain experiences but that these are experiences of a divine being and that this divine being is loving, just, all-powerful, and so on. Now to say that these are experiences *of* a divine being is to give an interpretation of these experiences. It is to say something about the nature of their occurrences and their significance for life as a whole. One who regards them as experiences of a divine being, that is, will hold certain *expectations* concerning these experiences and their place in experience as a whole which will not be held by those who interpret them differently. The realization or frustration of these expectations is the confirmation or falsification of this interpretation.

The meaning, then, of the predicates applied to God must be specified in terms that go beyond the encounter experience alone. The encounter theologian has typically maintained that the believer's choice of predicates as symbols to express the meaning of his encounters is governed by the expectation that although these symbols cannot be used to speak in some literal sense about God they will, if we choose them rightly, enable us to enter into direct relation with God. Our choice of the right symbols is based on our past encounters. The trouble is that, in breaking completely from the tests that apply when we use these words literally, the encounter theologian leaves us without knowledge as to what language rules are to govern the use of past experiences in selecting these symbols. How are we to use past encounters as a test or measure of the right symbol?

The encounter theologian, then, focuses upon the religious experience called "encounter with God" as fundamental to the meaning of "God." Just as one encounters the personal depth of another human being, so the personal depth of the whole of reality may also be experienced. The difficulty is that, although our experience of another as "Thou" is *more than* an experience of his observable public behavior, this personal experience of another is *inseparable from* this observable activity. Our knowledge of the other "Thou" is inseparable from our experience of his objectively knowable personality and the tests connected with it. Consequently, since the meaning of the terms we apply to God is derived from the meaning that they have when applied to human beings, this meaning cannot be entirely separated from observable activity.

This necessity for some sort of "empirical anchorage" for the assertions made in connection with religious experience has received special attention in the work of Ian Ramsey. According to him,

theological assertions must have a logical context which extends to, and is continuous with, those assertions of ordinary language for which sense experience is directly relevant. From such straight-forward assertions, theological assertions must not be logically segregated: for that would mean that they were pointless and, in contrast to the only language which has an agreed meaning, meaningless.[237]

Religious language, as Ramsey sees its use, attempts to refer to the observable world in such a way as to evoke and express an awareness of a personal depth to that world. Moreover, "with this discernment there now goes a personal commitment" to that which is disclosed, a commitment which the purely objective, impersonal experience of reality could not elicit.[238] This personal depth is something "which we discern as having a claim on us."[239] Religious language attempts to serve this function of "bringing alive" our objective situations by referring to them in ways that are logically "odd." This logical oddness takes three different forms. First, there are "the attributes of negative theology: such as 'immutable,' 'impassible.'"[240] These attributes function to negate and negate and negate the characteristics of the finite world until we discern that which is beyond the finite: "Features of the perceptual situation are progressively obliterated in an endeavor to bring about that discernment which is the basis for talking about God."[241]

Second, there is "the characterization of God by 'Unity,' 'Simplicity,' 'Perfection.'"[242] Here the attempt is to discover religious meaning by starting with contrasting meanings and gradually moving away from them until "at some point or other the penny drops, the light dawns, [and] there is a characteristic 'disclosure'."[243] We may start, for example, with situations of diversity and move progressively toward an awareness of their unity, such as the unity that many rooms possess in being part of one house, or many houses in being part of one city.[244]

Third, there is still another set of "traditional attributes and characterizations: e.g., 'First CAUSE'; 'Infinitely WISE'; 'Infinitely GOOD'; 'CREATOR ex nihilo'; 'eternal PURPOSE.'"[245] In each of these cases, we have a "model" ("Cause," "Wise," "Good," etc.), which expresses a meaning with which we are familiar, and a "qualifier" ("First," "Infinitely," etc.), which suggests a way of "developing" this meaning which may lead to a religious disclosure. For example, "we take goodness as a model—a word which gives us at once some picture of good behaviour, of a good man."[246] The qualifier "Infinite" bids us to move through a sequence of "stories of good lives" in the direction of greater and greater goodness and "to continue long enough

[237] "Contemporary Empiricism," p. 181.
[238] Religious Language, p. 29.   [239] Ibid.   [240] Ibid., p. 30.
[241] Ibid., p. 53.   [242] Ibid., p. 50.   [243] Ibid., p. 54.
[244] Ibid.   [245] Ibid., p. 50.   [246] Ibid., p. 68.

with the sequence to evoke a situation characteristically different from the terms which preceded it; until we have evoked a situation not just characterized by a goodness which we admire or feel stirred to follow, but a situation in relation to which we are prepared to yield everything, 'soul, life and all.' " [247]

What Ramsey does not make clear, however, is just what cognitive status these disclosures have—in just what way they are subject to some sort of test. He does strongly insist that these discernments, "when they occur, have an *objective* reference," [248] but he does nothing to support this claim. As Frederick Ferré comments, "He is quite correct in asserting that religious experience has a high degree of 'intentionality,' . . . but is he not confusing 'experiencing-*as*-objective' with having experience *of* the objective?" [249]

We have been considering, then, the discussion among Oxford philosophers about the meaning of those assertions about God in which God is conceived of as a divine being who though outside of human experience manifests himself in that experience. In following this discussion we have taken the standpoint that the logic of religious assertions is to be studied on its own terms but must have significant similarities with the logic of other sorts of assertion, for we would otherwise simply be equivocating on the meaning of "assertion" in applying that term to religious utterances. Since assertions express expectations that under certain conditions experience will be of one sort rather than another, the basic question is what difference in expectation distinguishes those who believe in a divine being from those who do not.

Mitchell's position that the occurrence of evil is contrary to the believer's expectations finds its logical culmination, we have argued, in Hick's eschatological verification view; for the believer obviously does expect evils to happen in this life and lives accordingly. But even in the next life God remains outside of experience and consequently, we have argued, the expectations have to do not with God but with the experienced world. This means that religious assertions are not about God but about the experienced world.

The accounts we have considered, then, of this model of God as a divine being outside of human experience do not provide a basis for meaningful assertions about God. This model presents the relation of God to the evidence for God as analogous to the relation of the thief to the missing jewels and broken lock or of the gardener to the garden. But we can speak meaningfully of the missing jewels and broken lock as effects of the actions of the thief because we know

---

[247] *Ibid.*   [248] *Ibid.*, p. 28.   [249] *Language, Logic and God*, p. 141.

what it would be like to see the thief performing such actions. We cannot analogously speak meaningfully of aspects of the experienced world as effects of the actions of God because we do not know what it would be like to see or somehow experience God performing such actions. Talk about such actions does not express expectations about what, under certain conditions, experience will and will not be like.

For a meaningful conception of divine transcendence, then, we need to explore other models. The ways, for example, in which a person transcends our experience of him and in which an order of nature or history transcends our experience of it are quite different from the way in which a thief transcends our experience of the broken lock and missing jewels. We shall explore such an alternative model in our final chapter.

PART FOUR: *Dialogue With Existentialism*

Analysis

&

Existentialism

Chapter Nine

Religion is inherently existential, and the nature of religious assertions involves the relation of existential and cognitive meaning. On the whole, however, analytic philosophers have given very inadequate attention to this relation; consequently, we shall conclude our study in Chapter X by an examination of the existential theology of Paul Tillich. In preparation for this it will be helpful if we explore briefly the relation of the existential and analytic approaches to philosophy.

The existential and analytic orientations dominate our contemporary philosophic thought and yet have had very little to do with each other. The existentialists tend to regard the analysts as perpetuating some of the more problematic aspects of life today. Caught up in the perspectives of science and often concerned with problems that seem trivial, the work of the analysts appears symptomatic of our troubles. In return, analytic thinkers believe the existentialists are poets or psychologists more than they are philosophers. Because they fail adequately to understand or to concern themselves with the logical aspects of knowledge and the problems and pitfalls of language, the existentialists' work seems filled with confusion and unable to withstand careful analysis. How, then, are we to understand this split in contemporary thinking?

Philosophers do not think in isolation from the culture that molds their understanding of themselves and their world. The tensions they now display arose within the context of our cultural situation, and we must seek to understand them in these terms.

Fundamentally, ours is a period of profound cultural change. A culture is simply the way of life of a particular people. It is expressed in their science and technology, their art and social system, their religion and philosophy. In a cultural transformation men find their old way of life inadequate to cope with changing conditions. The old images of self and world become increasingly unreliable guides for behavior; they fail to provide meaningful patterns of response to the new situations. God had been conceived as guaranteeing an objective and everlasting purpose to life. That god has died. But man cannot live without a sense of meaning in what he experiences, and if he clings to them the old forms become death-dealing. Out of the old way of life, then, a new way of life must be created. Increasingly dissociated from the old, unclear about the new, Western man is caught in a crisis in meaning.

The driving forces of this transformation are the unprecedented achievements of technology and science. The institutionalization of scientific research and technological development has so accelerated the growth and application of knowledge that the changes seem destined to be as far-reaching as those which marked the birth of civilization. In the judgment of many, it is in science that we find the most authentic and creative expression of the contemporary human spirit. In the impact of science they find cause for celebration, for it has brought to man a new sense of strength and creativity, and a new humility before the truth. Others are more impressed by the relation between science and that progressive dehumanization that marks the situation of modern man. Existentialism and analytic philosophy may be interpreted as divergent responses to our crisis in meaning generally and, to some extent, to the role of science in that crisis specifically.

Neither of these movements, however, constitutes a school in the sense that a set of philosophic doctrines are held in common. We shall be discussing, then, tendencies within these groups rather than points of consensus.

As we might expect, our crisis in meaning is reflected with particular clarity in our language. Apart from our technical languages in which we deal with the objectifiable and measurable, men experience much difficulty in communicating with one another. Even in the areas of the quantifiable, as science pushes ever more deeply into areas involving philosophical perplexities (for example, the Heisenberg uncertainty principle) it becomes increasingly difficult to relate ever more specialized pursuits. On an individual level one often finds himself speaking two or more unrelated languages—perhaps one reflecting the old meanings, another reflecting the new. It is striking, then, to find a major group of philosophers preoccupied with language, devoting most of their energies to the clarification of meaning through the analysis of language. As communication is confused and disrupted men turn to examine the tool of communication. They do this by analyzing the ways in which the tool is actually used in specialized areas and, particularly, in everyday life in dealing with our purposes and concerns.

Turning to the existentialists, one is impressed to find that they also typically pay considerable attention to our everyday ways of speaking. But they construe the question of meaning rather differently. They speak, not of a confusion of meaning, but of a loss of meaning. The fundamental problem is not to work for greater clarity and consistency in our uses of basic concepts. It is to uncover sources of meaning which, in our experience, we have progressively lost sight of under contemporary conditions. It is to the dehumanizing effect of science and technology that the existentialists are particularly sensitive. Under the impact of these forces experience has become more and more restricted and trivialized as the perspectives of science and technology have been allowed to usurp a deeper more human perspective apart from which life loses all significance.

Science has this depersonalizing effect because it is an expression of our concern to manipulate and control and because the attitudes attendant upon this concern have been allowed to become increasingly dominant in life as a whole. Prediction and control require an impersonal, detached attitude that reduces all of reality to its impersonal, quantifiable dimensions. The world becomes a conglomeration of things and man simply another of these things. Man's humanity disappears from view. The conviction fades that man is to be treated as an end in himself and not merely as a means that can be manipulated and controlled to some other end. Without a qualm the social scientist typically accepts as proper to the study of man the aim fundamental to the physical sciences—control; the Freudian analyst encourages his patients to regard themselves as the passive victims of forces from outside the conscious self.

The existentialist also sees technology as dehumanizing in many ways, fundamentally because it is geared to the production and consumption of consumer goods. Our economy requires a standardized man whose buying habits can be manipulated to insure ever greater consumption and whose living and working habits can be molded to make him an efficient unit on the assembly line or smoothly adjusting member of the administrative team. Educated to blend in, exposed increasingly to the banalities and carefully packaged truths of the mass media, victimized by political and social forces beyond his control, the individual loses his sense of uniqueness, of inner freedom, of personal responsibility. We seek the meaning of life, in varying degree, in the security of belonging, the pleasure of consuming, the achievement of producing. But we discover less and less of ourselves in a belonging that surrenders individuality or in pleasure isolated from other ends; we invest less and less of ourselves in productive processes that are devoid of compelling goals.

Because he sees our situation in terms such as these, the existentialist protests; he calls each man to break the patterns of conformity and create the authentic existence of a unique, free, responsible individual. Through the eyes of the existentialist we see ourselves thrown back upon our own individual resources. We must seek consciously to recover awareness of those fundamental relationships in which we stand to our world, for it is in these relationships that meaning has its source. Consequently, many of the existentialists employ the phenomenological method that has as its aim the description of such phenomena as time, concern, freedom, anxiety, guilt, wonder, and the sense of the holy which are understood as revealing the basic structure of man's relation to his world. Lacking such awareness our experience is drained of significance. The existentialist, then, seeks to penetrate beneath the superficialities that characterize our experience of ourselves and our world as a step toward the recovery of the human in a dehumanizing age.

Those who employ this phenomenological approach maintain that the life-world, the world of our ordinary, everyday experience, is more basic and inclusive than the scientific world. Against those such as the logical atomists and logical positivists who see the life-world as a subjective and less reliable version of the world described by science, the phenomenologists argue that the scientific world is really an abstraction from the rich concreteness of our everyday world. As William James put it, science presents us with the menu rather than with the dinner. The facts of our everyday world cannot be reduced to the facts of science.

How, then, are the linguistic philosophers related to this approach? We should note at the start that there is considerable agreement at several points. Both reject any dualism of mind and body. Consciousness is understood more in terms of doing than of seeing, although this is less consistently true of the analysts. Both are empiricist and distrust talk of anything beyond what we can experience. Ordinary language is studied seriously as expressing fundamental meanings on which all of our more technical meanings must finally depend.

The empiricism of these groups, however, is of two rather different sorts. The analysts show a great, although not uncritical, respect for David Hume and his famous dictum "Our ideas reach no farther than our experience." One finds in Hume much reference to sensory experience and to the "operations of the mind," while little attention is given to those experiences which are steeped in emotion. On the other hand, the existentialists make numerous references to the starting point of Descartes's philosophy, "I think therefore I am." Although Hume could find no basis in experience for affirming his existence as a self, Descartes began with what he regarded as a logical certainty of this existence. However little they may agree with Descartes's metaphysics, the existentialists see in him the discovery of immediately given personal or "subjective" experience as the basis for a truly experiential philosophy. Their concern, then, is primarily with the emotion-laden, personal experiences from which the analysts seem to shy away; existential philosophers believe that the emotional sides of human experience reveal the fundamental level of the human situation.

This difference in their empiricism helps us to understand why the linguistic philosophers on the whole tend not to give the clear-cut priority to the life-world over the scientific world which the existentialists and phenomenologists do. On the one hand, the break by the linguistic philosophers with their earlier analytic practices and beliefs concerning the systematic uniformity of language and the adoption by them of the view that language uses are inseparable from our everyday forms of life certainly evidence a new respect for the life-world. On the other hand, the linguistic philosophers are far less critical than the existentialists are of the impact of science on modern life, and, as Basil Mitchell indicates, they frequently share a "tendency to distrust any but scientific explanation." [1] In those areas of language, such as the religious, where scientific and technological change has led most markedly to confusion and even devitalization of language use, the linguistic philosophers often seem in a sense to be working out the conceptual implications of the scientific world view.

The sense in which this is true is not that the analysts still believe that ordinary statements are reducible to scientific statements but rather that they seem to look at ordinary statements in a context that is ultimately that of the scientific world view. The phenomenologist John Wild, for example, makes this sort of criticism of G. J. Warnock's essay "Analysis and Imagination." After apparently having recognized the relevance of facts in the life-world to the study of ordinary language "Warnock ridicules the whole idea that philosophers might be 'discoverers,' and asserts that any claim to factual evidence will bring them onto ground from which they are 'liable to be destructively expelled.'" [2] "Factual" seems here to be restricted to its scientific

[1] Faith and Logic, p. 8. In contrast, however, is John Passmore's "Explanation in Everyday Life, in Science, and in History" in History and Theory, ed. G. H. Nadel, Vol. II, No. 2 (Middletown, Conn.: Wesleyan University Press, 1962).
[2] Existence and the World of Freedom, p. 45.

meaning. Warnock allows only that "a metaphysical system . . . may have many virtues, such as elegance, simplicity, originality, comprehensiveness, depth, or power to give psychological satisfaction"; [3] Wild maintains that versions of the life-world also may be judged true or false according to the tests of whether they "fit the world facts" and "call forth authentic existence in history." [4]

The similarities in the approaches of these two groups, though, are more important than their differences. In fact, these approaches are complementary, and each finally requires the other. To get at this let us consider the sorts of meaning with which each is concerned.

We have seen that the empiricism of each of these two groups is of different sorts. This difference is reflected in the different levels of meaning with which the analyst and existentialist are concerned. The linguistic philosopher focuses on linguistic or conceptual meaning, whereas the existentialist searches out a more fundamental level of meaning presupposed by the linguistic which we may term existential or preconceptual or life meaning.

Existential meaning refers to our basic way of looking at the world, the way of organizing and making sense of experience which is operative in everything we do. Fully to understand what someone is saying, the existentialist maintains, we must be able to enter into his way of looking at things. It is, for example, a difference in existential meaning which makes it impossible to translate the full meaning of one language into another or even completely to understand a language other than one's own (how can one really belong to more than one world?). Or, as Merleau-Ponty shows, it is to existential meaning that one must refer if one is to understand a speech disorder such as aphasia in which certain ways of using words are lost.[5]

The linguistic philosophers recognize, however, that these two levels of meaning are not finally separable. Wittgenstein emphasized that a language-game is part of a form of life and cannot be understood apart from that form of life. According to Wittgenstein: "How words are understood is not told by words alone. (Theology)"; [6] "Only in the stream of life and thought do words have meaning"; [7] "What belongs to a language-game is a whole culture"; [8] "In order to get clear about aesthetic words you have to describe ways of living"; [9] "To describe [aesthetic words'] use . . . you have to describe a culture." [10] This

---

[3] "Analysis and Imagination," *The Revolution in Philosophy*, p. 122.
[4] *Existence and the World of Freedom*, p. 75.
[5] *Phenomenology of Perception* (New York: Humanities Press, 1962), p. 182.
[6] *Zettel*, sect. 144.   [7] *Ibid.*, sect. 173.
[8] Barrett, *Lectures and Conversations*, p. 8, sect. 26.   [9] *Ibid.*, p. 11, sect. 35.
[10] *Ibid.*, p. 8, sect. 25.

inseparability of language and form of life is dramatically illustrated by Wittgenstein in the case of a judge in a court of law, for "if the being that he is to judge is quite deviant from ordinary human beings, then e.g., the decision whether he has done a deed with evil intent will become not difficult but (simply) impossible." [11] Or as S. N. Hampshire has put it, "The significance of any statement . . . presupposes some constant background of ordinary human interests and purposes and of ordinary human experience." [12]

The clarification of language use, then, may be achieved without careful attention to a form of life only insofar as the philosopher can presuppose a common understanding with his readers of the form of life involved. In cases where some description of the form of life is necessary just what this description will include will vary from case to case: "Whether this or that belongs to a complete description will depend on the purpose of the description." [13]

A striking case in point is the discussion by one of Wittgenstein's leading followers, Norman Malcolm, in "Anselm's Ontological Arguments." Malcolm concludes this discussion by asking: "Why is it that human beings have even *formed* the concept of an infinite being? . . . I am sure there cannot be a deep understanding of that concept without an understanding of the phenomena of human life that give rise to it." [14] Among these phenomena, Malcolm suggests, is that spoken of by Kierkegaard: "There is only one proof of the truth of Christianity and that, quite rightly, is from the emotions, when the dread of sin and a heavy conscience torture a man into crossing the narrow line between despair bordering upon madness—and Christendom." Concerning this Malcolm says only that

there *is* that human phenomenon of an unbearably heavy conscience and that it is importantly connected with the genesis of the concept of God, that is, with the formation of the "grammar" of the word "God." I am sure that this concept is related to human experience in other ways. If one had the acuteness and depth to perceive these connections, one could grasp the *sense* of the concept. [15]

It is precisely phenomena of this sort, facts in our life-world with their existential meaning, with which the existential phenomenologists are concerned. And it is just such phenomena with which we shall find Tillich concerned in our final chapter. For Tillich, the grammar of the word "God" is rooted in the experience of a source of courage

[11] *Zettel*, sect. 350.
[12] "Metaphysical Systems," *The Nature of Metaphysics*, p. 27.
[13] *Zettel*, sect. 311.
[14] "Anselm's Ontological Arguments," reprinted in Malcolm, *Knowledge and Certainty*, p. 160.
[15] *Ibid.*, p. 161.

by which we may overcome the anxieties of guilt, death, and meaninglessness.

Now in seeking to understand "the phenomena of human life" that give rise to a concept the philosopher will often be engaged less in clarification than in discovery or rediscovery. The existential phenomenologists, especially, are seeking to recall us to the awareness of wonder, anxiety, freedom, concern, and many other phenomena which we have buried beneath the superficialities of contemporary life. Many of our language uses have become nearly useless, for the concepts involved have been uprooted from the life phenomena that gave rise to them. To reclaim these uses we must not simply remind ourselves of their logic but recover an active awareness of the phenomena that gave them life. This seems particularly true of our religious language uses.

Many efforts at such discovery or rediscovery are labelled "analysis," and so we need to look once again at this term. Contemporary philosophers present us with "logical," "linguistic," "situational," "existential," "phenomenological," and "ontological" analyses, while others outside of philosophy present us with literary, chemical, economic, sociological, and psycho- analyses, to mention a few. In each of these cases we look at the subject matter from a particular perspective so that we may come to see something that cannot be seen from any other perspective. Each perspective is that provided by a special language-game, and so it may be helpful if we think of an analysis as a kind of translation from an everyday language-game into a technical language-game.

To use translation as a model for conceiving analysis will prove misleading, however, if we think primarily in terms of the reductive analysts' conception of their method as a translation of one sentence into another of an exactly equivalent meaning. Analyses typically are non-reductive translations, translations with remainder of meaning. Such a translation may clarify or bring to awareness one dimension involved in the complex meaning of a statement, other translations illuminating other dimensions. One translation, that is, may call attention to some of the life phenomena in which the use of a concept is rooted, while another translation may enable us to see other of these phenomena. We may think, for example, of Freudian and Marxist analyses of the term "God."

This approach to analysis will also be misleading if it encourages the belief that all those engaged in analysis actually conceive of their work in terms of this sort of model or that they literally translate one statement into another. Nor should the idea of translation suggest to us that analysis is undertaken only after the analyst has fully developed the language to be used in making it. Often it will be in the process of making the analysis that the analyst's own perspective becomes clarified. The idea of translation will be useful if it simply draws our attention to the perspective from which an analysis is made so that we may be open to its potential illumination yet on guard against the distortions that often accompany reductive uses of analyses.

This model of analysis as translation with or without remainder of meaning can be applied to both reductive and non-reductive analyses. As we have seen in our study of logical positivism, Paul Holmer provides for the term "God" what he quite explicitly regards as a translation. Statements about God are to be translated without remainder of meaning into statements about certain possibilities that a person may become. The theist, however, may find that this translation is helpful in bringing out one important dimension of the meaning of his statements about God but insist upon the necessity of other translations to bring out the remainder of what he means in talking about God. The proposed model would leave the nature of the relation between the two languages an open question to be examined in each particular case.

Quite different from a reductive translation, then, is what we might term an enriching translation in which the aim is to bring to fuller awareness a dimension of experience to which, frequently, little or no attention is paid. We may recall here the statement of Austin Farrer that the theist "exhibits his account of God active in the world and the world existing in God, that others may recognize it to be the account of what they themselves apprehend—or, if you like, that others may find it to be an instrument through which they apprehend, for perhaps apprehension here is not separable from interpretation." [16] Translation into the theistic perspective aims, at the very least, to bring to conscious recognition a sense of the finitude and contingency of the world.

As another example of an enriching analysis, we may consider Paul Tillich's "ontological analysis" of the ethical meanings of "love," "power," and "justice." [17] The basic purpose of translating these terms into the perspective of his ontological language is to bring to awareness a sense of the Holy or being-itself as a dimension of the experiences to which these terms are applied. "Man cannot solve any of his great problems if he does not see them in light of his own being and of being-itself." [18] We are placed, then, before portraits of love, power, and justice on Tillich's ontological canvasses so that we may come to experience these things differently from before. This makes under-

[16] *Finite and Infinite*, pp. 9-10.
[17] *Love, Power and Justice* (London. Oxford University Press, 1954), p. 17.
[18] *Ibid.*, p. 125.

standable the fact that although Tillich claims simply to be giving a description[19] there are critics who report that they cannot see that he is describing anything at all.

We may think, too, of G. E. Moore's pioneering work in philosophical analysis. We have seen that there were many problems connected with his view of philosophical analysis as definition and that many of these problems find a solution in Wittgenstein's way of doing philosophy. Yet Moore, unlike Wittgenstein, thought of philosophy as involving discovery. It was Wittgenstein's complaint that what Moore, among others, saw himself concerned with was "not something that already lies open to view and becomes surveyable by a rearrangement, but something that lies *beneath* the surface . . . and which analysis digs out." [20] Wittgenstein was doubtless right that many of the answers Moore was seeking did not involve discovery at all; but insofar as discovery has a place in philosophy, then, as we earlier proposed, some of Moore's concerns may require a revised conception of analysis. Analysis may be conceived as providing a point of view leading to discovery.

We have been examining, then, two very different philosophical responses to our cultural crisis. From one perspective we seem caught up in a confusion of meaning, from the other in a loss of meaning. It would be surprising, in view of their influence, if there were not important insights in both views and analytic philosophy has been moving onto more common ground with existentialism. But the analytic philosopher accepts too uncritically those contemporary patterns of life which have been shaped by the impact of science and technology; while the existentialist is so extremely critical of and withdrawn from those patterns that he fails to discern their authentically human dimensions. In the final analysis, the split between these philosophies is symptomatic of a schizophrenic condition of our culture in which reason and emotion have become separated. On the one hand, we are asked to live by two kinds of knowledge—knowledge of persons and knowledge of things—which are left largely unrelated. On the other, although we are not asked to equivocate on the meaning of "know," too little attention is paid to the cognitive role of feeling and emotion. One suspects that in a dialogue between existentialist and analyst each would encounter in the other a reflection of the stranger in himself.

---

[19] *Ibid.*, p. 23.
[20] *Philosophical Investigations*, par. 92.

A TILLICHIAN
ANALYSIS OF *God*
Acts
in History

Chapter Ten

The primary question for a theologian concerning the analysis of religious language is whether an objective, non-reductive reference is to be retained for "God." Most Christians, it seems safe to say, take the word "God" to have objective reference and understand God's nature primarily in terms of their conviction that God acts in history. In this chapter we shall consider Paul Tillich's interpretation of this conviction for, although many dismiss (or embrace) Tillich as failing to give the word "God" more than a subjective, non-cognitive use, I join many others in interpreting Tillich as having achieved just that—a grammar in which "God" has cognitive use, a transcendent, objective reference—although not just the sort of transcendence looked for by those who dismiss Tillich at this point. To argue this in terms of our study of the linguistic philosophers is to use Wittgenstein's view that "grammar tells us what kind of object a thing is"; to describe a grammar of the word "God" is one way of describing a view of the nature of God. This Wittgensteinian approach enables us to attempt to clarify the sense in which Tillich understood God as transcendent by comparing and contrasting his grammar with the grammars by which we speak of things whose transcendence we understand more clearly.

Our approach is also that of John Wisdom in his contention that "ontology and epistemology are one"; in describing the epistemological rules governing a way of talking of God we *are* describing a way of conceiving of the nature of God. A belief is genuine, I have contended, if it expresses expectations about what, under certain conditions, future

337

experience will and will not be like. *One who believes in an objectively real God will differ cognitively from one who does not in certain expectations that he has concerning future experience.* Our aim in this chapter is to describe Tillich's view of the transcendent nature of God by describing the sort of expectation concerning experience that is part of Tillich's grammar for "God." [1]

Consider, for example, the way in which a Robinson Crusoe will, in coming upon a mark in the sand, have certain expectations if he judges it to be a human footprint which he will not have if he decides that it only looks a little like one and really is not. If he decides that it is a human footprint he anticipates that he may meet that human being and become the object of some sort of action by him, perhaps a friendly action or perhaps a hostile one. If, on the basis of further clues, he determines that this person is probably a friendly sort, his expectation will be that companionship rather than harm will result from such a meeting.

Similarly, if I say that God exists, that he is forgiving, etc., I anticipate the possibility of meeting God and I entertain certain expectations about the nature of his actions toward me. Words like "exist" [2] and "forgives" do not, of course, imply just the same sort of expectations when applied to God that they do when applied to a human being. To say that these two sorts of expectation differ is simply to say that our understanding of the nature of man differs from our understanding of the nature of God. We do not expect literally to see God taking children into his arms or to hear him uttering words of forgiveness. But some sort of expectation there must be. We may recall the parable of two jungle explorers who come upon a clearing in which both flowers and weeds are growing. One is impressed by the flowers, their arrangement, etc., and believes that they are the work of a gardener. His skeptic companion, being more impressed by the weeds, disagrees with this belief. When, in spite of the fact that no gardener is ever encountered, the believer continues to insist that there is a gardener, the skeptic asks, "Just how does an eternally elusive gardener differ from an imaginary gardener?" How, in other words, does a forgiving God that one never encounters differ from an imaginary

---

[1] Beyond this philosophical aim of determining the cognitive meaningfulness of this position there remains, of course, the religious goal of determining its truth. Although this latter aim is beyond our present scope, in attempting to answer a question, as Moore stressed, it is important to understand clearly the nature of that question and the sorts of reason that count for and against its possible answers.

[2] It may be, as some have argued, that too much confusion results from any attempt to apply the term "existence" to other than finite entities. It is used here simply because it does convey to most the idea of some sort of objective reference.

forgiver? Surely to refer to someone as forgiving is to have certain expectations concerning forgiving actions.

Underlying this approach to the cognitive status of talk of God is the belief that man is not primarily a spectator looking at life but an actor on the stage, deeply involved in what is going on. He has expectations or beliefs about things that he experiences as important. His beliefs function as guides for action in the pursuit of interests and concerns. A true belief is a reliable guide for action in achieving the purposes of the believer; it expresses expectations that can be realized under certain conditions. If "the cat is on the chair in the next room" expresses a true belief, then the expectations of seeing the cat will be realized if I enter the next room and look at the chair. We call "real," then, only that which makes a difference to our concerns—a difference about which we can have reliable or unreliable expectations. If we wish to sit on the chair it will make a difference whether the cat is sitting there. We do not, that is, first come to know things in our everyday world quite apart from their value or disvalue for us and then add to this knowledge our value judgments about them. Rather a thing's value is part of its very nature, part of what we mean in referring to that thing. When we know something is a potato, or desk, or rain cloud or person, our knowledge includes the sort of concern or interest we have in that thing.

Cognition, then, may be seen in terms of a dialogue between a man and his world. A man acts in pursuit of certain interests and discovers his action to be effective or ineffective. In acting he asks a question and, in the results of his action, his world answers. He may, indeed, find no actions to be effective in realizing his aim or find those actions which are effective in terms of one aim to be damaging in terms of other aims; in his dialogue with his world he learns something about the appropriateness of his goals and concerns.

This dialogue, however, is also a dialogue with other men. It is three-cornered. This is a correlate of the Wittgensteinian contention that language is not private. A man learns from others to use language to express beliefs about things that make a significant difference; he learns this use of language from others who use it in similar ways and so, by implication, grasp that significance or are grasped by it. In the case of the religious use of language, for example, Tillich stressed that the power of its key words to express religious or ultimate concern has its origin in the unconscious *of the group*.[3]

In other words, truth—the reliability of certain expectations—is intersubjective. The expectations must be understandable to the other. He

[3] "The Nature of Religious Language," *Theology of Culture*, p. 58.

must know what sort of experience counts for and what sort of experience counts against the assertion being made.

Closely related to the contention that language is not private is the contention that man is essentially a social being. He is a self only in relation to others; he needs to find that others share with him those concerns which are important to him.

Expectations about things that matter cannot, then, be understood simply in terms of sense experience. As Freud has stressed, a man also knows the world in terms of what is pleasure-giving and what is not. Then, too, he is concerned about those things which provide a basis for being a person; particularly he needs intimacy with individuals and status with groups. Few beliefs match the importance of those concerning what offers intimacy or offers status and what denies intimacy or denies status. These needs seem universal. Is there also a universal need, fundamental to being a person, which is the basis of talk about God?

To put all this another way, many things are important to the human being. He is concerned with biological survival and with pleasure. He is also concerned with self-identity, with a sense that his involvement with the world is meaningful, and the achievement of adequate self-identity seems to require status and intimacy. Moreover, as the existentialists have emphasized, identity is something each person must actively achieve through the use of his own powers. Above all, identity is achieved and maintained by the act of self-affirmation. It is Tillich's view that the experience of acceptance from others and from God is necessary if one is to achieve a truly fulfilling, meaning-giving self-identity—an unconditional affirmation of self and of others and of life. From this point of view, then, talk about God will be cognitive if it expresses expectations about this concern which will be either reliable or unreliable as guides for action.

In Tillich's terminology, these beliefs concerning man's quest for self-identity and affirmation concern facts in the world of persons, and these facts cannot be reduced to facts in the world of things. Some, however, make this reduction. For them, as Tillich put it, "the 'I-Thou' relation is delivered over to emotion and subjective feeling." [4] The issue here seems to be whether the concerns and needs of which we are speaking in terms of the world of persons are universal—rooted in our basic human nature so that however much we turn away from them we cannot escape them—or whether these concerns and needs are simply the result of conditioning and so are merely a matter of subjective feeling.

[4] "An Evaluation of Martin Buber" (1948), reprinted in Tillich, *Theology of Culture*, p. 191.

The question of God's transcendence, however, concerns more than the believer's expectations concerning future experience as that bears upon "the one thing needful," for there are differing senses in which we may speak of transcendence. In our discussion of Wisdom we considered three of these senses. We may say, first, that a person is more than his footprints in the sand and the arrangement of flowers in his garden, or, second, that a book is more than its manifestations, or third, that Jones is more than his behavior. Now in dealing with the question of God's transcendence the linguistic philosophers have focused almost exclusively on the picture of God as a being who is beyond the world we experience while manifesting himself in it much as the gardener exists beyond his manifestations in the garden, except that the gardener can be experienced directly while God cannot. Wisdom, however, has presented us with an alternative account of the logic of God's transcendence in which God is something we experience and yet is more than that experience in a sense analogous to that in which a book or energy or another's mind is more than our experiences of them or, in other words, more than the evidence by which we support our statements about them. Consider that the dagger that Macbeth sees before him is merely a subjective experience and not an objectively real dagger because it does not transcend his experience of it. Others cannot see it, and he himself cannot use it to defend himself or to whittle wood. The dagger is not something more than Macbeth's experience.

"Something more," in Wisdom's sense, concerns our way of grouping phenomena according to certain patterns in our experience which (1) are important to our concerns, (2) make possible certain inferences beyond those immediate experiences, and (3) keep us open to the possibility both of new inferences and of a grasp of still other patterns of significance. In "Gods," for example, Wisdom refers to those "unseen worlds which some philosophers 'believe in' and others 'deny', while non-philosophers unconsciously 'accept' them by *using them as models with which to 'get the hang of' the patterns* in the flux of experience." When the reductionist, then, in his fight against the skeptic and the transcendentalist, insists that "a book is nothing but sensations and possibilities of more" or that "a mind is nothing but a pattern of behavior" he gets at part of what we mean in saying that books and minds transcend any particular experience we have; but he fails to take into account the models involved in our talk of books and minds by which we (1) bring to mind the way certain experiences hang together—the kind of hanging together this is—and (2) license certain kinds of inferences from our statements about these things. Concerning point one, we may think of how experiences of a book hang together in one way, those of a person in another way (e.g. there may be changes and surprises and deceptions in this pattern), those of an order of nature in yet another way. Concerning point two, we may consider that the model of God as a divine, loving, all-powerful being usually licenses inferences that God will act to prevent anything from happening which is, in the long run, not for the best; for example, since God is loving he will resurrect men to a new life after their earthly life.

The model of material substances is our way of grouping certain patterns such as those of trees, chairs, and animal bodies and so of emphasizing their similarities. The model of mental substance groups other patterns according to the way in which these "things," as Wisdom put it, "behave so cunningly all by themselves unlike even the most ingenious machines."

When we ask, then, whether the relation of God to the evidence for God is closer to the relation of books or minds to the evidence for them than it is to the relation of the clever thief or elusive gardener to the evidence for them, we are asking about the relative appropriateness of these models in enabling us to "get the hang of" religious patterns in our experience. Here we may recall our discussion in the chapter on Bertrand Russell of models adequate to our talk of books and chairs. According to Wisdom, Russell

substituted for an old and muddling model of the connection between realities and appearances a new model. For to say that a chair is a logical construction out of appearances of a chair is to say that a chair is related to its appearances *not* as a thing is related to the images of it in a mirror,[5] not as a member of parliament to his constituents, but as the average plumber to plumbers, as a family to its members, *as energy to its manifestations,* as electrons to the evidence for electrons.[6]

The application of the model of logical constructions provides us with comparisons by which we are helped to see that it is silly to lament "Confined as we are to our sensations how can we claim knowledge of spades?" The use of this model also throws doubt upon the appropriateness of the question "Confined as we are to the manifestations of God in our experience of the finite world how can we claim knowledge of God?" Wisdom has argued accordingly that the relation of God to his manifestations in finite events is more like the relation of energy to its manifestations than it is to the relation of objects

[5] Wisdom has earlier noted that "philosophers had often represented us as seated sadly guessing from the image in the mirrors of our minds at what was happening in reality." ("Bertrand Russell and Modern Philosophy," p. 204.)
[6] "Bertrand Russell and Modern Philosophy," p. 205. Italics mine.

to their shadows on the wall of a cave or to the relation of the watchmaker to his watches or to the relation of an elusive gardener to his garden. Of course, the logic of God must also be compared with the logic of mind, and so we see finally that no one of these models is entirely adequate. Talk of God draws attention to a certain kind of order in nature (including the events of history and personal life), and we must finally come, through comparisons and contrasts, to see that this kind of order simply is what it is and cannot be reduced to any other kind of order. For Tillich, I shall contend, talk of God draws attention to a pattern in the totality of events that may be seen only from the perspective of the existential quest for a truly fulfilling self-identity and self-affirmation.

The question at issue between Wisdom and the reductionist is whether we can here follow the reductionist in equating meaning and verification or whether "God" is used in ways that are not served by talk about the evidences of God. Do we employ a model in our talk about God which makes possible a use to which we do not put talk about the manifestations of God, so that it becomes meaningful to say, "I mean God himself and not just religious phenomena"? Or, rather, can any statement about God be reduced to a set of corresponding statements about religious phenomena—reduced in the sense that this set of sentences could serve, if less efficiently, the same purposes as the statement about God? To argue that statements about God are ultimate and irreducible is really to argue that religious-phenomena statements cannot serve all the same functions as statements about God. The reductionist argues that they can. But if we use Wisdom's method of comparison and contrast we can come to see that in some ways the same functions are served and in some ways they are not.

In dealing with this problem of transcendence the analytic philosophers not only have focused mainly on the picture of God as a being who is beyond the world we experience—somewhat as the gardener is beyond his garden—but also have paid little attention to the existentialists or to the phenomenological method. In the work of Tillich we not only find an alternative picture of God but also find fundamental use of the existentialists and of the phenomenological method. I conclude our look at the analytic philosophers by a discussion of Tillich mainly because I believe that religion belongs basically to the existential dimension of life and that an adequate philosophy of religion must combine both the analytic and existential approaches. Beginning, then, with some basic elements in Tillich's position, I shall attempt to sketch the outlines (1) of a cognitive and existential application of his picture of God as the ground or depth of everything that exists and (2) its relation to the biblical conception of God as acting in history. The aim, then, of this chapter will be twofold: first, to throw light on the problem of the cognitive status of talk about God; second, to encourage a reconsideration of the relevance of Tillich in light of this problem.

It may be helpful to have in mind at the start some of the ideas that will be guiding our discussion. First and foremost, it is difficult to see how we can ever understand, or be concerned about, or take an attitude toward, or commit ourselves to, or talk meaningfully about something we do not experience or do not know what it would be like to experience. If God is pictured to be beyond what we experience yet manifesting or giving evidence of himself in what we experience there seems to be no way to know what the evidence is evidence of. Reasons for this conclusion have been given in preceding chapters. Tillich, however, meant by "God" something of which the believer is immediately aware.[7] Religious discourse is interwoven with that form of life to which this awareness is central and cannot be understood apart from it.[8] Talk about God, then, presupposes that religious experience or awareness is distinguishable from moral, aesthetic, and all other sorts of experience and is not reducible to any of them.[9] The sort of awareness this is finds its classical phenomenological description, Tillich believed, in Rudolf Otto's *Idea of the Holy*.[10] In picturing God as the depth of everything that exists Tillich was saying that we may become aware of the holy in our encounter with any of these things.[11] To say that God is personal is to say that we may become aware of the holy in encounters with other persons.[12] Finally, Tillich believed that God may be encountered *only* in connection with our encounters with finite things. Religious awareness that is not rooted in one's existential situation is mere projection or "subjective emotion"—reducible to the purely psychological.[13] Consequently, it is best to speak of religious awareness or of the religious dimension of experience rather than of

---

[7] "The Two Types of Philosophy of Religion," *Theology of Culture*, p. 22.

[8] "The Nature of Religious Language," p. 58; "An Evaluation of Martin Buber," p. 189.

[9] "Religion as a Dimension in Man's Spiritual Life," *Man's Right to Knowledge*, foreward by J. B. Brebner, 2nd ser. (New York: Columbia University Press, 1954); reprinted in Tillich, *Theology of Culture*, pp. 6-8.

[10] *Systematic Theology*, I, 215.

[11] "Science and Theology: A Discussion with Einstein," *Theology of Culture*, p. 131.

[12] *Systematic Theology*, I, 245; "An Evaluation of Martin Buber," p. 189; *The Courage to Be*, pp. 165-66.

[13] *Systematic Theology*, I, 218; "An Evaluation of Martin Buber," p. 189.

religious experience, especially since "experience" suggests a subject observing a finite object.[14]

The Experiential Basis of Tillich's Position

Tillich's theology starts with the act of self-affirmation[15] and asks, first, what it is that makes this act difficult, and, second, in light of this difficulty what it is that makes it possible. More technically, Tillich provides a phenomenological description or analysis of the experience of self-affirmation including what he often calls the element of "in-spite-of" which shows itself in this experience.

It is difficult for a man to affirm himself. It is difficult because he is finite. His existence as a self is threatened in many ways and, indeed, must inevitably come to an end. He must affirm himself, then, *as finite*, and awareness of his finitude produces anxiety.[16] This anxiety takes different forms depending upon the way in which he is threatened. He is anxious about death, the final loss of his being; about condemnation, the failure to become his true self; about meaninglessness, the collapse of that core of meanings and values around which he integrates his personality.[17] To affirm one's self in-spite-of one's anxiety in the face of threats to his existence is an act of courage. But courage is not something a man is capable of apart from his relationships. It is rooted in these relationships.

It was Tillich's contention that the act of self-affirmation is possible only in the context of acceptance offered by another person or persons. An act of acceptance is an act of overcoming the estrangement or separation of oneself from another—an act of reconciliation. Only acceptance by another makes it possible, Tillich believed, for a man to accept and affirm himself in the face of condemnation or of guilt (the less severe form in which failure to become one's true self is experienced). But acceptance by another, although necessary, is not sufficient to make possible the courage to accept oneself.[18] He must, at the same time, be aware of the presence of the holy (technically, the presence of that which has the quality of being holy), or God, which, because one is aware of him "in, with, and under" a human act of

[14] "The Two Types of Philosophy of Religion," p. 23.
[15] *The Courage to Be*, pp. 155-56; or see the following in the order listed: *Systematic Theology*, II, 165-66; *The Shaking of the Foundations*, pp. 106-7; *Systematic Theology*, I, 112-13; II, 8.
[16] *The Courage to Be*, p. 35.
[17] *Ibid.*, pp. 41-57.
[18] Or, one could say that acceptance by another is not sufficient to make possible the courage to receive that acceptance, for the act of receiving acceptance *is* the act of affirming oneself.

acceptance, is himself "experienced" as accepting. The holy, in other words, is "experienced" in this context as *the ultimate source of the courage to accept and affirm one's self.*[19] This is why that which is holy is the true object of what Tillich calls our ultimate concern. What concerns us in a life and death way, that is, is the source of our courage to become persons through self-affirmation. Or, as Tillich explains, "ultimate concern is the abstract translation of the great commandment: 'The Lord, our God, the Lord is one; and you shall love the Lord your God with all your heart, and with all your soul and with all your mind, and with all your strength.'" (Mark 12:29 RSV) [20]

Self-affirmation meant, for Tillich, eternal life, salvation, loving God, loving one's life, loving one's destiny, fulfilling the ultimate meaning of one's existence.[21] It also meant Paul's experience of receiving a new being. We can best understand these equations in terms of Tillich's treatment of Paul's doctrines of law and grace—especially as these are expressed in Romans 8, which begins with the condemnation experienced under law and ends with the acceptance experienced under grace:

For to be carnally minded is death; but to be spiritually minded is life and peace. Because the carnal mind is enmity against God: for it is not subject to the law of God, neither indeed can be. So then they that are in the flesh cannot please God. But ye are not in the flesh, but in the Spirit, if so be that the Spirit of God dwell in you. . . . For I am persuaded, that neither death, nor life, nor angels, nor principalities, nor powers, nor things present, nor things to come, nor height, nor depth, nor any other creature, shall be able to separate us from the love of God, which is in Christ Jesus our Lord.

All men, Tillich believed, bear an unconscious hostility toward God for the same reason that children unconsciously hate their fathers. In both cases the hostility is directed toward the representative of the moral law which one accepts but fails to fulfill. In failing to fulfill the law one is guilty, and the father [22]—human or divine—is experienced as the cause of this inner split.[23] Tillich gave powerful expression to this experience:

One is hostile, consciously or unconsciously, toward those by whom one feels rejected. Everybody is in this predicament, whether he calls that which rejects him "God," or "nature," or "destiny," or "social conditions." Everybody carries a hostility toward the existence into which he has been thrown, toward the hidden powers which determine his life and that of the universe.

[19] *The Courage to Be*, pp. 165-66.
[20] *Systematic Theology*, I, 11.
[21] See, for example, *ibid.*, III, 398; II, 165.
[22] Or whoever in fact exercised the early voice of moral authority.
[23] *The Shaking of the Foundations*, pp. 133-35.

. . . This happens often unnoticed by ourselves. But there are two symptoms which we hardly can avoid noticing: The hostility against ourselves and the hostility against others. One speaks so often of pride and arrogance and self-certainty and complacency in people. But this is, in most cases, the superficial level of their being. Below this, in a deeper level, there is self-rejection, disgust, and even hatred of one's self. Be reconciled to God; that means at the same time, be reconciled to ourselves. But we are not; we try to appease ourselves. We try to make ourselves more acceptable to our own judgment and, when we fail, we grow more hostile toward ourselves. And he who feels rejected by God and who rejects himself feels also rejected by others. As he grows hostile toward destiny and hostile toward himself, he also grows hostile toward other men.[24]

Passages such as this, which recur again and again in Tillich's sermons, reveal his sense of the overwhelming importance of receiving God's acceptance. He thought of salvation not in terms of a divine being whom we cannot experience or of a life after death which can only be a matter of future experience but in terms of the present experience of self-affirmation or reconciliation with God, with oneself, and with others.

The difference may be seen quite pointedly if we recall Antony Flew's question, after pointing to "a child dying of inoperable cancer of the throat," "what is this assurance of God's (appropriately qualified) love worth, what is this apparent guarantee really a guarantee against?"[25] The expectations that Tillich understood to be expressed by belief in God's love are not that a divine being will act to prevent evil or to prevent death from being the final end of our existence but that, once we have been reconciled with God as he grasps us in the depths of our being, not even the terrible death of a child has the power to break our reconciliation with God, our affirmation of life.

Providence means that the daemonic and destructive forces within ourselves and our world can never have an unbreakable grasp upon us, and that the bond which connects us with the fulfilling love can never be disrupted. . . . Providence and the forgiveness of sins . . . are one and the same.[26]

To put this another way, the existential problem that both moral and natural evil pose is what evil does to our capacity to love. The fact that men do evil and suffer evil means that love must always be love in-spite-of what is unlovable. But this does not mean that we must love God in-spite-of the fact that he is "a guilty bystander" (Camus) who although he has the power to prevent evil yet, for reasons

---

[24] *The New Being* (New York: Scribner's, 1955), pp. 20-21.
[25] *New Essays* . . . , pp. 98-99.
[26] *The Shaking of the Foundations*, pp. 106-7. See also *The New Being*, pp. 58-59.

that are often inscrutable, does not prevent it. There is nothing in our awareness of God, Tillich believed, which makes legitimate the inference that God is a Person who can act to intervene in the course of things. Such an inference, Tillich said (in terms that have otherwise proved rather misleading), is a failure to see that references to God as personal must be taken symbolically rather than literally. To make this inference that God is a person is to conceive of God as subject to the categories of finite being—such as the category of causality—which reduces God to a god who, by implication, is subject to the threat of nonbeing. He is then subject, for example, to the threat of condemnation as a guilty bystander who fails to use his power to prevent evil. On Tillich's view, God is "experienced" rather as the source of courage to face the threat of nonbeing, a courage that we learn that finite beings are unable to provide.

Because our account must be so compressed it would be prudent to avoid direct reference to a subject as abstruse as ontology. But it is so prominent in the writings of both Tillich and his critics that it must be at least touched on here. Tillich's use of the terms "being," "nonbeing" and "Being-itself" must be understood in terms of one's experience of self-affirmation in-spite-of the inescapable threat to one's existence as a self. We are aware of the threat of nonbeing, and so we have a sense of being. What is threatened is our being, our very existence as selves. When, shocked by this awareness, we nonetheless are able to affirm ourselves, we become aware at that moment of a presence that gives us the courage required. "Being-itself" is Tillich's label for what we experience as the source of this courage. The term is chosen to reflect the fact that relations with other finite beings do not make possible this courage until this presence becomes a dimension of those relations.

However, all of our experience, all of our thought about ourselves and our world, involves certain basic concepts; these concepts Tillich calls ontological because in seeking to describe them we are seeking to describe the structure of our experienced world. Without such conceptual structure, experience would be unintelligible or blind; in other words, without such structure it could not be an experience *of* anything. The theologian, then, should make explicit his use of these concepts in speaking of those revelatory experiences in which God has been decisively encountered, relating his use of them to the metaphysician's description of the use of these concepts throughout the other areas of experience. He should, for example, show the relation of his use of "cause" in referring to God as "first cause" to the sort of uses "cause" has outside of religious discourse. In doing this, the theologian should make explicit the metaphysical picture that guides his understanding of the relation of God to the finite world and the rules governing its application. Tillich's metaphysical picture is centered in the metaphor "depth."

In making explicit his metaphysical picture, Tillich spoke in terms of what he called "the depth of reason." By this he meant the way in which our use of reason sometimes expresses our awareness of something that we cannot grasp by reason. With particular reference to Kant, Tillich argued that although reason can only deal with the finite world man "also discovers that his reason does not accept this bondage and tries to grasp the infinite with the categories of finitude . . . and that it necessarily fails." [27] It is worth noting that although Tillich contends that "in post-Kantian metaphysics reason forgot its bondage to the categories of finitude" [28] he is often accused of adopting this approach himself by critics who lean toward Karl Barth.[29] Let us consider an alternative interpretation of Tillich.

To get at what Tillich meant, we may consider the work of one of those linguistic philosophers who are interested in this phenomenon of reason attempting to push beyond its limits.[30] Stephen Toulmin discusses it in terms of what he calls "limiting questions." These are questions that cannot be taken literally for, unlike literal questions, there are no "genuinely alternative answers" to select from.[31] We may, for example, ask literally about the purpose of pieces of antler found in an archaeological excavation because we can conceive of alternative answers to this question, and we know the sorts of things that would count in favor of one answer or in favor of another. But if we ask about the purpose of the universe the question is not literal, for "the ordinary procedure for answering questions about 'purpose' is no longer applicable." [32] Other examples of limiting questions are "Why did the Jones children have to die so young; and all on their birthdays, too?" or the famous passage from Pascal:

When I consider the short duration of my life, swallowed up in the eternity before and after, the little space which I fill, and even can see, engulfed in the infinite immensity of spaces of which I am ignorant, and which know

---

[27] *Systematic Theology*, I, 82.

[28] *Ibid.*

[29] See esp. Kenneth Hamilton, *The System and the Gospel: Critique of Paul Tillich* (New York: Macmillan, 1963), pp. 197 ff. (Esp. p. 200, n.).

[30] Among the others are John Wisdom, "Philosophy, Metaphysics, and Psycho-Analysis," pp. 281-82; Ludwig Wittgenstein, *Tractatus*, 6.4312 ff.; Ian Ramsey, *Freedom and Immortality* (London: SCM Press, 1960), pp. 72-74.

[31] *Reason in Ethics* (Cambridge: The University Press, 1964), p. 205.

[32] *Ibid.*, p. 216.

me not, I am frightened. . . . Who has put me here? By whose order and direction have this place and time been allotted me? [33]

Still another example cited by Toulmin is from Dmitri's dream in Dostoevski's *Brothers Karamazov*:

> "Why are they crying? Why are they crying?", Mitya [Dmitri] asked, as they dashed gaily by.
> "It's the babe", answered the driver, "the babe weeping." . . .
> "But why is it weeping?" Mitya persisted stupidly, "why are its little arms bare? Why don't they wrap it up?"
> "Why they're poor people, burnt out. They've no bread. They're begging because they've been burnt out."
> "No, no," Mitya, as it were, still did not understand. "Tell me why it is those poor mothers stand there? Why are people poor? Why is the babe poor? . . . Why don't they feed the babe?"
> And he felt that, though his questions were unreasonable and senseless yet he wanted to ask just that; and he had to ask it in just that way. And he felt that a passion of pity, such as he had never known before, was rising in his heart.[34]

Concerning such questions Toulmin contends that "the feeling of urgency behind so many of them, the insistence with which they recur, itself suggests that no good is done by bottling them up." [35] Rather we must understand the motives behind them and then, quite often, we shall discover that they are religious questions whose purpose is to seek the help afforded by religion in accepting the world. Religious answers function variously to reassure us, or to help us to resign ourselves to things like the deaths of the Jones children, or to "help us to put our *hearts* into" our moral duty.[36] Consider, for example, the following:

> "Why ought I to give back this book?"
> "Because you promised."
> "But why ought I to, really?"
> "Because it would be sinful not to."
> "And what if I were to commit such a sin?"
> "That would be to cut yourself off from God," etc.[37]

J. J. C. Smart and Paul Tillich both discuss another question of this sort, the question "Why should anything exist at all?" Unlike Toulmin, Smart has not decided how questions of this sort are to be understood, but something Toulmin has stressed is echoed in Smart's comment that

---

[33] *Thoughts*, trans. W. F. Trotter (New York: Collier, 1910), sect. III, no. 205.
[34] Trans. C. Garnet (New York: Macmillan, 1912), pp. 546-47.
[35] *Reason in Ethics*, p. 209.
[36] *Ibid.*, p. 219.
[37] *Ibid.*

"indeed, though logic has taught me to look at such a question with the gravest suspicion, my mind often seems to reel under the immense significance it seems to have for me." [38] It is, Smart believes, a question we ought to ask, for it expresses "a matter of the deepest awe." [39]

Tillich regarded this question as "the ultimate question," for, although strictly speaking it is meaningless when put in the form "Why should anything exist at all?", "fundamentally it is the expression of a state of existence." [40] It expresses, he believed, the shock of the possibility of nonbeing, and so it raises the question of a source of courage adequate to facing this shock—metaphorically, the question of a ground of being or depth of being. The theologian's treatment of any of the ontological concepts must be understood in light of the awareness expressed by this ultimate question. Concerning the concept "cause," for example, when one asks the "limiting" or religious question about a first cause, Tillich understood this in terms of asking for a ground of all causes as an "answer" to the wonder that there are any causes at all.[41] Our sense of the finitude and contingency of all things, including their causal relations, points to a contrasting awareness of something ultimate.

Our discussion of limiting questions now enables us to focus more clearly the question of Tillich's use of ontology. We have seen that man asks questions with which reason is not equipped to deal, for the conventions or procedures it normally follows are not applicable. Indeed, by the very nature of the questions no conventions of this sort could conceivably be applicable. We have further seen, however, that if we take careful notice of the circumstances in which such questions are asked we find that often[42] they are expressions of the questioner's existential situation. But how does one interpret what they mean and the sort of response that is relevant to them? How does one understand the difference in the interpretations given by Toulmin and by Tillich, Toulmin speaking of religious answers in terms of psychological effects, Tillich speaking of them in terms of ultimate concern?

Toulmin does not discuss how interpretations of the sort he has given are to be evaluated and justified; he seems to believe, in fact, that no convictions about the human situation are assumed by his account. We are asked not to assume from his discussion of religious answers that he personally finds or does not find value in them, for this does not enter into the discussion of their logic. "There are many

---

[38] "The Existence of God," p. 46.   [39] Ibid.
[40] Systematic Theology, I, 163-64.
[41] Ibid., p. 21.
[42] Some of them may, of course, be simply a product of confusion. See Toulmin, Reason in Ethics, p. 209.

people," he argues, "who do not play bridge, and who in fact consider it a shameful waste of time and energy; but they do not conclude . . . that all solutions of bridge problems are therefore invalid." [43] The implication seems to be that no more personal involvement is required in understanding religious problems than is required in understanding bridge problems or, in other words, that no personal convictions are involved in interpreting religious questions.

Tillich took the very different view that we interpret religious questions in light of certain convictional experiences, experiences of such an overwhelming impact that they become the perspective from which we view the whole of life. This means particularly that they become the touchstones for determining those things which are of first importance. For Tillich this was the experience of the act of self-affirmation or of receiving ultimate acceptance. Tillich spoke of this experience as receiving the revelation of Jesus as the bearer of the new being or the new life rooted in self-affirmation; he spoke of it in this way because as a member of the Christian community he had been nurtured to understand his experience in light of this revelatory event, and this event came alive for him only through his experience.

Tillich's ontological picture of God as the ground or depth of being makes explicit the conceptual structure of the experience of receiving ultimate acceptance. It shows the structure that makes the experience intelligible—makes it an experience *of* something. To picture God as the depth of being is to indicate that we may become aware of the holy in and only in our experience of the finite. "It is through the finite alone," Tillich contended, "that the infinite can express itself." [44] The sole basis for this belief is the existential experience of the community of believers.

Terms such as "non-being," "being," and "being-itself" were not used by Tillich to discover and express truths through the exercise of some sort of absolute power of reason. These terms were used by him rather as a kind of shorthand abbreviation for his analyses of our existential experience. "Not arguments but the courage to be reveals the true nature of being-itself." [45]

In describing awareness of the holy Tillich frequently employed the phenomenological description given by Rudolf Otto in *The Idea of the Holy*.[46] In Otto's terminology, the holy is inherently mysterious and has the qualities of *tremendum* and *fascinosum*. "Mysterious" here does not mean something not yet known, something of which one

---

[43] *Reason in Ethics*, p. 220.
[44] *Systematic Theology*, I, 218.
[45] *The Courage to Be*, p. 181.
[46] Trans. John W. Harvey, 2nd ed. (London: Oxford University Press, 1950).

is ignorant. It means that the holy cannot become an object of knowledge for us in the sense that finite things can be objects of knowledge. The holy transcends this subject-object type of experience, for we cannot separate ourselves from it. In the words of the mystic, Meister Eckart, "The soul is not only equal with God but it is . . . the same that He is." [47] Eckart did not mean that "God" is only another name for the self but rather that one cannot be aware of God without being aware of oneself. Metaphorically, one is aware of God as the depth of the self.[48] The experience is ecstatic rather than subject-object.

Awareness of God as the depth of oneself, however, cannot finally be separated from awareness of God as the depth of one's world, and primarily, as the depth of other selves; for we are selves only in relation to our world, and we understand self and world by the structure of experience which we share with our community. Indeed, the truly human self is born in moments of dialogue with others. "There is no depth of life without a depth of the common life." [49] The holy is mysterious, then, in that when we are aware of the holy in our relation with another we are aware of something that stands on both sides of the relation. Just as our self-awareness is necessary to our awareness of the behavior of others as the actions of conscious selves, so our immediate awareness of the holy is necessary to our awareness of the behavior of others as the actions of conscious selves to whom the holy is immediately present. But in the latter case we experience something that is both present to us through the actions of the other and immediately present to us in the depths of our being. Our experience of reunion or reconciliation with the other is the experience that he "belongs to the same Ground to which we belong." [50] In the act of self-affirmation, then, we are immediately aware of God, but our awareness of his acceptance is inseparable from the act of acceptance on the part of the other.

"*Tremendum*" refers to the qualities of awefulness and majesty. Awefulness is an "absolute unapproachability." Majesty is an "absolute overpoweringness" [51] which gives rise to a "creature consciousness" (Otto) or feeling of "absolute dependence" (Schleiermacher). In one of its forms, this is the experience of an "unconditional demand"

[47] Quoted by Tillich, "The Two Types of Philosophy and Religion," p. 15. Martin Buber speaks of God as "nearer to me than my I" (*I and Thou*, p. 79.) and as "the Being that is directly, most nearly, and everlastingly over against us, that may properly only be addressed, not expressed." (Pp. 80-81)

[48] Concepts such as the social unconscious or archetypal memory similarly represent the self as individuated only at the surface level of consciousness.

[49] Tillich, *The Shaking of the Foundations*, p. 57.

[50] *Ibid.*, p. 162. See also *The New Being*, p. 17. "in the light of ultimate acceptance we are united."

[51] *The Idea of the Holy*, p. 19.

upon us to become our true selves, a demand by which we feel condemned unless we experience God's acceptance. As we have seen, this quality of majesty or distance, this quality of God as the abyss of being, is of fundamental importance in Tillich's thought. It is often asked whether Tillich's position is really significantly different from naturalistic positions such as that of Erich Fromm or John H. Randall, Jr.[52] And it is this quality to which Tillich pointed in answering that it is. "The main argument against naturalism," Tillich contended, is "the failure of naturalism to understand a decisive element in the experience of the holy, namely, the distance between finite man . . . and the holy." [53] And elsewhere Tillich insisted that, "when God is identified with an element in human nature, as in humanism, the terrifying and annihilating encounter with majesty becomes an impossibility"; [54] "a man who has never tried to flee God has never experienced the God who is really God." [55] The naturalist fails to understand what traditionally has been called the wrath of God.

In addition to these qualities of unapproachability and overpoweringness there is the element of "urgency" or "energy" which has been expressed as "vitality, passion, emotional temper, will, force, movement, excitement, activity, impetus." [56] Closely related is the experience of the community of faith that the presence or absence of the holy is not subject to human will; one cannot take the initiative in somehow bringing about this presence, anymore than one can compel another person to be present in certain ways. We may invite and encourage the personal response of another, yet it may not be given; or another may say "Thou" to us in a moment when we least expect it or are least able to invite it. Similarly we may seek to adopt an attitude of openness and receptivity to the presence of God and yet not become aware of that presence; or we may be grasped by God's presence when we least expect it or are least able to open ourselves to it. That this experience is not controlled by us led Tillich to speak of being "grasped by" the holy. "God acts," he contended, "beyond human expectations. . . . He acts surprisingly, unexpectedly, paradoxically." [57]

This sense of the "divine initiative" was not even hinted at in our earlier statement that "to picture God as the depth of being is to indicate that we may become aware of the holy in and only in our experience of the finite." This way of putting it does not guard against the impression that the holy is a kind of inert quality of things, our

[52] See for example, John Hick, *Philosophy of Religion*, pp. 69-70; 86-87.
[53] *Systematic Theology*, II, 7.
[54] *The Shaking of the Foundations*, pp. 89-90.
[55] *Ibid.*, p. 42.
[56] Otto, *The Idea of the Holy*, p. 23.
[57] *The Shaking of the Foundations*, pp. 17, 20.

awareness of which simply depends upon our directing our attention to it. We may now revise this statement and say rather that to picture God as the depth of being is to indicate that men are grasped by the holy in and only in their relations with the finite world. "Depth" means abyss as well as ground; God is neither the same as nor separate from our finite world.

In addition to *tremendum*, Otto described the holy as having the quality *fascinosum*. The holy, that is, not only repels but also attracts and fascinates.[58] If it is abyss it is also ground. The awareness of its presence, on this side, is characterized by bliss, beatitude, wonderfulness, rapture. God is experienced as the source of ultimate courage, of ultimate acceptance, of ultimate meaning, of ultimate beatitude. We may note here that the experience of the courage to accept acceptance may also be described as the experience of that which gives ultimate meaning to life. It is true that our relations with the finite world do have meaning for us quite apart from any act of *full* self-affirmation on our part. Yet the limitation of this sense of meaning is expressed when we find ourselves asking the limiting question, "But what does it all finally add up to?" "What is the meaning of life as a whole?" As Augustine put it, "Our hearts are restless until they find rest in thee." Or, we may think here of Kierkegaard: "In the beginning was boredom."

Such descriptions of the holy, however, must be understood in the context of the existential situation in which man encounters the holy. Tillich emphasized this by his use of the metaphor "depth" and by his insistence that one does not know God apart from his relations with the finite world. In the encounter with God, man is totally involved, and, since man is man only in relation to his world, nothing of his finite relations is excluded from this involvement. This means that the experience of God as unconditional demand and as the source of ultimate courage to affirm oneself is not something that is in addition to or distinct from the experience of the holiness of God; it is one and the same experience.[59]

Man meets God only in his meeting with the finite. This means also that a "religious" feeling that is not a dimension of one's encounter with his concrete, physical environment is based on mere projection— purely subjective or psychological. "Only something subjective happens in a state of religious overexcitement," Tillich argued; "therefore, it has no revelatory power." [60] In contrast, "the holy is a 'quality in encounter', . . . and not an emotional response without a basis in the

[58] *The Idea of the Holy*, p. 31.
[59] To believe otherwise "transforms the holy into something aesthetic-emotional." (*Systematic Theology*, I, 215).
[60] *Systematic Theology*, I, 113. See also III, 117-18.

whole of the objects." [61] Awareness of the holy, that is, has its basis
in the objective world. It is authentic only in the appropriate concrete
situations. Drawing out the implications of Tillich's position, we may
say that appropriateness is judged here by whether the situation is the
sort that (1) involves the whole man and (2) justifies the use of
the predicate term by which the encounter is described. Let us look
more fully at these two points.

John E. Smith has given a phenomenological description of characteristics of situations involving the whole man in which the holy
is experienced.[62] Foremost among these are birth and death, the
natural boundaries of the total self. Then there are those crucial
junctures in life—marriage, initiation into adulthood, serious illness,
beginning a long journey, war, choice of vocation—in which the whole
meaning and direction and worth of that life are at stake. Smith
draws attention particularly to the temporal characteristics of these
events. Typically they are unrepeatable and occur at times when decisions must be made that involve the shape of one's destiny. Spatial
characteristics are also significant. We seek to live through such events
in spaces other than those of the ordinary, routine activities of life,
for such spaces have associations and distracting characteristics that
work against the felt need to view our life as a whole. We turn
to spaces which "have historic associations which remind us of the
experience of the Holy had by others in the past" and which are "so
structured as to direct our thoughts to ourselves . . . and at the same
time away from ourselves to an awareness of the Holy." [63] Much more
needs to be said here but this will at least suggest what is meant by
situations involving the whole man.

The situation must also be such as to justify the use of the predicate
by which the revelatory encounter is expressed. For example, the belief
that "God was in Christ reconciling the world unto himself" cannot
be separated from Jesus' acts of reconciling love; one cannot, then,
appropriately say "God was in Nero reconciling the world." Nor is
the belief that God delivered his people out of bondage in Egypt
understandable apart from Moses' act of deliverance; one cannot appropriately say that God delivered his people out of bondage in
Buchenwald. When may one say, then, according to the grammar of
the Christian language game as Tillich described it and employed

---

[61] "The Meaning and Justification of Religious Symbols," in *Religious Experience and Truth*, ed. Sidney Hook (New York: New York University Press, 1961),
p. 6.
[62] "The Experience of the Holy and the Idea of God," in *Phenomenology in
America*, ed. James M. Edie (Chicago: Quadrangle Books, 1967). See also Mircea
Eliade, *The Sacred and the Profane* (New York: Harcourt, Brace and Co., 1959).
[63] "The Experience of the Holy and the Idea of God," p. 303.

it in his preaching, that God has delivered me out of the bondage of guilt and self-condemnation? What, in other words, is the paradigm case [64] for Tillich's use of "God forgives"? One may properly say this only in a situation (1) in which the whole self is involved—for the very question concerns the whole man—and (2) in which one experiences a human act of forgiveness. "No self-acceptance is possible," Tillich contended, "if one is not accepted in a person-to-person relation." [65] Consider the believer who has a feeling of being forgiven while praying in church and yet has no relation of confession and acceptance with another human being. Then consider the person who believes that John loves him although nothing in John's behavior indicates this, or alternatively, the person who feels hated by John although John does not act in hostile ways toward him. In these latter two cases the feeling has no known basis in fact and so we say this person is projecting, reading something into the situation. But how is the situation of our believer essentially different? His feelings are equally without any known basis in the facts of his life; they find no basis, that is, in the world of his experience. And since his feelings are not rooted in his relations with his world how could they be relevant to those relations? [66] How could they bring healing or wholeness to one's life in the world or, as Tillich might put it, how could they provide the basis for affirming the self since the self exists only in relation to its world?

Freud's explanation of such feelings is fully compatible with this point of view. Faced with difficulties in the adult world which his pattern of life as an adult does not provide adequate resources for handling, the believer regresses to his childhood situation and projects into his present life some of the feelings he had as a child toward his father and perhaps also the "oceanic feeling" of oneness with the world that he experienced before coming to distinguish the self from what is not the self.[67] Since, in the case of the believer we are considering, these feelings are not rooted in the believer's present life in the world they play no constructive role in his present ways of relating. Does not some such interpretation throw light on the apparent gracelessness of so much of the life of the institutional church? And

[64] See Chap. 8 for a discussion of this concept.

[65] *The Courage to Be*, p. 166.

[66] His feelings do, of course, often constitute a kind of protective buffer between the person and his relationships; but the protection will again and again be dashed upon the hard realities of those relationships for, like it or not, he is related in just those ways.

[67] See *Civilization and Its Discontents*, trans. Joan Riviere (New York: Jonathan Cape and Harrison Smith, 1930), Chap. 1; also *The Future of an Illusion*, trans. W. D. Robson-Scott (New York: Liveright Publishing Corp., 1928).

does it not also illuminate the prophetic mistrust of any emphasis on religious awareness because this endangers the proper emphasis on responsibility before God? Religious feeling that is mere projection is inherently escapist—often a kind of irresponsible aestheticism.

Just as our need for human love is not met by hearing about human love, so our need for God's acceptance seems not to be met if we only hear about that acceptance. And since God has no body, no spatial location, we cannot encounter him by turning away from the things of this world which do have spatial location, for there is no place to turn to. If we say that we turn within we must ask, with Wittgenstein, whether there is an inner life that is not dependent on our life in the world. But we need not repeat here our discussion of Wittgenstein.

This interpretation of Tillich must not be taken to mean that experiences we have in solitude are necessarily suspect. T. S. Eliot has somewhere suggested that our experience is like a partially developed roll of film. Later moments may bring out more fully the meaning of an experience. Paul's Damascus Road experience, for example, was not without a basis in the relations that constituted his life at that time, for it was clearly rooted in his encounter with Christians, such as Stephen, whom he was persecuting.

Verification

With this sketch of the experiential base of Tillich's thought, we may consider more fully the fundamental expectations concerning future experience in terms of which religious belief, as Tillich interprets it, is subject to verification or falsification. That these are genuine expectations that are incompatible with certain conceivable states of affairs may be brought out by showing the conflict of Tillich's beliefs with those of Freud and of Harvey Cox. If Freud or Cox are right, the paradigm cases of what Tillich means by an experience of God do not actually exist; they have connotation but no denotation.

We need here particularly to remind ourselves that the verification problem does not take the same form in the case of Tillich's view of God as it does in the case of those who think of God as a divine being who is beyond the world of our experience but manifests himself through events or characteristics of that world. If verification is logically possible only where one expects to experience this rather than that, then verification is *not* logically possible in the case of "something" in principle beyond all possible experience.[68] The issues, however,

---

[68] We can, of course, verify things that we cannot experience—e.g., that Jesus was crucified. But we know in this case what it would be like to experience these

between Tillich and Freud, and between Tillich and Cox, are issues about this world and not about something beyond all experience. More pointedly, they are issues about the nature of religious awareness.

According to Tillich, in the act of self-affirmation we experience the courage-giving presence of the Holy as a dimension of our experience of receiving acceptance from another. To call this an act of self-affirmation or of receiving the courage to accept acceptance is not simply to hang a label on an experience. If this is truly an act of self-affirmation we will not be the same in the future for we will have received a new being. A reconciliation has taken place which nothing in the future has the power to break. This reconciliation makes possible an ultimate courage by which to face the anxieties of finite life. We can face death differently, for reconciliation has removed its sting. We need not be overwhelmed by a loss of meaning in our situation for in reconciliation we become aware of an ultimate meaning that no situation can remove. Above all we can offer unconditional love which, before receiving God's total forgiveness, it was not possible to do because "he who is forgiven little, loves little." (Luke 7:47 RSV) [69]

But we must bear in mind the ecstatic nature of the act of self-affirmation and so of the expectations and of the idea of God which are based on it. According to Tillich, "the term 'ecstatic' in the phrase 'ecstatic idea of God' points to the experience of the holy as transcending ordinary experience without removing it." [70] We experience God as that power which enables us to transcend our limiting finitude while yet remaining finite. As Tillich put it, we live in two orders: the historical and the eternal.[71] Our expectations, then, are that the problems and distortions of our finite existence have been conquered but not that they have been removed; conquered means that (1) we face them very differently when we see them in the context of such ecstatic experiences and (2) we have hope that at moments in the future we shall again be able to act in a way that transcends the ordinary limitations of our actions. We find both these points expressed in the writings of Martin Buber: "everything tells you that full mutuality is not inherent in men's life together. It is a grace, for which one must always be ready and which one never gains as an assured

---

things and so we understand how documents, etc., are related to them as evidence for them. But if we do not know what it would be like to experience God we do not know how manifestations of God are related to God—i.e., we do not know what it means to call them manifestations.

[69] See Tillich, *The New Being*, pp. 12-13.
[70] *Systematic Theology*, II, 8.
[71] See for example, *The Shaking of the Foundations*, pp. 12-23.

possession." [72] However, from such moments of mutuality we see that

because this human being exists, meaninglessness, however hard pressed you are by it, cannot be the real truth. Because this human being exists, in the darkness the light lies hidden, in fear salvation, and in the callousness of one's fellow-men the great Love.[73]

Rollo May, too, in his distinction between ordinary and creative or ecstatic consciousness of self expresses something paralleling Tillich's belief: although, for most of us, moments of ecstatic consciousness are not common, "the fact that at some instant we have been able to see truth unclouded by our own prejudices, to love other persons without demand for ourselves, and to create in the ecstacy that occurs when we are totally absorbed in what we are doing—the fact that we have these glimpses gives a basis of meaning and direction for all our later actions." [74]

The other side of these expectations defining the reconciled life are the contrasting expectations concerning the unreconciled life—life prior to self-affirmation. In the natural law tradition of Plato, Aristotle, Aquinas, Spinoza, Marx, Fromm, Brunner, the Niebuhrs, et al., to which Tillich belongs, the active man and the passive man are contrasted. Every man is born with certain distinctively human potentialities—potentialities, that is, which are rooted in the distinctively human capacity for self-awareness. In developing and actively using these powers one finds joy and liberation; he finds the liberation of actions in which his true nature is expressed. In failing to use these powers one experiences despair and the bondage of pseudo-actions or passions in which he is pushed around by forces strange to his true nature. Rollo May, for example, analyzes the emptiness, loneliness and anxiety of modern man in terms of our passive conformity.[75] Erich Fromm sees the passive obedience of authoritarian religion as resulting in weakness and self-destruction.[76] David Roberts points to the hidden price paid by the moralistic man who passively subjects himself to external moral authority: "The price may include a sacrifice in whole-heartedness, deep friendship, full experience of both the bodily and the spiritual riches of human love, steady joy in living, the unforced employment of talents he already possesses, and the development of interests which have never been given a chance," not to mention

[72] *I and Thou*, p. 131.
[73] *Between Man and Man*, trans. Ronald Gregor Smith (Boston: Beacon Press, 1955), p. 98.
[74] *Man's Search for Himself*, p. 142.
[75] *Man's Search for Himself*.
[76] *Psychoanalysis and Religion* (New Haven: Yale University Press, 1950).

psychosomatic ills.[77] And Joseph Wood Krutch relates the unhappiness of our affluent civilization to his belief that "men who have been conditioned to think or behave unnaturally are unhappy—as unhappy and as inefficient as swimming robins." [78] Thoroughly conditioned to the life of the *Brave New World*, Helmholtz can still reject it in the name of a dimly felt need for something more meaningful. The slate may be blank, but it seems to possess contours to which the lines of experience must be made to conform. But the metaphor of a blank slate is too static, used as it typically is to express the contrasting expectations of relativism. William Blake put it better. "Energy is Eternal Delight," he said. "He who desires but acts not breeds pestilence."

Now for Tillich the fundamental potentiality is the capacity of finite man for the infinite. It is in the act of self-affirmation made possible by God's acceptance that we experience the full meaning of being the active, truly human man. It is in this ecstatic act that we become aware of the full meaning of freedom, of being the author of our own actions, and of having an ultimate goal or aim or destiny for our existence. Tillich's expectations were that, failing this self-affirmation, we pay the price of the ultimately passive life; particularly we pay the price of idolatrous relations in which we look to something finite to furnish the ultimate meaning and acceptance and courage which we cannot do without and which come only from God.

Freud's expectations concerning the nature of religious experience are in marked contrast to those of Tillich except, as we have contended, in those cases where such experience is not an appropriate part of our interaction with our world. According to Tillich, when awareness of the holy is rooted in the believer's present life in the world the result is an ultimate courage to live honestly and creatively. Freud, however, believed that all such awareness is simply a regression to the child's dependency feelings toward the father—feelings of awe, of helplessness, of a desperate need to be protected by the strength of another, and of a security under that protection. The projection of these feelings into the present is a way of refusing to face reality and so strengths that might have been developed remain dormant. Contrary to Tillich, Freud believed that the result of centering life in such awareness is to block courage and perpetuate a dishonest and infantile way of

---

[77] *Psychotherapy and a Christian View of Man* (New York: Scribner's, 1950), p. 98.
[78] "Life, Liberty and the Pursuit of Welfare," in the *Saturday Evening Post*, July 15, 1961, reprinted in *Contemporary Moral Issues*, ed. Harry K. Girvetz (Belmont, California: Wadsworth Publishing Company, 1963), p. 370.

life. Even concerning the mystical element in such awareness, it was Freud's conviction that it "seeks to reinstate limitless narcissism" and is "another way taken by the ego of denying the dangers it sees threatening it in the external world." [79]

Believing that "infantilism is destined to be surmounted," Freud urged an "irreligious education" that would encourage this result.[80] Again contrary to Tillich, Freud believed that religion will be shown, in this way, to be rooted merely in the contingencies of history—personal and perhaps also social—rather than in human nature itself.

Tillich's reply to Freud is that religion does commonly involve projection of the father image but that the screen onto which the image is projected is that which is ultimate, the true object of man's ultimate concern. By "ultimate," though, Tillich meant the source of ultimate courage and meaning, so that the metaphor of a screen simply expresses Tillich's belief that awareness of the holy does in fact provide resources of courage and strength as opposed to Freud's belief that this awareness is the expression of an infantilism that blocks courage. The point to be emphasized is that Tillich and Freud have conflicting expectations concerning the nature of religious awareness. The issue between them is cognitive.

One of Tillich's critics, in fact, has argued that belief in God based on alleged awareness of God is more vulnerable to Freud's attack than is belief in God based on reasons of the sort offered by traditional theism.[81] But the point of our discussion has been this very vulnerability, for cognitive statements are falsifiable, and falsifiable means vulnerable. By conceiving of God as somehow outside of experience, belief in God is made less vulnerable, but as belief is made less vulnerable its cognitive status becomes more doubtful.

Tillich's belief concerning religious experience is also attacked by those who contend that the anxieties of which he speaks, and so the religious question of a source of courage by which to face these anxieties, are due to the conditions of past ages and are not an inescapable part of the human situation. Harvey Cox expresses this by saying:

we are pragmatic men whose interest in religion is at best peripheral. It *is* true that at the center of our pragmatic questions we can hear echoes of older ones about how to be saved, how to overcome guilt and insufficiency, how to discern significance, and how to live purposefully. But . . . secular

[79] *Civilization and Its Discontents*, p. 21.

[80] *The Future of an Illusion*, pp. 84-86.

[81] William P. Alston, "Psychological Explanations of Religious Belief," in *Faith and the Philosophers*, ed. John Hick (New York: St. Martin's Press, 1964), pp. 87-92.

man relies on himself and his colleagues for answers. He does not ask the church, the priest, or God.[82]

In the final analysis, those who hold this sort of view see nature as man's fundamental problem and nature is rapidly being mastered. Man is not inherently a problem to himself; there is nothing beyond his mastery. On this assumption, history can be read by Marx as a march toward fully human man in the classless society, by Cox as a march from tribal-man through town-man to secular-city man, by Comte as a march from religious-man through metaphysical-man to scientific-man.

Tillich agreed that the trend of Western culture, at least in the last three hundred years, has been a trend "towards ever increasing loss of religious consciousness." He saw this, however, not as a mark of modern man's liberation but as a mark of modern man's dehumanization of himself—his ever deepening alienation from himself and also from nature and from others. "How indeed," asked Maritain, "could God still live in a world from which his image, i.e., the free and spiritual personality of man is fading away?" Or, as Buber viewed it, "The fact that it is so difficult for present-day man to pray . . . and the fact that it is so difficult for him to carry on genuine talk with his fellow-men are elements of a . . . lack of trust, . . . an innermost sickness."

Tillich found evidence for his view of our situation "in all the various cultural forms which express modern man's interpretation of his existence" [83]—especially in depth psychology. Indeed, one of the functions of the metaphor "depth," for Tillich, is to express the belief that God is the depth of man's cultural life, the belief that man's awareness of God and of the question of God implicit in his sense of finitude find expression throughout his cultural activity. "The unconditioned of which we have immediate awareness without inference, can be recognized in the cultural and natural universe." [84] As we said in relating Tillich to John Wisdom, for Tillich, talk of God draws attention to a pattern in the totality of events that may be seen only from the perspective of an awareness of the unconditioned or the ultimate or the dimension of depth. But we cannot develop here Tillich's analyses of the orders of culture[85] and of nature except to note that the existentialist self-understanding or style of culture which Tillich shared was seen by him as, above all, a protest against the dehumanization of man under the dominant style of Western

[82] *The Secular City* (New York: MacMillan, 1965), p. 70.
[83] *Systematic Theology,* I, 5.
[84] "The Two Types of Philosophy of Religion," p. 26.
[85] See esp., *Theology of Culture.*

culture—the spirit of industrial society—to which Cox's pragmatic man belongs.[86] As Joseph Haroutunian has said of Tillich,

either he or the irreligionists are right, and it makes much difference who is right. If it is true that human existence and anxiety are inseparable one from the other, the secularists are wrong, and their wrongness is a deadly thing. If man is a religious animal under any conceivable culture, then the advocates of a religionless society are doing humanity a dangerous disservice.[87]

This certainly provides a rather pointed answer to the question whether future experience can count for or against Tillich's belief. The issue is a cognitive one.

To avoid confusion, however, it ought to be remembered that Tillich was as critical as the irreligionists are of most of what the latter mean by "religion." But, if dependency means running away from reality by asking another to do for us what we have the power to do for ourselves, then feeling a need for God's love and forgiveness as a source of courage is no more an expression of dependency than is feeling a need for human love and forgiveness. The issue is rather about resources for human courage and strength; it is whether the grace of God—the enabling presence of the Holy Spirit—is fundamental among these resources, or, more accurately, is the depth dimension of all finite resources. As the Marxist, Roger Garaudy, has put it, "If we reject the very name of God, it is because the name implies a presence, a reality, whereas it is only an exigency which we live, a never-satisfied exigency of . . . omnipotence as to nature and of perfect loving reciprocity of consciousness." [88] It is instructive that although Cox speaks often of God as acting in history this turns out, at least in *The Secular City*, not to mean anything more than this sense of exigency coupled with the belief that "there are no powers anywhere which are not essentially tameable and ultimately humanizable" [89]—a belief certainly shared by Garaudy. Although Cox charges that "van Buren is wrong when he states that modern, secular man does not experience the transcendent" [90] he does not succeed in giving any meaning to "transcendent" that van Buren would reject; nor is it clear how he could possibly provide

---

[86] See "Aspects of a Religious Analysis of Culture" (1956), reprinted in *Theology of Culture*, pp. 43-47; also "The Theological Significance of Existentialism and Psychoanalysis" (1955), reprinted in *Theology of Culture*, pp. 113-16.
[87] "The Question Tillich Left Us," *Religion in Life* (Winter, 1966), p. 540; reprinted in *Paul Tillich: Retrospect and Future*, Nels F. S. Ferré, et al. (Nashville: Abingdon Press, 1966), p. 56.
[88] *From Anathema to Dialogue* (New York: Herder and Herder, 1966), p. 94. On page 92 we read, "For the Marxist, the infinite is absence and exigency, while for the Christian, it is promise and presence."
[89] *The Secular City*, p. 112.   [90] *Ibid.*, p. 228.

such a meaning if he rejects the experience of the transcendent as an enabling, courage-giving presence. The issue, then, is not whether God is abyss, absence and exigency—the hidden God—but whether God is also ground, presence, and grace—the revealed God.

We have been attempting to interpret and, at points perhaps, to develop Tillich's thought to show that it does express expectations concerning experience and, so, is not consistent with all possible states of affairs or even with other widely held beliefs. It may be asked, though, whether Tillich's own discussion of religious knowledge is not incompatible with our account, and we must consider briefly the sort of reply that can be made. Tillich's way of putting these things seems to invite misinterpretation, especially if it is not understood in the context of his work as a whole, including his sermons. It is, after all, in his sermons that we see Tillich actually using religious language rather than reflecting on it.

According to Tillich all religious statements are non-literal and symbolic except the statement that God is Being-itself.[91] But, a common criticism goes,[92] if the only thing we can say of God literally is that he is Being-itself, just what it is that the word "God" refers to must remain hopelessly obscure. Those who are not trained to understand ontological talk would have no way at all of knowing what "God" refers to since none of the predicate terms they do understand could be taken literally. Those who think they understand Tillich's sermons, it seems, must be taking something that he says literally and so they really do not understand him. Yet even an understanding of Being-itself does not help much, for we are talking here of something that is beyond all differentiation and so we still do not know what is meant by any of the other terms. Tillich, it seems, has completely segregated the logic of his religious use of terms from the logic of their use in ordinary language. But, as William P. Alston rightly argues, if a system of belief is to provide "an effective identification" of its referent, then "the component assertions in such a system must at some points yield implications concerning experienceable states of affairs."[93] And such assertions, Alston believes, must be literal.

However, Tillich meant by "literal" the meaning a term has in ordinary nonreligious language. In saying that statements about God are non-literal, Tillich was contending their predicate terms do not have just the same meaning that they have in statements about finite persons. But it does not follow from this that such statements fail

---

[91] *Systematic Theology*, I, 238-39. A different formulation is given in II, 9, but the difference does not affect our discussion.

[92] See William P. Alston, "Tillich's Conception of a Religious Symbol," in *Religious Experience and Truth*, ed. Sidney Hook, pp. 13-19.

[93] *Ibid.*, p. 14.

to "yield implications concerning experienceable states of affairs." If "literal" is used to mean yielding implications concerning experienceable states of affairs, then, as I have tried to show, many statements are used literally in Tillich's language-game; they do refer to experience and do express expectations concerning experienceable states of affairs. They are able to function in this way because the logic of their predicates is not unrelated to the logic these predicates have in ordinary use; as I have tried to show, these predicates are applicable only in situations where they would also be applicable in terms of the logic of their ordinary use concerning finite persons.

But there is here another, closely related problem. Tillich contended that true religious symbols—symbols that effectively point to that which is ultimate—have a self-evident or self-verifying character, for they express revelation, and "revelation claims to give a truth which is both certain and of ultimate concern." [94] In other words, revelatory experience gives cognitive certainty.[95] But we have contended that Tillich's belief is vulnerable to future experience and that it is incompatible with the beliefs both of Freud and of Cox concerning religious experience. How can belief be both certain and vulnerable? In reply we must consider (1) that Tillich did not fail to understand the problem, (2) that warranted certainty and vulnerability are often not incompatible, and (3) that the question of what warrants certainty is a meaningful question only in the context of a community of persons in whose language game the word "certain" has the use in question.

Tillich recognized that "the verifying test belongs to the nature of truth"; knowledge of the truth "prevents wrong expectations and consequent disappointments." [96] Verifying tests, he maintained, are of two sorts, experimental and experiential. The repeatable experiment presupposes "isolation, regularity, generality" and so is limited to "separable elements of life-processes"; but life processes themselves "have the character of totality, spontaneity, and individuality" [97] and so knowledge of these processes is verified or falsified only by their cumulative results. To refer once more to John Wisdom, talk of God draws attention to a pattern in the totality of events. The issues between Tillich and Freud, or Tillich and Cox, then, are experiential rather than experimental, for they concern the relation of religious awareness to the life-process as a whole; in each case a different answer is given concerning the sort of life that is most fulfilling. And yet,

[94] Systematic Theology, I, 105.
[95] Religious symbols are rooted in revelatory experience, for "the knowledge of revelation cannot be separated from the situation of revelation." (Ibid., p. 129).
[96] Systematic Theology, I, 102.
[97] Ibid., p. 103.

after emphasizing that no experience within the life-process can give certainty about one's belief, Tillich sees the ecstatic experience of revelation as the exception. In Russell's terminology, ecstatic experience is of a different logical type.

The crucial point to be made here, to defend our contention that Tillich's beliefs are cognitive, is that we do have certainty about all sorts of beliefs which nonetheless are really beliefs—beliefs, that is, which really do exclude certain possible future states of affairs. This, of course, is the important lesson we learned from G. E. Moore. If I am standing before a tree gazing at it, I know with certainty that it is a tree. If I glance away I know with certainty that when I look back I will again see a tree and not a stone pillar or a telephone pole or a rosebush or nothing at all. How could I sensibly doubt that these are reliable expectations? The question, then, is not whether Tillich's contention about the certainty of revelation carries the logical consequence that revelation can have no implications concerning future states of affairs, but whether such certainty is warranted.

The certainty of revelation is a convictional certainty in the sense that we have seen Zuurdeeg use that term. According to Tillich, the believer is simply overwhelmed [98] by the experience of God's forgiveness. He is grasped by something of such power and significance that nothing in the past is even comparable. The believer finds inexhaustible power, ultimate meaning, eternal reconciliation, ecstatic certainty. But this is not simply a matter of the believer feeling a certain way, for certainty is not warranted or justified by feelings. I know with certainty this is a tree, that is a house, there is cheese on the table, yet often have no feeling at all in this connection. As we have seen earlier, criteria for certainty are given as part of the rules of whatever language-game we are playing when we express our certainty. Certainty about this being a tree is one thing, about the next roll of the dice is quite another thing, and about a friend's forgiveness is yet another thing.

The believer makes his judgments as a member of a two-thousand-year-old community of believers. It is in the life-processes of this community that the criteria of its revelations have been established and the expectations have been witnessed to as reliable. Salvation and its ecstatic certainty come not to the isolated individual but to the individual in community.

Tillich's position concerning the ecstatic nature of revelation, however, must be distinguished in one important respect from that of Zuurdeeg, Hordern, and others who have stressed the convictional

[98] *The New Being*, pp. 22, 59.

nature of belief. Tillich's convictions about God concerned a dimension of his experience and not something somehow beyond experience. We can know and believe only what has happened to us in our community. This means that our certainty does not concern any special content of revelation if, by "content," we mean those meanings taken from nonreligious experience by which we symbolize the "object" of religious awareness; in other words, our certainty is not that any particular symbol will continue to function effectively in our lives, not even the symbol of God as a person. The experience of the community, Tillich believed, does not support certainty about symbols—certainty, that is, about the content of its spiritual life.[99] "There are," he argued, "many examples of people . . . who in moments (and even periods) of their lives experienced the failure of the faith they had risked, and who preserved the ontological certainty, the unconditioned element in their faith." [100] Faith, then, involves a genuine risk, a risk "based on the fact that the unconditioned element can become a matter of ultimate concern only if it appears in a concrete embodiment." [101]

The awareness of a certainty that remains when the symbols of one's faith have lost their meaning Tillich called the experience of absolute faith, faith in the God beyond the God symbolized by theism, faith in the God who grasps us with healing power even when we can no longer address him as God. "It is the accepting of the acceptance without somebody or something that accepts." [102] The failure of symbols, in other words, does not undercut the power of self-affirmation, the reconciliation with the holy. This failure does not remove the ultimate courage by which the believer conquers the destructive power of anxiety. However symbolized, revelatory experience is the experience of that power whereby we are enabled to love our lives and, so, to love the other apart from whom life is an empty abstraction. It is this experience which we symbolically express and it is this experience which sustains us when, for the time being, we can no longer express it. In the words of T. S. Eliot, the believer must then

> . . . wait without hope
> For hope would be hope of the wrong thing; wait without love

---

[99] "The message of the new reality in the Christ . . . does not contain an easy answer and . . . does not guarantee any spiritual security." (*The Shaking of the Foundations*, p. 75). "Spiritual," for Tillich, refers to the meanings by which man lives. "Spiritual self-affirmation occurs in every moment in which man lives creatively in the various spheres of meaning." Therefore nonbeing "threatens man's spiritual self-affirmation, relatively in terms of emptiness, absolutely in terms of meaninglessness." (*The Courage to Be*, pp. 46, 41.)

[100] "The Two Types of Philosophy of Religion," p. 28.

[101] *Ibid.*

[102] *The Courage to Be*, p. 185.

For love would be love of the wrong thing; there is yet faith
But the faith and the love and the hope are all in the waiting.[103]

"The God above the God of theism," Tillich believed, "is not the devaluation of meanings which doubt has thrown into the abyss of meaninglessness; he is their potential restitution." [104]

This loss of symbols, it must be emphasized, does not imply the death of those expectations which are the basic cognitive content of the conviction that nothing can separate us from the love of God. The believer is convinced that he continues in the power of reconciliation which overcomes his enmity toward life or, more broadly, that he continues to receive an ultimate courage by which he conquers the anxieties of death, condemnation, and meaninglessness. He actively affirms himself, that is, in-spite-of these threats to his selfhood. The very act of facing his loss of meaning is, in fact, an expression of this courage. As Tillich put it, "revelation claims to give a truth which . . . includes and accepts the risk and uncertainty of every significant cognitive act, yet transcends it in accepting it." [105]

This is what Tillich meant in calling the believer's certainty "ecstatic." It is the certainty that he is empowered to accept uncertainty. And, in transcending his uncertainty, the believer discovers himself grasped by that in which he finds the ultimate meaning and aim of his life. Such certainty belongs to a different order of experience than do our ordinary certainties: "the certainty that . . . we are united with the eternal meaning of our life, is either itself eternal or is nothing." [106] On the matter of certainty, then, the difference between this belief and ordinary beliefs is not that this belief is consistent with every possible future state of affairs; it is rather that many of our ordinary beliefs concern things about which we are or may become anxious, whereas this belief concerns that which overcomes these anxieties.

To speak of certainty as ecstatic is to say that doubt is overcome without being removed; the believer remains in the situation of doubt while transcending it. "Every theologian," said Tillich, "is committed *and* alienated; he is always in faith *and* in doubt; he is inside *and* outside the theological circle." [107]

It is an important point concerning the vulnerability of belief to remember that its expectations concern more than the life of the community of believers. Jesus' followers "had the certitude that they were healed, *and* that the healing power amongst them was great

[103] "East Coker," *The Complete Poems and Plays* (New York: Harcourt Brace Jovanovich, 1952), pp. 126-27.
[104] *The Courage to Be*, p. 186.
[105] *Systematic Theology*, I, 105.
[106] *The Shaking of the Foundations*, p. 138.
[107] *Systematic Theology*, I, 10.

enough to conquer individuals and nations all over the world." [108]
That God is the father of all men, then, involves two certainties both
of which are incompatible with certain possible states of affairs:

One dwells in every soul which knows about itself. It is the certainty which
the law imposes that no life and no death, no courage and no flight, can
liberate us from the command to be what we ought to be and the impossibility to be so, the condemnation of which is despair. . . . The other
certainty dwells in those who have the Spirit; they are beyond their own
finiteness and they cannot use arguments, for their eternity is present to
them. It is not a matter of a future life after death; it is the convincing
presence of the Spirit Who is Life, beyond life and death.[109]

If the word "God" were used in this community to refer to something
that was of consequence for some men but not for others, belief would
concern a god rather than the one God. "God," that is, would refer
not to a transcendent reality but to some aspect of finite life—say,
a quality of life in a certain community.

There is, of course, no justification offered here for attempting to
impose this belief on others or for relating to them with an attitude
of spiritual superiority. "We point," Tillich insisted, "to the truth
which possesses us, but which we do not possess." [110] It is God alone
who convinces.

With this sketch of some of the fundamentals of Tillich's position,
I have tried to indicate the experiential basis of his thought; everything stands or falls, finally, with his view of the nature of religious
awareness. Lack of agreement concerning religious awareness has important roots (1) in the projective nature of much that is labeled
religious awareness, (2) in those cultural factors contributing to the
loss of religious sensitivity, (3) in the sheer complexity of human
experience, (4) in the fact that we interpret our experience in light
of those personal and historical events which have had a particularly
great impact on us, and, (5) in the turning away from God which
expresses our unwillingness to be man—particularly to be guilty man.
But one further observation needs to be made about religious awareness
and this concerns the long tradition of those who do not necessarily
deny an immediate awareness of God, but maintain, rather, that such
awareness is much too vague or ambiguous to be the focal point of
faith. To borrow an analogy used by Aquinas, "to know that someone
is approaching is not the same as to know that Peter is approaching,
even though it is Peter who is approaching." [111] Tillich was saying

---

[108] *The New Being*, p. 39. Italics are mine.
[109] *The Shaking of the Foundations*, pp. 137-38.
[110] *Ibid.*, p. 125.
[111] *Summa Theologica*, I, P. I., Q. II, a. 1.

that what we mean by "Peter" must be what we are aware of in those situations symbolized by "Peter approaching." For Aquinas, then, very little of God is revealed in religious awareness; for Tillich everything that concerns us ultimately is revealed in religious awareness. This difference in evaluation of religious awareness suggests that the evaluators have their hearts set on different things. If, for the believer, the eschaton is an ecstatic reconciliation with God in-spite-of the conditions of estrangement which mark life in this world, the experience of reconciliation will be very differently evaluated by him—evaluated as an overwhelming experience of God—than it will be by the believer for whom the eschaton is life with God in the world to come, a life qualitatively different from this present life. As one critic has put it, Tillich speaks of the *anxieties* of death, of condemnation, and of meaninglessness as being overcome while we believe that death, condemnation and meaninglessness will themselves be removed. Since we may here and now experience immediately an empowering to face anxiety creatively but may not here and now experience immediately the removal of those conditions of finitude which create this anxiety, if one believes that God promises the latter then one will think of God in terms only loosely tied to what we immediately experience. Of course, to speak of God as outside of our experience raises all the problems of logic that we have examined at length in preceding chapters. We can wonder if it is Peter who is approaching only if we have had, or at least know from experience what it would be like to have, a fuller, clearer experience of Peter. But the point in our present discussion is that we judge religious experience in light of our convictions. Just as the distinction touched on earlier between active man and passive man rests on having been overwhelmed by the experience of the joy of using one's own powers, so the contention that we are immediately aware of God rests on having been overwhelmed by the experience of being enabled completely to affirm oneself and others. By "God" Tillich meant this enabling presence which concerned him ultimately.

The Prophetic–Biblical Concept of God Acting

If, as we have tried to show at least in outline, Tillich's position does meet the logical requirements for talking meaningfully "about" God, then it is important to show the relation of Tillich's position to the biblical concept of God as acting in history. We have said that to picture God as the depth of being is to indicate that men are grasped by the holy in and only in their relations with the finite world. We have further said that to speak of God as personal is to indicate that men are sometimes grasped by the holy in their encounters with other persons as persons.

As Martin Buber expressed it, "Every particular *Thou* is a glimpse through to the eternal *Thou*; by means of every particular Thou the primary word addresses the eternal Thou." [112] To speak of God as personal means not that he is *a person* who can be spoken about in language having a logic closely similar to the logic of our language about persons but that in those moments of relation with others which are most personal the religious dimension may become a part of our conscious awareness. The belief that the divine ground is personal, that is, involves the expectation that we may become aware of the divine in those relations with other persons which are marked by empathy and agapeistic concern rather than in those relations with others which are marked by a distant, objectifying, and impersonal attitude. This talk, however, of the religious dimension in our experience of the finite should not be taken to suggest that the religious is in some way subordinate to the other aspects. Buber says of one's relation with God that "everything is gathered up in the relation. For to step into pure relation is not to disregard everything but to see everything in the *Thou*, not to renounce the world but to establish it on its true basis." [113]

If, then, to speak of God as personal is to mean that our most personal relations may be experienced as having an ultimate depth, it follows that *to speak of God as acting is to mean that certain actions of finite persons may be experienced as having this religious depth.* One might express it that God acts through the actions of a human being. To speak of God as loving me or forgiving me means, then, that in the love or forgiveness of another person I may experience not just that person's love or his forgiveness but the holy depth of all love and forgiveness. That experience of finite love is permeated with a sense of ultimacy, a sense of being grasped by something wholly other. As Tillich expressed it in *The New Being*, "We do not merely love others, but we love the Love that is in them and which is more than their or our love." [114]

This interpretation, we have argued, provides us with a solution to the problem of how one can meaningfully apply terms like "loving" and "forgiving" to God when their ordinary meaning is tied to the physical activity of the human body—taking one's children into one's arms, uttering appropriate words, etc. Since God is not conceived of

[112] *I and Thou*, p. 75.   [113] *Ibid.*, pp. 78-79.   [114] *The New Being*, p. 173.

as corporeal, he cannot meaningfully be conceived of as another being even with the exception that various imperfections have been whittled away from our concept of human beings. Rather one speaks of God as "loving" and "forgiving" because it is in the "love" and "forgiveness" of another human being that one may experience God rather than in actions opposite to these. In other words, *one may use of God the language used of human beings because we become aware of God in our experience of those human beings.*

To show that this interpretation is meaningfully related to the biblical perspective, it will be helpful if we first relate the concept of God acting to the two closely related concepts of God speaking and God revealing himself.[115] A person reveals himself through his actions, loving actions revealing a loving person, hostile actions a hostile person, etc. One may speak, then, of God revealing himself in those actions of finite persons in which he is experienced or, more correctly, through which he grasps us. But divine revelation involves not only action but a response to that action. It is not simply that, as is also true of the revelation of one finite person to another, actions have the power to reveal only to the extent that they are understood by the recipient. To respond to an act as an act of God is not merely a matter of interpretation. It is also to see in that act a norm for one's own actions. In Donald Evans' terminology,[116] this response finds expression in a self-involving utterance. We shall see at a later point how this is entailed by what has already been said concerning the logic of statements about God acting.

On the face of it, there would seem to be no point in making the further distinction of God speaking. Speaking is, after all, a form of acting, and, so, statements about speaking do not involve any significantly different rules than do statements about other forms of acting. Consistent with our interpretation of statements about God acting, one could merely say that statements about God speaking mean that we become aware of God in certain verbal actions of finite persons. There is, however, another aspect of the logic of the prophetic concept of God acting which warrants a special use of the concept of God speaking. In the prophetic concept, God calls men to be the means by which he acts in the lives of others. Whenever one is sensitive to another's need for God and to the possibility of being an agent

[115] While it is true that the biblical writings are varied in perspective the concept of God acting in history belongs to the prophetic tradition, and it is to this perspective that we allude. We shall consider the J, E, and D writings in the Pentateuch as within this tradition.

[116] See Chap. VIII.

in meeting that need by allowing God to act through him, this may be expressed as God speaking. The norm for this judgment, of course, will be those previous actions to which one responds as divine revelation. This may best be elucidated by considering the way in which the interpretations we have offered are meaningfully related to the biblical (prophetic) perspective.

Those occurrences which are seen by the biblical writers as acts of God center in the acts of human beings. In that act which is central to the Old Testament, the exodus, it is Moses who leads the people out of Egypt. The prophets saw in this an act of God; others, such as the Egyptians, did not. The "J" writer is representative of prophetic thought in seeing it to be Israel's mission to be the means through which God acts to heal the Gentile nations: "The Lord said to Abram '. . . I will make of you a great nation, . . . and by you all the families of the earth will bless themselves.'" (Gen. 12:1-3 RSV) The book of Jonah, in which the hero attempts to evade God's will that he be God's instrument in behalf of the hated Assyrians, may be seen as a criticism of post-exilic Judaism for turning away from her mission as the means by which God might act in the lives of other nations, and withdrawing instead to preserve an alleged purity brought about by the suffering of the exile and furthered by strict adherence to the Law. In the central event of the New Testament, God acts through the actions of Jesus to "reconcile the world to himself."

If the exodus, then, is seen to be an act of God, it follows that God is seen to reveal something of himself in this act. Since this is an act of deliverance, God is seen to be a deliverer. But to respond to an act as an act of God is also to see in that act a norm for one's own actions. In Deuteronomy 10:15, 19, for example, we read: "The Lord set his heart in love upon your fathers; . . . love the sojourner therefore, for you were sojourners in the land of Egypt." (RSV) Or, we may take a similar passage, Exodus 22:21, in which the writer admonishes: "You shall not wrong a stranger or oppress him, for you were strangers in the land of Egypt." (RSV) Similarly, in the case of the New Testament, since the acts of Jesus were those of reconciling love, God is revealed as a God of reconciling love. These actions become normative for those who see them as an act of God, as is evident, for example, in Philippians 2:5: "Let this mind be in you, which was also in Christ Jesus." We may take as another example the First Letter of John: "If God so loved us, we ought also to love one another." (4:11) It is perhaps of interest to note some striking passages to this effect in Martin Luther's "Treatise on Christian Liberty."

A Christian . . . ought to . . . in every way deal with his neighbor as he sees that God through Christ has dealt . . . with himself.[117]
I will do and suffer all things, just as Christ did and suffered far more for me.[118]
I will therefore give myself as a Christ to my neighbor.[119]

The special sense that we have given to God speaking—i.e., the sensitivity of the "hearer" to another's need for an act of God for which he can be the agent, allowing God to act through him—is quite justified by the central place in the biblical drama occupied by the experience of being "called" by God to be the means by which God acts in the lives of others. This is given classic expression in Isaiah's account of his call which ends: "And I heard the voice of the Lord saying, 'Whom shall I send, and who will go for us?' Then I said, 'Here I am! Send me.'" (Isa. 6:8 RSV) Similarly, Moses' return to Egypt to lead the exodus was occasioned by his burning bush experience or encounter with God on Mount Sinai: "The Lord said, 'I have seen the affliction of my people who are in Egypt, . . . and I have come down to deliver them out of the hand of the Egyptians. . . . Come, I will send you to Pharaoh that you may bring forth my people . . . out of Egypt.'" (Exod. 3:7-10 RSV) As Bernhard Anderson puts it, "God's word came to Moses in a moment when he was acutely conscious of the historical situation of his people in Egypt." [120] In Jesus' case there were, of course, the forty days spent in the wilderness directly preceding the beginning of his ministry.

We have so far limited our interpretation of the biblical concept of God acting to his redemptive acts. God acts through or is experienced as the depth in the redemptive actions of human beings. But preceding these acts of healing are often said to occur acts of judgment. Thus, to reconcile his people to himself and to his task for them, God visits upon the Israelites the terrible judgment of defeat at the hands of the cruel Assyrians and upon the Judeans the Babylonian exile. How, in our account, are these "acts" to be interpreted?

An act of divine judgment is here interpreted in terms of that moment in which destructive elements within the recipient(s) can no longer be covered up but erupt into the surface into plain view. These destructive elements may precipitate this crisis themselves, as, for example, in the case of the crucifixion in which elements of hostility toward love are made visible. Or, we may take as another example a point made by Rollo May concerning neurotic attitudes:

[117] In Martin Luther, *Three Treatises* (Philadelphia: Muhlenberg Press, 1947), pp. 277-78.
[118] *Ibid.*, p. 282.   [119] *Ibid.*, p. 278.
[120] *Rediscovering the Bible* (New York: Association Press, 1951), p. 58.

No matter how clearly the neurosis may be shown to be based on sheer falsehood, the patient will not give it up until his suffering becomes insupportable.

Fortunately the wheels of life do grind relentlessly on and bring a just portion of suffering as a penalty for every neurotic attitude. When this misery becomes so great that the individual is willing to give up his wrong attitude . . . he has arrived at that state of desperation which Kunkel says is prerequisite for any cure at all.[121]

The moment in which this suffering becomes so great that one can no longer avoid facing the negative elements that produce it is the moment of judgment. It is a moment in which one experiences acutely his estrangement from others. When one experiences this separation from the finite as, at the same time, a separation from its depth or God, one experiences this as a moment of divine judgment. Or, rather, this is at least a fundamental part of what is involved.

The crisis in which these disruptive elements become visible is not always precipitated by those elements themselves, however. In the case of God's judgment of Israel and Judah, it was the aggression of Assyria and Babylon which created a situation in which the nation's true spiritual condition became evident. As Anderson says, for example,

Before Israel could understand the depth of God's forgiveness, his people had to know the reality of their sin, the fact of their estrangement from him. And, for some strange reason, people do not readily acknowledge their need for God's love and their dependence upon him until their self-centered and self-sufficient way of life has been shaken to its foundations.

Israel's change of attitude would not necessarily have prevented Assyrian aggression, but it would have made a difference, in the way the people faced the political situation.[122]

In the words of Hosea, "I will return again to my place, until they acknowledge their guilt and seek my face, and in their distress they seek me, saying, 'Come, let us return to the Lord; for he has torn, that he may heal us; he has stricken, and he will bind us up.'" (5:15–6:1 RSV)

In our analysis so far, then, the logic of the term "act" used in connection with moments of divine judgment is significantly different from that of its use with respect to moments of reconciliation in which we become aware of God as present within the reconciling acts of finite persons. In moments of judgment our interaction with others expresses our alienation from them and so our alienation from

---

[121] *The Art of Counseling* (Apex ed.; Nashville: Abingdon Press, 1967), p. 157.
[122] *Rediscovering the Bible*, pp. 110, 115.

God. These actions are marked by the *absence* rather than by the *presence* of God. God is absent, that is, in his personal dimension, for in failing to relate to the finite as personal, we fail to relate to God as its personal depth. To quote again from Hosea: "'The pride of Israel testifies to his face; Ephraim shall stumble in his guilt; Judah also shall stumble with them. With their flocks and herds they shall go to seek the Lord, but they will not find him; he has withdrawn from them." (5:5-6 RSV) God is here experienced as abyss but not as sustaining ground, as we have interpreted the logic of these spatial metaphors. So far, then, in our analysis such moments cannot properly be spoken of as acts of God, since, in rejecting the interventionist interpretation of the logic of "act of God," we have rejected any *impersonal* meanings of "act" when used of God, such as a miraculous contravening of the laws of nature so as to walk on water, or to cause the sun to stand still, or to cause water-soaked wood to burst into flame. "Act," in our account, is properly to be used only with reference to our experience of God as personal—as the depth experienced in our personal encounters with others. We must, then, further distinguish between personal and impersonal meanings of the term "judgment."

The distinction we have in mind is well made by C. H. Dodd in his interpretation of Paul's doctrine of justification by faith through grace. Moffatt translates Rom. 3:23-24: "All have sinned, all come short of the glory of God, but they are justified for nothing by his grace." What Paul is doing in this use of the term "justification," says Dodd, "is to appeal to the prophetic strain in biblical religion against the legalistic strain which prevailed in the Judaism of his own time." [123] Paul is using the term primarily in its Greek meaning of legal acquittal.[124] His use of this legal (and so impersonal) term with respect to God, however, according to Dodd, is paradoxical:

To say that men are acquitted before the divine tribunal is sheer paradox. Paul meant it to be so. If the dealing of God with sinful men is to be described in legal terms at all (as Paul and his fellow-Pharisees were accustomed to describe it), then it can be described only in terms of paradox. For the fact is that, though men have deserved ill of God, He does not give them their deserts. . . . We may note that in the Old Testament the very phrase, "to justify the wicked," is constantly used of unjust judges (e.g. Isa. v. 23; Prov. xvii. 15; Exod. xxiii. 7). Paul, therefore, was fully aware what a daring thing he was doing in attributing such a thing to God.

[123] *The Epistle of Paul to the Romans*, a volume of *The Moffatt New Testament Commentary*, ed. James Moffatt (New York: Harper, n.d.), p. 50.
[124] This meaning is flavored, however, by an Old Testament use found in Isa. 46:13 and 51:5 in which it means "an act by which a wronged person is given his rights, is vindicated, delivered from oppression." (*Ibid.*, p. 51.)

The real moral is that *the personal relations of God to men cannot be described in legal terms at all.*[125]

The *impersonal* side of judgment is expressed in terms of the "wrath": "in due time sin would by the law of cause and effect bring its own retribution—the wrath." [126] On the *personal* side, "God's righteousness is revealed if, over and against the terrible spectacle of the wrath at work (as Paul has described it in chap. i.), there is a divine intervention by which man is delivered from sin and wrath," delivered that is, from his destructive condition and its consequences.[127]

Insofar, then, as the relationships involved in a moment of judgment are not impersonal, legalistic, and condemning, but *personal*, it becomes possible to speak of a divine *act* of judgment. Unless judgment is experienced in a context of personal relationship, it cannot become part of a healing, meaning-restoring process. Thus Roberts observes that "many of the attempts to convict men of sin which the Church has used are harmful." [128] One of the reasons for this is that "this facing of shortcomings is never constructive unless it can be carried through in a situation *where a man is accepted* in spite of them." [129] The "in spite of" expresses the element of judgment which is not removed by the acceptance offered in the personal relationship but which can be faced creatively in the context of such a relationship. A divine act of judgment means experientially that one experiences God's acceptance-*in-spite-of*. In other words, one experiences the depth of the acceptance-*in-spite-of* which is enacted by another human being.

Let us consider, for example, the moment of judgment between persons in which that which is disruptive of their relationship erupts into the open and their lack of personal relationship and trust is brought to a crisis. Faced impersonally the division cannot be overcome. But there is another possibility which Martin Buber describes:

That which never reveals itself outside of crisis, the power of turning, begins to work when he who is gripped by despair, instead of allowing himself to fall, calls forth his primal powers, . . . [calls forth] that which moves secretly in the depths—the latent healing and solution.[130]

When the estranged persons turn toward each other to establish a personal relationship, they are speaking what Buber terms "the living

---

[125] *The Epistle of Paul . . .*, p. 52. Italics mine.
[126] *Ibid.*, p. 60.
[127] *Ibid.*
[128] *Psychotherapy and a Christian View of Man*, p. 111.
[129] *Ibid.* Italics mine.
[130] "Genuine Conversation and the Possibilities of Peace," *Cross Currents*, 1957, p. 295.

word" which "draws the poison out of the differences in interests and convictions" so that they face their situation "not overlooking what divides them, but determined to bear it in common." [131]

The aggression of the Assyrians against the Israelites or of the Babylonians against Judah does not in itself qualify as an act of God on other than an interventionist view of the logic of this concept. Under these external threats, the behavior of the Israelites and Judeans was such as to uncover the true character of their economic and religious practices. And this "uncovering" is certainly a moment of judgment, but it is a moment of the *absence* of God (as personal) and not of the *active presence* of God. God could be encountered as personally present only insofar as these crises successfully motivated a personal turning toward each other in which the "primal powers of healing" were discovered in a depth to which the disruption could not reach.

In our analysis, a moment of judgment—a moment in which disruptive elements find open expression—involves an act of God when it becomes not simply a moment of the absence of God, but also a moment of acceptance-in-spite-of. In this act, one is offered reconciliation in spite of what separates. In our view of man, acceptance must always include an element of in-spite-of. For this reason, the offer of acceptance—unconditional, unearned acceptance—is commonly rejected, for it is painful to face the in-spite-of. Only as one is no longer able to hide these disruptive elements behind a facade of defense "mechanisms" or stratagems can one allow himself to become conscious of God acting in his situation. Acceptance in-spite-of, then, involves both judgment and acceptance. The two are inseparably united in an act of God. Our awareness of the holy, we may say, involves both a mystical side, in which we become aware of the ultimate meaning that is relationship with the ground of our being, and a judging-transforming side, in which we become aware of the imperative that reconciliation replace alienation and estrangement. In terms of our earlier discussion of biblical language, it involves both a divine acting in which meaningful relationship is offered and a divine speaking in which we experience a call to move against the disruptive elements in which we are involved.

The solution that our analysis offers to the problem of how the religious and ordinary use of terms are related is based on the premise that the basic cognitive function of religious language is to relate religious awareness to the various areas of our experience; in other words, talk of God functions cognitively in drawing attention to—and

---

[131] *Ibid.*, pp. 295, 296.

so either directly or indirectly, asserting the existence of—a pattern in the totality of events that may be seen only from the perspective of an awareness of the unconditioned or ultimate. In the account that we have given of this function, the picture of God as a being has been replaced by the spatial metaphors "ground" and "depth." If God is pictured as the depth of the finite world, then references to God do not cease being references to the finite world, but become references to its depth dimension. The words used retain their original logic insofar as they refer to the finite world. They take on their religious function insofar as in referring to the finite world they refer to its relation to its depth. To refer to God as personal means that we may become aware of him as the depth in finite persons. To refer to God as acting means that he may grasp us through finite actions.

In this view, the *expectation* that we may become aware of a religious depth in our experiences of the finite—a depth that enables one to affirm himself, others, and life—defines one of the basic differences or "contrasts" between believing God to be objectively real, believing God to "exist," and believing that "God" does not have a reference transcending the finite. In this view, God does not exist as a being. The expectations accepted by our analysis as properly attendant upon the use of the term "God" are not the sort that one has in connection with the existence of particular beings.

This expectation has as its corollary the expectation that one will not find his relationships with the finite world adequately meaningful unless he is at the same time relating to its depth. At some level of his awareness, the autonomous man knows an emptiness, a meaninglessness, an ultimate estrangement to which he has no answer. He must either erect defenses against allowing himself to be consciously aware of this emptiness or succumb to conscious despair over the lack of meaning, i.e., to nihilism. Basic to these defenses is idolatry, the attempt to substitute something finite for God—the attempt to find adequate meaning for one's life in a relationship with the finite. To treat something finite as more than finite has had several consequences. If the idol is destroyed, the result is a collapse of meaning. Challenges concerning the idol's adequacy which threaten to uncover the idolater's own doubts on the matter must be fanatically resisted. In cases of conflict, all other finite interests must be sacrificed to the absolutized interests of the idol.

The work of Reinhold Niebuhr is among the more penetrating attempts to verify this expectation that, failing to accept a relationship with God, man falls into one of the closely related conditions of nihilism or idolatry—"the worldly wisdom which either makes sense out of life too simply or which can find no sense in life at all." [132] He marshalls evidence concerning the idolatrous autonomy of our day, that "the hidden despair, which is never absent from complacency, is beginning to reveal itself." [133] Offered as representative is the pilgrimage of H. G. Wells from evolutionary idealism through "desperate optimism" to the complete despair to which he gave the following expression shortly before his death:

A frightful queerness has come into life. Hitherto events have been held together by a certain logical consistency as the heavenly bodies have been held together by the golden cord of gravitation. Now it is as if the cord had vanished and everything is driven anyhow, anywhere at a steadily increasing velocity. . . . The writer is convinced that there is no way out, or around, or through the impasse. It is the end. [134]

These and related expectations contain far-reaching implications for the church. If we experience God as personal only as we experience finite persons,[135] we must *expect* talk of the reconciling love of God to remain mere cliché to those who do not experience reconciling love from another human being. Merely to be told that this love of God was once experienced in the love of Jesus becomes irrelevant because Jesus no longer exists to offer this love. What is required is that the love of God be given concrete expression in the life of the church as its members respond to the life of Jesus as a revelatory event by making it the ideal pattern for themselves. In this way the church becomes the *body* of Christ, the concrete expression of this reconciling love.

If reconciling love is to be enacted between finite persons, whatever is necessary to this must similarly be enacted. Genuine confession, for example, cannot be made to God "alone." As Dietrich Bonhoeffer has put it:

Confess your faults one to another (Jas. 5:16). He who is alone with his sin is utterly alone. It may be that Christians notwithstanding corporate worship, prayer, and all their fellowship in service, may still be left to their loneliness. The final breakthrough to fellowship does not occur, because, though they have fellowship with one another as believers and as

---

[132] *Faith and History* (New York: Scribner's, 1949), p. 163.

[133] *Ibid.*, p. 160.

[134] *The Mind at the End of Its Tether* (London: W. Heinemann, 1945). pp. 4-5.

[135] Having once encountered God in a finite personal relation, we doubtless carry over this knowledge of God into our encounter with him in other areas, say, as the depth of nature. One does not first come to know God as personal, however, in his experience of nonpersonal dimensions of nature. Similarly, once one encounters another as personal, this experience doubtless colors subsequent relations with the other.

devout people, they do not have fellowship as the undevout, as sinners. The pious fellowship permits no one to be a sinner. So everybody must conceal his sin from himself and from the fellowship. We dare not be a sinner. Many Christians are unthinkably horrified when a real sinner is discovered among the righteous. So we remain alone with our sin, living in lies and hypocrisy. The fact is that we *are* sinners.

In confession the break-through to community takes place. Sin demands to have a man by himself. . . . The unexpressed must be openly spoken and acknowledged.[136]

If one is to experience acceptance-in-spite-of, one must experience both the acceptance *and* the in-spite-of.

These are the sorts of expectation, then, which *contrast* our interpretation of the logic of "God acting" from interventionist and reductionist accounts. Many will raise the question whether in leaving behind expectations concerning particular actions of a divine being we do not end up with a kind of pantheism. Although space will not allow a full discussion of this, it may be well, in closing, at least to point out that our analysis has neither denied human freedom, nor identified God with anything that is experienced as finite, nor conceived of God as something impersonal. Rather we have emphasized that we become aware of God as the depth of or as present in our most personal relations, completing and fulfilling them. As Tillich has expressed it,

the depth of being cannot adequately be symbolized by objects taken from a realm which is lower than the personal. . . . A neutral subpersonal cannot grasp the center of our personality; it can satisfy our aesthetic feeling or our intellectual needs, but it cannot convert our will, it cannot overcome our loneliness, anxiety, and despair. For as the philosopher Schelling says: "Only a person can heal a person." [137]

---

[136] *Life Together*, trans. John W. Doberstein (New York: Harper, 1954), pp. 110, 112.
[137] "Science and Theology," pp. 131-32.

Bibliography*

Alston, William P. "The Elucidation of Religious Statements," *Process and Divinity*. Ed. by William Reese and Eugene Freeman. Lasalle, Ill. Open Court, 1964.
———, and Nakhnikian, George, eds. *Readings in Twentieth-Century Philosophy*. New York: The Free Press, 1963.
Austin, John. *How to Do Things with Words*. Ed. J. O. Urmson. Cambridge: Harvard University Press, 1962.
Ayer, A. J. *et al*. *The Revolution in Philosophy*. London: Macmillan, 1956.
Bambrough, Renford. *Reason, Truth and God*. London: Methuen, 1969.
Barrett, Cyril, ed. *Wittgenstein: Lectures and Conversations on Aesthetics, Psychology, and Religious Belief*. London: Basil Blackwell, 1966.
Black, Max. *A Companion to Wittgenstein's Tractatus*. Ithaca: Cornell University Press, 1964.
Blackstone, William T. *The Problem of Religious Knowledge*. Englewood Cliffs, N. J.: Prentice-Hall, 1963.
Britton, Karl. "Portrait of a Philosopher," *The Listener*, June 16, 1955. Reprinted in K. T. Fann, ed. *Ludwig Wittgenstein: The Man and His Philosophy*. Delta Book; New York: Dell, 1967.
Buber, Martin. *I and Thou*. Trans. Ronald Gregor Smith. New York: Scribner's, 1937.
Carnap, Rudolf. *Philosophy and Logical Syntax*. London: Routledge & Kegan Paul, 1935.
Cavell, Stanley. "The Availability of Wittgenstein's Later Philosophy" (1962), reprinted in George Pitcher, ed. *Wittgenstein: The Philosophical Investigations*. Garden City, N. Y.: Doubleday, 1964.

*References selected are those which, because they occur in widely separated places in the text, might be difficult to find full bibliographical information on from the footnotes alone.

Charlesworth, Maxwell John. *Philosophy and Linguistic Analysis.* ("Duquesne Studies: Philosophical Series," ed. A. G. van Melsen and H. J. Koren, Vol. IX.) Pittsburgh: Duquesne University Press, 1959.

Crombie, Ian. "Theology and Falsification," *New Essays in Philosophical Theology.* Ed. Antony Flew and Alasdair MacIntyre. New York: Macmillan, 1955.

Drury, M. O'C. "Ludwig Wittgenstein: A Symposium" (1960) Erich Heller, *et al.*, reprinted in K. T. Fann, ed., *Ludwig Wittgenstein: The Man and His Philosophy,* Delta Book; New York: Dell, 1967.

Fann, K. T., ed. *Ludwig Wittgenstein: The Man and His Philosophy.* Delta Book; New York: Dell, 1967.

Farrer, Austin. *Finite and Infinite.* London: A. & C. Black, 1959.

Ferré, Frederick. *Language, Logic and God.* New York: Harper, 1961.

Flew, Antony G. N. ed. *Logic and Language.* 1st and 2nd Series. Oxford: Basil Blackwell, 1959 and 1960.

————, and MacIntyre, Alasdair, eds. *New Essays in Philosophical Theology.* New York: Macmillan, 1955.

————. "Theology and Falsification" (1950-51), reprinted in *New Essays in Philosophical Theology.* Ed. Antony Flew and Alasdair MacIntyre. New York: Macmillan, 1955.

Foster, Michael. "Contemporary British Philosophy and Christian Belief," *The Christian Scholar,* Fall, 1960.

————. *Mystery and Philosophy.* ("The Library of Philosophical Theology," ed. Alasdair MacIntyre and Ronald Gregor Smith.) London: SCM Press, 1957.

————. " 'We' in Modern Philosophy," *Faith and Logic.* Ed. Basil Mitchell. Boston: Beacon Press, 1957.

Gellner, Ernest. *Words and Things.* Boston: Beacon Press, 1960.

Hallett, Garth. *Wittgenstein's Definition of Meaning as Use.* New York: Fordham University Press, 1967.

Hampshire, S. N. "Metaphysical Systems," *The Nature of Metaphysics.* Ed. D. F. Pears. London: Macmillan, 1957.

Hepburn, Ronald W. *Christianity and Paradox.* London: C. A. Watts, 1958.

————. "Poetry and Religious Belief," *Metaphysical Beliefs.* Stephen Toulmin, Ronald W. Hepburn, and Alasdair MacIntyre. London: SCM Press, 1957.

Hick, John. *Philosophy of Religion.* ("Foundations of Philosophy Series," ed. Elizabeth and Munroe Beardsley.) Englewood Cliffs, N. J.: Prentice-Hall, 1963.

Hook, Sidney, ed. *Religious Experience and Truth: A Symposium.* New York: New York University Press, 1961. (Published proceedings of the fourth annual New York University Institute of Philosophy, held October 21-22, 1960).

Hutchison, John. *Faith, Reason, and Existence.* New York: Oxford University Press, 1956.

MacIntyre, Alasdair. "The Logical Status of Religious Belief," *Metaphysical Beliefs.* Stephen Toulmin, Ronald W. Hepburn, and Alasdair MacIntyre. London: SCM Press, 1957.

Malcolm, Norman. "Moore and Ordinary Language," *The Philosophy of G. E. Moore.* Ed. Paul A. Schilpp. ("The Library of Living Philosophers.") New York: Tudor Publishing Co., 1952. (Now published by The Open Court Publishing Co., LaSalle, Ill.)

May, Rollo. *Man's Search for Himself.* New York: W. W. Norton, 1953.

Mitchell, Basil, ed. *Faith and Logic.* Boston: Beacon Press, 1957.

——. "Introduction," *Faith and Logic.* Ed. Basil Mitchell. Boston: Beacon Press, 1957.

Moore, George E. "A Defence of Common Sense," *Contemporary British Philosophy.* Ed. J. H. Muirhead. Second Series ("Library of Philosophy.") London: Allen and Unwin, 1925.

——. *Philosophical Studies.* London: Routledge and Kegan Paul, 1922.

——. "A Reply to My Critics," *The Philosophy of G. E. Moore.* Ed. Paul A. Schilpp. ("The Library of Living Philosophers.") New York: Tudor Publishing Co., 1952. (Now published by The Open Court Publishing Co., LaSalle, Ill.)

——. *Some Main Problems of Philosophy.* New York: Macmillan, 1953.

——. "Wittgenstein's Lectures in 1930-33," *Mind,* 1955.

Morick, Harold, ed. *Wittgenstein and the Problem of Other Minds.* New York: McGraw-Hill, 1967.

Muirhead, J. H., ed. *Contemporary British Philosophy.* First & Second Series ("Library of Philosophy.") London: Allen and Unwin, 1924, 1925.

Murdoch, Iris. "Metaphysics and Ethics," *The Nature of Metaphysics.* Ed. D. F. Pears. London: Macmillan, 1957.

Pears, D. F. "Logical Atomism," *The Revolution in Philosophy.* A. J. Ayer *et al.* London: Macmillan, 1956.

——, ed. *The Nature of Metaphysics.* London: Macmillan, 1957.

Perkins, Moreland. "Two Arguments Against a Private Language" (1965), reprinted in Harold Morick, ed. *Wittgenstein and the Problem of Other Minds.* New York: McGraw-Hill, 1967.

Pitcher, George. *The Philosophy of Wittgenstein.* Englewood Cliffs, N. J.: Prentice-Hall, 1964.

——, ed. *Wittgenstein: The Philosophical Investigations.* Anchor Books; Garden City, N. Y.: Doubleday, 1966.

Pole, David. *The Later Philosophy of Wittgenstein.* London: The Athlone Press, University of London, 1958.

Ramsey, Ian. "Contemporary Empiricism," *The Christian Scholar,* Fall, 1960.

——. *Religious Language.* ("The Library of Philosophy and Theology," ed. Alasdair MacIntyre and Ronald Gregor Smith.) London: SCM Press, 1957.

Rhees, Rush. "Can There Be a Private Language?" *Proceedings of the Aristotelian Society.* Supplementary Vol. XXVIII (1954). Reprinted in George Pitcher, ed. *Wittgenstein: The Philosophical Investigations.* Anchor Books; Garden City, N. Y.: Doubleday, 1964.

Roberts, David. *Psychotherapy and a Christian View of Man.* New York: Scribner's, 1950.

Russell, Bertrand. "Knowledge by Acquaintance and Knowledge by Description" (1910-11), reprinted in *Mysticism and Logic.* London: Allen and Unwin, 1917.

————. "Logical Atomism," *Contemporary British Philosophy*. Ed. J. H. Muirhead. First Series. ("Library of Philosophy.") London: Allen and Unwin, 1924.

————. "Reply to Criticisms," *The Philosophy of Bertrand Russell*. Ed. Paul A. Schilpp. ("The Library of Living Philosophers.") New York: Tudor Publishing Co., 1951. (Now published by The Open Court Publishing Co., LaSalle, Ill.)

Ryle, Gilbert, Warnock, Mary, and Quinton, A. M. "Final Discussion," *The Nature of Metaphysics*. Ed. D. F. Pears. London: Macmillan, 1957.

————. "Ordinary Language," *The Philosophical Review*, 1953.

Schilpp, Paul A., ed. *The Philosophy of Bertrand Russell*. ("The Library of Living Philosophers.") New York: Tudor Publishing Co., 1951. (Now published by The Open Court Publishing Co., LaSalle, Ill.)

————, ed. *The Philosophy of G. E. Moore*. ("The Library of Living Philosophers.") New York: Tudor Publishing Co., 1952. (3rd ed. by The Open Court Publishing Co., LaSalle, Ill., 1968.)

Smart, J. J. C. "The Existence of God," *New Essays in Philosophical Theology*. Ed. Antony Flew and Alasdair MacIntyre. New York: Macmillan, 1955.

Smart, Ninian. *Reasons and Faiths*. New York: Humanities Press, 1959.

Strawson, P. F. "Construction and Analysis," *The Revolution in Philosophy*. A. J. Ayer *et al.* London: Macmillan, 1957.

Tillich, Paul. *The Courage to Be*. New Haven: Yale University Press, 1952.

————. "The Nature of Religious Language" (1955), reprinted in *Theology of Culture*. Ed. Robert C. Kimball. New York: Oxford University Press, 1959.

————. *The New Being*. New York: Scribner's, 1955.

————. "Science and Theology: A Discussion with Einstein" (1940), reprinted in *Theology of Culture*. Ed. Robert C. Kimball. New York: Oxford University Press, 1959.

————. *The Shaking of the Foundations*. New York: Scribner's, 1955.

————. *Systematic Theology*. Vols. I, II, and III. Chicago: The University of Chicago Press, 1951, 1957, 1963.

————. *Theology of Culture*. Ed. Robert C. Kimball. New York: Oxford University Press, 1959.

————. "The Two Types of Philosophy of Religion" (1946), reprinted in *Theology of Culture*. Ed. Robert C. Kimball. New York: Oxford University Press, 1959.

Torrance, Thomas F. "Faith and Philosophy," *The Hibbert Journal*, April, 1949.

Toulmin, Stephen. *The Uses of Argument*. Cambridge: The University Press, 1964.

Urmson, J. O. *Philosophical Analysis*. Oxford: The Clarendon Press, 1958.

Warnock, G. J. "Analysis and Imagination," *The Revolution in Philosophy*. A. J. Ayer *et al.* London: Macmillan, 1957.

————. *English Philosophy Since 1900*. ("Home University Library of Modern Knowledge.") London: Oxford University Press, 1958.

Wellman, Carl. "Wittgenstein's Conception of a Criterion" (1962), reprinted in Harold Morick, ed. *Wittgenstein and the Problem of Other Minds*. New York: McGraw-Hill, 1967.

Wild, John. *Existence and the World of Freedom*. Englewood Cliffs, N. J.: Prentice-Hall, 1963.

Wisdom, John. "Bertrand Russell and Modern Philosophy: *History of Western Philosophy and Its connection with Political and Social Circumstances from the earliest times to the Present Day*" (1947), reprinted in John Wisdom, *Philosophy and Psycho-Analysis*. Oxford: Basil Blackwell, 1957.

————. "Eternal Life," *Talk of God*. G. N. A. Vesey, *et al*. ("Royal Institute of Philosophy Lectures," Vol. II). New York: St. Martin's Press, 1969.

————. "A Feature of Wittgenstein's Technique" (1961), reprinted in John Wisdom, *Paradox and Discovery*. Oxford: Basil Blackwell, 1965.

————. "Gods" (1944), reprinted in John Wisdom, *Philosophy and Psycho-Analysis*. Oxford: Basil Blackwell, 1957.

————. "The Logic of God," *Paradox and Discovery*. John Wisdom. Oxford: Basil Blackwell, 1965.

————. "The Metamorphosis of Metaphysics," reprinted in John Wisdom, *Paradox and Discovery*. Oxford: Basil Blackwell, 1965.

————. "Metaphysics and Verification" (1938), reprinted in John Wisdom, *Philosophy and Psycho-Analysis*. Oxford: Basil Blackwell, 1957.

————. "Moore's Technique" (1944), reprinted in John Wisdom, *Philosophy and Psycho-Analysis*. Oxford: Basil Blackwell, 1957. Also reprinted in *The Philosophy of G. E. Moore*. Ed. Paul A. Schilpp.

————. "Note on the New Edition of Professor Ayer's *Language, Truth and Logic*" (1948), reprinted in John Wisdom, *Philosophy and Psycho-Analysis*. Oxford: Basil Blackwell, 1957.

————. "Other Minds I," reprinted in John Wisdom, *Other Minds*. Oxford: Basil Blackwell, 1965.

————. "Paradox and Discovery," in John Wisdom, *Paradox and Discovery*. Oxford: Basil Blackwell, 1965.

————. "Philosophical Perplexity" (1936), reprinted in John Wisdom, *Philosophy and Psycho-Analysis*. Oxford: Basil Blackwell, 1957.

————. "Philosophy, Anxiety and Novelty" (1944) reprinted in John Wisdom, *Philosophy and Psycho-Analysis*. Oxford: Basil Blackwell, 1957.

————. "Philosophy, Metaphysics and Psycho-Analysis," in John Wisdom, *Philosophy and Psycho-Analysis*. Oxford: Basil Blackwell, 1957.

————. "Religious Belief," reprinted in John Wisdom, *Paradox and Discovery*. Oxford: Basil Blackwell, 1965.

————. "Symposium: Other Minds," reprinted in John Wisdom, *Other Minds*. Oxford: Basil Blackwell, 1965.

Wittgenstein, Ludwig. *Philosophical Investigations*. Trans. G. E. M. Anscombe. 2nd ed. Oxford: Basil Blackwell, 1953.

————. *The Blue and Brown Books*. 2nd ed. Ed. R. Rhees. Oxford: Basil Blackwell, 1960.

————. *Philosophische Bemerkungen*. Ed. R. Rhees. Oxford. Basil Blackwell, 1965.

————. *Remarks on the Foundations of Mathematics.* Ed. G. H. von Wright, R. Rhees, and G. Anscombe. Trans. G. Anscombe. Oxford: Basil Blackwell, 1956.

————. "Some Remarks on Logical Form," *Aristotelian Society Supplementary Volume.* (1929).

————. *Tractatus Logico-Philosophicus.* ("International Library of Psychology, Philosophy and Scientific Method," ed. C. K. Ogden.) London: Routledge and Kegan Paul, 1922.

————. *Zettel.* Ed. G. Anscombe and G. H. von Wright. Trans. G. Anscombe. Berkeley: University of California Press, 1967.

Zuurdeeg, Willem. *An Analytical Philosophy of Religion.* Nashville: Abingdon Press, 1958.

Index

Page numbers in italics refer to footnotes.

Addis, Laird, *Moore and Ryle: Two Ontologies* (with Lewis), *30*

Aeschylus, 251

Alston, W. P., 205-10
  language use criteria, 275-76, 294
  writings
    'The Elucidation of Religious Statements," 205, 206, *295*
    The Philosophy of Language, 276
    "Psychological Explanations of Religious Belief," *362*
    Readings in Twentieth-Century Philosophy (with Nakhnikian), *39, 43, 62*
    "Tillich's Conception of a Religious Symbol," *365*

Analysis
  analytic vs. synthetic propositions, 29-30, 33
  in atomism, 56-57
  epistemological, 32, 34
  existentialism and, 327-36
  limitations of, 222-23
  and logical atomism, 55-89
  in logical positivism, 90 ff.
  as method in Moore, 27-45

Anderson, Bernhard, *Rediscovering the Bible,* 375, 376

Anscombe, G. E. M.
  An Introduction to Wittgenstein's Tractatus, 129
  "What Wittgenstein Really Said," *196*

Anselm, 283, 284, 285

Aquinas, Thomas, 360, 371
  Summa Theologica, 35, 46, 370

Aristotle, 61, 209, 263, 360
  Aristotelian categories, 46

Arius, 86

Atomism, 55-58. *See also* Logical atomism

Augustine of Hippo, 174, 195, 239, 257, 285

Austin, John, 12, 262
  performative vs. constantive utterances, 277-79, 293
  "value/fact fetish," 272
  writings
    How to Do Things with Words, 272, 277
    "Other Minds," 265, 277

Ayer, A. J., *39,* 224, 228
  on analyticity, 93, 96, 99
  on ethical statements, 94
  on existence of God, 101 ff., 114
  writings
    "Can There Be a Private Language?" *194*
    Language, Truth and Logic,

Ayer, A. J.—cont'd
    92, 94, 95, 96, 98, 101,
    102, 104, 107
    The Revolution in Philosophy,
    93

Bach, Johann Sebastian, 211
Baier, Kurt, 264
    "The Ordinary Use of Words,"
    264
Baillie, Donald, 316
    God Was in Christ, 14
Bambrough, Renford, 232
    logic of God, 247-49, 255-56
    Reason, Truth and God, 247,
    248, 250, 251, 255, 259
    on Wisdom, 247-48, 250-52
Barrett, Cyril, 150, 157, 196, 197,
    332
Barth, Karl; Barthianism, 289-91,
    349
Belief, genuine, 337-38
Bendall, Kent, *Exploring the Logic
    of Faith* (with Ferré), 99
Bentham, Jeremy, 65
Berkeley, Bishop, 31, 78, 277
    *Three Dialogues Between Hylas
    and Philonous*, 35
Black, Max, 56, 128
    *A Companion to Wittgenstein's
    "Tractatus,"* 127, 129, 131
    Language and Philosophy, 123
    "Russell's Philosophy of Lan-
    guage," 70, 71
Blackstone, William T.
    falsifiable assertions, 295, 299,
    301
    *The Problem of Religious Knowl-
    edge*, 295, 300, 309
Blake, William, 361
Bonhoeffer, Dietrich, 381
    Life Together, 382
Bosanquet, Bernard, 28
Bradley, F. H., 28, 31, 46, 59, 176
    The Principles of Logic, 56
    *Translations from the Philosoph-
    ical Writings of Gottlob
    Frege*, 56
Brahms, Johannes, 139
Braithwaite, R. B., 90, 224, 250
    An Empiricist's View of the

Braithwaite, R. B.—cont'd
    Nature of Religious Belief,
    13
Brebner, J. B., 344
Brightman, Edgar, "Russell's Phi-
    losophy of Religion," 80
Britton, Karl, 183
    "Portrait of a Philosopher," 183,
    184, 186, 263
Brunner, Emil, 316, 360
Buber, Martin, 316, 359, 363
    Tillich on, 340
    writings
        Between Man and Man, 360
        "Genuine Conversation and
        the Possibilities of Peace,"
        378
        I and Thou, 104, 353, 360,
        372
Bultmann, Rudolf, 255
    Jesus Christ and Mythology, 51
Butler, Bishop, 29, 219

Cambridge philosophy, 215, 262.
    See also philosophers by name
Camfield, W. F.
    The Collapse of Doubt, 290
    religious language, 290
Camus, A., 347
Carnap, Rudolph, 71, 95, 142
    Philosophy and Logical Syntax,
    70, 94
Carroll, Lewis, *Through the Look-
    ing Glass*, 147
Casserley, J. V. L., 20
    The Christian in Philosophy, 21
Cavell, Stanley, 183
    "The Availability of Wittgen-
    stein's Later Philosophy,"
    152, 177, 180
Charlesworth, Maxwell John, 69,
    124, 186
    on Moore, 40
    *Philosophy and Linguistic Analy-
    sis*, 34, 36, 39, 40, 68, 123,
    125, 244, 275
    on Wisdom, 243-44
Chirico, 258
Christology, strict vs. free, 289
Classification, categories of, 73

Common sense
  language of, 93-94
  Moore and, 28-34, 38-43, 47, 49,
    50, 51
  Russell and, 59
Comte, Auguste, 363
Correct language, 276
Cox, Harvey, 358, 359, 362, 366
  The Secular City, 363, 364
Crombie, Ian, *15*
  religious language, 312-15
  writings
    "The Possibility of Theologi-
      cal Statements," 312,
      313, 314, 315
    "Theology and Falsification,"
      *206, 210, 295, 312, 313,
      314*

Deists, 209
Demythologizing, biblical, 51, 89,
  256, *260, 261*
Descartes, René, 170, 331
Dodd, C. H., *The Epistle of Paul
  to the Romans,* 377, 378
Dodgson, Charles. *See* Carroll,
  Lewis
Dostoevsky, Feodor, 195, *258*
  Brothers Karamazov, 350
Drury, M. O'C., *183, 195,* 211

Eckhart, Meister, 353
Edie, James M., *356*
Einstein, Albert, *107, 231, 235*
Eliade, Mircea, *The Sacred and
  the Profane,* 356
Eliot, T. S., 358, 368
  "East Coker," 369
  "The Hollow Men," 17
Empiricism
  analytic vs. phenomenological
    approaches, 330-32
  classical, 56
  classical British, 11, 55, 170
Englemann, Paul, *Letters from
  Ludwig Wittgenstein,* 132
Epimenides, *61*
Epistemology
  Moore and, 32, 34 ff.
  subject matter of, 83

Evans, Donald, 373
  biblical performatory utterances,
    293
  The Logic of Self-Involvement,
    293
Existentialism
  phenomenological method in,
    330, 334
  religious language and, 87, 327-
    36

Fann, K. T., *118, 183, 195*
Farmer, 316
Farrer, Austin, 204, 335
  *Finite and Infinite, 52, 106, 202,
    203,* 335
Farrer, Katherine, *105*
Feigle, Herbert, *105*
Ferré, Frederick
  Exploring the Logic of Faith
    (with Bendall), 99
  Language, Logic and God, 105,
    *250, 251, 259, 291, 292,
    303,* 322
Feyerabend, Paul, *186*
Fitch, Frederic, *Symbolic Logic,* 71
Fletcher, Joseph, "Six Propositions:
  The New Look in Christian
  Ethics," 223
Flew, Antony, *48, 249, 282,* 300,
  301, 307, 347
  gardener parable, 296, 308
  paradigm-case argument, 266 ff.
  writings
    "Divine Omnipotence and
      Human Freedom," *267,
      268, 269, 271*
    "Philosophy and Language,"
      266, 268, 271
    "Theology and Falsification,"
      295, 296, 307
Foster, Michael, *11, 18, 52, 133*
  positivistic analysis, 104-5
  on use of moral language, 50-51,
    272
  writings
    "Contemporary British Philos-
      ophy and Christian Be-
      lief," *134*
    *Mystery and Philosophy, 14,
      15, 105, 134*

Foster, Michael—*cont'd*
"'We' in Modern Philoso-
phy," 42, *51*, 272
Frege, Gottlob, 56
Foundations of Arithmetic, 60
Freud, Sigmund, 19, 111, 113, 183,
184, 185, 197, 198, 224, 236,
237, 238, 251, 256, 258, 334,
340, 358, 359, 361, 366
Civilization and Its Discontents,
357, 362
The Ego and the Id, 210
The Future of an Illusion, 357,
362
Fromm, Erich, 354
Marx's Concept of Man, 19
Psychoanalysis and Religion, 360

Garaudy, Roger, *From Anathema
to Dialogue,* 364
Gardener parable, 234-35, 296, 308
Gasking, D., "Ludwig Wittgen-
stein" (with Jackson), 263
Geach, Peter, 56
Gellner, Ernest, 180
Words and Things, 178, 179,
294
God, acting in history
prophetic tradition, 373-82
Tillichean interpretation, 337-73
See also Religious language
Grice, H. P., 77

Hallett, Garth, *Wittgenstein's Defi-
nition of Meaning as Use,*
151, 158, 192, 193
Hamilton, Kenneth, *The System
and the Gospel: Critique of
Paul Tillich,* 349
Hampshire, Stuart, 264
"Metaphysical Systems," 264,
280, 333
Thought and Action, 279
Hare, R. M., 250
blik concept, 297-300, 301
writings
The Language of Morals, 271
"Religion and Morals," 297,
298, 301, 302
"Theology and Falsification,"
295, 297, 298, 299, 300

Haroutunian, Joseph, "The Ques-
tion Tillich Left Us," *364*
Hartshorne, Charles, 211
Hegel, G. W. F., 12, 59
Heidegger, Martin, 87
Heim, Karl, *Christian Faith and
Natural Science,* 104
Heisenberg uncertainty principle,
328
Heller, Erich, 183
Henson, Richard G., "Ordinary
Language, Common Sense
and the Time-Lag Argument,"
275
Henze, Donald, *The Private-Lan-
guage Problem* (with Saun-
ders), 174
Hepburn, Ronald W., 88, 250
religious language, 288-90, 291
writings
Christianity and Paradox, 287,
288, 289, 291, 317, 319
"Poetry and Religious Be-
lief," 288, 291, 301
Hick, John, 300, 322
divine Gardener parable, 308
existence of God, 281-83, 308-12,
315
writings
Faith and Knowledge, 308,
309, 310, 311
Philosophy of Religion, 48,
281, 282, 300, 310, 311,
315, 354
Hitler, Adolf, 298
Hodges, H. A.
*Languages, Standpoints and At-
titudes,* 53
*Wilhelm Dilthey: An Introduc-
tion,* 20
Holmer, Paul, 106
"Kierkegaard and Religious
Propositions," 103
"The Nature of Religious Propo-
sitions," 103
"Philosophical Criticism and
Christology," 103
Homer, 247, 251
Hook, Sidney, 356, 365
Hordern, William, 367

Hume, David, 56, 111, 223, 224, 330, 331
A Treatise of Human Nature, 297
Hutchinson, John, 136
Faith, Reason, and Existence, 87, 137, 287
Huxley, Aldous, *Brave New World*, 361

Idealism, 55, 56, 58, 275
basic confusion in, 28
Moore's critique of perception in, 28 ff.
Isaacs, Susan, 238

Jackson, A., "Ludwig Wittgenstein" (with Gasking), 263
James, William, 240
The Varieties of Religious Experience, 195, 211
Job, 299, 306
Johnson, Samuel, 31

Kafka, Franz, 183, 258
Kant, Immanuel, 18, 31, 42, 63, 76, 196, 223, 264, 280, 349
Critique of Pure Reason, 177
transcendental knowledge, 177
Kaufmann, Walter, *Critique of Religion and Philosophy*, 20
Kierkegaard, Søren, 103, 133, 183, 184, 185, 195, 197, 208, 211, 333, 355
Kimball, Robert C., 18, 21
Kneale, W. C., "Gottlob Frege and Mathematical Logic," 57
Kraus, Karl, *Language*, 183
Krutch, Joseph Wood, "Life, Liberty and the Pursuit of Welfare," 361
Kuhn, Helmut, *Encounter with Nothingness*, 239
Kunkel, Fritz, 376

Language
confusion of, in Western culture, 16-23
criteria for use (Oxford philosophy), 275-76
effect of science on grammar, 270

Language—*cont'd*
meaning as use, 263 ff., 274 ff., 332-33 (*see also* Wittgenstein, Ludwig)
See also Correct language; Linguistic philosophy; Metaphysics; Moral language; Ordinary language; Religious language; Wittgenstein: Private language
Lewis, Douglas, *Moore and Ryle: Two Ontologies* (with Addis), 30
Linguistic philosophy
definition, 11
on religious uses of language, 13-14
Locke, John
dualism of, 165
An Essay Concerning Human Understanding, 165
Logical atomism, 55-89, 219
analytic vs. synthetic, 73
extensional logic, 66
and metaphysics, 67 ff.
See also Wittgenstein: *Tractatus Logico-Philosophicus*
Logical positivism, 90-114
emotion vs. understanding, 94, 98-99
evaluation of, 94-101
kinds of statements in, 94
verification principle, 91-92
Loos, 183
Luther, Martin, "Treatise on Christian Liberty," 374

MacIntyre, Alasdair, 14, 48, 84, 249
"The Logical Status of Religious Belief," 88, 288, 301
religious language, 288
McKeon, Richard, 43, 44
McPherson, Thomas, 135
"Religion as the Inexpressible," 134, 136
McTaggart, John, 28, 30, 31, 44
Malcolm, Norman, 42, 183, 186
on existence of God, 285-87
on Moore, 40

Malcolm, Norman—cont'd
"ordinary expression," 276
writings
"Anselm's Ontological Argu-
ments," 284, 286, 333
Knowledge and Certainty, 38,
39, 40, 101, 333
Ludwig Wittgenstein: A Mem-
oir, 195
"Moore and Ordinary Lan-
guage," 276
Manet, Edouard, 236, 251
Marcel, Gabriel, 105, 251
Being and Having, 105
Maritain, Jacques, 363
Marquand, John P., 239
H. M. Pulham, Esq., 240
Martin, Charles B., Religious Be-
lief, 13
Martin, C. G., 319
"A Religious Way of Knowing,"
317
Martin, James A., Jr., The New
Dialogue Between Philosophy
and Theology, 309
Marx, Karl, 19, 184, 197, 334, 360
Mascall, E. L., 203
Existence and Analogy, 201, 202
Materialism, 275
Mathematics, philosophical theory
and, 56-58
Maugham, Somerset, Of Human
Bondage, 240
May, Rollo, 375
The Art of Counseling, 376
"Contributions of Existential
Psychotherapy," 318
Man's Search for Himself, 16,
20, 21, 23, 360
Meinong, Alexius, 63
Merleau-Ponty, Maurice, Phenom-
enology of Perception, 332
Metaphysics
language of, 60-65
logical positivism and, 90, 94 ff.
in Oxford philosophy, 274-79
See also God; Religious language;
philosophers by name
Mill, John Stuart, 56, 63
A System of Logic, 225

Mitchell, Basil
religious vs. ordinary language,
287, 302-8, 313, 322
writings
Faith and Logic, 14, 17, 42,
287, 302, 304, 312, 313,
331
"Theology and Falsification,"
295, 302, 303
Moore, G. E., 12, 27-54, 55, 58, 59,
75, 79, 81, 139, 149, 161, 178,
185, 197, 209, 216, 219, 226,
262, 272, 336, 338
agnosticism of, 45
analysis in, 27-34, 45-54
common sense, 28-34, 38-43, 47,
49, 50, 51
definition, theory of, 35-36
epistemology, 32, 34 ff.
evaluation of, 34-45
on meaning of "God," 51
metaphysics, 34
methods of, 27
ontology, 34
on perception in idealism, 28 ff.
on theory of descriptions, 72
use of "we," 42
and views of others, 43-45
writings
"An Autobiography," 30, 37,
43, 45
"The Conception of Reality,"
30
"Defence of Common Sense,"
31, 32, 38-39, 40, 41, 42,
44, 51
"Hume's Philosophy," 36
Philosophical Studies, 28, 29,
30, 36, 46
Principia Ethica, 27, 29, 33,
37
"Proof of an External World,"
30, 40
"The Refutation of Idealism,"
27
"A Reply to My Critics," 32,
34, 39, 40, 44, 73
Some Main Problems of Philosophy, 33, 38, 51
"Wittgenstein's Lectures in
1930-33," 179, 195

Moral language
   "Natural Law Moralists," 273-74
   use of, 50-51, 272, 273
Moses, 374, 375
Muirhead, J. H. II, 31
Murdoch, Iris
   "Metaphysics and Ethics," 144,
      273
   on use of moral language, 273,
      274

Nadel, G. H., 331
Nakhnikian, George, Readings in
   Twentieth-Century Philosophy
   (with Alston), 39, 43, 62
Natural Law Moralists, 273-74
Naturalistic fallacy, 33, 271
Newton, Sir Isaac, 224, 235
Niebuhr, Reinhold, 360, 380
   Faith and History, 381
Nielsen, Kai, "Eschatological Veri-
   fication," 311
Nietzsche, Friedrich, 184
Novak, Michael, Belief and Unbe-
   lief, 198

O'Brien, Dennis, "The Unity
   of Wittgenstein's Thought,"
   118, 160
Ogden, Schubert, 211
Ontology
   Russell on, 64
   in Tillich, 335-36, 351 ff.
Ordinary language
   Oxford philosophy of, 265-81
   science and, 331
   use of, in philosophical issues,
      265-81
Orwell, George, 1984, 296
Otto, Rudolf, 136, 138
   The Idea of the Holy, 134, 135,
      137, 344, 352, 353, 354, 355
   qualities of the holy, 353-55
Oxford philosophy, 215, 262-323
   correct language, 276 ff.
   descriptive and revisionary meta-
      physics, 274-79, 280
   language use and usage, 265-81
   logic of religious assertions, 281-
      316
   meaning as use, 263 ff.

Oxford philosophy—cont'd
   ordinary-language theory, 265-81
   See also philosophers by name

Paradigm-case argument, 266 ff.
   existence of God, 281-87
Pascal, Blaise, Thoughts, 350
Passmore, John A.
   religious language, 291
   writings
      "Christianity and Positivism,"
         291
      "Explanation in Everyday
         Life, in Science, and in
         History," 331
Paton, H. J., "The Alleged Inde-
   pendence of Goodness," 37
Paul, 257, 299, 306, 346, 358, 377,
   378
Paul, G. A.
   "G. E. Moore: Analysis, Com-
      mon Usage, and Common
      Sense," 39
   "Wittgenstein," 263
Pears, D. F., 18, 77, 122, 139, 144
   "Logical Atomism," 58, 68, 75,
      123, 140
Perception, Moore on, 28 ff.
Perkins, Moreland, 195
   "Two Arguments Against a Pri-
      vate Language," 186
Phenomenology, 255, 330, 334. See
   also Tillich, Paul
Pitcher, George, 152, 186
   The Philosophy of Wittgenstein,
      129, 187, 188, 189, 192, 195
Plato, 64, 76, 195, 263, 360
   Parmenides, 61
   Republic, 298
   Theaetetus, 145
Pole, David, 178-80, 243
   The Later Philosophy of Witt-
      genstein, 164, 178, 180,
      185, 186, 242
   on Wisdom, 242-43
Popper, Karl
   falsifiability principle, 295
   The Logic of Scientific Discov-
      ery, 295

Price, H. H., *Some Aspects of the Conflict Between Science and Religion,* 52
Proust, Marcel, 236, 251

Quine, W. V. O., 71
  Mathematical Logic, 71
Quinton, Anthony
  revisionary metaphysics, 280
  writings
    "Final Discussion," 280
    "Philosophy and Belief," 294

Ramsey, Frank P., 90
Ramsey, Ian, 47, 86, 87
  on religious language, 287, 320-22
  writings
    "Contemporary Empiricism," 201, 287, 321
    Freedom and Immortality, 349
    Religious Language, 84, 88, 321
Randall, John H., Jr., 354
Realism, Greek, 122
Religion, philosophy of: Moore's methodology and, 45-54
Religious language
  in Bambrough, 247-49
  Barthian, 289-91
  cognitive use of word "God," 337-82
  "convictional" language, 109 ff.
  definition, 13
  encounter theology, 316 ff.
  existentialism and, 87, 327-36
  falsifiability principle, 295
  grammatical vs. logical form, 83-89
  language about Jesus, 85-86
  logic of God (Wisdom), 234-41
  logical positivism and, 101-14
  Oxford philosophy and, 281-316
  relevance of Wittgenstein to, 195-211
  Russell's theories and, 80-89
  Tillich's understanding of "God," 337-73
  verification of (Tillich), 358-73
  in Wisdom, 228-41, 250-61

Religious language—*cont'd*
  Wittgenstein's *Tractatus,* 118-19, 132-40
  Zuurdeeg on, 108-13
  See also God; Metaphysics
Rhees, Rush, *183*
  "Can There Be a Private Language?" *160,* 194
  on language use and conditioned response, 160
Roberts, David, 360
  Psychotherapy and a Christian View of Man, 361, 378
Robinson, John A. T., *Honest to God,* 306, 307
Russell, Bertrand, 12, 30, 31, *118,* 120, 122, 123, 145, 168, 176, 235, 342, 367
  common sense, 59
  evaluation of, 65-80
  extensional logic, 66
  linguistic philosophy of, 58-65, 275
  metaphysical language, 34, 60-65, 76
  ontology and, 64
  "particulars," 62
  theory of definite descriptions, 63-65, 72, 73
  theory of logical constructions, 65 ff., 77-80, 254
  theory of types, 61-63, 64, 71
  on Wittgenstein's religious attitude, 132
  writings
    "A Free Man's Worship," *129*
    A History of Western Philosophy, 64
    "Knowledge by Acquaintance and Knowledge by Description," 65, 76
    "Logical Atomism," 59, 60, 62, 64, 65, 74, 88
    "Ludwig Wittgenstein," *132*
    "My Mental Development," 59, 66
    The Philosophy of Logical Atomism, 62, 64, 76
    Principia Mathematica (with Whitehead), 55, 57, 61, 63

Russell, Bertrand—*cont'd*
"Reply to Criticisms," *59, 72*
Ryle, Gilbert, 12, 18, 19, *56,* 166, 262, 271
"category mistakes," *265*
concept of mind, 265-66
language use, 274, 275
writings
The Concept of Mind, 265, 266
Dilemmas, 265
"Final Discussion," *74, 280, 281*
"Ludwig Wittgenstein," *262*
"Ordinary Language," *274*

Sartre, Jean-Paul, 251
Saunders, John, *The Private-Language Problem* (with Henze), 174
Schelling, Friedrich, 382
Schilpp, Paul A., *30, 59*
Schleiermacher, F., *353*
Schlick, Moritz, *94,* 128
"Meaning and Verification," *105*
"Notes on Talks with Wittgenstein," *133*
Schönberg, Arnold, *183*
Sellars, Wilfred, *105*
Smart, J. J. C., 50, 350
"The Existence of God," *48, 351*
Smart, Ninian, *Reasons and Faiths, 14, 139*
Smith, John E., "The Experience of the Holy and the Idea of God," *356*
Smith, Ronald Gregor, *14, 84, 104,* 360
Socrates, 61, 145, *153*
Sophocles, 251
Spinoza, Baruch, 22, 59, 196, 240, 241, 256, 257, 360
Spranger, Eduard, *183*
Lebensformen, 183
Stebbing, L. Susan, "Moore's Influence," *36, 37, 39*
Stephen the Martyr, 358
Stevenson, Charles L.
Ethics and Language, 97
"Persuasive Definitions," 97

Strawson, P. F., 71, 77, 186, 187, 192, 193, 194, 198
concept "person," 173-74
revisionary metaphysics, 280
writings
"Construction and Analysis," *69, 279*
Individuals, 174, 272, *279*
Introduction to Logical Theory, 72, 76
"Persons," *174*

Tillich, Paul, 13, 15, 18, 22, 50, 106, 255, 256, 258, 261, 327, 333
existence of God, 285-86
experiential basis of thought, 345-58
God in history, 337-82
ontology, 335-36, 351 ff.
verification of religious language, 358-73
writings
"Aspects of a Religious Analysis of Culture," *364*
The Courage to Be, 257, 344, 345, 346, 352, 357, 368, 369
"An Evaluation of Martin Buber," *340, 344*
Love, Power and Justice, 335
"The Meaning and Justification of Religious Symbols," *356*
"The Nature of Religious Language," *339, 344*
The New Being, 347, 353, 359, 367, 370, 372
"Religion as a Dimension in Man's Spiritual Life," *344*
"Science and Theology: A Discussion with Einstein," *107, 305, 307, 344, 382*
The Shaking of the Foundations, 318, 346, 347, 353, 354, 359, 368, 369, 370
Systematic Theology, I, 23, 35, 46, 285, 344, 345, 346,

Tillich, Paul—cont'd
  349, 351, 352, 355, 363,
  365, 366, 369
  Systematic Theology, II, 138,
  309, 345, 354, 359
  Systematic Theology, III, 346
  "The Theological Significance
  of Existentialism and Psychoanalysis," 364
  "The Two Types of Philosophy of Religion," 49,
  52, 285, 344, 345, 353,
  363, 368
Tolstoy, Leo, 195, 258
  War and Peace, 237
Torrance, Thomas F., 20
  religious language, 290
  review of Warfield's *Inspiration
  and Authority of the Bible*,
  290
Toulmin, Stephen, 88, 183, 190,
  279
  "substantial" argument, 222-23
  writings
    Reason in Ethics, 349, 350,
    351, 352
    The Uses of Argument, 223,
    279
Tournier, Paul, 317
  The Meaning of Persons, 316,
  318
Turbayne, Colin M., 35

Upanisad: Isa Upanisad, 139
Urmson, J. O., 64
  on atomism, 72
  writings
    Philosophical Analysis, 57, 63,
    65, 66, 72, 74, 75, 77, 79,
    93, 95, 96, 118, 121, 126,
    142, 215, 219, 225
    "Some Questions Concerning
    Validity," 272
Ussher, Archbishop, 18

Van Buren, Paul, 364

Waismann, Friedrich, "Verifiability," 264
Warfield, 290

Warnock, G. J.
  correct language, 276-77
  writings
    "Analysis and Imagination,"
    280, 331, 332
    Berkeley, 277
    "Criticisms of Metaphysics,"
    264
    *English Philosophy Since
    1900*, 31, 39, 277
Warnock, Mary, 74
Watkins, J. W. N., "Farewell to
  the Paradigm-Case Argu-
  ment," 267, 268, 270
Wellman, Carl, 186, 194
Wells, H. G., *The Mind at the
  End of Its Tether*, 381
Whitehead, Alfred North, 65, 311
  Principia Mathematica (with
  Russell), 55, 61, 63
Wild, John, 53
  *Existence and the World of
  Freedom*, 54, 331, 332
Williams, B. A. O.
  "Metaphysical Arguments," 280
  "Tertullian's Paradox," 105
Wilson, John, *Philosophy and Re-
  ligion*, 15
Wisdom, John, 12-15, 23, 32, 45,
  63, 64, 73, 77, 88, 106, 113,
  162, 266, 279, 310, 311, 312,
  331, 342-43, 363, 366
  on Ayer's analysis of ethical statements, 98-99
  evaluation
    of overall position, 241-50
    of philosophy of religion, 250-
    61
  "invisible gardener" parable,
    234-35, 308
  kinds of philosophers, 232
  on knowledge of other people's
    feelings, 217-22
  on Moore, 40, 44, 45
  paradox-platitude classifications,
    216 ff., 227-34
  rational processes, 222-27
  religious language, 228-41, 250-
    61
  on Wittgenstein, 215

Wisdom, John—*cont'd*
  writings
    "Bertrand Russell and Modern Philosophy," 69, 78, 233, 254, 342
    "Eternal Life," 239, 240, 241, 243, 257, 258, 260
    "Gods," 224, 230, 234, 235, 238, 239, 241, 251, 253, 256, 259, 260, 298, 301, 341
    "The Logic of God," 237, 238, 239, 248, 260
    "Logical Constructions," 57
    "The Metamorphosis of Metaphysics," 174, 233, 244
    "Metaphysics and Verification," 216, 217, 220, 222, 225, 226, 228, 254
    "Moore's Technique," 40, 44, 233
    "Note on the New Edition of Professor Ayer's *Language, Truth and Logic*," 34, 228, 234, 246
    Other Minds, 221, 223, 229, 230, 231, 238, 239, 240, 245, 258
    Paradox and Discovery, 225, 231, 233, 235, 238, 239, 245, 246, 260
    "Philosophical Perplexity," 182, 215, 216, 218, 220, 222, 225, 226, 227, 228
    Philosophy and Psycho-Analysis, 14, 19, 65, 96, 100, 198, 221, 227, 231, 257
    "Philosophy, Anxiety and Novelty," 216, 217, 226, 228
    "Philosophy, Metaphysics and Psycho-Analysis," 216, 217, 218, 220, 221, 224, 227, 231, 232, 234, 238, 241, 243, 249, 258, 261, 349
    "The Philosophy of G. E. Moore," 31
    "Religious Belief," 239, 241, 246, 249, 256, 257, 258, 259, 260

Wisdom, John—*cont'd*
    "Tolerance," 231, 237, 238, 241, 260
Wittgenstein, Ludwig, 12, 23, 35, 36, 38, 40, 44, 48, 55, 57, 71, 90, 215, 216, 217, 233, 238, 251, 266, 280, 285, 286, 287, 336
  contrast principle in language, 155-64, 276
  dualism, 164-70
  evaluation of, 122-32, 142-94 *passim*
  extensional logic, 66
  formal vs. proper concepts, 120
  forms of life and critical evaluation, 177-85
  language-games analogy, 145-55, 220-21, 294
  limits of language, 155-57, 176-77 (see also *Tractatus*)
  on meaning as use, 143, 191-93, 263, 267, 268, 269, 270, 271, 278
  metaphysical language, 76
  nonobservable phenomena, 184-91
  private language, 170-74, 193-94, 339
  religious language and, 118-19, 132-40, 195-211
  vs. Russell, on meaning, 118
  self-evaluation, 279
  writings
    The Blue Book, 146, 148, 149, 150, 152, 153, 154, 159, 161, 162, 165, 176, 178, 181, 182, 220, 279
    The Brown Book, 145, 149, 156, 158, 175, 191
    Lectures and Conversations, 150, 157, 190, 196, 197, 332
    "Lectures on Ethics," 128, 130, 132, 133
    Philosophical Investigations, 37, 39, 41, 49, 80, 117, 125, 142-211 *passim*, 220, 262, 336
    Philosophische Bemerkungen, 131, 152, 156

Wittgenstein, Ludwig—*cont'd*
  *Remarks on the Foundations
    of Mathematics*, 141,
    151, 178, 182, 183, 191,
    194
  "Some Remarks on Logical
    Form," 131, 156
  *Tractatus Logico-Philosoph-
    icus*, 58, 62, 70, 75, 76,
    77, 117-40 *passim*, 142,
    143, 150, 152, 155, 156,
    157, 162, 170, 176, 179,
    186, 349
  Wittgenstein Notebooks, 129,
    130, 132
  works available, 142

Wittgenstein, Ludwig—*cont'd*
  Zettel, 154, 168, 178, 179,
    181, 182, 186, 187, 188,
    190, 191, 220, 269, 332,
    333
Wolheim, R. A., "F. H. Bradley,"
    176
Woolf, Virginia, *Jacob's Room*,
    240
Wordsworth, William, 235-36

Zeno, 30
Zuurdeeg, Willem, 367
  *An Analytical Philosophy of Re-
    ligion*, 19, 53, 108
  on religious language, 108-13